'This powerful book takes a close look at the relationship between the Bolshevik party and the democratic aspirations of rank-and-file workers in Moscow in the crucial early years of the Russian revolution. Simon Pirani's prodigious utilization of local party and secret police archives allows him to show how the Bolshevik party leadership systematically destroyed democratic voices on the shop floor: the party offered a "social contract" that promised improving standards of living in exchange for the loss of a political voice. Paying close attention to the material reality of the post-revolutionary period and to moments of intense shop floor dissent, this book goes beyond Robert Daniels's classic *The Conscience of the Revolution* in emphasizing the importance of independent and non-party socialist worker activists. He instructs careful readers about the complex, fragile thing called democracy, exploring its origin and demise in economically and politically fraught conditions of revolutionary change.'

Diane P. Koenker
University of Illinois at Urbana-Champaign

'Why did the Russian revolution, a mass uprising for justice and democracy, end in a single Party dictatorship? This gripping tale of workers in revolution and retreat is essential reading for anyone interested in an answer. Pirani follows Russian workers as they seize power, fight for a democratic revolution, and lose to a Bolshevik Party bureaucracy intent on consolidating control. Using exciting new sources, Pirani takes us into the factories of Moscow to understand relations among activists, workers, bureaucrats, and a multiplicity of revolutionary parties.'

Wendy Goldman
Carnegie Mellon University

The Russian Revolution in Retreat, 1920–24

The Russian revolution of 1917 was a defining event of the twentieth century, and its achievements and failures remain controversial in the twenty-first. This book focuses on the retreat from the revolution's aims in 1920–24, after the civil war and at the start of the New Economic Policy – and specifically, on the turbulent relationship between the working class and the Communist Party in those years. It is based on extensive original research of the actions and reactions of the party leadership and ranks, of dissidents and members of other parties, and of trade union activists and ordinary factory workers. It discusses working-class collective action before, during and after the crisis of 1921, when the Bolsheviks were confronted by the revolt at the Kronshtadt naval base and other protest movements. This book argues that the working class was politically expropriated by the Bolshevik party, as democratic bodies such as soviets and factory committees were deprived of decision-making power; it examines how the new Soviet ruling class began to take shape. It shows how some worker activists concluded that the principles of 1917 had been betrayed, while others accepted a social contract, under which workers were assured of improvements in living standards in exchange for increased labour discipline and productivity, and a surrender of political power to the party.

Simon Pirani studied Russian at the University of London and wrote a doctoral dissertation at the University of Essex. He writes about the economy and politics of the former Soviet Union as a journalist. He is currently a senior research fellow at the Oxford Institute for Energy Studies, and is working on book projects on the post-Soviet period.

BASEES/Routledge Series on Russian and East European Studies

Series editor: Richard Sakwa, Department of Politics and International Relations, University of Kent

Editorial Committee:
Julian Cooper, Centre for Russian and East European Studies, University of Birmingham
Terry Cox, Department of Central and East European Studies, University of Glasgow
Rosalind Marsh, Department of European Studies and Modern Languages, University of Bath
David Moon, Department of History, University of Durham
Hilary Pilkington, Department of Sociology, University of Warwick
Stephen White, Department of Politics, University of Glasgow

Founding Editorial Committee Member:
George Blazyca, Centre for Contemporary European Studies, University of Paisley. This series is published on behalf of BASEES (the British Association for Slavonic and East European Studies).

The series comprises original, high-quality, research-level work by both new and established scholars on all aspects of Russian, Soviet, post-Soviet and East European Studies in humanities and social science subjects.

1 **Ukraine's Foreign and Security Policy, 1991–2000**
   Roman Wolczuk

2 **Political Parties in the Russian Regions**
   Derek S. Hutcheson

3 **Local Communities and Post-Communist Transformation**
   Edited by Simon Smith

4 **Repression and Resistance in Communist Europe**
   J.C. Sharman

5 **Political Elites and the New Russia**
   Anton Steen

6 **Dostoevsky and the Idea of Russianness**
   Sarah Hudspith

7 **Performing Russia – Folk Revival and Russian Identity**
   Laura J. Olson

8 **Russian Transformations**
   Edited by Leo McCann

9 **Soviet Music and Society under Lenin and Stalin**
   The Baton and Sickle
   Edited by Neil Edmunds

10 **State Building in Ukraine**
   The Ukranian parliament, 1990–2003
   Sarah Whitmore

11 **Defending Human Rights in Russia**
Sergei Kovalyov, Dissident and Human Rights Commissioner, 1969–2003
Emma Gilligan

12 **Small-Town Russia**
Postcommunist Livelihoods and Identities A Portrait of the Intelligentsia in Achit, Bednodemyanovsk and Zubtsov, 1999–2000
Anne White

13 **Russian Society and the Orthodox Church**
Religion in Russia after Communism
Zoe Knox

14 **Russian Literary Culture in the Camera Age**
The Word as Image
Stephen Hutchings

15 **Between Stalin and Hitler**
Class War and Race War on the Dvina, 1940–46
Geoffrey Swain

16 **Literature in Post-Communist Russia and Eastern Europe**
The Russian, Czech and Slovak Fiction of the Changes 1988–98
Rajendra A. Chitnis

17 **Soviet Dissent and Russia's Transition to Democracy**
Dissident Legacies
Robert Horvath

18 **Russian and Soviet Film Adaptations of Literature, 1900–2001**
Screening the Word
Edited by Stephen Hutchings and Anat Vernitski

19 **Russia as a Great Power**
Dimensions of Security Under Putin
Edited by Jakob Hedenskog, Vilhelm Konnander, Bertil Nygren, Ingmar Oldberg and Christer Pursiainen

20 **Katyn and the Soviet Massacre of 1940**
Truth, Justice and Memory
George Sanford

21 **Conscience, Dissent and Reform in Soviet Russia**
Philip Boobbyer

22 **The Limits of Russian Democratisation**
Emergency Powers and States of Emergency
Alexander N. Domrin

23 **The Dilemmas of Destalinisation**
A Social and Cultural History of Reform in the Khrushchev Era
Edited by Polly Jones

24 **News Media and Power in Russia**
Olessia Koltsova

25 **Post-Soviet Civil Society**
Democratization in Russia and the Baltic States
Anders Uhlin

26 **The Collapse of Communist Power in Poland**
Jacqueline Hayden

27 **Television, Democracy and Elections in Russia**
Sarah Oates

28 **Russian Constitutionalism**
Historical and Contemporary Development
Andrey N. Medushevsky

29 **Late Stalinist Russia**
Society Between Reconstruction and Reinvention
Edited by Juliane Fürst

30 **The Transformation of Urban Space in Post-Soviet Russia**
Konstantin Axenov, Isolde Brade and Evgenij Bondarchuk

31 **Western Intellectuals and the Soviet Union, 1920–40**
From Red Square to the Left Bank
Ludmila Stern

32 **The Germans of the Soviet Union**
Irina Mukhina

33 **Re-constructing the Post-Soviet Industrial Region**
The Donbas in Transition
Edited by Adam Swain

34 **Chechnya – Russia's "War on Terror"**
John Russell

35 **The New Right in the New Europe**
Czech Transformation and Right-Wing Politics, 1989–2006
Seán Hanley

36 **Democracy and Myth in Russia and Eastern Europe**
Edited by Alexander Wöll and Harald Wydra

37 **Energy Dependency, Politics and Corruption in the Former Soviet Union**
Russia's Power, Oligarchs' Profits and Ukraine's Missing Energy Policy, 1995–2006
Margarita M. Balmaceda

38 **Peopling the Russian Periphery**
Borderland Colonization in Eurasian History
Edited by Nicholas B Breyfogle, Abby Schrader and Willard Sunderland

39 **Russian Legal Culture Before and After Communism**
Criminal Justice, Politics and the Public Sphere
Frances Nethercott

40 **Political and Social Thought in Post-Communist Russia**
Axel Kaehne

41 **The Demise of the Soviet Communist Party**
Atsushi Ogushi

42 **Russian Policy towards China and Japan**
The El'tsin and Putin Periods
Natasha Kuhrt

43 **Soviet Karelia**
Politics, Planning and Terror in Stalin's Russia, 1920–39
Nick Baron

44 **Reinventing Poland**
Economic and Political Transformation and Evolving National Identity
Edited by Martin Myant and Terry Cox

45 **The Russian Revolution in Retreat, 1920–24**
Soviet Workers and the New Communist Elite
Simon Pirani

The Russian Revolution in Retreat, 1920–24

Soviet workers and the new communist elite

Simon Pirani

LONDON AND NEW YORK

First published 2008
by Routledge
2 Park Square, Milton Park, Abingdon, Oxon OX14 4RN

Simultaneously published in the USA and Canada
by Routledge
270 Madison Ave, New York, NY 10016

Routledge is an imprint of the Taylor & Francis Group, an informa business

Transferred to Digital Printing 2009

© 2008 Simon Pirani

Typeset in Times New Roman by
Taylor & Francis Books

All rights reserved. No part of this book may be reprinted or reproduced or utilised in any form or by any electronic, mechanical, or other means, now known or hereafter invented, including photocopying and recording, or in any information storage or retrieval system, without permission in writing from the publishers.

British Library Cataloguing in Publication Data
A catalogue record for this book is available from the British Library

Library of Congress Cataloging in Publication Data
Pirani, Simon, 1957–
The Russian revolution in retreat, 1920-24 : Soviet workers and the new Communist elite / Simon Pirani.
p. cm. – (Basees/Routledge series on Russian and East European studies ; 45)
Includes bibliographical references and index.
  1. Labor policy–Soviet Union. 2. Working class–Soviet Union. 3. Elite (Social sciences)–Soviet Union. I. Title.
   HD8526.P54 2008
   331.0947'09042–dc22
                  2007036600

ISBN10: 0-415-43703-2 (hbk)
ISBN10: 0-415-54641-9 (pbk)
ISBN10: 0-203-93029-0 (ebk)

ISBN13: 978-0-415-43703-5 (hbk)
ISBN13: 978-0-415-54641-6 (pbk)
ISBN13: 978-0-203-93029-8 (ebk)

Contents

Acknowledgements xi
Abbreviations, acronyms and Russian words used xiii
Map: Moscow in 1922 xv
Note on names and biographical information xvi

Introduction: workers and the Soviet state 1

1 Struggling to survive: workers in July–December 1920 19

2 Sweet visions and bitter clashes: the party in July–December 1920 44

3 The revolution that wasn't: workers and the party in January–March 1921 72

4 The NEP and non-partyism: workers in 1921 90

5 Renegades, oppositionists, suicides and administrators: the party in 1921 115

6 Mass mobilization versus mass participation: workers in 1922 138

7 The party elite, industrial managers and the cells: the party in 1922 166

8 The social contract in practice: workers in 1923 192

9 The elite takes charge: the party in 1923–24 211

Conclusions: the impact on socialism 233

Appendix 1. Biographical information 242
Appendix 2. Districts and workplaces 253
Appendix 3. Wages and currency rates 257

Appendix 4. Party membership 259
Appendix 5. Communists' occupations 261
Bibliography 264
Index 282

Acknowledgements

I owe a special debt to Steve Smith, who supervised the PhD dissertation on which this book is based, and gave support to my research that went far beyond anything I might have expected. Barbara Allen, Donald Filtzer, Aleksei Gusev and Viktoriia Tiazhel'nikova have given generously of their time. I also thank for comments on my research and correspondence Robert Argenbright, Robin Blackburn, Sally Boniece, Terry Brotherstone, Paul Flenley, Wendy Goldman, Gijs Kessler, Diane Koenker, Lars Lih, Konstantin Morozov, Kevin Murphy, Brian Pearce, Jon Smele, Tony Swift, Leonid Vaintraub, Suzi Weissman and Sergei Zhuravlev.

I thank the organizers of, and participants in, conferences where I presented research material: the British Association of Slavonic and East European Studies conference (2003 and 2004), the American Association for the Advancement of Slavic Studies convention (2004 and 2006), the Russian labour history conference at the International Institute of Social History in Amsterdam (2005) and the BASEES Study Group on the Russian Revolution (2005 and 2006). Discussions arranged by Workers Liberty and by the Praxis group in Moscow, seminars in the 'Individuals and Society' series at Birkbeck College, London, a session at the Historical Materialism conference in London and meetings of the Iranian Socialist Forum and of the South Place Ethical Society also helped me to clarify my ideas.

I thank the archivists at the Central Archive of the Social-Political History of Moscow, the Central Archive of the City of Moscow, the Central State Archive of the Moscow Region, the Central Moscow Archive/Museum of Personal Collections, the State Archive of the Russian Federation and the Russian State Archive of Social and Political History, and the librarians at the University of Essex, the Russian State Public History Library in Moscow, the Russian State Library, the library of the School of Slavonic and Eastern European Studies of the University of London, the British Library, Woolwich Reference Library and the European Resource Centre at the University of Birmingham.

Thanks to Sholpan Goronwy for help with Russian idioms and expressions, to Brian Eley for the graphics, and to friends who have discussed the issues with me, or helped me in other ways, including Janos Borovi, Sebastian

Budgen, Christine Cooper, Peter Court, David Crouch, Wendy Derose, William Dixon, Raouf Fateh, Paul Flewers, the late Peter Fryer, David Gorman, Trevor Goronwy, Iuliia Guseva, Hilary Horrocks, Natasha Kurashova, Yassamine Mather, David Maude, Anthony McIntyre, Jonas Nillson, Ali Reza, William Rowe, Torab Saleth, Keith Scotcher, Cyril Smith, John Spencer, the late Ngo Van, Vladimir Yefstratov and Chris Wright. I am also grateful to commissioning editors and others with whom I have worked in journalism while researching this book, especially Taimur Ahmad, Jonathan Bell, Andy Beven, David Eldridge, John Elkins, Robbie Firth, Bob Jones, Caroline Palmer, Andrew Pendleton, Sudip Roy and Mike Topp.

I am very grateful to my friends with whom I stayed in Moscow during my research trips: the Goriachev family (Konstantin and Inna, Dima, Anya and Ilyusha), and the Arkhangelov family (Natalia, Nikolai, Anton, Andrei and Aleksandra Nikolaevna). In London, Felix Pirani and the late Marta Monteleoni, John Ballantyne and Marta Cocco, and Elizabeth Cooper and Roger Keyse have been endlessly supportive. So has our daughter, Nadine. The biggest thanks of all, though, are to my partner, Monika, without whom I could not have written this book.

Some material in Chapters 1 and 3 was first used in my article, 'Class Clashes With Party: Politics in Moscow between the Civil War and the New Economic Policy', *Historical Materialism* 11: 2, 2003: 75–120, and material in Chapter 4 in 'The Moscow Workers' Movement in 1921 and the Role of Non-partyism', *Europe-Asia Studies* 56: 1, 2004: 143–60. An earlier version of Chapter 7 was published as 'The Party Elite, the Industrial Managers and the Cells: Early Stages in the Formation of the Soviet Ruling Class in Moscow, 1922–23', *Revolutionary Russia* 19: 2, 2006: 197–228. These are reproduced with permission.

Photographs have kindly been supplied by the Russian State Archive of Cinematic and Photographic Documents, the Central Archive of the Social-Political History of Moscow and the David King Collection.

Abbreviations, acronyms and Russian words used

Russian words that are not easily translated have been left in the original, as have the abbreviations of less well-known bodies. The names of some well-known and easily translatable bodies (e.g. Central Committee or Moscow Committee) have been anglicized and then abbreviated.

AMO	(Avtomobil'noe Moskovskoe Obshchestvo) — Moscow Automobile Company.
CC	Central Committee of the Russian Communist Party (Bolshevik).
CCC	Central Control Commission of the Russian Communist Party (Bolshevik).
CEC	the Central Executive Committee of soviets.
Cheka	(from *chrezvychainie kommissii*) — special commissions (full title, special commission for the repression of counter-revolution and sabotage). From 1922, the Cheka's name was changed to the State Political Administration (Gosudarstvennoe Politicheskoe Upravlenie); I have used the abbreviation GPU. In late 1923 it was further renamed Unified State Political Administration (Ob"edinnenoe Gosudarstvennoe Politicheskoe Upravlenie or OGPU), but for simplicity I have continued to use GPU.
Comintern	Communist International.
DCs	Democratic Centralists (grouping in the Bolshevik party).
glavk	(pl. *glavki*, from *glavny komitet*) — chief committee. Bodies established by VSNKh after 1917 to manage industries; largely replaced by trusts in 1922.
GPU	see Cheka.
kollektivnoe snabzhenie	collective supply. A system of collective payment in kind introduced to some workplaces in 1921.

MC	Moscow committee of the Russian Communist Party (Bolshevik).
MGSPS	(Moskovskii gubernskii sovet professional'nykh soiuzov) — the Moscow regional council of trade unions.
MSNKh	(Moskovskii sovet narodnogo khoziaistva) — the Moscow council of the economy.
naznachenstvo	appointism. The appointment, as opposed to election, of party and state officials.
naturpremiia	the establishment of stockpiles of an enterprise's own products to be traded for food.
NEP	New Economic Policy.
otvetstvennye rabotniki	responsible officials.
partstroitel'stvo	party building, a broad political/organizational concept.
rabfak	workers' faculty, set up in universities to streamline access for workers.
RKSP	(Rabochaia-krestianskaia sotsialisticheskaia partiia) — the Workers and Peasants Socialist Party.
sluzhashchie	(pl. *sluzhashchii*) — white-collar staff or employees, also extended to other service workers.
sovmestitel'stvo	the holding of two or more official posts simultaneously.
Sovnarkom	(Sovet narodnykh kommissarov) — Council of People's Commissars.
sovznaky	soviet currency notes.
spets (pl. *spetsy*)	technical specialist, often referred to as 'bourgeois specialist'.
SRs	Socialist Revolutionaries.
STO	(Sovet truda i oborony) — Council of Labour and Defence.
subbotnik	Saturday voluntary work.
tsentry	(*tsentral'nye komitety*) — central committee. In this context, industrial management bodies, similar to the *glavki* (see above).
udarnyi	adjectival form of 'shock', in the sense of shock work. Came into use during the civil war to describe factories whose production was prioritized.
udarnichestvo or *udarnost'*	the system of shock work.
VSNKh	(Vysshii sovet narodnogo khoziaistva) — Supreme Council of the Economy.
VTsSPS	(Vserossiiskii tsentral'nyi sovet profsoiuzov) — All-Russian Central Council of Trade Unions.
WO	Workers Opposition.

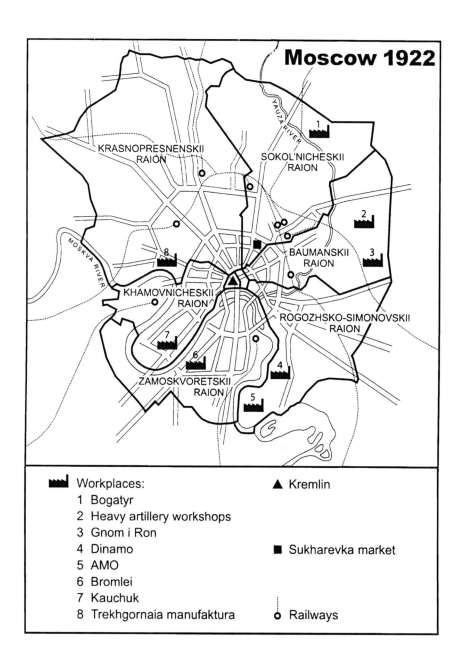

Note on names and biographical information

Individuals are referred to by their names, with profession and political affiliation where known. The use of first names or initials is preferred; if these are missing it is because I have not found them. There are biographical sketches of some important individuals, and a note on source material, in Appendix 1. In other cases, briefer information appears in footnotes.

Introduction
Workers and the Soviet state

The Russian revolution was a defining event, maybe *the* defining event, of the twentieth century. It was a turning point in the history of European and Asian empires and in the history of class struggles and movements of social liberation. The overthrow of the old Russian regime, and the successful establishment of a government that claimed to represent the working class, towered over the century as a whole, influencing social movements across the world. The retreat from, or failure of, the revolution's aims – aspects of which are discussed in this book – have, no less than its achievements, been a central problem for all those concerned with progressive social change.

The two Russian revolutions of 1917, which in February brought down tsarism and in October replaced the short-lived provisional government with the Bolsheviks, were the crucial outcome of the First World War. Whereas the Ottoman and Austro-Hungarian empires disintegrated, the Russian empire was swept away in the course of a social movement in which millions of people participated: workers who aspired to run their factories, peasants who wanted to take the land from those who had owned it down the ages, soldiers who didn't want to fight. Whereas the German and Hungarian revolutions of 1918–19 were reversed violently, the brutal Russian civil war of 1918–20 resulted, narrowly, in a Bolshevik victory. Once in power, the Bolsheviks presided over industrialization and modernization, not, as in nineteenth-century Europe, under the banner of capitalism and the market, but for the first time in history by means of a supposedly socialist state. All the subsequent workers' movements that challenged capitalist state power, from Spain in the 1930s to France in 1968 or Iran in 1979, were influenced by Bolshevik ideology; so too were the Chinese and Vietnamese revolutions, which were more peasant wars than workers' uprisings, and many nationalist movements in the period after the Second World War. The methods of property nationalization and state planning adopted in the Soviet Union were spread across Eastern Europe by the Red army.

While the revolution's influence continued to spread for decades, in Russia, within months of the October uprising, the revolution was in retreat from the aims of social liberation it had proclaimed. It was confounded by circumstances, and pushed back by the state. The retreat, like the revolution, was not uniform or unidimensional. Workers, communists and others kept trying to push the revolution forward, long after passing the points that they, or historians, later defined as the crucial moment of reversal (1918, 1921 or even 1928–29). This book views this process – and specifically, the way that it was manifested in the Bolsheviks' fraught relations with workers in Moscow after the civil war – from a socialist standpoint. 'Socialism' is here meant in the original sense used by Marx, a movement to recreate society by superceding alienated labour,[1] private property and the state. On this view, the Russian revolution, and all the twentieth-century revolutionary workers' movements, may be characterized as a series of unsuccessful attempts to break through and overturn the complex of social relationships based on alienated labour, which has the state at its head. Given that collective, participatory democracy is a necessary part of any movement towards socialism, the turning-back of strivings towards such democracy is seen as inherent in its failures.

The efforts by large numbers of people to develop such democracy, in the first place through the soviets and factory committees that emerged during the 1905 uprising, was a central feature of the Russian revolution. Soon after the February 1917 revolution – which brought about the legislation of universal suffrage and freedom of the press, abolition of the death penalty and other democratic measures – the soviet movement spread from the towns to the countryside and army. It grew still stronger in late 1917, in the build-up to the October uprising. During the civil war of 1918–20, the revolution as a socialist project began to turn back. Its heartlands were geographically isolated by White armies. The economy collapsed, peasants resisted grain requisitioning, famine and disease spread unhindered and the population suffered unprecedented hardship. Society was close to breaking down. In industry, most of which was nationalized within weeks of the Bolsheviks taking power, attributes of alienated labour – labour discipline and top-down management – were imposed, as the Bolshevik government struggled to revive the broken economy. Indeed, under these conditions of desperate shortage, labour could *only* be alienated labour, and on that basis social relationships were formed that could only be exploitative. Experiments with workers' inspection and management of production were short-lived. Labour compulsion was tried out. The Bolshevik party soon turned its back on the principle of collective working-class democracy that had been practiced in 1917. Where the soviets survived, their decisions were

1 Alienated labour means activity, the product of which is outside the creator's control and stands hostile to her or him. Marx's complex concept of alienation, i.e. a loss of control, embraced human beings' alienation from nature, from their 'species being' as members of the human species, and from each other, as well as the alienation inherent in wage labour. The best concise summary remains K. Marx, *Wage Labour and Capital*, Moscow: Progress Publishers, 1952, pp. 20–22, and the best discussion I. Meszaros, *Marx's Theory of Alienation*, London: Merlin, 2005, especially pp. 8, 14–22 and 122–61.

usually subordinated to edicts by party or military bodies. Non-Bolshevik socialist parties were subject to repression. The death penalty was partly reimposed and the special security commissions (the Cheka) became stronger.

There was and is no consensus among socialist writers about whether the Russian revolution was defeated, retreated or failed; nor about the time frame within which it turned back, or was turned back. The civil war is often at the centre of the debates, though. For many, it was the principal factor that forced the Bolsheviks to abandon many of the aspirations of 1917; for others, the worst of it could have been avoided, had the Bolsheviks, Socialist Revolutionaries (SRs) and others acted differently; for some, it merely reinforced anti-socialist tendencies already prevalent in Bolshevism. The historiography, too, emphasizes the civil war as a cause of the trend towards dictatorial rule. Some arguments (for example Sheila Fitzpatrick's) underline the role of political and cultural practices developed in the Red army and carried over into peacetime construction. Others (for example Malvin Helgesen's, which reflects a view of the origins of Bolshevik authoritarianism common on the left) suggest that material circumstances denied the Bolsheviks opportunities to develop democracy that they would otherwise have taken.[2] This book focuses instead on the period straight after the civil war, when the factors on which the revolution's future depended – both objective (economic collapse, demographic changes) and subjective (Bolshevik ideology, workers' movements) – were present in a different configuration. The terrible weight of adverse conditions that forced the hands of the Bolsheviks, workers and other historical actors during the civil war was lifted – not sufficiently for any of them to be able to roll back the retreat of the revolution, but enough, at least, for them to make clearer choices about how to build the new society. The force of circumstance was still strong, even overwhelming, but worked over a longer time scale. The Bolsheviks' choices – notwithstanding such crises as the transport breakdown of 1920–21, and even the catastrophic rural famine of 1921–22 – were now less about how to stave off a military or supply emergency within days

2 Fitzpatrick argues that the civil war militarized the Bolsheviks' 'revolutionary political culture', leaving a heritage that included 'readiness to resort to coercion, rule by administrative fiat ..., centralized administration and summary justice'. She sees this, together with the propositions that a minority dictatorship was almost bound to be authoritarian and that the Bolsheviks' worker supporters were unlikely to worry about dictatorial methods, as central to the origins of Soviet authoritarianism. Helgesen, whose work is unfortunately unpublished, concludes that the emergence of one-party rule and the concentration of political power, particularly in the party apparatus, was 'the result of individual pragmatic policy decisions made ... in an effort to cope with the manifold crises of the civil war'. S. Fitzpatrick, *The Russian Revolution 1917–1932*, Oxford: Oxford University Press, 1982, p. 64; M.M. Helgesen, *The Origins of the Party-State Monolith in Soviet Russia: Relations between the Soviets and Party Committees in the Central Provinces, October 1917 – March 1921* (PhD diss., State University of New York at Stony Brook, 1980), p. 525.

or weeks, and more to do with how people would live and work in future months, years and decades.

This book argues that one of the most important choices the Bolsheviks made at this point was to turn their backs on forms of collective, participatory democracy that workers briefly attempted to revive. It challenges the notion, persistent among left-wing historians, that political power was forced on the Bolsheviks because the working class was so weakened by the civil war that it was incapable of wielding it. In reality, non-party workers were willing and able to participate in political processes, but, in the Moscow soviet and elsewhere, were pushed out of them by the Bolsheviks. The party's vanguardism, i.e. its conviction that it had the right, and the duty, to make political decisions on the workers' behalf, was now reinforced by its control of the state apparatus. The working class was politically expropriated; power was progressively concentrated in the party, and specifically in the party elite. These were the most important features of the new political order established by the Bolsheviks after the adoption of the New Economic Policy (NEP) in 1921, and on the basis of a dynamic economic revival. Workers benefited from this set-up – most significantly by regaining, and starting to surpass, the living standards achieved on the eve of the First World War. But the *quid pro quo* for this was the surrender of political power to the party. In terms of the development of the workers' movement and socialism, this latter aspect of the party-worker relationship was the most important, and the most destructive.

These arguments are made from a standpoint that views the working class in the sense used by Marx and E.P. Thompson: as a class formed in a process of struggle and self-definition against the ruling class; 'a social and cultural formation' understandable 'in terms of its relationship with other classes' (Thompson), rather than as a 'structure' or category; a 'happening', the understanding of which must deal with consciousness, experience and collective action.[3] Labour history has included a constantly widening array of aspects of workers' experience in the study of working-class formation: the social history (history 'from below') pioneered in the 1970s and 1980s has been enriched more recently by the approaches of cultural history and the methods of the 'linguistic turn'. Hopefully, this book reflects the influence of all this work, but its main focus is comparatively 'traditional': on working-class politics – not in the narrow sense of concern with government,

---

3 K. Marx and F. Engels, *The German Ideology. Part One* (ed. C.J. Arthur), London: Lawrence & Wishart, 1977, pp. 82–83; E.P. Thompson, *The Making of the English Working Class*, especially pp. 10–11 and p. 939. See also E.P. Thompson, *The Poverty of Theory and Other Essays*, London: Merlin, 1978, pp. 298–99, and I. Katznelson, 'Working Class Formation: constructing cases and comparisons', in I. Katznelson and A. Zolberg (eds), *Working-Class Formation: Nineteenth-Century Patterns in Western Europe and the United States*, Princeton: Princeton University Press, 1986, pp. 3–41.

but in a broader sense of collective action that seeks to change, or question, power relations – as an integral part of class formation.[4] Working-class politics is taken to be not solely or principally about workers' parties, but about the political strivings of the working class in general.

The process of working-class formation in Russia took a sharp turn when the Bolsheviks, having been swept into government on an unprecedented wave of working-class action, dispossessed the capitalists, nationalized industry, and made the state, which claimed to express workers' interests, the driver of economic development. Henceforth, this state was a key factor in the process of working class formation. The working class had to articulate its collective interests in the face of this 'workers' state'. The dilemmas that resulted have been considered by those historians who brought the labour history of the Russian revolution to the foreground, and have strongly influenced my work.[5] The editors of an important volume on labour history wrote: 'Soviet workers, coming together and working within a system called by its leaders "socialist", were quickly proletarianized, but they did not then constitute themselves as a conscious proletariat in Marx's sense of a class-for-itself'. In the same volume, Moshe Lewin referred to a

---

4 A useful definition of 'collective action' is by Charles Tilly: it applies 'more or less equally to actors who are determined to tear down the system and those who seek minor reforms, to the outcast and the privileged, to the successful and the ineffectual', and argued that it 'covers a wide range of behaviour whose connection and common properties deserve attention: not only almost all behaviour which authorities call "protest", "rebellion" or one of the other disparaging epithets, but also petitioning, parading, bloc voting, and any number of other ways of acting together'. C. Tilly, 'Introduction', in L. Tilly and C. Tilly (eds), *Class Conflict and Collective Action*, Beverly Hills: Sage, 1981, pp. 9–20.

5 For example D.P. Koenker, *Moscow Workers and the 1917 Revolution*, Princeton: Princeton University Press, 1981; D.P. Koenker and W.G. Rosenberg, *Strikes and Revolution in Russia, 1917*, Princeton: Princeton University Press, 1989; A. Rabinowitch, *Prelude to Revolution: the Petrograd Bolsheviks and the July 1917 Uprising*, Bloomington: Indiana University Press, 1968; A. Rabinowitch, *The Bolsheviks Come to Power: the Revolution of 1917 in Petrograd*, New York: W. Norton, 1976; S.A. Smith, *Red Petrograd*, Cambridge: Cambridge University Press, 1983; D. Mandel, *The Petrograd Workers and the Fall of the Old Regime: from the February Revolution to the July Days, 1917*, London: Macmillan, 1983; D. Mandel, *The Petrograd Workers and the Soviet Seizure of Power: from the July Days 1917 to July 1918*, London: Macmillan, 1984. An overview of this work is R.G. Suny, 'Towards a Social History of the October Revolution', *American Historical Review* 1 (1983), pp. 31–52. On Moscow, as well as Koenker's book, there are e.g. V.E. Bonnell, *Roots of Rebellion: Workers' Politics and Organizations in St. Petersburg and Moscow, 1900–1914*, Berkeley: University of California Press, 1983; R.E. Johnson, *Peasant and Proletarian: the Working Class of Moscow in the Late Nineteenth Century*, Leicester: Leicester University Press, 1979; L. Engelstein, *Moscow 1905: Working Class Organization and Political Conflict*, Stanford: Stanford University Press, 1982.

'riddle': 'we have a working class reminiscent of the old capitalist system but a ruling stratum (later, class) reminiscent of what?'[6]

This stratum, as it existed during the Russian civil war, could not meaningfully be called a ruling *class*: a ruling elite formed around the party, Red army commanders and state officials, yes, but no social class with clearly defined collective interests. Nevertheless, despite this absence of a ruling class, exploitative social relationships based on alienated labour reappeared. The state played a central role in this. As the Bolsheviks contended with the economic breakdown, they campaigned, and turned the trades unions and factory committees to campaign, for labour discipline; and they combined labour mobilization techniques with labour compulsion measures, including militarization. Often, workplace organizations – and presumably workers themselves – supported these measures, and in some cases proposed still harsher ones. Most of the time, most anti-Bolshevik workers' parties supported such measures too, although the Mensheviks and others bridled at labour compulsion. Organized independent workers' action had peaked in the spring of 1918 in Petrograd, with a strike wave and the convening of an independent factory representatives' assembly, and was soon suppressed. In the two years that followed, workers' reactions to the labour regime and the supply crisis were as often individual as collective. There were scattered strikes and protests, mostly over rations, but more often there was absenteeism, skilled workers quitting the job and moving elsewhere, and the use of factory machinery to make objects for sale or home use.[7]

Workers were in many respects reduced to a struggle for survival. The impact of such events on the process of working-class formation and the development of political consciousness was overwhelmingly negative. That having been said, the provocative challenge by Michael Seidman to historiographical assumptions about workers' reactions to post-revolutionary chaos deserves comment. Traditionally, historians, especially those on the left, have assumed that workers' aversion to labour discipline indicated a lack of political consciousness. Their individual survival strategies have been categorized as acts of desperation that bear little or no relation to the class struggle. Seidman has questioned this: he opposes the 'productivist' vision that assumes the factory to be an 'arena of liberation' and abstention from work as, by implication, negative. In his books on the Spanish civil war and the French popular front – situations in which, as in revolutionary Russia,

---

6 L. Siegelbaum and R.G. Suny, 'Class Backwards? In Search of the Soviet Working Class', pp. 1–26, and M. Lewin, 'Concluding Remarks', pp. 376–89, here p. 383, in L. Siegelbaum and R.G. Suny (eds), *Making Workers Soviet: Power, Class and Identity*, London: Cornell University Press, 1994.

7 D. Brower, '"The City in Danger": the civil war and the Russian urban population', in D.P. Koenker, W.G. Rosenberg and R.G. Suny (eds), *Party, State and Society in the Russian Civil War: Explorations in Social History*, Bloomington: Indiana University Press, 1989, pp. 58–80; M. McAuley, *Bread and Justice: State and Society in Petrograd 1917–1922*, Oxford: Clarendon, 1991, especially pp. 239–258.

workers faced a crisis of capitalist rule and governments claiming to impose labour discipline in the workers' name – Seidman argues that workers' 'resistance to work' had a 'utopian', anti-wage-labour aspect. He produces little evidence that such a stance was articulated, and neither have Russian labour historians found much. The relative importance in workers' motivation of such utopianism, and of survival strategies, needs further research. On the other hand, Seidman makes a convincing case that state and quasi-state authorities' hierarchical tendencies were aggravated by their reaction to workers' resistance to work. He shows that it 'contributed to the bureaucratization and centralization' of the anarcho-syndicalist labour confederation in revolutionary Barcelona, and that workers' unwillingness to conform to labour discipline brought out the worst authoritarian streak in the anarcho-syndicalist leaders.[8] A similar tendency was evident during the Russian civil war, when workers' foot-dragging and absenteeism provoked ever-more draconian reactions from many Bolsheviks. The common features in the Russian and Spanish cases were: a revolutionary breakthrough led to the formation of a government that ruled in the name of the working class; due to the limited scope of the breakthrough, alienated labour was reimposed; the state, even where it was rudimentary, and the workers' organizations, were instrumental in this process; and even in the absence of a capitalist or other ruling class, that state became rapidly bureaucratized, and hierarchical social relations were soon reproduced. While many strands of utopianism were no doubt present, it also seems incontrovertible that, as a result of the civil war, the process of working-class formation and development of workers' consciousness were severely disrupted.

The period covered by this book opens in 1920, immediately after the civil war. There was a revival of working-class collective action that culminated in February–March 1921 in a widespread strike movement and the revolt by sailors at the Kronshtadt naval base. The political character of these movements is a key to understanding working-class formation, and there is no consensus about it among historians. The Bolsheviks condemned these movements as, at best, expressions of backward self-interest, and, at worst, as supportive of counter-revolution. Among western historians working in the Soviet period, Isaac Deutscher and others accepted some of this argument, while Paul Avrich, Israel Getzler and others questioned it. Jonathan Aves's study of the workers' movement in 1920–21 concluded that 'resilient traditions of organization' had survived the civil war; I argue that a variety of political trends in the workers' movement did too. Russian and western historians working in the post-Soviet period, when access to

---

8 M. Seidman, *Workers Against Work: Labor in Paris and Barcelona During the Popular Fronts*, Berkeley: University of California Press, 1991, pp. 11–15, 96–100 and 133–55; and M. Seidman, *Republic of Egos: a Social History of the Spanish Civil War*, Madison: University of Wisconsin Press, 2002, especially pp. 7–8, 14 and 67–69.

archives improved, built up a more detailed picture of these movements.[9] Two prominent historians writing in the 1990s, Richard Pipes and Orlando Figes, both suggested that the spring of 1921 amounted to a 'revolutionary situation', in which the Bolsheviks could have been overthrown, and I argue against this. That is not to say that this movement was apolitical or anti-socialist. On the contrary, while frustration over food supply motivated many of the strikes, some sections of the non-party workers' movement put a premium on political participation. This became very clear at the Moscow soviet elections of April-May 1921, which provided an opportunity to revive working-class political participation. The Bolsheviks turned it down.

The political crisis of 1921 pushed the Bolsheviks to adopt the NEP, which in turn paved the way for economic recovery. The Bolsheviks' chosen path was to conduct the economic revival under the leadership of the party and the state; the working class was consigned to the area of production and kept out of the process of political decision-making. A social contract, as I describe it in Chapter 4, took shape, and was accepted by most workers: living standards improved consistently, in exchange for both increased labour discipline and productivity, and the surrender of political power to the party. This is a central theme of this book. The working class gained in terms of living standards, but paid a heavy price in terms of its collective consciousness and political development.

The evolution of the Soviet state and the party that controlled it is another major theme. During the civil war, the new state started to be built on the foundations of the 'war communist' economy described above. As efforts were made to intensify the rate of exploitation in the factories, and the Red army undertook economic and administrative, as well as military, functions, tsarist and post-February systems of government were junked – although chunks of the old apparatus and its methods were retained, hardly altered. The organs of active, collective democracy experimented with in 1917 – soviets, factory committees, workers' militia, bodies for workers' inspection and manage-

---

9 Deutscher dismissed the idea that the Kronshtadt revolt was led by White generals, but repeated sympathetically Trotsky's contention that the sailors were a new intake with no revolutionary traditions, 'blinded' to the consequences of their actions. I. Deutscher, *The Prophet Armed. Trotsky 1879–1921*, London: Oxford University Press, 1970, pp. 510–14. P. Avrich, *Kronstadt 1921*, Princeton: Princeton University Press, 1970; I. Getzler, *Kronstadt 1917–1921: The Fate of a Soviet Democracy*, Cambridge: Cambridge University Press, 1983; J. Aves, *Workers Against Lenin*, London: Tauris, 1996, p. 186. More recent works include S. Iarov, *Gorozhanin kak politik: revoliutsiia, voennyi kommunizm i NEP glazami petrogradtsev*, St Petersburg: 'Dmitrii Bulagin', 1999; V.Iu. Cherniaev and E.I. Makarov (eds), *Piterskie rabochie i 'Diktatura Proletariata'. Oktiabr'1917–1929: ekonomicheskie konflikti i politichestkii protest*, St Petersburg: Russko-baltiiskii informatsionnyi tsentr BLITs, 2000; D.J. Raleigh, *Experiencing Russia's Civil War: Politics, Society and Revolutionary Culture in Saratov, 1917–1922*, Princeton: Princeton University Press, 2002.

ment – were subordinated to hierarchical, often militaristic, authority. Rights to free speech, assembly and judicial process were trampled by the Cheka, whose actions were often justified by party leaders in terms of necessity. It is obvious that the Bolshevik government had nothing but its ramshackle state machine with which to confront one emergency after another – and equally obvious that all this was a complete break with the movement to socialism envisaged in outline by Marx, for example in his writings on the 1871 Paris commune. Circumstances shaped the Bolsheviks' ideology. They became the most fervent statists. They found themselves gutting their socialism of the means of social change that had been inherent in Marx's: the movement of collective democracy to supercede the state. Marx's phrase, the 'dictatorship of the proletariat', stripped of its context, was misused to justify the drastic expansion of state power. Lenin's 1917 pamphlet that discussed the 'withering away' of the state, *The State and Revolution*, was published, but neither he nor any other party leader seriously revisited the questions he had raised. On the contrary, they justified what they were doing in theoretical terms, e.g. in whole books by Bukharin and Trotsky.[10] In the Bolshevik ranks, the classical Marxist concept of socialism as the negation of the state scarcely crossed many people's minds. A worker who quit in protest at his comrades bowing before 'the new God That They Call the State', mentioned in Chapter 2 below, was in a tiny minority. Henceforth, for most Bolsheviks, state power, state control over the economy, and increasing productivity in state industry, became synonymous with the struggle for 'socialism'.

It has been argued above that Russia during the civil war had no ruling class. The gap was not properly filled in the post-civil-war period either. The landed gentry and capitalist class had been broken up. The new Soviet ruling class had not yet coalesced from the groups of officials who would join its ranks. The working class ruled in name only, ceding political power to the Bolshevik party. That party found itself, and the state that it controlled, playing an extraordinarily important role, not only in rebuilding the economy, but in recreating a ruling class. Moshe Lewin observed that it was a superstructure, 'suspended temporarily in a kind of vacuum', that had to recreate its own base.[11] Bolshevism, having become so decidedly statist during the civil war, now turned to state-building and economy-building. This, for the party, was the logic of NEP and of the 'great break' that followed in 1928–30. The state had to be strong enough to oversee an economic transformation that would enable the Soviet Union – as the Bolshevik-ruled territories became in late 1922 – to hold its own against the

10 L. Trotsky, *Terrorism and Communism: a Reply to Karl Kautsky*, London: New Park, 1975, especially pp. 140–82; N. Bukharin, *Ekonomika perekhodnogo perioda*, in N. Bukharin (ed.), *Izbrannye proizvedeniia*, Moscow: Ekonomika, 1990, pp. 81–239, especially pp. 189–98.
11 M. Lewin, *The Making of the Soviet System: Essays in the Social History of Interwar Russia*, New York: The New Press, 1994, p. 260.

capitalist powers. This was also nation-building: Stalin acquired his 'unbreakable hold' over party, government and administration by combining the aims of industrialization and modernization with that of 'revival of the power and prestige of the Russian nation', as E.H. Carr wrote of the 'great break'.[12]

Some discussions of the Soviet state have focused on its use of social mobilization. Thomas Remington defined mobilization during the civil war as 'a means of subjecting social resources to state control'. It was used to 'draw the independent initiative and organizational authority of the working-class and industrial bodies into the new state' and 'place them under its formal authority', depriving the regime of the potential support of a broader range of civil society organizations.[13] Remington assumes socialism to be state-building, and proposes pluralism, as opposed to mobilization, as the way to mediate between state and society. In contrast, I argue that the movement towards socialism must involve participatory democratic forms that, through history, transcend the state. I endeavour to interpret events in early Soviet Russia as the conflict of these forms, however embryonic, with the state forms. Mobilization techniques were the other side of the coin of political expropriation of the working class. They were not a spur to workers' initiative in any meaningful sense, but a substitute, imposed as initiative was stifled. From very early on (1918–19), the Bolsheviks' state was anathema to socialist creativity, emasculating soviets and trades unions, and laying down strict boundaries on workers' political activity, enforced by repressive measures. In Chapter 6 I advance this argument with reference to mobilization campaigns in the early NEP period.

David Priestland's recent book argues that ideologically inspired mobilization – in support of labour discipline, or in campaigns against 'bureaucratism', and resting latterly on a 'fusion of nationalist and Marxist ideas' – was at the centre of Bolshevik state-building efforts from the civil war to the purges.[14] In his interpretation, ideology was the fount from which mobilization techniques sprang. He puts internal party discussions in the foreground, as though the party was the only significant subjective force. I view mobilization techniques from a different angle. Working-class political interests were articulated not in the shadow of Bolshevik politics, but independently; as well as being impacted by what went on in the party, workers' struggles influenced the party. Mobilization techniques were as much a reaction to the challenge of independent working-class politics as a product

12 E.H. Carr, *The Russian Revolution from Lenin to Stalin, 1917–1929*, Basingstoke: Palgrave, 1979, pp. 75 and 171.
13 T. Remington, *Building Socialism in Bolshevik Russia: Ideology and Industrial Organization 1917–1921*, Pittsburgh: University of Pittsburgh Press, 1984, pp. 12–13 and 176–88.
14 Remington, op. cit., especially p. 11; D. Priestland, *Stalinism and the Politics of Mobilization: Ideas, Power and Terror in Inter-war Russia*, New York: Oxford University Press, 2007, especially pp. 189–92 and 407–8.

Moscow factory workers. Top: a speaker addresses workers, mostly women, at the Trekhgornaia cotton combine (early 1920s). Above: workers at the AMO motor works discuss an engine repair (1924).

of ideology. This interpretive issue is relevant not only to the post-civil-war period but also to the 'great break' of 1928–30. Priestland's account, in which shifts in Bolshevik ideology are at the centre, describes how the apparatus called on workers to criticize 'bureaucratism', and how workers made effective use of this right against managers. But that is less than half the story of working-class action at that time. More significant were the gigantic protests organized independently of and in opposition to the Bolsheviks, which began by resisting speed-up and wage cuts and moved on to the political plane before being repressed. Jeffrey Rossman's work on the textile workers' movement in Ivanovo region has brought these to the centre of attention.[15]

This book endeavours to place changes in Bolshevik politics and ideology, including the use of mobilization techniques, in the context of changing class relations. In counterpoint to working-class formation, the new Soviet ruling class was taking shape. The party elite acted as a centre of gravity around which this class gathered, and the party as a whole adapted its policies to the elite's interests. The later chapters of this book trace this process as it unfolded in the first years of NEP. Industrial workers and other party activists were sucked into the party-state apparatus, a process that the Moscow party secretary compared despairingly to the action of a pump. Other social groupings that went on to become constituent elements of the Soviet ruling class – factory managers, party cell leaders and specialists – found themselves, from the start, in an antagonistic relationship with workers. Notwithstanding the discomfort felt by many party members at these hostilities, the party as an organization reinforced the evolving hierarchy. At the same time, the party elite consolidated its control of the whole party, a process that culminated in the defeat of the left opposition in 1923. Between the civil war and the mid 1920s, the party was transformed from a military-political fighting organization to an administrative machine for implementing decisions taken at the top. In terms of socialist theory, it is concluded that, in view of the role that the state played in these events, the characterization of it as a 'workers' state' needs to be questioned.

The writing of the labour history of the early Soviet period has been defined by three major developments in recent decades: the assertion of the role of the working class in the Russian revolution; the 'revisionist' arguments about working-class support for the Stalinist transformations of the late 1920s, and responses to them; and the impact on the field of cultural history and the 'linguistic turn'. The labour history of the revolution came to the fore with the work of Diane Koenker, Alexander Rabinowitch, William Rosenberg and many others in the 1970s and 1980s.[16] From the late 1980s, a

---

15 Priestland, op. cit., especially pp. 201–5; J. Rossman, *Worker Resistance Under Stalin: Class and Revolution on the Shop Floor*, London: Harvard University Press, 2005.
16 See note 5 above.

great deal of attention was paid to the civil war and early NEP periods.[17] The 'revisionist' trend, which asserted that sections of the working class formed the social basis on which Stalin carried out his 'revolution from above', and the controversies around it, centred initially on the 'great break'. But it also found its reflection in the historiography of the first Soviet decade. William Chase, for example, asserted in his monograph on Moscow that, in the mid 1920s, 'the historic alliance [between party and class, formed in 1917] began to re-form on a tentative basis'. Lewis Siegelbaum's book on state and society under NEP took a more sceptical view.[18] I propose in this book that the social contract between the Bolsheviks and workers depended on the workers ceding political power to the party; the accent, in contrast to Chase, is on the deepening gulf between the two sides.

More recently, Soviet labour history, reflecting broader historiographical trends, has widened its focus from its 'traditional' subjects (male manual workers, organized in unions and parties) and studied hitherto-neglected sections of it and aspects of its experience, for example Wendy Goldman's writing on women workers and Daniel Orlovsky's on the *sluzhashchie*.[19] Latterly, the 'cultural turn' has also impacted strongly on the Soviet labour history, and its potential shown by work as diverse as Orlando Figes's and Boris Kolonitskii's on 1917, Mark Steinberg's on worker writers and Eric Naiman's on the NEP period. Its influence on Russian historians of the period is evident in the work, e.g., of Sergei Zhuravlev and Natalia Lebina.[20] Labour history *per se* of the early Soviet period is also undergoing something of a revival; recent examples include Diane Koenker's book on the printers' union, Kevin Murphy's on the Serp i Molot factory and Jeffrey Rossman's, cited above, on workers' movements during the first five-year plan.[21]

---

17 See, for example, articles in D.P. Koenker, W.G. Rosenberg and R.G. Suny (eds), *Party, State and Society in the Russian Civil War: Explorations in Social History*, Bloomington: Indiana University Press, 1989, and S. Fitzpatrick, A. Rabinowitch and R. Stites (eds), *Russia in the Era of NEP: Explorations in Soviet Society and Culture*, Bloomington: Indiana University Press, 1991. See also McAuley, op. cit.
18 The initial statement of the 'revisionist' position was in S. Fitzpatrick, *Education and Social Mobility in the Soviet Union 1921–1934*, Cambridge: Cambridge University Press, 1979; W. Chase, *Workers, Society and the Soviet State: Labour and Life in Moscow 1918–1929*, Urbana: University of Illinois Press, 1990, p. 297; L. Siegelbaum, *Soviet State and Society Between Revolutions, 1918–1929*, Cambridge: Cambridge University Press, 1992, especially p. 100 and p. 226.
19 W. Goldman, *Women, the State and Revolution: Soviet Family Policy and Social Life, 1917–1936*, Cambridge: Cambridge University Press, 1993; W. Goldman, *Women at the Gates: Gender and Industry in Stalin's Russia*, Cambridge: Cambridge University Press, 2002; D. Orlovsky, 'State building in the civil war era: the role of the lower middle strata', in D. Koenker et al. (eds), op. cit., pp. 180–209; Orlovsky, 'The Hidden Class: White Collar Workers in the Soviet 1920s', in Siegelbaum and Suny (eds.), op. cit., pp. 220–52.

14 *Introduction*

Political history has moved at a different tempo. In the last two decades, comparatively little has been published by western historians, especially on the immediate post-revolutionary period, although a considerable amount has been written about the party rank and file. Sheila Fitzpatrick even went so far as to assert, in a recent historiographical survey, that 'Soviet political history has been under a cloud for the past 20 or 30 years'.[22] But Russian historians, initially in the context of Gorbachev-era discussions about the breakdown of the USSR, have produced a great deal of research on political changes under Lenin and Stalin.[23] I have found of particular value monographs by E.G. Gimpel'son, Irina Pavlova and others who have sought to reinterpret the birth of the Soviet ruling class as a primarily political process, and work on the early 1920s by Sergei Pavliuchenkov, Sergei Tsakunov and others.[24]

This book deals with events in the city of Moscow and the Moscow region. This approach has allowed me to pay attention to events 'at the grass roots', particularly in the factory-based organizations, and, in the sections on the party's internal affairs, has made possible a consideration of

20 O. Figes and B. Kolonitskii, *Interpreting the Russian Revolution: the Language and Symbols of 1917*, New Haven: Yale University Press, 1999; M.D. Steinberg, *Proletarian Imagination: Self, Modernity and the Sacred in Russia, 1910–1925*, Ithaca: Cornell University Press, 2002; E. Naiman, *Sex in Public: the Incarnation of Early Soviet Ideology*, Princeton: Princeton University Press, 1997; S.V. Zhuravlev, *'Malenkie liudi' i 'bol'shaia istoriia'. Inostrantsy moskovskogo Elektrozavoda v sovetskom obshchestve 1920-kh – 1930-kh gg*, Moscow: Rosspen, 2000; N.B. Lebina, *Povsednevnaia zhizn Sovetskogo goroda 1920–1930 gody: normy i anomalii*, St Petersburg: izd. 'Letnii sad', 1999; V. Tiazhel'nikova, 'Povsednevnaia zhizn' moskovskikh rabochikh v nachale 1920-kh godov', in A.K. Sokolov and V.M. Koz'menko (eds), *Rossiia v XX veke: liudi, idei, vlast'*, Moscow: Rosspen, 2002, pp. 194–218.
21 D. Koenker, *Republic of Labor: Russian Printers and Soviet Socialism, 1918–1930*, Ithaca: Cornell University Press, 2005; K. Murphy, *Revolution and Counterrevolution: Class Struggle in a Moscow Metal Factory*, Oxford: Berghahn Books, 2005; Rossman, op. cit. See also a collection that followed the 2005 Amsterdam conference on Russian labour history, D. Filtzer, W. Goldman, G. Kessler and S. Pirani (eds), *A Dream Deferred: New Studies in Russian and Soviet Labour History*, Amsterdam: Peter Lang, forthcoming.
22 S. Fitzpatrick, 'Politics as practice: thoughts on a new Soviet political history', *Kritika*, 5: 1, 2004: 27–51. On the rank and file, see, e.g., S. Fitzpatrick, 'The Bolsheviks' Dilemma: Class, Culture, and Politics in Early Soviet Years', *Slavic Review* 47, 1988: 599–613; S. Fitzpatrick, 'The Problem of Class Identity', in S. Fitzpatrick et al., op. cit., pp. 12–33; and P. Kenez, *The Birth of the Propaganda State: Soviet Methods of Mass Mobilization 1917–1929*, Cambridge: Cambridge University Press, 1985. Igal Halfin has also written on the party rank and file; see p. 45. Studies of the Komsomol, and particularly A.E. Gorsuch, *Youth in Revolutionary Russia: Enthusiasts, Bohemians, Delinquents*, Bloomington: Indiana University Press, 2000, have discussed similar issues. The earlier work of T.H. Rigby on the party ranks remains of great value.
23 Notable Russian monographs and articles of the last 20 years are listed in note 5 to Chapter 7, p. 169.

the politics of the rank and file. On the other hand, in a study of the Soviet capital rather than an outlying region, the interaction between events on the ground and decisions taken at the top can be more readily discerned. Moscow, and its party organization, was the first among the regions. It felt the impact of, and impacted upon, the Bolshevik leadership, more than any other. While the city is already served by John Hatch's articles on its labour history, Chase's social history, work on labour under Stalin, Timothy Colton's work on municipal government, and histories of the Bolshevik organization during the civil war and late NEP,[25] this book is the first with a focus on working class politics, and the dynamics of workers' relationships with the party, in the aftermath of the civil war.

The chapters are arranged chronologically. Chapters 1 and 2 cover, respectively, the class and the party in 1920, straight after the civil war, when peacetime construction was being envisaged by the Bolsheviks as a continuation of 'war communism'. Chapter 3 covers the crisis of January–March 1921, which culminated in the Kronshtadt revolt. Further pairs of chapters deal alternately with the actions and reactions of workers and the

24 E.G. Gimpel'son, *Formirovanie sovetskoi politicheskoi sistemy 1917–1923 gg.*, Moscow: 'Nauka', 1995; E.G. Gimpel'son, *Sovetskie upravlentsy 1917–1920 gg.*, Moscow: Institut istorii RAN, 1998; E.G. Gimpel'son, *Novaia ekonomicheskaia politika i politicheskaia sistema 20-e gody*, Moscow: Institut istorii RAN, 2000; I. V. Pavlova, *Stalinizm: stanovlenie mekhanizma vlasti*, Novosibirsk: Sibirskii khronograf, 1993; G.F. Olekh, *Povorot, kotorogo ne bylo: bor'ba za vnutripartiinuiu demokratiu 1919–1924 gg.*, Novosibirsk: izd. Novosibirskogo universiteta, 1992; S.A. Pavliuchenkov, *Krestianskii Brest, ili predystoriia bol'shevistskogo NEPa*, Moscow: Russkoe knigoizdatel'skoe izdatel'stvo, 1996; S.V. Tsakunov, *V labirinte doktriny: iz opyta rarabotki ekonomicheskogo kursa strany v 1920-e gody*, Moscow: Rossiia molodaia, 1994; V.S. Tiazhel'nikova, 'Samoubiistvo kommunistov v 1920-e gody', *Otechestvennaia istoriia* 6, 1998: 158–73; V.S. Tiazhel'nikova, '"Voennyi sindrom" v povedenii kommunistov 1920-kh gg.', in E.S. Seniavskaia (ed.), *Voenno-istoricheskaia antropologiia. Ezhegodnik 2002. Predmet, zadachi, perspektivu razvitiia*, Moscow: Rosspen, 2002, pp. 291–305.
25 J. Hatch, 'Labour Conflict in Moscow 1921–25', in S. Fitzpatrick et al. (eds), op. cit., pp. 58–71; J. Hatch, 'The Politics of Mass Culture: Workers, Communists and Proletkult', *Russian History/Histoire Russe* 13: 2–3, 1986: 119–48; J. Hatch, 'Working-class politics in Moscow during the early NEP', *Soviet Studies* 34: 4, 1987: 556–74; J. Hatch, 'The Lenin Levy and the Social Origins of Stalinism', *Slavic Review* 48: 4, 1989: 558–78; W. Rosenberg, 'The Social Background to Tsektran', in Koenker et al. (eds), op. cit., pp. 349–73, is concerned with Moscow labour during the civil war; W. Chase, op. cit.; D.L. Hoffman, *Peasant Metropolis: Social Identities in Moscow, 1929–1941*, London: Cornell University Press, 1994; K.M. Strauss, *Factory and Community in Stalin's Russia: the Making of an Industrial Working Class*, Pittsburgh: University of Pittsburgh Press, 1997; T.J. Colton, *Moscow: Governing the Socialist Metropolis*, Cambridge, MA: Harvard University Press, 1995; R. Sakwa, *Soviet Communists in Power: a Study of Moscow During the Civil War*, London: Macmillan, 1988; C. Merridale, *Moscow Politics and the Rise of Stalin: the Communist Party in the Capital 1925–32*, Basingstoke: Macmillan, 1990.

16 *Introduction*

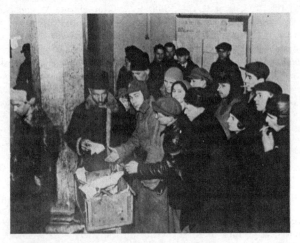

Small privileges amidst scarcity provoked resentment. Top: delegates to the second congress of the Communist International at dinner (1920), while, above, workers had to queue for rations.

party: Chapters 4 and 5 cover the events of mid to late 1921, including the non-party workers' movement that grew after the Kronshtadt crisis, and the first moves towards the NEP. Chapters 6 and 7 cover 1922, when the party moved to refashion its relationship with workers through mobilization campaigns and changes in the unions, while, in the party itself, the contours of groups that would make up the future Soviet ruling class became clearer.

Chapters 8 and 9 cover 1923–24, during which workers' industrial action revived, while working-class political dissidence was further isolated, and the defeat of the Left Opposition marked a turning point in the party elite's consolidation of control over the party as a whole.

The basic archival source materials used are: minutes of the Bolshevik party's Moscow committee (MC), and its secretariat and bureau; reports by Cheka-GPU agents in Moscow; trade union records, including those of the Moscow regional trade union federation and the metalworkers' and chemical workers' unions; and minutes of mass meetings, and records of factory committees, party cells and other workplace organizations. The workplaces whose records I consulted most fully are listed in Appendix 2. In researching events at the AMO car factory and the Bromlei machine building works, unpublished interviews taken during the 'history of factories' project were valuable. This project, headed by Maksim Gor'kii, aspired to write the history of the Soviet working class in its own words. It was launched in 1931, but run down from 1934 and scrapped abruptly in 1938. The interviews were often detailed and surprisingly frank. After the Second World War, some of the material was consulted by Soviet historians – for example the authors of a history of AMO – but much of it was never used.[26]

The value of the Cheka-GPU agents' reports as a source has been a subject of considerable discussion among historians.[27] They are best regarded not as objective reflections of events – in which their authors were, after all, often active participants – but as material that says as much about its authors as about those whom they were surveying. Most of the reports I read were collected by the Moscow Cheka's Workers Group, which was responsible not only for gathering information about what was going on in the factories, but also for working together with party and workplace organizations to solve disputes, and, in particular, to deal with supply failures and apparatus corruption.[28] The summary reports, in which Cheka officers attempt to interpret workers' political mood, bear particularly heavy marks

26 On the history of the project, S.V. Zhuravlev, *Fenomen 'istorii fabrik i zavodov': gor'kovskoe nachinanie v kontekste epokhi 1930-kh godov*, Moscow: Institut rossiiskoi istorii RAN, 1997. See also A.P. Churiaev, N.V. Adfel'dt and D.A. Baevskii (eds), *Istoriia Moskovskogo avtozavoda im. I.A. Likhacheva*, Moscow: izd. 'Mysl'', 1966; Strauss, op. cit., pp. 331–35.
27 P. Holquist, 'Information is the Alpha and Omega of Our Work', *Journal of Modern History* 69, 1997: 415–50; V.S. Izmozik, *Glaza i ushi rezhima: gosudarstvennyi politicheskii kontrol' za naseleniem Sovetskoi Rossii v 1918–1928 gg.*, St Petersburg: izd. Sankt-Peterburgskogo universiteta ekonomiki i finansov, 1995, pp. 106–37; G.L. Olekh, *Krovnye uzy: RKP(b) i ChK/GPU v pervoi polovine 1920-kh godov: mekhanizm vsaimootnoshenii*, Novosibirsk: Novosibirskaia gosudarstevennaia akademiia vodnogo transporta, 1999, pp. 58–80.
28 V.I. Alidin, A.S. Velidov, I.E. Polikarenko and V.G. Ushakov (eds), *MChK: iz istorii Moskovskoi chrezvychainoy kommissii: sbornik dokumentov (1918–1921 gg)*, Moscow: Moskovskii rabochii, 1978, pp. 244 and 255–58.

of the normative standards applied to workers' behaviour by Cheka agents and other Bolsheviks.[29] If the agents approved of the workers' attitude, they would deem it 'conscious' or 'satisfactory'; at the other end of the scale it would be judged 'hostile'. The idea that workers might at the same time be politically conscious and opposed to the government policy of the day was rarely, if ever, admitted. Agents regarded expressions of concern about supply as evidence of a lack of class consciousness: workers who complained about it were often dismissed as *obyvatel'skoe*, i.e. 'concerned with small everyday questions' or 'philistine'. The agents were blind to the contradiction that the same workers might well concern themselves with wider political issues. This having been said, the reports often contain useful detail. Minutes of party, trade union and factory committee meetings also reflect the opinions and prejudices of minute-takers, as well as those they record – although, where stenographic reports of larger gatherings are available, these give relatively accurate accounts of speeches, and sometimes, invaluably, of interjections and heckling. I have endeavoured to build up a picture of events by checking the reports, minutes and interviews against each other and against other archival and published sources.

29 On the summary reports, see S. Kotkin, Review of S. Davies, *Popular Opinion in Stalin's Russia, Europe-Asia Studies* 50: 4, 1998: 739–42.

1 Struggling to survive
Workers in July–December 1920

The conditions for the development of the workers' movement in Russia in 1920, when the civil war had ended but New Economic Policy (NEP) had not yet begun, were uniquely difficult. The main White armies were defeated in October-November 1919, and after that the Bolsheviks' hold on the most important areas of Russia was relatively secure. But for another 15 months, until March 1921, they pressed ahead with economic policies developed during the civil war and based on state regulation and compulsion, which later became known as 'war communism'. The fighting was not all over, of course, and the 'breathing space' in the spring of 1920 lasted only until the Polish invasion of Ukraine in May. The Red army launched a counter-offensive, which came to a disastrous halt just outside Warsaw in mid August. Peace talks with Poland began in that month, and resulted in an armistice being signed in October. The only significant White Russian army still operating by this time, that of Vrangel' in southern Russia, was in continuous retreat from September 1920 until its final defeat in mid November. In the autumn, peasant revolts erupted in central Russia and Siberia; these increased the Bolsheviks' sense of isolation. Nevertheless, discussions on industrial recovery and peacetime construction were underway. Most Bolshevik party leaders, and members, assumed that in peacetime the existing economic policies – state direction of production and distribution, a degree of labour compulsion, food requisitioning, the minimization of trade and experimentation with non-monetary forms of exchange – would continue, albeit with modifications. Some Bolsheviks, although not all, made super-optimistic assumptions about a possible forced march to 'socialism', whatever that meant in this context, by building on civil-war methods.

Characteristic of 1920 was a yawning gap between the perceptions, on one hand, of such super-optimists, whose belief in victory enabled them to undertake seemingly impossible tasks, and, on the other, of workers who may well have sided with the revolutions of 1917, but were now exhausted. In Moscow, their suffering was bearable only in comparison with the Russian provinces, where millions of people lived in conditions of social breakdown and with the imminent threat of famine. Moscow's population had been halved since 1917, mainly by migration to the countryside, to about 1 million.

Food supply was precarious. There were desperate shortages of fuel, and 'self-supply', i.e. the burning of any timber people could lay their hands on, was widespread. The city itself was ruined: about one-third of its houses had been destroyed, and the number of dwellings unfit for habitation had doubled. Soap and hot baths were terribly scarce, and this aggravated regular epidemics. The city's trams were carrying one-twelfth of their 1913 passenger volume, as most had been diverted to freight duties; shortages of fuel and oats meant there were few trucks or horse-drawn carts around.[1] Industry was battered but not beaten. In late 1919, most enterprises with fewer than 10 employees were closed – but 91 per cent of those with 100–500 employees, and all but one of the 65 enterprises with more than 500 employees, were open. Lack of fuel and raw materials interrupted production incessantly. The phenomenon should not be exaggerated, though: labour commissariat statisticians estimated that the average Moscow industrial worker lost only 7.9 working days in 1920 because of down-time (i.e. lack of fuel and raw materials); far more was lost due to absenteeism, which is discussed below.[2] Production in 1920 in 'civilian' industries was at only 15 per cent of its 1913 level, although, as the Soviet historian Iurii Poliakov pointed out,[3] this oft-quoted statistic did not include military supply factories, many of which were running at full steam. Much of Moscow industry suffered serious shortages of labour, particularly some types of skilled labour, mainly because workers had left the city for the countryside or joined the Red army. In other cases, factories ran out of fuel and raw material first, leaving workers the choice of hanging around dormant workshops or leaving the city. This chapter will discuss some related demographic issues that have been significant for labour historians; then supply problems and their impact on working-class politics; and finally, workers' attitudes to the Bolshevik state and party.

Workers and *sluzhashchie*

The exodus of workers from Russian cities during the civil war has been the subject of political and historiographical dispute. According to Bolshevik

---

1 M. Gorinov, 'Moskva v 20-kh godakh', *Otechestvennaia istoriia* 5, 1996: 3; *Moskovskii sovet rabochykh, krestianskikh i krasnoarmeiskikh deputatov 1917–27*, Moscow: izd. Moskovskogo soveta, 1927, p. 237; *Pravda*, 26 January 1921; Z.P. Korshunova (ed.), *Ocherki istorii Moskovskoi organizatsii KPSS, kn. II, noiabr' 1917–1945*, Moscow: Moskovskii rabochii, 1983, p. 195; T.J. Colton, *Moscow: Governing the Socialist Metropolis*, Cambridge, MA: Harvard University Press, 1995, p. 125.

2 N.M. Aleshchenko, *Moskovskii sovet v 1917–1941 gg.*, Moscow: Nauka, 1976, p. 222; Iu.A. Poliakov, *Moskovskie trudiashchiesia v oborone sovetskoi stolitsy v 1919 godu*, Moscow: izd. Akademii nauk SSSR, 1958, p. 9; F.D. Markuzon, 'Polozhenie truda v g. Moskve v 1921 godu', *Voprosy truda* 2, 1922: 136–81, here 144.

3 Poliakov, op. cit., p. 10.

discourse, the dispersal of urbanized male workers to the Red army or the countryside, and their substitution in the factories by women, younger workers, and new migrants, had 'deproletarianized' the working class. This resulted in a lack of political consciousness, to which the party attributed much of the working-class opposition it faced in 1920–21. But the demography has been shown to have been far more complex than the Bolsheviks allowed. And once consciousness is measured otherwise than by the Bolsheviks' primary standard, workers' degree of acceptance of government policy, the interpretation of lack of consciousness as the main cause of worker-government conflict fails.

Demographically, early twentieth-century Moscow had much in common with other urban centres during industrialization. Migration from the countryside was at first mainly by young, single males; married males who moved to the city often left their families behind in the village; large-scale migration of whole families started only in the 1920s. The movement from countryside to city was not one-way, though. There was a high level of temporary migration. Workers who settled in the city often sent their children back to be cared for by relatives in the countryside, and they themselves retained plots of land and/or returned periodically to the village.[4] Civil war brought about the drastic reduction in Moscow's population, from about 2 million to about 1 million between 1917 and 1920.[5] The number of industrial workers also fell by approximately half, to about 200,000, but the number of *sluzhashchie* (a census category that often translated as 'white-collar staff' or 'employees', but which also extended to other service workers) fell only slightly, to about 220,000.[6] The contraction of the labour force was not even. By 1920, the number of workers in the metalworking sector fell to less than half of its wartime peak, i.e. to below 30,000, partly because skilled

---

4 R.E. Johnson, *Peasant and Proletarian: the Working Class of Moscow in the Late Nineteenth Century*, Leicester: Leicester University Press, 1979, pp. 28–66; Koenker, 'Urbanization and Deurbanization in the Russian Revolution and Civil War', *Journal of Modern History* 57, 1985: 424–50; D.L. Hoffman, *Peasant Metropolis: Social Identities in Moscow, 1929–1941*, London: Cornell University Press, 1994, pp. 15–72; W.J. Chase, *Workers, Society and the Soviet State: Labour and Life in Moscow 1918–1929*, Urbana: University of Illinois Press, 1990, pp. 81 and 88–95; O.I. Shkaratan, *Problemy sotsial'noi struktury rabochego klassa SSSR*, Moscow: 'Mysl'', 1970, pp. 246–49.

5 Census statisticians counted the population of the city of Moscow as 2,017,173 in 1917 and 1,027,336 in 1920. Statisticheskii otdel Moskovskogo soveta, *Statisticheskii atlas gor. Moskvy i Moskovskoi gub. Vyp. 1. Naselenie.*, Moscow, 1924, p. 7.

6 Labour department statisticians counted 411,070 industrial workers in Moscow region in 1917 and 208,158 in 1920; census statisticians counted 460,800 and 202,700, respectively, and 258,427 *sluzhashchie* in 1918 and 223,375 in 1920. Markuzon, 'Polozhenie truda'; Statisticheskii otdel Moskovskogo soveta, *Statisticheskii atlas gor. Moskvy i Moskovskoi gub. Vyp. 3. Promyshlennost' i torgovlia*, Moscow, 1925, p. 16.

22 Struggling to survive

workers gravitated to other manufacturing centres.[7] In the textile industry, the largest in terms of numbers employed, the workforce had shrunk to less than half its 1913 size, from around 250,000 to around 120,000.[8] Food processing plants' workforces also contracted drastically. But in the garment sector the workforce expanded by nearly a third, to about 18,000, mainly in response to demand from the Red army. And about 8500 chemical workers were working in Moscow – fewer than in 1916, but as many as there had been in 1913, partly because some production had been transferred from Petrograd and Riga.[9]

In the 1950s, citing the reductions, Isaac Deutscher argued that, at the end of the civil war, the working class was 'pulverized' and that 'the proletarian dictatorship was triumphant but the proletariat had nearly vanished'. This interpretation has been disputed. From the 1970s, western social historians drew a more complex picture. Diane Koenker argued that, among the most urbanized workers, i.e. urban families, there was 'no place to go except the Red army' and that the young men went to the front while others remained in Moscow; that among the least urbanized Moscow workers, for example fathers with families in the countryside, the exodus had often started 'even before the serious [supply] crises began'; and that among the middle layers with one foot in the city and one in the village, and first-generation migrants, some stayed while others left.[10]

The reader's attention is drawn to two issues that have arisen in the discussions among historians. The first concerns the impact of these demographic changes on the political character of the working-class movement. Deutscher's picture of working class politics in 1920–21, copied by some

---

7 Industry statisticians counted 42,500 metalworkers in 1913; 82,600 in 1916; 63,300 in 1917; and 29,200 in 1920 (excluding military enterprises and workplaces with 15 employees or less). *Fabrichno-zavodskaia promyshlennost' g. Moskvy i Moskovskoi gubernii, 1917–1927 gg.*, Moscow, 1928, p. 15. Census statisticians counted 38,800 metalworkers in 1913; 83,600 in 1917; and 28,600 in 1920 (in Moscow region, excluding metallurgy and transport). Statisticheskii otdel Moskovskogo soveta, *Statisticheskii atlas. Vyp. 3.*, p. 23.

8 Census and industry statisticians, respectively, counted the number of textile workers in the Moscow region falling from around 250,000 in 1913–17 to 113,000–128,000 in 1920. Statisticheskii otdel Moskovskogo soveta, *Statisticheskii atlas. Vyp. 3.*, p. 21, and *Fabrichno-zavodskaia promyshlennost'*, p. 15.

9 On the garment industry, Chase, op. cit., p. 34; Poliakov, op. cit., p. 10. Trade union statisticians counted 4594 workers in Moscow in 'production of clothing and shoes' in 1913; 21,210 in 1916; 14,030 in 1918; and 17,348 in 1921. They counted 19,680 food workers in 1913 and 12,046 of them in 1921. Markuzon, 'Polozhenie truda', p. 138.

10 I. Deutscher, *The Prophet Unarmed. Trotsky 1921–1929*, London: Oxford University Press, 1970, pp. 6–10; Koenker, 'Urbanization and deurbanization', particularly p. 433 and p. 442. See also D.R. Brower, '"The City in Danger": the civil war and the Russian urban population', in D. Koenker, W.G. Rosenberg and R. G. Suny (eds), *Party, State and Society in the Russian Civil War: Explorations in Social History*, Bloomington: Indiana University Press, 1989, pp. 58–80.

more recent socialist writers,[11] is so one-sided as to be misleading: the movement was 'an empty shell'; 'here and there, small groups of veterans of the class struggle met and argued about the prospects of the revolution', but could not see behind them 'the main force of their class'. My research shows, in contrast, that the workers' movement in Moscow was, despite its numerical weakness and the burdens of civil war, engaged with political as well as industrial issues. While most textile mills were closed in 1920, much of the metalworking industry was active, often supplying the military. Political discussion continued at factory mass meetings and at the regular city-wide assemblies of metalworkers' union delegates, a largely pro-Bolshevik bastion of organization. The records of these meetings suggest that, even though thousands of the Moscow workers who supported the October revolution had gone to the front, many others remained active in the factories; in this respect my research bears out Koenker's conclusions. Koenker describes a 'middling out' of the working class, with the most politically committed going to the front, the least committed returning to the countryside, and a middle group remaining in Moscow, including the male workers mentioned and women, some of whom were their family members, joining the workforce. For Deutscher, the soviets became 'creatures of the Bolshevik party' because they 'could not possibly represent a virtually non-existent working class'. On the contrary: the working class was far from nonexistent, and when, in 1921, it began to resuscitate soviet democracy, the party's decision to make the Moscow soviet its 'creature' was not effect but cause.

The second issue concerns the *sluzhashchie*, who the Bolshevik leadership characterized as a petty-bourgeois grouping that diluted the proletarian character of the state and played a negative role in the revolution. In the early NEP period, when worker communists were moved in large numbers into the state institutions where the *sluzhashchie* worked, and usually into positions of authority, these ideological presumptions about the class position of the *sluzhashchie* sometimes merged with workerist prejudice. This discourse was subject to criticism by Daniel Orlovsky, who argued that the white-collar workers, to whom the label *sluzhashchie* was most readily applied, had played a dynamic role in the revolution that had been 'invisible' for previous historians.[12] The census category *sluzhashchie*, inherited from tsarist Russia, included not only white-collar staff but also a range of other

---

11 E.g., John Rees in J. Rees, S. Farbman and R. Service, *In Defence of October*, London: Bookmarks, 1997, p. 77.
12 Orlovsky, D.T., 'State building in the civil war era: the role of the lower middle strata', in D. Koenker, W.G. Rosenberg and R.G. Suny (eds), *Party, State and Society in the Russian Civil War: Explorations in Social History*, Bloomington: Indiana University Press, 1989, pp. 180–209; D. Orlovsky, 'The Hidden Class: White Collar Workers in the Soviet 1920s', in L.H. Siegelbaum and R.G. Suny (eds), *Making Workers Soviet: Power, Class and Identity*, London: Cornell University Press, 1994, pp. 220–52.

social groups that may be regarded as part of, or having close affinity with, the working class. In the case of Moscow, it is striking that during the civil war, when the number of industrial workers fell so sharply, the number of *sluzhashchie* remained almost constant. It hardly changed during early NEP, either. The 1920 census counted in the city's working population 205,427 workers and 223,375 *sluzhashchie*; the figures did not change significantly in the 1923 census.[13] At first sight, these figures appear to bear out oft-repeated Bolshevik complaints that the working class was being elbowed aside by armies of petty bourgeois. But the category *sluzhashchie* covered not only white-collar staff, but also 'cultural-educational personnel', almost all university staff and school teachers (16,634 of the 223,375 *sluzhashchie*), and people best described as service workers: medical and health workers (22,557); communications staff such as postal, telephone and telegraph workers (9140); and security staff, mostly watchmen (15,402). The census also counted, in a category separate from industrial workers and *sluzhashchie*, 46,828 domestic servants (*prislugi*), mostly house-helps to groups of working-class families. Bolshevik ideology deemed all these groups to be either partly or completely non-proletarian, and the census methodology reflected that. Indeed many of these people may not have considered themselves to be workers. Teachers, for example, were usually thought of as members of the intelligentsia. However, in keeping with the interpretive framework proposed in the Introduction, such people may be regarded as part of the working class or as its allies. By adding to the 205,427 industrial workers the 63,733 educational and service workers, and the 46,828 domestic servants, a total of 315,988 workers is reached. These outnumber by nearly two to one the remaining 159,642 *sluzhashchie*, most of whom were white-collar staff.[14] This group included top- and middle-ranking administrative officials who had been in similar positions under the old regime, and industrial specialists and managers.[15] But its majority comprised badly-paid office

13 The 1923 census counted 219,059 workers, 225,886 *sluzhashchie*, plus 94,953 unemployed. Statisticheskii otdel Moskovskogo soveta, *Statisticheskii atlas. Vyp. 1.*, p. 15, and F.D. Markuzon (ed.), *Polozhenie truda v Moskovskoi gubernii v 1922–1923gg.: sbornik materialov biuro statistika truda*, Moscow: MGSPS, 1923, p. 6.
14 The remaining categories of *sluzhashchie* were 'administration and the courts', 'technical personnel' (mostly in government offices), 'trade and distribution staff', 'accounting and inspection staff', 'filing personnel' and 'other'. In all categories, auxiliary personnel are included, who were often manual workers. *Perepis' sluzhashchikh sovetskikh uchrezhdenii g. Moskvy 1922 g.*, Moscow, 1922, p. V.
15 An analysis of the results of the 1922 census of *sluzhashchie* showed that among senior and specialist *sluzhashchie*, respectively, working in the people's commissariats in 1922, the most common pre-revolutionary occupations had been 'state administrative service' (28.2 per cent and 10.9 per cent), 'junior personnel' (12.2 per cent and 7.2 per cent), 'free professions' (12.0 per cent and 21.7 per cent) and 'students' (15.3 per cent and 25.2 per cent). V.I. Vasiaev, V.Z. Drobizhev, L.B. Zaks, B.I. Pivovor, V.A. Ustinov and T.A. Ushakova, *Dannie perepisi sluzhashchikh 1922g. o sostave kadrov narkomatov RSFSR*, Moscow: izd. Moskovskovskogo universiteta, 1972, pp. 148–52.

workers, many of whom, along with others in urban middle layers, had been active in the revolutions of 1917. The divisions between industrial workers and *sluzhashchie* were real enough – the latter performed mental, rather than manual, labour – but these differences were not absolute, as Bolshevik ideology suggested. And self-perceptions among the *sluzhashchie* differed greatly: while many regarded themselves as non-proletarian, those in the factories saw themselves as close to their blue-collar colleagues. The minutes of mass meetings show that the two groups often assembled and voted together.[16]

The Bolshevik party's discussions about the *sluzhashchie* and their class position often merged with, or became confused with, those about the state apparatus in which many of them worked. 'Bureaucratism' was recognized by all as a serious defect of the state, but whereas to some it had a political meaning, i.e. it signified a lack of participatory democracy, to others it meant inefficiency and red tape (*volokita*). The *sluzhashchie*, as bearers of alien class pressure, were an important cause of bureaucratism, according to the view prevalent in the Bolshevik leadership.[17] While this analysis was not universally accepted, there was broad agreement among the Bolsheviks and their political opponents that the state apparatus was far too big, and disastrously ineffective, and that staff numbers should be cut. Moscow's role as the Soviet capital exacerbated this problem in the city. For example in 1920 Moscow had, among those 159,642 white-collar staff, 58,185 'filing personnel', who outnumbered the metalworkers by nearly two to one.[18] Central government offices, which employed up to 100,000 *sluzhashchie*, multiplied like triffids: in January 1921, the Supreme Council of the National Economy (VSNKh) and the transport commissariat were registered at 200 and 130 addresses in the city, respectively.[19] The party leadership constantly made energetic, but unsuccessful, efforts to reduce the numbers of *sluzhashchie*. In February 1921 Lenin signed an order forbidding commissariats to open new departments without permission from the Council of People's Commissars (Sovnarkom); in May that year he wrote to Gleb Krzhizhanovskii, head of the new planning agency, Gosplan, proposing to reduce the soviet apparatus

---

16 TsAGM, 100/5/78, 84, 99; 337/2/39; 415/16/314, 317, 318; TsAOPIM, 432/1/4; 465/1/4; TsGAMO, 186/1/598/3–40; 609/1/107.
17 The case is stated in Iu. Larin, *Intelligentsiia i sovety: khoziaistvo, burzhuaziia, revoliutsiia, gosapparat*, Moscow: Gosizdat, 1924.
18 Statisticheskii otdel Moskovskogo soveta, *Statisticheskii ezhegodnik g. Moskvy i Moskovskoi gubernii. Vyp. 2. Statisticheskie dannye po g. Moskvy za 1914–1925 gg.*, Moscow, 1925, p. 52. See also S. Sternheimer, 'Administration for Development: the emerging bureaucratic elite, 1920–30', in W. Pintner and D.K. Rowney (eds), *Russian Officialdom: the Bureaucratization of Russian Society from the Seventeenth to the Twentieth Century*, London: Macmillan, 1980, pp. 316–54, here pp. 320–21.
19 *Perepis' sluzhashchikh*, p. 122; *Izvestiia*, 25 January 1921.

'possibly by 25 per cent, or 50 per cent'; and in June Sovnarkom called officially for a 50 per cent reduction. But at the eleventh party congress in March 1922, Lenin announced disgustedly that since 1918 the number of *sluzhashchie* in Moscow had *risen* slightly, to 243,000.[20]

The battles for food supply and productivity

During the civil war and through 1920, relations between workers and 'their' state were determined, more than anything, by the food shortage in the cities, which made inequality in distribution inevitable. The food shortage resulted from the constant decline in the proportion of land sown for food production, itself caused by civil war, peasant hostility to state requisitioning of grain, and the contraction of trade. The main method of food supply in Moscow, from 1918 until 1922, was the rationing system, under which grain and other agricultural products requisitioned from the peasantry were centralized by the food supply commissariat and distributed to the Red army and the urban population. There were fierce disputes over how rationing should be organized, which amounted, essentially, to competitions between different types of inequality. Many workers responded individually to the crisis. Those with sought-after skills took advantage of the acute labour shortage, caused by the exodus to the front on one hand and the countryside on the other, and moved frequently from one workplace to another to drive up the price of their labour. Some others resorted to absenteeism and theft. But traditions of collective organization and struggle were far from destroyed, and underwent a revival in the metalworkers' union in particular.

Under the rationing system introduced in 1918, more food was supposed to go to soldiers at the front, those doing heavy physical work and other priority groups. Industrial workers were prioritized over *sluzhashchie*. But special rations and exemptions were introduced endlessly, and then attempts made to redress the inequalities created. Rations were distributed late or not at all, and then efforts made to ensure that priority groups received what they were due more reliably. In 1919, an additional 'labour ration' was introduced for factory workers; then factories of 'special importance' were upgraded to military ration status; then the principle of 'reserved' (*bronnirovannye*) rations was introduced, under which the food supply authorities were supposed to ensure that those thus designated received their rations no matter what; then came an academic ration, a special ration for Red army men's families, and so on. Corruption, and trade in fake ration cards, was rife. An early manifestation of Soviet state officials' privilege was corrupt access to extra rations, which fuelled working-class resentment and demands

---

20 Colton, op. cit., pp. 100–101; A.B. Nenin, *Sovnarkom i Novaia Ekonomicheskaia Politika (1921–23gg)*, Nizhnii Novgorod: izd. Volgo-Viatskoi akademii gosudarstvennoi sluzhby, 1999, pp. 59–65.

for 'equalization of rations'.[21] In April 1920, the Sovnarkom established another new 'unified' ration system with three categories. But the pressure to make exceptions was as strong as ever: the decree stated that workers in 'enterprises of special state importance', those who worked long shifts and 'persons doing specially qualified mental labour' would have special norms. Implementation of the decree was postponed until September, and by that time, differentials had been exacerbated by new trends in industrial administration, principally the use of bonuses in kind as productivity incentives, and the 'shock working' system (*udarnichestvo*), under which factories denominated as 'shock' (*udarnyi*) were entitled to priority supplies.[22] Rations were supplemented by food acquired directly from the countryside, either on the black market, which thrived in spite of blockade detachments patrolling the railways, or on procurement trips, made by individual workers under an important exemption from the ban on trade that allowed them to go into the countryside and purchase 1.5 puds (24.6 kilos) of grain each, or by workplace collectives organized by factory committees.[23]

Even when centrally and locally procured food supplies were added together, there was simply not enough food arriving in Moscow. The nadir had been reached in 1919, and by mid 1920 the food situation had improved: year on year, consumption per head of bread was up by 45 per cent, of groats by five times and of potatoes by 1.5 times, according to the Soviet historian N.M. Aleshchenko. Nevertheless, the food available was insufficient to supply all the rations due. In June 1920, only 57.6 per cent of rations due were issued, and that figure fell steadily to 26.5 per cent in September before it improved again. Some rations had been cancelled altogether and workers exhorted to form groups to dig for potatoes in nearby rural areas. Although Aleksei Badaev of the supply commissariat had to report to the Bolshevik party's Moscow committee (MC) 'the complete absence of milk in Moscow', deliveries of grain and other food

---

21 S.S. Khromov et al. (eds), *Grazhdanskaia voina i voennaia interventsiia v SSSR: entsiklopediia*, Moscow: Sovetskaia entsiklopediia, 1983, pp. 396–97; L. Lih, *Bread and Authority in Russia 1914–1921*, Berkeley: University of California Press, 1990, pp. 162–92; M. McAuley, *Bread and Justice: State and Society in Petrograd 1917–1922*, Oxford: Clarendon, 1991, pp. 282–97; S. Malle, *The Economic Organization of War Communism 1918–1921*, Cambridge: Cambridge University Press, 1985, pp. 322–73.
22 *Dekrety sovetskoi vlasti*, Moscow: Gos. izd. polit. literatury, 1986, vol VIII, p. 135; T. Remington, *Building Socialism in Bolshevik Russia: Ideology and Industrial Organization 1917–1921*, Pittsburgh: University of Pittsburgh Press, 1984, pp. 157–61; Khromov et al., op. cit., p. 608.
23 M. Borrero, *Hungry Moscow: Scarcity and Urban Society in the Russian Civil War, 1917–1921*, New York: Peter Lang, 2003, pp. 89–96; L.N. Suvorova, 'Za 'fasadom' "voennogo kommunizma": politicheskaia vlast' i rynochnaia ekonomika', *Otechestvennaia istoriia* 4, 1993: 48–59; and Brower, op. cit., especially pp. 68–72.

stocks were stabilized.[24] In the city of Moscow, the improvement persisted in November-December, but there were acute supply shortages in the surrounding rural districts. Only in January 1921 did the overall situation deteriorate again, producing strike waves in Moscow and Petrograd and support for the Kronshtadt revolt.

The way in which food was supplied to factory workers was in large part dependent on labour policy. In the face of economic breakdown, this policy not only provided for the forms of alienated labour common throughout Europe, but also for extreme measures to enhance productivity under conditions where monetary incentives were unworkable. Compulsory labour mobilization had been introduced in some industries in 1919, and adopted as a general principle in January 1920. But it had largely failed either to ensure that workers with necessary skills went to the factories where they were most needed, or to contain the more general problem of chronic absenteeism – much of which was caused by workers spending time procuring food supplies. Many industrial managers and trade union leaders found that ensuring a regular supply of better-than-average rations was a more effective way of keeping workers at work than military or administrative compulsion. But the shortage of skilled engineering workers in the armaments and other metallurgical factories was particularly acute. A survey of 35 armaments plants, covering the first nine months of 1920, showed that nine-tenths of those conscripted (34,939 out of 38,514) had not shown up. In Moscow, a list of 37,400 workers employed outside their own profession was drawn up; 10,700 of them were mobilized to the places where they were needed.[25] At two metalworkers' union conferences, discussion focused on the exodus of workers from physically demanding professions. Iron founders', blacksmiths' and hammerers' skills were 'literally dying out', one speaker, Sangovich, complained.[26]

Absenteeism, and the use of factory resources to make goods to trade with peasants, were widespread. Labour commissariat statisticians estimated that in 1920 the average Moscow worker lost 71.2 working days due to absences, and broke these down as 15 days 'business trips and organizational

24 TsAOPIM, 3/1a/6/33; *Pravda*, 1 October 1920; *Moskovskii sovet*, pp. 93–95; Aleshchenko, op. cit., pp. 189–90, Borrero, op. cit., pp. 77–81.
25 Among the metalworkers working in the wrong places, there were 1023 in small workshops, 4643 working as garment workers and 1353 as tanners. V.N. Sarab'ianov, *Metallopromyshlennost' Rossii*, Moscow: Gosizdatel'stvo, 1921, pp. 71–75; Chase, op. cit., pp. 46–47; W.G. Rosenberg, 'The Social Background to Tsektran', in D. Koenker, W.G. Rosenberg and R.G. Suny (eds), *Party, State and Society in the Russian Civil War: Explorations in Social History*, Bloomington: Indiana University Press, 1989, pp. 349–73, here pp. 359–60; M. Dewar, *Labour Policy in the USSR, 1917–1928*, London: Royal Institute of International Affairs, 1956, pp. 46–50; and A.M. Sinitsyn et al. (eds), *Istoriia rabochykh Moskvy 1917–1945 gg.*, Moscow: 'Nauka', 1983, pp. 92–93.
26 TsGAMO, 186/1/460/24.

work', 11 'additional days off', 20 days sickness and 25.4 days absence without excuse (*proguly*). In the metal processing plants, illness and 'absences without reason' were predominant, whereas in the textile plants downtime caused by lack of fuel and raw materials was a greater problem.[27] Further research is needed into the reasons for these absences. Michael Seidman, in the work referred to in the Introduction, has suggested that in post-revolutionary situations in Spain and France, workers' 'resistance to work' had a 'utopian' aspect, in opposition to socialist political parties who glorified work. I have seen no clear evidence of such a trend in Russia. On the other hand, Daniel Brower has shown that in 1919–20 workers were strongly motivated to take time off to engage in trade, on which they often relied more heavily than their regular jobs to make a living.[28]

The labour market became completely distorted, particularly in the metalworking industry, where the whip hand was held not by the government, with its draconian slogans of labour compulsion, but by workers whose skills were in short supply. In response, managers competed feverishly for the 'shock' label and for better bonuses in kind. The number of 'shock' enterprises proliferated, and the concept was devalued. In the second half of 1920 the number of 'shock' metal plants rose 12-fold from 20 to 240, and by the end of the year there were 1716 'shock' enterprises all together. In Moscow, chemical and textile factories, along with metallurgical ones, were labelled 'shock'. A speaker at the 4th trade union congress in May 1921 said there were more 'shock' enterprises than 'non-shock' ones.[29] Along with the 'shock' system, the payment of bonuses in kind mushroomed; the union leaders fought an inter-institutional battle with industrial managers, soviets and the food supply commissariat for the right to administer the bonuses, and in June 1920 the all-Russian trade union council (VTsSPS) was given control of them.[30]

Managers and factory committees engaged in a competitive scramble for supplies, to provide huge bonuses for scarce types of labour. Electrical engineering trust managers who sent a rail engine for repair at the cable

---

27 Markuzon, 'Polozhenie truda', here 144–46. See also *Ekonomicheskaia zhizn'*, 16 October 1920.
28 M. Seidman, *Workers Against Work: Labor in Paris and Barcelona During the Popular Fronts*, Berkeley: University of California Press, 1991, pp. 16–17; Brower, op. cit., pp. 72–74.
29 Remington, op. cit., pp. 157–61; A.A. Matiugin, *Rabochii klass SSSR v gody vosstanovleniia narodnogo khozaistva, 1921–1925*, Moscow: izd. Akademii nauk SSSR, 1962, p. 49; E.H. Carr, *The Bolshevik Revolution 1917–1923*, London: Macmillan, 1978, vol. 2, pp. 216–17.
30 Malle, op. cit., pp. 423 and 481–86; J. Bunyan, *The Origin of Forced Labor in the Soviet State 1917–1921: Documents and Materials*, Baltimore: Johns Hopkins Press, 1967, pp. 175–78; J. Aves, *Workers Against Lenin*, London: Tauris, 1996, pp. 98–100.

30 *Struggling to survive*

factory added employees at the Dinamo factory in Rogozhsko-Simonovskii district[31] to the list of those to receive bonus grain supplies 'for (fictional) participation in the repair'. The factory committee was not ashamed to record this ruse in its minutes.[32] The lengths to which managers went to bribe skilled workers to stay at the 1886 power station in Zamoskvorech'e were uncovered by a joint union-soviet commission, which in March 1921 inspected, and ordered the abolition of, 'payments, on various pretexts, to workers and *sluzhashchie* above the stated norms', labelled 'bonus', 'overtime', 'watch duty', 'transport', 'work outside normal duties', 'carriage of meters', 'piece-work payments' and 'individual bonuses', that brought some pay packets to 30 times the average.[33] The divisiveness of the 'shock' system was highlighted at a Moscow metalworkers' union delegate conference in September 1920. A report by Boris Stiunkel of the VSNKh on improved production and reduced absenteeism at 'shock' factories provoked complaints by delegates from elsewhere. Nikolai Gavrilin, a leading party member from the AMO car factory, said:

> There's no way anyone on the Moscow hunger ration [i.e. the regular non-'shock' ration] will meet targets. If all the factories were supplied as [the] Podol'sk [engineering works] is [i.e. with 'shock' rations], they would fulfil norms too. ... Podol'sk is so well-supplied that they sell part of what they receive.

This accusation that 'shock' rations were finding their way onto the market drew an angry denial from Georgii Tarasov, chairman of the Moscow metalworkers' union.[34]

The divisions exacerbated by 'shock working' overwhelmed neither the metalworkers nor the workers' movement as a whole. The perception was spreading that workers needed to unite against inequalities in the rationing system that benefited party officials and high-up *sluzhashchie*. The administrative bodies that ran individual industries and reported to VSNKh, the chief committees and central committees (*glavki* and *tsentry*), were accused by worker activists of using *udarnichestvo* not only to promote their industrial sectors' interests, but also to accumulate material benefits for their Moscow office staff. At the metalworkers' delegate conference in December, one speaker, Buravtsev, criticized the VTsSPS for tolerating the payment of inflated wages and bonuses to officials in the *glavki* and *tsentry*. Trade union activists both inside and outside the

---

31 Rogozhsko-Simonovskii was one of Moscow's seven urban administrative districts. There were also 17 rural districts. The districts are listed in Appendix 2.
32 TsAOPIM, 412/1/4/16; TsAGM, 100/5/78/15.
33 GARF, 5469/5/29/130.
34 TsGAMO, 186/1/460/25–27ob. On Gavrilin and Tarasov, see Appendix 1.

Bolshevik party believed that inequalities could be better combated by bringing wages and ration distribution more firmly under the control of individual unions. Proposals made in October 1920 by the trade union leader Abram Gol'tsman, to shift from individual unions to the VTsSPS the task of setting wage rates, ran into opposition at the metalworkers' national union conference in November, and at the Moscow metalworkers' December conference. D.S. Gol'tsev, an AMO worker recently expelled from the party, protested at the latter that the scheme 'sidestepped the factory committees'.[35]

'Equalization of rations'

There was widespread concern among workers that inequalities in the rationing system worked in favour of party officials and the embryonic ruling elite – and this inspired the demand for equalization of rations , i.e. that all urban wage-earners should receive the same. The supposed beneficiaries of inequality were not always clearly defined by their accusers, but 'responsible officials' (*otvetstvennye rabotniki*), i.e. party officials, were often mentioned, as were the *glavki* and *tsentry*. Non-party workers fought strikes for 'equalization'. In the metalworkers' union the slogan was taken up by non-Bolshevik workerists, who linked it to calls for union control over food distribution. Within the party, it was supported both by left-wingers, who linked it to their demands for 'equality between communists', and by the Moscow regional leadership, who saw it as a means to restrain the divisive use of *udarnichestvo*. In the spring of 1921, the formula was adopted on one hand by the Moscow soviet, with support from the government, and on the other by the Kronshtadt rebels. It was opposed, though, by the Socialist Revolutionaries (SRs), who considered that tinkering with distribution mechanisms was a diversion from the main issue, i.e. the need to scrap civil-war methods of food procurement, such as forcible requisitioning.

The 'equalization' demand had obvious inconsistencies. The Moscow metalworkers supported 'equalization of rations' while simultaneously demanding greater bonuses – implying that hard work, as opposed to sitting in government offices, could justifiably be rewarded unequally. Moreover, workers did not take the 'equalization' demand to mean that the advantages they enjoyed over other sections of the population should be scrapped. For example in November 1920, peasant delegates at a Moscow regional conference 'reproached' the Bolsheviks for 'giving workers 2 funt [of bread per day], and the peasants half a funt' – and while workers may have been sympathetic to their plight, it was rarely addressed during discussions of

---

35 TsGAMO, ibid., 40ob.

'equalization'.³⁶ Nevertheless, the slogan had the merit of focusing on the accumulation of material wealth by the embryonic elite. Many of the slogan's supporters believed that, however small the quantity of food being unfairly distributed at the top, that was a breach of the socialist principles to which the Soviet state aspired.

The 'equalization' issue was raised in the largest strike in Moscow in the summer of 1920, by tram workers. The immediate trigger for this action, like many others, was late delivery of food supplies. It began on 12 August at the Zamoskvorech'e tram depot. The next day, three other depots, and a group of drivers based at the Sokol'niki vehicle building works, stopped work. Workers in other industries joined in too. The Simonov factory struck for two hours, protesting at a 10-day delay in distribution of rations. At the motor repair workshops in Zamoskvorech'e, a threat to join the strike, without actually doing so, was enough to win concessions from a commission set up to deal with workers' demands.³⁷ The tram workers themselves stayed out a further two days before being driven back to work by arrests and threats of mass sackings. The strike's political character was highlighted by the Krasnopresnia party district committee, whose minutes recorded:

> There is a desire among workers to destroy all extra rations for responsible officials, and [the strikers] propose to ask the Moscow soviet and the Moscow council of the economy [MSNKh] urgently to put an end to all existing inequalities. They proceed from the consideration that in a working people's republic, every worker and member of office staff should receive a ration, but only a working person's ration.³⁸

A Cheka agent reported that the strikers wanted negotiations on 'supply; rates and bonuses; uniforms (work clothes); on a general meeting of all depots; fines; distribution of salt from a supply train; increase in rations; current issues [i.e. the political situation]; [and] on bonus supplies of flour that were promised'. The demand for the right to hold a city-wide meeting is significant: here the workers' movement was trying to get on the first rung of the ladder of organization, and being knocked off by the Bolsheviks. The strike raised political issues, but was not led by members of any political party. No outside agitation was detected by the Cheka, and no opposition political organization comparable to the Menshevik groups in the printers' and chemical workers' unions, or the left SRs in the bakers' union, was

---

36 P. Avrich, *Kronstadt 1921*, Princeton: Princeton University Press, 1970, p. 73; TsGAMO, 180/1/236/64; TsAOPIM, 3/1a/2/84; *Sotsialisticheskii vestnik* 1921, no.1, p. 13.
37 TsAOPIM, 3/1a/11/12, 38, 40. See also S. Pirani, 'Class Clashes With Party: Politics in Moscow between the Civil War and the New Economic Policy', *Historical Materialism* 11:2, 2003: 75–120.
38 TsAOPIM, ibid., 38.

present. The commission in Krasnopresnia described the strike leaders as 'unconscious elements, both men and women' who 'in no way differed from other workers'.

The party responded to the strike in such a way as to undermine workers' organization and consciousness. Isaak Minkov, the MC secretary, had not long beforehand written a circular to industrial cells, advising that if strikes could not be averted by negotiation, then party members at workplaces should 'without the mass noticing, isolate it from the influence of actively counter-revolutionary persons'. The latter should be sacked by communist managers only if all other methods had failed.[39] Events among tram workers had obviously gone beyond this point, and on 12 August, the first day of the strike, the MC bureau not only declined to sanction a city-wide tram workers' meeting, but also decreed that depots still on strike by 9.00 am the next day would be closed. Gol'tsman and Grigorii Mel'nichanskii, leaders of the Moscow regional council of trades unions (MGSPS), were to announce that all strikers could be arrested. In each depot commissions were set up, with representatives from the party cell, union and management, to undertake 'filtration' of the workers into three categories: conscientious workers; those with 'unexplained absences'; and 'malicious leaders' of the strike, who should be arrested. The arrests were made on 14 August; one strike organizer, Aleksei Krylov, was later sentenced to a year in jail. The MC bureau's actions were approved by the full MC; no objection to the repression of the strike by means reminiscent of tsarism was recorded at meetings of either body.[40]

While thus throttling independent action for 'equalization of rations', the Moscow party leadership itself used the 'equalization' slogan against the *glavki*, whose endless efforts to out-bid each other in the market for scarce types of labour was fuelling the resentment of workers whose labour was not in short supply. The Moscow party conference in August 1920 decided, in line with Sovnarkom's ruling in April, on a centralized ration system, based on the type of labour a person performed, rather than the category of factory in which he/she worked, that would narrow some of the differentials widened by *udarnichestvo*. Vasilii Likhachev, a leading official of MSNKh, told the conference that it was 'imperative to set up a single supply organization' to end confusion and corruption, otherwise 'officials of various *glavki* will continue to receive, while children go hungry'. The *glavki* and *tsentry* should be 'subordinated to the general distribution system', Likhachev argued; 'shock' rations should be abolished and replaced with a more uniform bonus system. He also advocated reducing individual rations and increasing food distribution via public canteens – which were already regularly feeding about a quarter of Moscow's population (61,000 adults and 219,000

---

39 TsAGM, 415/16/587/16.
40 TsAOPIM, 3/1a/7/27; TsAOPIM, 3/1a/11/40, 48. On Mel'nichanskii, see Appendix 1.

34 Struggling to survive

children).⁴¹ The conference criticized the organization of procurement trips by individual factories on the authority of the *glavki*. After further discussion, on 4 October the Moscow soviet presidium adopted a plan to centralize bread distribution with a simple two-tier ration system.⁴²

The meaning of 'equalizing rations' was further discussed at the Moscow metalworkers' delegate conference of 2–4 February 1921,⁴³ which called for an 'equalized, unified' supply system for 'all labouring people'. On one hand the meeting resolved that all privileged rations 'be they Sovnarkom rations, academic rations, specialists' rations or whatever' should be abolished, and called for greater union involvement in distribution. On the other hand, in a separate resolution on wages, it called for restrictions on the bonus system to be abolished, in order to allow bonuses of up to 300 per cent. Such self-interest was articulated by Kolyshkin of the Ustinskii works, who spoke of 'equality of distribution, with advantages for the workers'. Resentment was expressed against the *spetsy*: a resolution on pay condemned the injustice of arbitrary rewards for them and the power of the *glavki* to bestow bonuses in kind as they saw fit. But non-party workers made clear that there was a principle, beyond self-interest, at stake: privileges for officials and specialists strengthened the apparatus and distanced the 'workers' state' from the workers. The instrument to deal with this was the union, not the party, they said. Portnov from the Motor factory urged: 'Clean out all the *glavki* and throw out all the bourgeois. The whole thing should be put under the metalworkers' union's control.' Kraevskii said 'all distribution and supply must be put into the hands of our association, our metalworkers' union; take it away from the bureaucratic *glavki*'. The factory committees should take charge of distribution; the union had to 'get its workers' hands on those *glavki*'. This was workerism not as self-interest, but as a conviction that social liberation will be achieved by the working class, as distinct from, and indeed in opposition to, the socialist parties or the intellectuals in any guise.

These workerist and egalitarian arguments on rationing were rejected by the pro-SR group at the meeting, whose leaders included Epifanov from the 1886 power station and Kazenkov of the Dobrovykh-Navgolts factory, both in Zamoskvorech'e. Epifanov said 'the root of evil is not the privileges in rationing, but the economic policy' – and, above all, grain requisitioning.

---

41 *Pravda*, 1 October 1920; Borrero, op. cit., pp. 150–57. Likhachev (1882–1924) was born in Kazan, where his father was a forester; joined the Social Democrats in 1902 and became a professional revolutionary, living in exile in the USA from 1911 to 1917; he was on the Moscow soviet presidium from 1918 and headed MSNKh in 1921–23.
42 Those doing hard physical labour would receive 1.5 funt (614 grammes) of bread per day; those doing light physical labour and soviet officials would receive 1 funt (410 grammes); so would a third 'intermediate' group and children under 16. TsAOPIM, 3/1;a/1 and 2ob-3ob; Aleshchenko, op. cit., p. 190; *Moskovskii Sovet*, p. 94.
43 There is an account of the meeting in Chapter 3 below, pp. 74–78.

Against them, Portnov stated his opposition to 'reopening the Sukharevka', Moscow's main market, the closure of which in December 1920 marked the high tide of 'war communist' fervour. The Bolsheviks, who clashed sharply with the egalitarians on other issues, lined up with them here: when Ivan Kireev, a member of the strong non-party group at AMO, denounced privileged rations, the Bolshevik party official Moisei Rafes supported him, citing the Moscow soviet's decision two weeks earlier to abolish all extra rations.[44]

The Polish war and working-class politics

In May 1920 Poland invaded Soviet Ukraine, and within weeks a Bolshevik counter-offensive was mounted. For three months, until the Red army's offensive was halted by a crushing military defeat, the war was seen by Lenin, and by many rank-and-file Bolsheviks – although not by many other party leaders – as an opportunity to spread the revolution westwards and bring closer the socialist transformation of Europe. Moscow workers recognized that the war was crucial to the fate of the revolution. Most participated in huge public displays of support for it, while in the factories, a significant minority voiced doubts about who might benefit, which merged with broader concerns about the party's position in the Soviet state.

In July 1920, a gigantic demonstration was staged to welcome to Moscow the delegates to the third congress of the Communist International (Comintern), and the war was at the front of participants' minds. The estimated attendance of 250,000 could only have been achieved on the basis of some worker support for the war and the government. On the other hand, most demonstrators did not just turn up of their own accord. Workers were given paid time off to participate, plus, in some cases, an unusually nutritious meal afterwards in workplace canteens. The SR memoirist V.F. Klement'ev, then working as a *sluzhashchii*, recorded both good humour and political scorn in the crowd. A colleague had remarked 'we're marching along like blockheads'; he, and other grumblers, were sacked the following day.[45] Such orchestrated displays cannot, therefore, be taken by themselves as a reliable indication of workers' mood. (This issue is further discussed in Chapter 6.) The minutes of factory meetings are more revealing, particularly from workplaces where Menshevik or non-party socialists were active, and challenges to the Bolsheviks more likely. At the Bogatyr chemical factory in Sokol'niki, where the Bolshevik cell constantly clashed with a vocal Menshevik group, mass meetings consistently supported the war, but were undecided about the issue of the Comintern that divided the two sides. In July 1920 a Bolshevik

---

44 TsGAMO, 180/1/236/6–66; TsGAMO, 180/1/235.
45 *Kommunisticheskii trud*, 29 July 1920; M. Farbman, *Bolshevism in Retreat*, London: Collins, 1923, p. 137; V.F. Klement'ev, *V bol'shevistskoe Moskve (1918–1920)*, Moscow: Russkii put', 1998, pp. 429–31.

resolution was rejected in favour of a Menshevik one that greeted 'the victory of the Red army' and 'the revolutionary upsurge in western Europe', but excluded mention of the Comintern; a subsequent meeting in September adopted a standard Bolshevik resolution, including support for the Comintern, unanimously.[46]

In September the party called for volunteers to go to the front, and for workers to work an extra two hours per day to support the war effort. This inspired active support at one extreme and hostility – not to the war as such, but to the party's role in it – on the other. In between, many workers appear to have been passively supportive of, or indifferent to, the war. Over the summer, 3000 Bolshevik volunteers had left Moscow for the western front; more than 3500 would go to the western and southern fronts later in the year; and thousands of Moscow party and Komsomol members who had been mobilized in 1919 were still at war.[47] Family and workplace connections with these large contingents must have raised the level of support for the Red army. Workers at the Bromlei machine-building factory – who in September 1920 were heard by a Cheka agent to 'pile insults on the communists for everything', and who in March 1921 were at the forefront of support for the Kronshtadt rising – agreed to do the two extra hours. So did those at the Duks aircraft factory in Krasnopresnia. Workers at the rail workshops in Rogozhsko-Simonovskii voted to work the two extra hours by 21 against 3, with 27 abstentions, suggesting little enthusiasm for the extra work, but an unwillingness to vote against the war effort. At a meeting of women members of the metalworkers' union, objections were expressed to the extra hours not on principle – on the contrary, speakers stressed their support for the war's aims – but on the grounds that they already had to work extra 'on the side', to make ends meet. In response to an appeal to sew uniforms for the Red army in the evenings at home, some speakers protested that they could not, because by the time they reached home each day it was dark.[48] There were reservations expressed about the war, often on the grounds that, since the party had chosen to exercise power on its own, it should defend that power, without appealing to workers for help. At the Soviet rolling mill no.1 in Sokol'niki, a Cheka agent reported speeches at a mass meeting to the effect that 'if the communists have power, then the communists must defend that power. We non-party people don't want to defend the revolution'. A Bolshevik resolution hailing the Red army, 'Red Poland' and the Communist Party was amended, and 'long live the Communist Party' replaced with 'long live the workers' party'. Workers had said they 'did not want any one party to rule on its own'.[49] Similar points were made during quarrels about finding volunteers for the front. Workers

46 TsAGM, 337/2/29/168–168ob, 174–174ob.
47 Korshunova et al., op. cit., pp. 165–66; *Pravda*, 23 October 1920; TsAOPIM, 3/1a/6/16; Poliakov, op. cit., pp. 87–120.
48 TsAOPIM, 3/1a/11/24, 57; TsGAMO, 186/1/481/2; TsGAMO, 186/1/492.
49 TsAOPIM, 3/1a/11/70.

expressed contempt for party members who avoided volunteering, such as the cell leaders at the Gabai tobacco factory in Krasnopresnia, who, on receipt of a telegram from their trade union asking for two people to do political work at the front, decided to send non-party volunteers. Their excuses for not going themselves were 'completely deceitful', a Cheka agent complained. A Menshevik woman worker, Krutetskaia, made copies of the telegram, and distributed them, telling workers: 'The communists start a war, and we carry the can'.[50]

These concerns merged with widespread resentment at incursions on democratic rights both inside and outside the workplace. No trace remained in Bolshevik practice of the ideas, widely discussed in 1917–18, that repression of the revolution's enemies, like other aspects of policy, was an issue subject to decision by the masses of the revolution's participants. The arbitrary exercise of power by party bodies and the Cheka, often justified during the civil war on military grounds, continued in 1920. One cause of the continuing repression was the party's extreme nervousness about its ability to retain power. Although the war with the Whites was by now confined to a small area of southern Russia, in Moscow the Bolsheviks felt vulnerable to armed opposition. In October 1920, for example, reports of events that turned out later to be unconnected – of a plot being prepared abroad to overthrow the government, of a right-wing conspiracy in Omsk, and of a threatened mutiny in the Moscow garrison over lack of supplies – caused them to believe that a coup was being prepared in the capital. They put the Cheka on full alert and made a wave of arrests.[51] But the Bolsheviks also suppressed, with similar gusto, workers' movements in which no such external or political threats were present – for example, the tram workers' strike mentioned above. The Bolsheviks' efforts to prevent strike action that disrupted transport were hardly exceptional, in the midst of an economic crisis. But their dismissive rejection of the tram workers' demand for a city-wide meeting spoke volumes about their hostility to the development of the workers' movement, and landed a blow at the type of collective democracy that might have been better able to confront supply problems.

The arrest and dismissal of workers who organized strikes – amongst whom there must have been, by definition, many of the most vocal and articulate workers' representatives – was not an exception, but the most likely response to any stoppage that lasted more than a day. Such arrests sometimes provoked knock-on protest strikes. At the Sytin print works, which had a strong tradition of organization by Mensheviks and other non-Bolshevik socialists, arrests in August 1920 triggered a strike. Two months earlier, the Bolsheviks had orchestrated a public campaign against the Menshevik-dominated Moscow printers' union board, and initiated its disbandment through the national union. Then, 40 union activists had been detained. In

---

50 TsAOPIM, ibid., 67ob.
51 TsAOPIM, 3/1a/6/44ob.

August, four Sytin workers – Voronin, Shlenskii, Triakin and Smirnov – were arrested for 'actively agitating for improvements in supply'. When a rumour spread that they were to be shot, a strike was immediately declared, on the pretext of lateness of bread supply, although a Cheka agent reported that 'the main issue was the liberation of the arrested workers'. The works was occupied for two days until the four were released.[52] A similar strike broke out at the Gustav List engineering factory in October 1920, after the Cheka arrested two workers and accused them of counter-revolution and/or SR party membership. A general meeting was called, a Cheka representative explained the grounds on which the arrests had been made, and three delegates were elected to testify to the workers' good character to the Cheka and to secure their release.[53]

The scale and direction of repression of non-Bolshevik parties – including those who had supported the soviet side during the civil war, such as left Mensheviks, left SRs and anarchists – were decided on by the Cheka, which reported to party committees. Workers' organizations had no say. In early 1920, Cheka action in Moscow was concentrated on the anarchist underground organization that had organized the bombing of a Moscow party meeting in September 1919; by August the Cheka felt that it had 'broken up' the anarchist groups and could concentrate on the right SRs, opponents of soviet power, who wielded 'disorganizing' influence among the *sluzhashchie* in soviet institutions. During August and September it arrested 175 people, including most of the SR central committee. Workplaces where the SRs were strong, such as the Aleksandrovskaia railway workshops, were affected. After a protest over labour compulsion, Gavrilin, an SR member who worked there, and Vavil'kin, a former Menshevik, were arrested and sentenced to two years' hard labour. Three other participants in the action were sentenced to one year's hard labour.[54] The left SRs were spared any such round-ups, but their demands for legal recognition met with little enthusiasm among the Bolsheviks. In July, the party's MC bureau, rather than any soviet body, discussed a request by the Moscow left SRs for legal status, and turned it down on the grounds of 'the complexities of the current situation'.[55] The Cheka also kept an eye on the left SR

---

52 TsAOPIM, 3/1a/11/38; *Sotsialisticheskii vestnik* 1921, no. 1, p. 15; D. Koenker, 'Labour Relations in Socialist Russia: Class Values and Production Values in the Printers Union 1917–21', in L. Siegelbaum and R. Suny (eds), *Making Workers Soviet: Power, Class and Identity*, London: Cornell University Press, 1994, pp. 171–73 and p. 188. See also Aves, op. cit., pp. 64–67.
53 TsAOPIM, 3/1a/11/87, 101.
54 TsAOPIM, 3/1a/11/12; Aves, op. cit., p. 47. See also M.S. Bernshtam, *Narodnoe soprotivlenie kommunizmu v Rossii: nezavisimoe rabochee dvizhenie v 1918 godu*, Paris: YMCA Press, 1981, p. 185, p. 208 and pp. 260–61.
55 In January 1921 the bureau relented slightly, suggesting that the left SRs be allowed to publish a paper, subject to pre-publication censorship. But this position was reversed again after the Kronshtadt rising, during a general clampdown on non-Bolshevik parties. TsAOPIM, 3/1a/7/22, 3/1a/6/15, 3/2/28/18.

internationalist group, 11 members of which were detained briefly in September 1920.[56]

Workers beyond the ranks of the opposition parties took what opportunities were available to challenge the Bolsheviks' drift to political dictatorship. Party speakers at the February 1921 metalworkers' conference were confronted over the use, and abuse, of Cheka repression. When Lev Kamenev, the leader of the Moscow party,[57] admitted that 'there are people who justly hate the [Cheka headquarters at] Lubianka', a heckler responded that he had been imprisoned despite having proof of his innocence. Kamenev's promise that 'the soviet will deal with such injustices' provoked uproar. Non-party workerists at the meeting, who on economic policy issues sided with the Bolsheviks against the SRs, clashed with the Bolsheviks over issues of workers' democracy. Pozden, a non-party worker who sympathized with the Workers Opposition (WO) in the Bolshevik party, said that industrial production required the involvement of the working masses, which in turn required 'the freedom of [political] action, without any pressure from anyone to prevent it'. Barkovskii, who was also close to the WO, demanded 'freedom of the press, freedom of speech and freedom of assembly'.[58]

These political concerns, as well as those about supply, told heavily on the Bolsheviks' workplace cells, whose members had to defend and explain government policy to their workmates. The workplace cells' weakness remained a concern for the Moscow party right through the post-civil-war period. In September 1920, only 9777 party members in the Moscow region, i.e. a little more than a quarter of the total, worked in industry and transport. These numbers fell gradually, while the proportion of them working in administration rather than on the shop floor rose, until late 1922.[59] At the November 1920 Moscow party conference, MC member Il'ia Tsivtsivadze said the cells were 'caught between two fires. We pressure them from above, demand that they carry out tasks, and they are under pressure from below'. Cell members were being 'choked' by 'millions of duties'. The expression of

---

56 TsAOPIM, 3/1a/11/58.
57 Kamenev (1883–1936), one of the Bolshevik CC's senior figures, was chairman of the Moscow soviet and political leader of the Moscow party organization from 1918 until his removal, after falling out with Stalin, in 1926. A recent biography is J. Ulrich, *Kamenev: Der gemassigte Bolschewik*, Hamburg: VSA-Verlag, 2006.
58 TsGAMO, 180/1/236/9, 11, 21, 28, 46–47.
59 In October 1920, out of a total of 35,226 party members in the Moscow region, there were 8071 members in industrial cells and 1706 in transport cells, of which most (7545 and 1247, respectively) counted themselves as 'workers or junior *sluzhashchie*' rather than administrators. The numbers 'at the bench' fell substantially by the national reregistration in January-February 1922. Sekretariat TsK RKP(b), *Materialy po statistike lichnogo sostava RKP*, Moscow, 1921, pp. 42–47. The issue is further discussed in Chapter 5, pp. 129–131. Statistics on party members' occupations are in Appendix 5, p. 261.

dissatisfaction, 'sometimes unconsciously', was 'natural' on the part of communists 'who are placed in such a rotten position'. A member of the AMO cell had told Tsivtsivadze that 'we get home late, when the family is already asleep. In the morning we leave early and they are still asleep. We can not live like this'.[60] Varvara Iakovleva, then the MC secretary, continued the theme at the tenth party congress in March 1921. Some factory-based communists, faced with an upsurge of 'petty-bourgeois spontaneity', felt themselves to be 'under greater threat at workers' meetings than they did when threatened by bullets and bayonets – and sometimes, taking the line of least resistance, going along with the masses' mood'. Many such members were 'on the verge of leaving the party'.[61]

There is further evidence of the pressure experienced by worker communists in the archives of the AMO cell mentioned by Tsivtsivadze, which faced strong political competition from the factory's non-party group. One cell member, P.A. Olenov, resigned in July 1920 rather than act as an informer. Workers had struck, demanding 'shock' status for the factory and a change in summer holiday arrangements to facilitate procurement trips. After the strikers returned to work, party members were required to compile reports on workers who were 'stirring up the unconscious masses'. Olenov refused to, resigned from the factory committee in protest, and was threatened with expulsion.[62] On the other hand, two party members on the factory committee who enjoyed considerable popularity in the workforce, Gol'tsev and Demidov, faced concerted attempts from within the party to remove them, on the grounds that they were unfit to represent it. The metalworkers' union regional executive refused to ratify their election. Lurid accusations that they were cheats, bribe-takers and drunkards, and that Gol'tsev was in the habit of brandishing a revolver, were then published in the party newspaper, *Pravda*. At least some of these charges were proved to the cell's satisfaction, and Gol'tsev and Demidov were expelled from it. Nevertheless the workforce reiterated its support for them at a mass meeting – and, until a group of AMO communists returned from the Red army in 1921, there were no

---

60 TsAOPIM, 3/1a/2/71. Tsivtsivadze (1881–1938) was born at Kutaissk (now Abkhazia) in Georgia; was educated at the local seminary, and expelled for revolutionary activity; joined the Bolsheviks in 1903 and from 1912 lived in Moscow; from 1917 was a member of the Moscow soviet, worked in the housing department from 1922 and in industrial administration from 1929.
61 *Desiatyi s"ezd RKP(b): stenograficheskii otchet*, Moscow: Gos. izd. polit. literatury, 1963, p. 280. On Iakovleva, see Appendix 1.
62 TsAGM, 415/16/317/20ob. Olenov, a native of Tver', started his working life there in the forge of a rolling stock manufacturer and took part in underground political activity, collecting funds for the Social Democrats; he moved to Moscow in 1916 and was recruited to the tsarist army; having quit the party in 1920 he rejoined in 1925.

Struggling to survive 41

party members available to replace them on the factory committee.[63] The cell also suffered from numerous resignations: on 4 January 1921 it discussed measures to counter 'the outflow of the worker mass from the party', which it blamed on 'the stifling of cells' self-activity', the 'great inequality' between communists, and the fact that the party tops were 'cut off from the ranks'.[64]

Calm before the storm

The prelude to the crisis of spring 1921 – when the Bolsheviks faced a revolt by the Kronshtadt sailors and strike waves in urban centres – was a brief period in November-December 1920, when a short-lived improvement in supply in Moscow eased some of the tensions between workers and the party. It coincided with the reopening of some key factories and a consequent improvement in production. All this reinforced illusions in the party about the viability of extending 'war communist' economic policies into peacetime construction. The soviet felt able to report:

> Compared to last year, we will spend this winter in much better conditions. The supply of bread and fuel, the number of schools working, and the number of factories and workshops that have restarted, all clearly confirm that for the Moscow workers the worst days have already passed.[65]

A Cheka report covering the second half of November said rations were being delivered reliably to almost all workers in the 'shock' and 'reserved' categories. In that period there were only two strikes over supply in the city of Moscow – a one-day stoppage at Dobrovykh-Navgolts and a half-day strike at the Bromlei works.[66]

There is abundant evidence that many Bolsheviks took the temporary improvement to mean that the worst supply problems had been overcome, and believed that further economic successes could be achieved by the continuation of 'war communist' methods. At the Moscow regional party conference on 20–22 November, the party leadership and the opposition, who were at loggerheads about almost everything else, agreed that the

---

63 TsAGM, 415/16/317/20, 415/16/39/9, 415/16/587/9, 415/16/47/11–14. Gol'tsev remained active in AMO's workers' organizations and was back on the factory committee by early 1922. In 1923–24, the AMO cell twice rejected his applications for readmission, but he rejoined later in the late 1920s. A.P. Churiaev, N.V. Adfel'dt and D.A. Baevskii (eds), *Istoriia Moskovskogo avtozavoda im. I.A. Likhacheva*, Moscow, izd. 'Mysl'', 1966, pp. 73 and 85; TsAGM, 415/16/47/11–14, 415/16/318/95, 415/16/587/9; TsAOPIM, 433/1/16/54 and 433/1/19/6.
64 TsAGM, 415/16/590/50.
65 *Moskovskii Sovet*, p. 95.
66 TsAOPIM, 3/1a/11/142. See also Aleshchenko, op. cit., p. 190.

supply crisis was over. Nikolai Bukharin, who led the attack on the opposition on behalf of the Bolshevik central committee (CC), told the conference that, whereas earlier in the year, speakers addressing workers' meetings were deluged with notes asking about supply, 'now everybody knows that at workers' meetings there are hardly any such notes. ... Now we have overcome all the difficulties. Rations are distributed regularly'. Bukharin, who had ideologed 'war communism' as a method of long-term economic construction, claimed that workers were no longer calling, as they had done earlier in the year, for the restoration of free trade. This 'principled step forward [in] mass psychology' was a starting point from which the superiority of 'our [war communist] methods' over free trade, 'private initiative' and other bourgeois methods in the economy could be demonstrated. Ivan Kutuzov, a leader of the opposition, said: 'Now our position ... has improved; we hear about the victories on the [military] fronts and, at last, feel an advance at home too. The workshops are going, the factories are starting up, and the workers' mood has improved.'[67] The illusions about economic progress were best expressed by the pride with which the Moscow party organization greeted the closure on 14 December of the capital's main market, the Sukharevka. This highly publicized blow to free trade was seen by some party members as symbolic of the republic's ability, at this early stage of its march forward to socialism, to liberate exchange between town and country from profiteering and speculation.[68] The decisions of the eighth congress of soviets in December 1920 reflected the same determination to press ahead. On agriculture, the congress rejected a proposition by the Menshevik David Dalin, that 'the peasantry should have the possibility to dispose of all surpluses', and passed a resolution drafted by Valerian Osinskii, a leader of the democratic centralist (DC) faction, that envisaged a centrally directed sowing campaign, carried out by sowing committees. There were vehement protests by delegates from rural areas, and after meeting with them, Lenin convinced the Bolshevik faction at the congress not to remove legislation permitting certain premiums for individual households. On industry, the congress approved Krzhizhanovskii's famous electrification plan, and envisaged the revival of heavy industry and extensive introduction of new technology by the following spring. The resolution on transport asserted, over optimistically, that the worst of the transport crisis

---

67 *Narodnoe khoziaistvo*, December 1920; TsAOPIM, 3/1a/2/32. Kutuzov (1885–1937) was born in a village in Smolensk region; his father was an *otkhodnik* who worked in Moscow in the winter; he became a dye-finisher and in 1907 set up a trade union organization at the mill where he worked; a Moscow soviet delegate from the first days of its existence in February 1917, he joined the Bolsheviks in that year; 1918–26 chairman of the textile workers' union; supported the WO; from 1926, chairman of the central soviet executive committee of the USSR.
68 *Kommunisticheskii trud*, 14 December 1920.

was passed. The party press celebrated Lenin's motto that 'communism = soviet power + electrification'.[69]

In fact the improvements were frail and temporary. Stocks of flour accumulated during September and October were used up, and warnings from the food supply commissariat about the resulting gap appear to have gone unheeded. The celebrations in Moscow of the steps forward, both real and apparent, were in stark contrast to the mood in villages just a few kilometres into the surrounding countryside, where peasants were close to starvation. From late October Cheka agents in some rural areas were reporting hunger, and warning of resentment at labour conscription and the requisitioning of draft animals. By December some reports indicated a hostile mood, caused by shortages of animal feed that were forcing peasants to slaughter cattle. The peasants had also lost horses.[70] In the textile manufacturing towns in the countryside around Moscow, there were large-scale strikes in November: in Orekhovo-Zuevo district, 1000 workers struck for four days; at Pavlova Posada, 500 workers at the Dreznenskaia mill struck because neither their 'reserved' rations nor September's wages had arrived, and 3000 workers from another nearby mill joined in. Party, soviet and union officials sanctioned 15 arrests.[71] Perhaps workers' resentment at their supply problems was aggravated by the suffering of their peasant neighbours. It took another two months – during which the peasant revolts intensified, the supply crisis threatened the Moscow and Petrograd workers with hunger, and unrest climaxed in the Kronshtadt revolt – before the Bolshevik leaders were forced into a fundamental change of strategy, the adoption of the initial NEP-type measures at the tenth party congress in March 1921.

69 *Dekrety sovetskoi vlasti*, vol. XII, pp. 80–86 and 113–16; *Doklady na VIII-m Vserossiiskom s'ezde sovetov*, Moscow: MK RKP(b), 1921. See also Farbman, op. cit., pp. 262–64, and S.A. Pavliuchenkov, *Krestianskii Brest, ili predystoriia bol'shevistskogo NEPa*, Moscow: Russkoe knigoizdatel'skoe izdatel'stvo, 1996, pp. 257–60.
70 TsAOPIM, 3/1a/11/128–29, 163–163ob, 168–168ob.
71 TsAOPIM, ibid, 142ob.

2 Sweet visions and bitter clashes
The party in July–December 1920

Communists who had joined the party during the civil war returned to Moscow in 1920 to begin peacetime construction, which many of them saw as an extension of the military struggle. They had high hopes about the new society they would build, and often reacted angrily to manifestations of authoritarianism and hierarchy back in the capital, and in particular to any evidence of material privilege among the new elite. The party they had joined was volatile, in contrast to the sullen organization it became after the tenth congress, when dissent was discouraged. The democratic centralist (DC) group, which had in 1919 won a majority for its policy of dispersing decision-making power down through the soviets, was joined in opposition by the Workers Opposition (WO). In Moscow, support for these and other dissident groupings brought the party organization close to a split. The numerical predominance in the party of the civil war communists, i.e. those who joined during the civil war, was illustrated by a survey of the Moscow regional party's 35,226 members in October 1920. It showed that 32 per cent of them had joined between the October revolution and August 1919, and another 51 per cent since then, mainly in the 'party week' recruitment drive of October 1919. Only a tiny minority (5 per cent, i.e. 1763 members), had joined the party before 1917, and another 10 per cent had joined in 1917 before October. The party was, literally, steeled in battle: nationally, 89 per cent of the membership was male, and of those, 70 per cent had completed military training, 'the majority in combatant units'. Many had just returned from, or were between turns of duty at, the front. As Viktoriia Tiazhel'nikova has shown, some persisted in their habit of carrying firearms when going about their office or factory jobs, not only in 1920 but for years afterwards.[1] The transfer of communists into administration, a tendency that continued into the mid 1920s, had begun: 27 per cent of the Moscow region's members were working

---

1 Sekretariat TsK RKP(b), *Materialy po statistike lichnogo sostava RKP*, Moscow, 1921, pp. IX and 62–63; V.S. Tiazhel'nikova, '"Voennyi sindrom" v povedenii kommunistov 1920-kh gg.', in E.S. Seniavskaia (ed.), *Voenno-istoricheskaia antropologiia. Ezhegodnik 2002. Predmet, zadachi, perspektivu razvitiia*, Moscow: Rosspen, 2002, pp. 291–305.

in soviet institutions and 4 per cent in party or trade union posts, as against 23 per cent in industry, 5 per cent in transport and 18 per cent in the Red army.[2]

The civil war communists

In the mood of the civil war communists, as distinct from the pre-1917 Bolsheviks in the party leadership, there was a streak of super-optimism, i.e. an exaggerated confidence, based on the victories achieved in 1917–19, in their own ability to change the world. The discussion that follows situates these moods in the specific, and rapidly changing, conditions. This may add to research by other historians whose conclusions I do not always share,[3] while striking a contrast with Igal Halfin's work on the party rank and file, in which he has taken the 'linguistic turn' to extremes, not only downplaying, but specifically rejecting, the need to consider the political and social changes to which linguistic expression is related. He argues that the 'conflation' of Bolsheviks' statements with 'what positivist historians consider the objective conditions of the tsarist empire or of early Soviet Russia' would be a 'serious mistake'. Elsewhere he asserts that historians have no need 'to explain what historical protagonists were saying or doing in terms of underlying economic interests or political struggles'.[4] In trying to explain what protagonists were doing in exactly this way, I approach the subject matter from a diametrically opposite standpoint.

The evidence of heightened optimism comes not from the party's factory-based worker members, but from middle-level officials who were racing from one military front, or civilian 'front', to the next. Pavel Lebedev-Polianskii, an official in literary organizations, recalled in 1929 that during the civil war he had lived by the 'deepest conviction' that the world revolution was about to explode. 'We all lived in a state of revolutionary romanticism: weary and exhausted but happy, festive; unkempt, unwashed, long-haired and unshaven, but clear and clean of thought and heart.'[5] His romanticism had been reinforced by the discussion in 1920 about the possible abolition of money. In that year, the hopes of such artificial leaps away

---

2 Sekretariat TsK RKP(b), op. cit., pp. 42–47. Details of communists' occupations in Appendix 5, p. 261.
3 E.g. S. Fitzpatrick, *The Russian Revolution 1917–1932*, Oxford: Oxford University Press, 1982, especially pp. 76–79; and S. Fitzpatrick, 'The civil war as formative experience', in A. Gleason, P. Kenez and R. Stites (eds), *Bolshevik Culture: Experiment and Order in the Russian Revolution*, Bloomington: Indiana University Press, 1985, pp. 58–76. Other works are cited in notes 22 and 24 to the Introduction.
4 I. Halfin, *From Darkness to Light: Class, Consciousness and Salvation in Revolutionary Russia*, Pittsburgh: University of Pittsburgh Press, 2000 (quotation from p. 86); I. Halfin, *Terror in My Soul: Communist Autobiographies on Trial*, Cambridge, MA: Harvard University Press, 2003; and I. Halfin, 'Introduction', and 'Intimacy in an Ideological Key', in I. Halfin (ed.), *Language and Revolution: Making Modern Political Identities*, London: Cass, 2002.
5 Lebedev-Polianskii in *Krasnaya nov'* 3, 1929, pp. 202–3.

from market relations, and the temporary successes achieved by the application of military methods to economic problems, intensified the impression that rapid advances were being made towards socialism. The writer Boris Pil'niak, politically inclined to anarchism but a personal friend of many senior and middle-level Bolsheviks, wrote:

> I know that – in the cities [an important qualification, SP] – 1920 was the most wonderful year in the history of Russia. ... It should be written about – not only for Russia, but for the entire world, because that year was the most wonderful in the history of humanity.[6]

It was the communists' sense of their own power to change the world and vanquish their enemies that was 'wonderful', Pil'niak stressed. And the authors of the Collectivist manifesto, a 1921 opposition document, in a self-critical retrospective on the 'military utopianism' of the WO, said:

> The military-consumer communism of the besieged fortress [had then] seemed to us like the genuine production communism of the proletariat. ... It never once entered our heads to check our perspectives and our view of the future against the facts, against reality.[7]

One aspect of super-optimism was the hope that, driven by sufficient willpower and self-sacrifice, the revolution could spread to western Europe and overcome domestic economic problems in the process. The advance into Poland by forces under Mikhail Tukhachevskii's command fed this illusion. The British journalist Michael Farbman wrote that at the second Comintern congress in July-August 1920, where western European delegates reported on communist advances in the labour movement and Tukhachevskii's progress was daily plotted on a map, 'the Bolsheviks were simply lifted off their feet by this demonstration of revolutionary solidarity and enthusiasm'. Not all super-optimist visions were contingent on the European revolution, though; some depicted transformations achieved independently of it. The Bolshevik historian M.N. Pokrovskii wrote:

> It seemed [in 1920] that our brilliant success on the military front would be repeated in education and in the economy. We ... were drunk with the speed of events. Things moved so fast that it seemed to us that we were very near to communism, communism that we would build with our own resources, without waiting for the victory of proletarian revolution in the west.'[8]

6 Pil'niak, in *Pisateli ob iskusstve i o sebe: sbornik statei. no.1.*, Moscow/Leningrad: 'Krug', 1924, p. 81. Pil'niak returned to the theme in his novel *Mashiny i vol'ki*, written in 1923.
7 RGASPI, 17/60/43/22.
8 M.N. Pokrovskii, *Sem' let proletarskoi diktatury*, Moscow: Gos. izdatel'stvo, 1924, p. 7; M. Farbman, *Bolshevism in Retreat*, London: Collins, 1923, p. 137.

National and regional party leaders. Top: CC members at the ninth party congress (March 1920), including Avel' Enukidze, Mikhail Kalinin and Nikolai Bukharin (sitting, 1st, 2nd and 3rd from left), Lev Kamenev and Evgenii Preobrazhenskii (sitting, 6th and 7th from left) and Lenin (sitting, right). Above: members of the Moscow commission to organise the 'trade union week' (March 1921).

48 Sweet visions and bitter clashes

The exaggerated voluntarism of the Bolsheviks' middle ranks was most clearly articulated by the proletarian poets and writers in the proletkult movement. Mikhail Gerasimov, a leading figure in the Kuznitsa group, formed in February 1920 as an alternative to the Moscow proletkult,[9] wrote: 'There's no limit to our bold daring. / We're Wagner, da Vinci, Titian'. Such chest-beating was neither ironic nor out of step with the prevailing mood. Il'ia Sadof'ev, another leading light in the Kuznitsa group, had written during the civil war:

> Brighter, happier and more infallible poets than us
> Our planet has never produced ...
>
> From our lips the songs of the uncountable masses
> First rang out with unprecedented grandeur.[10]

Platon Kerzhentsev, one of proletkult's leading theoreticians, insisted that this unbounded confidence was not 'self-glorifying boasting', but 'a profound consciousness that the proletariat will be victorious'.[11] Semen Rodov, the single middle-class intellectual in the Kuznitsa group, had in 1920 praised Gerasimov for his vision of 'the future victory of the collective, in whose name he [Gerasimov] pronounces that steely "we"'.[12] This 'we', i.e. the makers of the new world, was famously exalted by the proletarian poet Vladimir Kirillov, praised by Anatolii Lunacharskii, the commissar of enlightenment, and satirized by Zamiatin in his novella, *We*.

At the top of the party, although some Bolshevik leaders occasionally voiced super-optimistic sentiments, these were tempered by a generally sober outlook. And the leaders often had deep disagreements between themselves on aspects of military and economic policy that appeared to

---

9 The proletkult movement, formed in 1918, sought to encourage worker writers, musicians and actors as bearers of a new proletarian culture. In February 1920, Gerasimov had formed the Kuznitsa group as an alternative to the Moscow proletkult. The difference between the two groups centred on how to develop writing skills and the role of professionalism in literature rather than political questions. See L. Mally, *Culture of the Future: the Proletkult Movement in Revolutionary Russia*, Berkeley: California University Press, 1990; S. Fitzpatrick, *The Commissariat of the Enlightenment: Soviet Organization of Education and the Arts Under Lunacharsky 1917–1921*, Cambridge: Cambridge University Press, 1970, pp. 89–109; Z.A. Sochor, *Revolution and Culture: The Bogdanov-Lenin controversy*, Ithaca: Cornell University Press, 1988, pp. 125–57; M.D. Steinberg, *Proletarian Imagination: Self, Modernity and the Sacred in Russia, 1910–1925*, Ithaca: Cornell University Press, 2002, pp. 54–55.
10 *Kuznitsa* 1, p. 21.
11 P.M. Kerzhentsev, *K novoi kulture*, Petersburg, 1921, pp. 73–74.
12 On Rodov, see Steinberg, op. cit., p. 55.

some rank-and-filers to promise short cuts to socialism. There is a substantial historiographical discussion on the mood in the Bolshevik leadership. Cold-warrior historians argued that 'war communist' policies were 'not so much emergency responses to war conditions as an attempt as rapidly as possible to construct a Communist society' (Richard Pipes) fuelled by a 'veritable ideological delirium' (Martin Malia). Lars Lih and others have shown that the Bolshevik leadership remained collectively pragmatic, and that, as Christopher Read put it, 'the various barks were, in fact, considerably worse than the associated bite'. This point accepted, it nevertheless seems clear that the exotic ideological justifications for the forced march, by Trotsky, Bukharin and others, helped to prolong it. Karl Radek observed in 1922 that 'ideology, which had taken on its own dynamic [in 1918–20], very often transformed provisional, transitional measures into a system, which in its turn influenced the measures and prolonged them beyond what was necessary'.[13]

The political discussions of 1920 pointed up the contrast between the leadership's increasingly cautious assessment of the party's potential, and the profound belief of middle- and lower-ranking Bolsheviks in its ability to change the world by the force of will. So the communist oppositionists gave greater weight to the party as a subjective factor than the mainstream leaders did; they accepted the general proposition that the party was constrained by objective circumstances, but accused its leaders of too readily accepting those circumstances as inevitable and of underestimating the subjective factor. At the November 1920 Moscow regional party conference, at the high tide of inner-party dissent, the DC R.B. Rafail criticized leaders including Lenin and Stalin who 'blame[d] everything on objective conditions'

---

13 On Trotsky and Bukharin, see the Introduction, p. 9. R. Pipes, *Russia Under the Bolshevik Regime*, London: Harvill, 1994, pp. 370–71; M. Malia, *The Soviet Tragedy: a History of Socialism in Russia, 1917–1991*, New York: Maxwell Macmillan International, 1994, p. 130; L. Lih, 'Vlast' from the Past', in *Left Politics*, 6: 2, 1999: 29–52; L. Lih, 'The Mystery of the *ABC*', *Slavic Review* 56: 1, 1997: 50–72; C. Read, *From Tsar to Soviets: the Russian People and their Revolution 1917–21*, London: Routledge, 1996, p. 244; K. Radek, 'The Paths of the Russian Revolution', in Richardson (ed.), *In Defence of the Russian Revolution: a Selection of Bolshevik Writings, 1917–1923*, London: Porcupine Press, 1995, pp. 35–65. I thank Lars Lih for sending me his unpublished article '"Our position is in the highest degree tragic": Bolshevik euphoria in 1920'. See also M. Dewar, *Labour Policy in the USSR, 1917–1928*, London: Royal Institute of International Affairs, 1956, pp. 52–58; B.M. Patenaude, *Bolshevism in Retreat: the Transition to NEP 1920–22* (PhD diss., Stanford University, 1987), pp. 58–68, 92–98, 104–9 and 118–22; S.A. Pavliuchenkov, *Krestianskii Brest, ili predystoriia bol'shevistskogo NEPa*, Moscow: Russkoe knigoizdatel'skoe izdatel'stvo, 1996, pp. 117–67, 216–49 and 257–69; S.V. Tsakunov, *V labirinte doktriny: iz opyta rarabotki ekonomicheskogo kursa strany v 1920-e gody*, Moscow: Rossiia molodaia, 1994, pp. 50–63; and N.S. Simonov, 'Demokratichnaia alternativa totalitarnomu NEPu', *Istoriia SSSR* 1, 1992: 41–56.

50 Sweet visions and bitter clashes

instead of asking whether 'we could deliberately do something differently'. Another leading oppositionist, Nikolai Angarskii, said that instead of thinking about how to combat inequalities, party leaders 'try to justify everything with reference to objective conditions'. Petr Smidovich, a supporter of the leadership, argued that the 'bureaucratism' condemned by the oppositionists was just a formal attitude to tasks, 'often borne of the fact that our forces just don't correspond to the tasks they have to undertake'. To the DC Mikhail Boguslavskii, this was worship of the accomplished fact, by those who 'objectively support bureaucratism'.[14] The oppositionist Efim Ignatov developed this point further at the tenth congress, criticizing Bukharin in similar terms.[15]

Long after those leaders who had been enthusiastic about short cuts realized that they led nowhere, illusions about them persisted in the ranks. For example, Lenin, in sharp disagreement with Trotsky and other leaders, found attractive the idea that Tukhachevskii's pursuit of the retreating Polish army might open the road to Germany and hasten the European revolution. But very soon after Tukhachevskii started retreating, Lenin realized that this had been a serious miscalculation. On 6 September 1920, when Lenin was preparing to make his self-criticism about the Polish adventure at the ninth party conference,[16] a party agitator, Shpindler, reported to communists in Bauman district that the Russian revolution was spreading to western Europe and 'the infection of communism is flowing like a current through all the veins of the earth'.[17] Bauman district boasted Moscow's largest concentration of military industries and barracks, which were heavily represented in the party organization, bastion of the city's

---

14 TsAOPIM, 3/1a/2/35,39 and 63. On Angarskii and Boguslavskii, see Appendix 1. Rafail (1893–1966), a Bolshevik from 1910, was on the MC throughout the 1920s and headed the Moscow education department from 1922; participated in the DC group of 1920–21, the left opposition of 1923 and the united opposition of 1927; in internal exile from 1933. Smidovich (1874–1935) was born into a noble landowning family; joined the revolutionary movement at university in 1893 and the Bolsheviks in 1903; from 1920 held senior positions in education, industry, and on committees for the welfare of the Siberian native peoples.
15 *Desiatyi s"ezd RKP(b): stenograficheskii otchet*, Moscow: Gos. izd. polit. literatury, 1963, p. 234. On Ignatov, see Appendix 1.
16 Lenin's report on the Polish disaster was made public only in 1992. V.I. Lenin, 'Ia proshu zapisyvat' men'she: eto ne dolzhno popadat' v pechat'', *Istoricheskii arkhiv* 1, 1992: 12–30. For interpretations of Bolshevik motives, see Pipes, op. cit., p. 177; E.H. Carr, *The Bolshevik Revolution 1917–1923*, London: Macmillan, 1978, vol. 3, pp. 209–17; T.C. Fiddick, *Russia's Retreat from Poland, 1920: from Permanent Revolution to Peaceful Coexistence*, London: Macmillan, 1990, especially pp. 110–24 and 251–79; R.K. Debo, *Survival and Consolidation: the Foreign Policy of Soviet Russia, 1918–1921*, Montreal: McGill-Queen's University Press, 1992, pp. 241–47 and 408–10; S.A. Pavliuchenkov, *Voennyi kommunizm v Rossii: vlast' i massy*, Moscow: RKT-Istoriia, 1997, pp. 98–99.
17 TsAOPIM, 63/1/17/11.

strongest left opposition group.[18] At the heavy artillery workshops cell in the district, the oppositionist Vladimir Demidov kept up his optimistic commentary on the international revolution even after the armistice with Pilsudski was signed on 12 October, referring on 29 October to 'the hardships and the victories of the Red army' and on 11 November, after the German elections, to 'the failure of Menshevik propaganda against the communists, and the complete support of the German workers for proletarian power'.[19]

On the economic 'front', too, the mood of middle-level officials lagged behind changes in thinking at leadership level. The possibility of abandoning aspects of 'war communism' was under discussion in the party leadership from early 1920. In January the third national congress of economic councils adopted a proposal by Iurii Larin to abandon grain requisitioning, but the CC buried it. In February, the CC rejected a similar suggestion, by Trotsky. Then he took charge of transport and reversed his position completely, becoming the most extreme exponent of compulsive methods. Both he and Bukharin published their theoretical justifications of these methods in the middle of the year.[20] But when the transport crisis erupted in February 1921, Lenin and other party leaders very quickly concluded that the move towards market methods was unavoidable – while some middle-level Bolsheviks continued to regard such proposals as an unthinkable retreat. 'Should we put out the fire of revolution, then?' the middle-level Bolshevik official Moisei Rafes demanded of hecklers at the Moscow metalworkers' meeting of February 1921, where the majority called for grain requisitioning and other methods of market suppression to be scrapped.[21] An affirmative answer came from none other than Lenin, who told the meeting that worker-peasant relations should be 'reconsidered'. His proposals for the tax in kind, which opened the road to New Economic Policy (NEP), were drafted a few days later. Rafes must have been shocked.

For the civil war Bolsheviks, the subject of history, Gerasimov's 'we', was not the working class but the party – a select group, a band of communist brothers, united and made equal by shared beliefs and shared sacrifices. The pre-revolutionary Bolsheviks' conception of the vanguard party had been shaped by Lenin's theoretical arguments and the factional struggle with the Mensheviks; for the civil war Bolsheviks, the experience of the front was at

---

18 Baumanskii komitet VKP(b), *Ocherki po istorii revoliutsionnogo dvizheniia i bol'- shevistskoi organizatsii v Baumanskom raione*, Moscow, 1927, pp. 71–78. Bauman party membership lists, TsAOPIM, 63/1/23, 30, 62.
19 On Demidov, see Appendix 1. TsAOPIM, 465/1/3/47–48.
20 Larin in *Deiateli soiuza sovetskikh sotsialisticheskikh respublik i oktiabr'skoi revoliutsii: avtobiografii i biografii*, Moscow: Granat, 1925–26, cols. 279–80; I. Deutscher, *The Prophet Armed. Trotsky 1879–1921*, London: Oxford University Press, 1970, pp. 496–97; Patenaude, op. cit., p. 63; Pavliuchenkov, *Voennyi kommunizm*, pp. 93–94; Pavliuchenkov, *Krestianskii Brest*, p. 81.
21 TsGAMO, 180/1/236/13–14.

least as significant. It conditioned ideas and moral standards, and many instances of civil war communists trying to uphold these standards in peacetime will be mentioned in this book. That is the theme of the worker writer Iurii Libedinskii's novel *Kommissary*. Its heroes are civil war communists at a residential education course in late 1921, 'combative and capable people, people tempered in the civil war, educated in the fight against specialists' treachery, against kulak rebellions and against the poison of anarchist propaganda. They had been through it all, they themselves had triumphed'.[22] There is no happy ending, though: some of the commissars make a rancorous exit during a row about implementing NEP, and others struggle to adjust to peacetime tasks.

The civil war communists' vanguardism was combined with a strong belief in equality between communists, both materially and in terms of making decisions and exercising power. The corollary of the party's right and duty to make political decisions on behalf of the working class was the need for loyalty, trust, and consequently equality, between its members. At the front, this loyalty and trust were at a premium. Equality, on the one hand, implied equal prospects of death or serious injury, or military success, and, on the other, referred to the priority supplies to the Red army that shielded it from the worst food shortages. This equality was overwhelmingly between males, and did not often extend to women members of male communists' families. As Iakov Dorofeev, a member of the Bolshevik party's Moscow committee (MC), said in a candid moment:

> They [worker communists] don't understand freedom right. They split up with their wives. [Many, including full-time officials] leave them with five children. They split up even with wives who are communists, and this happens right at the top [of the party]. ... There are many such cases, and it can't be hidden. It doesn't get discussed at meetings, but it gets talked about in party circles all right, and I feel that it will all come out [into the open] soon.[23]

This equality, albeit limited in these ways, in 1920 became a cardinal principle for many party members. It served as a slogan through which rank-and-filers – often young, male activists who had served at the front and were now returning to the factories or to administrative posts – expressed distrust of, and disaffection with, the party elite. The way that this issue fuelled

22 Iu. Libedinskii, *Nedelia: Kommissary: Povesti*, Moscow: Voennoe izd., 1968, p. 138.
23 Dorofeev was participating in a round-table discussion that reviewed party life in the first two years of NEP in the light of Trotsky's book *Questions of Everyday Life* (*Voprosy byta*), which had just been published. *Rabochaia Moskva*, 5 August 1923. Dorofeev (1886–1979) was born into a poor peasant family and at the age of 14 migrated to Moscow with his brother and started work in an upholstery workshop; joined the Bolsheviks 1907; from 1922 was chairman of the Moscow soviet presidium and worked in industrial management.

political disputes is evident in a letter, denouncing material privileges among senior party officials, written to Lenin by the Red army commander Anton Vlasov. He returned to Moscow in September 1920 and was devastated at the contrast between the internal solidarity established by communists at the front and the absence of it in the city. Vlasov wrote that

> in the heart of every conscious comrade from the front, who at the front has become used to almost complete equality, who has broken from every kind of servility, debauchery and luxury – with which our very best party comrades now surround themselves – there boils hatred and disbelief

at the taste for the good life among some party leaders and, significantly, their wives.[24]

The sense of inner-party egalitarianism was not narrowly military, though. The AMO car factory cell sought to achieve egalitarian relations between communists with the help of communal living arrangements. The cell, whose strained relations with workers were mentioned in Chapter 1, held a series of discussions in January-February 1921 about strengthening the party organization. In addition to common tonics, such as organized reading of Bukharin and Preobrazhenskii's *ABC of Communism* and better turn-outs for *subbotniki* (volunteer Saturday working), it was decided to 'cure our organization's ills by means of communal living'. Thus:

> [T]he [domestic] situation of all members will be improved, as well as their education, as they will be living together with responsible comrades as one single family – and in this way we will destroy bureaucratism, self-seeking, slovenliness and dishonesty.

Such communes, which owe something to Chernyshevskii's naïve socialist utopia, were popular among Komsomol members and radical cultural groups from 1917 through to the mid 1920s, as they simultaneously offered a means for members to become 'new people' and a practical solution to the acute shortage of living space.[25]

Civil war communists' belief in a vanguard, bound together by equality between its members, was combined with views of the socialist future that often, on one hand, envisaged the abolition of private property, and,

---

24 A. Vlasov, 'My vse vidim i vse znaem: krik dushi krasnogo komandira', *Istochnik* 1, 1998: 85–87. On communist officials' wives, see Chapter 5, p. 121.
25 There is no record of whether the decision was implemented, although the AMO cell went on in 1928 to found Moscow's most high-profile communist commune. TsAGM, 415/16/590/51, 53–55. See also N. Chernyshevskii, *What Is To Be Done?: Tales About New People*, London: Virago, 1982, pp. 153–61; R. Stites, *Revolutionary Dreams: Utopian Vision and Experimental Life in the Russian Revolution*, Oxford: Oxford University Press, 1989, pp. 213–14 and 216–17.

on the other, looked to the state apparatus they had begun to build during the civil war as the means to achieve that. Uporov, the communist hero of a story by a worker writer from Rogozhsko-Simonovskii, believed that 'the time would soon come when property would not exist, and then people, brought together by common labour, would be happy'.[26] At a meeting in the same district in 1922, at which the definition of socialism was disputed, the AMO cell secretary, Gavrilin – expressing the way in which the civil war had taken party members further from Marx's view of socialism as the negation of the state, and closer to statism – described communism as something to which the party had got closest in 1920.

> We are only going towards it, as if up a great mountain. There was a time when we got up very high, but we couldn't stay at that level. We rolled down. And now we need to build an embankment, to give the hill a gentler gradient.[27]

Such positive views of 'war communist' methods were reinforced with ideas borrowed from statist trends in nineteenth-century socialism. The writings of Edward Bellamy, the American statist socialist, became popular among the civil war communists. *Looking Backwards*, Bellamy's utopian novel, describes a disciplined egalitarian state, with an economy dependent on universal labour service and political decisions taken by a hierarchy of elders; its authoritarian streak had incensed libertarian socialists from William Morris onwards. Bellamy's book, already hugely popular in the pre-revolutionary Russian workers' movement, was reprinted in comparatively large numbers in 1917–18 and party members often included it on their list of favourite books.[28] Its popularity dismayed some party leaders. In 1922, when Lenin compared the recruits joining the party under NEP unfavourably with the civil war communists

---

26 N. Bondarev, 'Riadovoi', in *Vagranka. Sbornik literaturno-khudozhestvennogo kruzhka pri Rogozhsko-Simonovskogo raikoma RKP(b)*, Moscow: Moskovskii rabochii, 1921, pp. 61–71. Bondarev belonged to a worker writers' group based in Rogozhsko-simonovskii district. The group was named Vagranka, the Russian term for a small iron-founding furnace. Victor Serge thought highly of the group, and believed that 'it means more for human culture than any exquisite literary salon in Paris'. See V. Serge, 'Une litterature proletarienne est-elle possible?', in Serge, *Littérature et révolution*, Paris: Maspero, 1976, p. 117.
27 TsAOPIM, 433/1/14/11ob. See also Chapter 7, p. 176.
28 *Looking Backward* was reprinted in 1917 (number of copies unknown) and in 1918 (10,000 copies). Bellamy's story, 'The Parable of the Water Tank', was reprinted in 200,000 copies, an exceptionally large run for those years. A. Nikoljukin, 'A Little-Known Story: Bellamy in Russia', in S. Bowman (ed.), *Edward Bellamy Abroad: An American Prophet's Influence*, New York: Twayne, 1962, pp. 67–85. See also Stites, op. cit., p. 32; S. Lapitskaia, *Byt' rabochikh trekhgornoi manufaktury*, Moscow: OGIZ, 1935, p. 78.

(see Chapter 6, p. 163), Aron Sol'ts, chairman of the party control commission, wrote to him:

> It's not always true that the old are better than the young. Don't overlook the fact that in the war communist period, many adventurist and naïve people practically forced their way into our ranks. They thought they would taste all the fruits of socialism, just the way it was portrayed in *In A Hundred Years' Time* [the Russian translation of *Looking Backward*].[29]

The Bolshevik educationalist Nadezhda Krupskaia (Lenin's wife) bemoaned Bellamy's 'barren picture of the future society without any struggle or collective'.[30]

While Bellamy's ordered, statist vision of socialism apparently appealed to the majority, the minority view was expressed by a party member from Viatka region, who resigned because:

> I can not be that sort of idealist communist who believes in the new God That They Call the State, bows before the bureaucracy that is so far from the working people, and waits for communism from the hands of pen-pushers and officials as though it was the kingdom of heaven.[31]

'The tops and the ranks'

The return of civil-war communists to the urban centres pushed the issue of material inequality within the party to the top of the political agenda. Their sense of communist egalitarianism was offended by the privileges, albeit meagre, that had begun to accumulate in the party elite. Perhaps the impact was reinforced in Moscow because there returning Red army men would have seen evidence of these privileges with their own eyes. But the issue of 'the tops and the ranks',[32] as it became known, was not driven by crude jealousy of superiors. Anger about privilege mingled with concern about the accumulation of political power at the top, the subject of a longer-term dispute initiated by the DCs a year and a half earlier.

The DC Il'ia Vardin had described as 'tops' communists who had become 'state functionaries [*chinovniki*], scattered around commissariats and *tsentry*'

---

29 A.V. Kvashonkin et al. (eds), *Bol'shevistskoe rukovodstvo. Perepiska. 1912–1927*, Moscow: Rosspen, 1996, p. 242.
30 Nikoljukin, op. cit., p. 75.
31 I am grateful for permission to use this citation, from Tsentr dokumentatsii noveishei istorii Udmurtskoi respubliki g. Izhevsk, 2/1/195/98–98ob, which has been shared with me by Viktoriia Tiazhel'nikova.
32 The standard expression used, '*verkhy i nizy*', translates literally, and awkwardly, as 'the tops and the bottoms' or 'the high-ups and the low-downs'.

and thus 'cut off from the masses'.[33] Mainstream party leaders frequently acknowledged the problem, too: in February 1921 Sol'ts pointed to the formation of 'a hierarchical communist caste with its own specific group interests', which practiced 'bureaucratism, extreme arrogance, uncomradely attitudes to rank-and-file communists and the non-party masses' and had 'monstrous' acquisitive greed.[34] The DCs' concern, though, was not only with the elite's material privileges, but also with the 'bureaucratic centralization' of the workers' republic. Unlike most party leaders – who understood 'bureaucratism' in the narrow sense of inefficiency and corruption in state institutions, and saw it as the product of alien class pressure, transmitted mainly by the *sluzhashchie* – the DCs believed that centralization of political power was dangerous in and of itself. They advocated separating party and soviet bodies; and shifting power away from the Sovnarkom to the soviet congresses and the Central Executive Committee (CEC) of soviets, and away from the *glavki* and *tsentry* towards local soviets and their executive committees. In industry, the DCs acknowledged that one-man management had been necessary during the civil war, but in 1920 called for collegial management to be reintroduced. At the eighth congress in March 1919, the DCs' proposals to amend the soviet constitution, to strengthen the CEC at the Sovnarkom's expense, was denounced as 'parliamentarism' by Lenin and defeated. The DC Konstantin Iurenev believed that that was the moment when the party 'capitulated before the state'.[35] But in December 1919, riding the tide of optimism produced by the defeat of the main White armies, the DCs turned the tables on the party leadership, gaining a majority for their proposals at a soviet congress and a party conference.[36]

During 1920 the party leaders, who saw centralization as the best means to combat 'bureaucratism', implemented neither the letter nor the spirit of

33 *Pravda*, 1 January 1919. See also Pavliuchenkov, *Voennyi kommunizm*, p. 183.
34 *Pravda*, 12 February 1921.
35 I. Iurenev, *Nashi nestroenie*, Kursk: 'Tsentropechat'', 1920, p. 7 and p. 19. See also R.V. Daniels, *The Conscience of the Revolution: Communist Opposition in Soviet Russia*, Cambridge, MA: Harvard University Press, 1960, p. 110; Pavliuchenkov, *Voennyi kommunizm*, pp. 183–84; D. Priestland, 'Bolshevik ideology and the debate over party-state relations, 1918–21', *Revolutionary Russia* 10: 2, 1997: 37–61; D. Priestland, *Stalinism and the Politics of Mobilization: Ideas, Power and Terror in Inter-war Russia*, New York: Oxford University Press, 2007, pp. 107–10; D. Orlovsky, 'The anti-bureaucratic campaigns in the 1920s', in T. Taranovski (ed.), *Reform in Modern Russian History: Progress or Cycle?* Cambridge: Cambridge University Press, 1995, pp. 290–315.
36 *Sed'moi vserossiiskii s"ezd sovetov: stenograficheskii otchet*, Moscow, 1920, pp. 196–245 and 247–53. The DCs' highly significant victory, acknowledged by soviet historians in the Gorbachev period, is not only completely absent from earlier soviet historiography but also largely ignored by western political historians. It is noted by L. Schapiro, *The Origin of the Communist Autocracy*, London: G. Bell & sons, 1955, p. 223. See also T.V. Sapronov, *Stat'i i doklady*, Moscow, 1920, p. 25 and p. 29; S.V. Kuleshov, O.V. Volobuev and E.I. Pivovar (eds), *Nashe otechestvo: opyt politicheskoi istorii*, Moscow: Terra, 1991, p. 78.

these democratizing resolutions. Where the DCs stressed the dangers arising from the Bolsheviks' own political and organizational methods, the party leaders saw an external source of danger: the *sluzhashchie*. Zinoviev reported to the eighth congress of soviets in December 1920 that a 'reserve army' of *sluzhashchie* 'presses down on our institutions, one way or another breaks through our defences, and ... brings with it this bureaucratism'. Zinoviev acknowledged the proletariat's lack of experience of government, the decline of soviet democracy and the predominance in the state apparatus of appointism (*naznachenstvo*) as additional causes of 'bureaucratism'. But for the DCs, political centralization was part of the problem, while for the mainstream leaders, it was the solution.[37] Those who came together in late 1920 to form the WO broadly shared the party leaders' view that 'bureaucratism' grew from the petty-bourgeois social composition of the apparatus. Their solutions centred on 'workerization', i.e. bringing workers straight into the apparatus, and the higher party committees, on a quota basis. This contrasted both with Lenin's view, that workers had to learn how to run the state apparatus before taking it over, and with the DCs' calls to democratize soviet bodies.[38] In practice, meanwhile, the tide was turning against both democratization and 'workerization'. The CC apparatus, which was to play such a vital role from 1922, was as yet only embryonic; the CC secretariat's staff grew from 30 in February 1919 to 150 in March 1920 and 602 in the year up to March 1921.[39] But during 1920 power was further concentrated in the Sovnarkom and people's commissariats, the work of which was controlled by the central party leadership, while local soviet bodies were fading, or collapsing. In industry, one-man management was by the end of 1920 in use in 86 per cent of enterprises.[40]

At the end of the civil war, the party elite – Vardin's 'state functionaries, scattered around commissariats and *tsentry*' – was still tiny. In the 1920 survey of Moscow party members referred to above, 4191 members described themselves as 'responsible officials' (3348 working in soviet institutions, plus small numbers in industry, transport and the trades unions) and 1930

---

37 *Doklady na VIII-m Vserossiiskom s'ezde sovetov*, Moscow: MK RKP(b), 1921, pp. 66–72.
38 *Deviatyi s"ezd RKP(b): stenograficheskii otchet*, Moscow: Gos. izd. polit. literatury, 1960, pp. 60–61; *Deviataia konferentsiia RKP(b), sentiabr' 1920 g.: protokoly*, Moscow: izd-vo politicheskoi literatury, 1972, p. 176.
39 *Desiatyi s"ezd RKP(b): stenograficheskii otchet*, Moscow: Gos. izd. polit. literatury, 1963, p. 56; G. Easter, *Reconstructing the State: Personal Networks and Elite Identity in Soviet Russia*, Cambridge: Cambridge University Press, 2000, p. 70; A. A. Timofeevskii (ed.), *V.I. Lenin i stroitel'stvo partii v pervye gody sovetskoi vlasti*, Moscow: Mysl', 1965, p. 139; I.V. Pavlova, *Stalinizm: stanovlenie mekhanizma vlasti*, Novosibirsk: Sibirskii khronograf, 1993, p. 42; E.G. Gimpel'son, *Sovetskie upravlentsy 1917–1920 gg.*, Moscow: Institut istorii RAN, 1998, p. 195.
40 Daniels, op. cit., pp. 110–13; S.A. Smith, *Red Petrograd*, Cambridge: Cambridge University Press, 1983, pp. 241–42 and 260; J.R. Azrael, *Managerial Power and Soviet Politics*, Cambridge, MA: Harvard University Press, 1966, p. 46.

as 'doing party work'. Many of these communists, who were in charge of state institutions and the non-communist *sluzhashchie* working in them, would have fitted Vardin's description. So would the 133 communists from Moscow's Red army garrison who described themselves as 'political leadership', 104 labelled 'high command', and senior Cheka officers who were exempted from the survey.[41] The elite's material privileges had both legal and illegal sources. The legal extras were modest compared to 1923, let alone the 1930s – leather jackets, good living quarters and better meals – but, in conditions of general poverty, seemed unjust to those who went without. The majority of party leaders, including Lenin and Trotsky, favoured in principle the award of these privileges to 'responsible officials', on the grounds that they needed them to work effectively. Senior Bolsheviks who tried to refuse extras, including Bukharin, Aleksandr Tsiurupa and Viktor Nogin, were instructed to accept them.[42] The illegal wealth was accumulated by, among other methods, bribery. *Pravda* described the string of bribes paid by every private entrepreneur requiring official paperwork and warned that 'the entire apparatus is at the speculators' service'. The Menshevik Fedor Dan noted that bribery was 'universal'. Mikhail Egorov, a Moscow party member who tried in early 1920 to expose corruption at the fuel authority, and as a result was threatened by fellow communists with jail, ended his appalled resignation letter: 'Communism is a great thing, but the communists can no longer be called true to it'.[43] The party conference in September 1920, at which the issue of privilege came to a head, acknowledged that the problem started from the very top, i.e. among party leaders based at the Kremlin. It set up a three-man commission to check on living standards there: Ignatov, the Dinamo cell leader Konstantin Ukhanov, and a CC apparatus official, M. Muranov. Its report to the tenth congress, which named and shamed senior Bolsheviks for abuses such as the receipt of multiple rations, luxurious apartments and extravagant use of cars, was quietly buried.[44]

It was both the emotion engendered by material inequality, and the principled dispute over political power initiated by the DCs, that fired the 'tops and ranks' debate of 1920. Discussions on 'party building' (*partstroitel'stvo*) – a broad subject, often the first agenda item at party gatherings, which covered the party's internal problems, its position in the soviet state and its relations with workers – became dominated by these issues. In July the MC set up a commission on bureaucratism, which reported 'a deep-going but far

---

41 Sekretariat RKP(b), op. cit., pp. 42–47. The table is reproduced in Appendix 5.
42 Gimpel'son, op. cit., pp. 189–90 and 199–207.
43 *Pravda*, 4 February 1921; F. Dan, *Dva goda skitanii 1919–1921*, Berlin: sklad izd. Russische Bucherzentrale Obrazowanje, 1922, p. 16; TsAOPIM, 63/1/62/38–39.
44 The commission's report was read only by a few CC members but kept from tenth congress delegates. G.A. Bordiugov (ed.), 'Kak zhili v Kremle v 1920 godu: materialy Kremlevskoi kommissii TsK RKP(b)', in *Neizvestnaia Rossiia* II, 1992: 261–71.

from clearly defined ferment among broad layers of the party rank and file', directed against 'the scandalous privileges of soviet and party tops, and against the bureaucratism that has provided fertile ground for these privileges to grow and for irresponsibility and careerism to flower'. The facts about privilege in central state departments were no longer secret 'either from wide circles of party officials and members in general, or from groups of non-party workers'. Speeches denouncing the 'tops' on this account drew 'thunderous applause' at party meetings, and in Krasnopresnia a speaker 'in defence of the bureaucracy' had been booed into silence.[45] Similar tensions rent party organizations at the front: in November, anger about Red officers' privileges became so widespread that special meetings of communist officials were held on each front to discuss it.[46]

The depth of feeling about privilege was summed up in Vlasov's letter to Lenin, mentioned above. He accused a string of senior Bolsheviks of graft, and cited the case of country estates earmarked by workers at the Motor engineering factory in Zamoskvorech'e to use as a children's holiday camp, but appropriated by the head of the Moscow garrison, Aleksandr Burdukov, and other communist officers, for their own use as country homes.[47] Vlasov expressed solidarity with the Moscow rank-and-file protests at inequality. The Bauman oppositionists, 'the best comrades', were being subject to surveillance and discipline 'for daring to express their dissatisfaction with the district committee'. He made explicit the connection between authoritarianism, bureaucracy and privilege. Drawing parallels with the degeneration of the French revolution, he told Lenin: 'Our communist workers' party is on the verge of bankruptcy; it has no authority, or rather, any it has is just fear of the Cheka. ... Our party committees have become bureaucratized. They are completely cut off from the masses'. Vlasov even threatened that 'if the [ninth party] conference, or CC, does not change the party's bureaucratic [*chinovnich'ei*] policy, if the Bonapartes are not subdued, then this winter we [Red army veterans] will do the bidding of the revolution, arms in hand' – and added that he had passed copies of the letter to friends, with instructions to distribute it if he were arrested. Vlasov was not alone in considering revolutionary action against bureaucratism;

45 RGASPI, 17/112/69/50–57.
46 L.V. Borisova, *Voennyi kommunizm: nasilie kak element khoziaistvennogo mekhanizma*, Moscow: Moskovskii obshchestvennyi nauchnyi fond, 2001, pp. 205–9; L.D. Trotsky, *How the Revolution Armed: the Military Writings and Speeches of Leon Trotsky* (tr. B. Pearce), London: New Park, 1981, vol. 2, pp. 115–20.
47 Vlasov, op. cit. While Vlasov provided convincing detail about corruption by Burdukov, a middle-ranking figure, his complaints against national party leaders – Trotsky, Lunacharskii, Kamenev, Viktor Taratuta and Efraim Sklianskii – were unsubstantiated. Jean-Jacques Marie suggests there may have been anti-semitic motivation, but I find this implausible. Vlasov's allegations were discussed by the party's MC, which found them 'three quarters untrue'. TsAOPIM, 3/1a/6/42ob; J.-J. Marie, *Cronstadt*, Paris: Fayard, 2005, p. 154.

Iurenev referred to – and distanced himself from – a radical tendency of 'fighters against the tops' who believed that a 'second October revolution' was necessary.[48]

Privilege, particularly if it was illicit, also troubled leadership loyalists. When a shipment addressed to the CC member Avel' Enukidze and labelled 'military supplies' – but found on inspection to contain rice, sugar, tobacco, wine, cognac and other luxuries – was sequestered at Kazan railway station, even the faithful apparatchik Rozaliia Zemliachka[49] was incensed. She protested to the CC organization bureau that Enukidze had brought the party into disrepute before non-party workers. (The bureau got Enukidze off the hook by accepting his implausible excuse that the wine was to be sent to the health commissariat.)[50] Zemliachka used non-party workers' anger to illustrate her point; she did not make common cause with them. Nor did most communist dissidents, until they started quitting the party in 1921. The party consensus was that non-party workers were a relatively unconscious reservoir of either support or opposition. Nevertheless, the embryonic elite was a common target for the party ranks and non-party workers: the 'inequality' abhorred by civil war communists bore a striking resemblance to the 'inequality' in the rationing system against which non-party workers protested. The DCs assumed that the non-party workers' protests were motivated solely by self-interest and distanced themselves from such 'shameful ... semi-consciousness'.[51] But in the factories where the cells were weak, communists felt trapped between workers with whose criticisms they partly sympathized and a leadership whose actions they could not fully endorse. Cheka agents not only forwarded reports of workers shouting 'our "comrades" in the soviet institutions are eating three helpings and we just don't get fed', but also warned that 'even communists' in some districts were joining in complaints about the excess of the 'tops'.[52] At the Moscow regional party conference in February 1921, an unnamed protester complained from the floor that 'we have heard the same orators who talk at all meetings, but no-one from the masses has spoken. ... We [i.e. the workers] are unable to put forward our point of view'. The heckler was particularly incensed that Kamenev had ridiculed the DCs' political reform proposals.[53]

---

48 Iurenev, op. cit., pp. 32–33.
49 Zemliachka (Zalkind) (1876–1947) was born in Kiev; 1893, joined the revolutionary movement; 1904, joined the Bolsheviks; repeatedly jailed and exiled; from 1915, worked with the underground Bolshevik organization in Moscow; in 1920 in Crimea, became notorious for her part in the brutal round-up and execution of White sympathizers; from 1922, member of the MC bureau; from 1924, on the CCC; from 1939, on the Sovnarkom.
50 RGASPI, 17/1/12/60/4, 50–50ob.
51 Iurenev, op. cit., p. 14. See also *Desiatyi s"ezd*, p. 250.
52 TsAOPIM, 3/1a/11/39, 43ob.
53 TsAOPIM, 3/2/2/46–47, 76.

The Moscow dissidents

The wave of rank-and-file anger about hierarchy and privilege strengthened the two best organized opposition groups in Moscow, the Bauman group and the supporters of Efim Ignatov. These operated at district and city level, respectively, and, although they had much in common with the DCs and WO, had their own political identities. The Bauman group was held together by resentment against the 'tops' rather than by a written platform. It came together in August 1920 with the stated purpose of taking control of the district party committee.[54] It did so, in October, and held on to it for a year. The place of the civil war experience in the group's formation is apparent from the background of its three leaders: Vasilii Paniushkin, a Baltic fleet seafarer who served on the Cheka collegium and as a special military commissar during the civil war; P.V. Zakolupin, an old navy comrade of his; and Demidov, who had headed the Bauman military-revolutionary committee in October 1917 and now led the heavy artillery workshops' factory committee.[55] Another group spokesman, Aleksei Sovetov, had returned from the front, suffering from tuberculosis, and was 'attached' to various local factory cells. (The 'attachment' of party members in administrative posts to workers' cells was one of the procedures used to counter their 'bureaucratization' and 'isolation from the masses'.) The group's main strongholds were military suppliers: the heavy artillery workshops, where Demidov, K.V. Burdakov, Anton Khotinovich, Samsonov and other oppositionists ran both management and factory committee; the Gnom i Ron aircraft factory, where leading positions were held by group members Aleksandr Baranov, an engineer, Glagol'ev, and Grigorii Korzinov, a full-time party official; and the Manometr engineering works.[56] Other members included party full-timers in the district, such as Maria Berzina, Ekaterina Kuranova, the agronomist Mikhail Rozenshtein and M.D. Shavtovalova, who worked in the apparatus of the soviet. Prominent Bolsheviks in Bauman who sympathized with the group included Kutuzov and Nikita Tul'iakov, a Moscow soviet executive member 'attached' to the artillery workshops cell.[57]

54 TsAOPIM, 3/1a/6/27–29.
55 On Demidov and Paniushkin, see Appendix 1. Zakolupin joined the party in 1908 and, like Paniushkin, was a marine navigator. TsAOPIM, 63/1/36/2.
56 TsAOPIM, 3/1a/6/27ob, 3/4/37/101, 63/1/61/38, 465/1/3/12–54, 465/1/4/15. Baranov returned from the front in 1920 and became deputy head of the technical bureau at Gnom i Ron; in spite of his badly needed technical skills, his political enemies in the MC tried to have him reassigned to the front, but he refused to leave; in 1923 he was expelled from the party for association with the Workers Group, and arrested. Glagol'ev stayed at Gnom i Ron as chairman of the factory committee, but was ousted in 1924. Korzinov (1888–1926) was a native Muscovite worker, a toolmaker; he joined a workers' circle at the Dobrovykh and Navgol'ts factory in 1903; spent time in exile and returned in 1917; worked as a full-time party official; from 1921, director of the Proletarskii Trud factory.
57 On Berzina, Kuranova and Tul'iakov, see Appendix 1. Rozenshtein was born into the family of a Jewish doctor; joined the revolutionary movement as a student in 1905; participated in the 1920 and 1923 oppositions; 1924, served briefly on the Moscow control commission; from 1925, worked as an agronomist in Uzbekistan.

For many of these men and women, resisting hierarchy and corruption, and ensuring working-class predominance in the soviet state, were deeply held moral imperatives. Although some of them, such as Konstantin Ostrovitianov,[58] later renounced the opposition and went on to careers in the party apparatus, many of them resolved the moral dilemma posed by the party's degeneration the hard way – by quitting it. Paniushkin led a breakaway group, and Sovetov and Burdakov were expelled, in 1921; three oppositionists at the Basmanny fire station, S.G. Beregovoi, V.G. Gerasimov and Ivan Kuznetsov, quit together in early 1922;[59] and in 1923 four former leaders of the Bauman opposition (Baranov, Berzina, Demidov and Il'in) were expelled, and one (Shavtovalova) censured, as supporters of the Workers Group.[60] They believed they were resisting a corrosion eating away at the party's principled foundations. When the Bauman oppositionists were called to the MC in September 1920 to answer charges of conspiratorial activity, Demidov denounced the shut-up-and-obey-orders attitude of party officials. 'The words "keep quiet" and "that's not for discussion" are heard too often', he said. At the Bauman district delegate meeting in October, at which the oppositionists won control of the district committee, Sovetov launched a blistering tirade against corruption: the Lefortovo sub-district had expelled a former tsarist colonel, Kindarzhan, but he had inexplicably been readmitted by district organizers; a good woman comrade, Vysotskaia, had been unjustly expelled and had committed suicide as a result; a district organizer, Levit, had been accused of misappropriating food supplies from a hospital but nothing had been done.[61] The Bauman group's anger at corruption was married to a narrow, puritanical workerism, which saw petty-bourgeois party members as a key source of the party's ills and factory communists as the only effective antidote. Some of Demidov's outbursts on this subject were preserved by minute-takers. In August 1920 he insisted that Slavina was 'incapable' of doing the job of soviet sub-district organizer to which she had been appointed; she was 'unable to influence the masses, since she is the daughter of a big factory owner'. In September 1921 Demidov rounded on Gavriil Alikhanov, a former student appointed as an organizer during a CC campaign to pack out Bauman with its loyalists: 'He [Alikhanov] is undermining [our] working-class psychology. ... Our party is being overwhelmed by the intelligentsia's petty-bourgeois [*meshchanskaia*] psychology'.[62] While the Baumanites were decidedly workerist, they were

---

58 Ostrovitianov (1892–1969), a Bolshevik since 1914, suffered a three-month expulsion for his oppositional activities; after rejoining the party in 1922 he worked as an economics lecturer and rose through academia to become a member of the Communist Academy (from 1930), vice-president of the academy of sciences (1953–62) and candidate member of the party CC (1952–59).
59 TsAOPIM, 3/3/34/66, 78.
60 See Chapter 8, pp. 196–7.
61 TsAOPIM, 3/1a/6/27–29; 63/1/7/18–19.
62 TsAOPIM, 3/1a/6/28; 63/1/45/40.

not necessarily for 'workerization' of the apparatus. Demidov and his comrades at the heavy artillery workshops wanted to stay in the factories, rather than try to proletarianize the state machine. In August 1922, when the MC asked the workshops cell bureau for a volunteer to take an apparatus post – the sort of invitation many factory communists greeted as a comfortable option – it declined, because 'we workers, closely linked to state production, have no wish to break off contact with production'.[63]

Ignatov's group was formed at the same time as the DCs, in the run-up to the eighth congress of March 1919. The two groups were politically close. Ignatov, N.V. Lisitsyn and others won a majority at the Moscow city party conference in January 1919 for a proposal, similar to Osinskii's at the eighth congress, mentioned above, for powers to be transferred from the Sovnarkom to the CEC; the congress delegates from Moscow then supported Osinskii.[64] The DCs and Ignatovites were united in favour of democratizing soviet structures, but disagreed on 'workerization', which the DCs considered an irrelevance at best. In the discussion on 'party building' prior to the tenth congress, the Ignatov group advocated 'workerization' of the party, by reserving two-thirds of the places on every party committee for workers, and by reregistering the entire membership, with all who joined since January 1919, and 'non-worker/peasant elements' who joined since November 1917, being made to reapply. The DCs concentrated instead on pressing for wider party democracy, for example by opening CC meetings to other party members, as observers, and by guaranteeing freedom of expression.[65]

The Ignatovites' platform, like the DCs', was concerned with internal party reform and ascribed no active role to non-party workers. But Ignatov embraced the non-party workers' movement as a key force for change; he was the only leading oppositionist to do so consistently. At the Moscow regional party conference in February 1921, Ignatov specifically rejected the prevalent Bolshevik assumption that non-party strikers were treasonous or anti-soviet. The problem was that 'the party, being the proletarian vanguard, often does not understand the masses'. The workers 'often have practically to drag this vanguard by the scruff of the neck, when it is a question of whether to strike or not to strike'. At the tenth congress, where alarm at the February strike wave and the Kronshtadt revolt was rampant and many oppositionists were in retreat before false allegations that they sympathized with the rebels, Ignatov was on the offensive. The party was losing touch with the class, he argued – the proof of which was 'a series of strikes during which the workers throw the communists out of the factories', and workers quit the party 'on a mass scale'. Nothing would be changed

---

63 TsAOPIM, 465/1/5/7.
64 R. Sakwa, *Soviet Communists in Power: a Study of Moscow During the Civil War*, London: Macmillan, 1988, p. 188; Pavliuchenkov, *Voennyi kommunizm*, pp. 183–85.
65 *Des'iatyi s"ezd*, pp. 644–622; *Kommunisticheskii trud*, 12 February 1921.

'without the self-activity of the communist "base" and the proletarian masses'.[66]

In 1920 the Ignatov group took on a formal title, the 'group of active workers in the Moscow districts', took control of the Gorodskoi district party committee and joined with other dissidents in attempting to take control of the MC. The group's most illustrious member was the 'old Bolshevik' Angarskii; most others were full-time party officials working at district level. Among the 17 signatories of Ignatov's platform on 'party building' were the Gorodskoi district secretary I. Maslov; worker Bolsheviks who had returned from the civil war to take up full-time organizers' jobs, such as the engineers Aleksandr Orekhov and Ivan Stefashkin; the AMO car worker Semen Smirnov; and the railway worker Vasilii Fonchenko. Two Baumanites (Korzinov and Kuranova) also signed the platform, while Andrei Lidak, who in November 1920 was sent to Bauman to regain a foothold there for the Moscow leadership, signed Ignatov's platform on the trade union issue.[67]

The DCs were organized more tightly. They worked as a pressure group inside the national party leadership, producing in September 1920 a set of theses that warned of the 'moral breakdown' of the party elite ('luxurious life-style, drunkenness, gluttony, debauchery, squandering of state resources, etc'); the emergence of cliques within the apparatus such as those of Trotsky, Smilga and Stalin in the Red army; and the problems caused by Lenin surrounding himself with bureaucratic 'business-like types'.[68] Their contingent on the MC was headed by Boguslavskii, deputy chairman of the Moscow soviet; Rafail, head of the city's education department; and Andrei Bubnov.[69] In 1920, they joined the attempt to dislodge the Moscow leadership.

66 TsAOPIM, 3/2/2/50; *Desiaty s"ezd*, pp. 236–38.
67 *Kommunisticheskii trud*, 12, 13 and 15 1921. On Semen Smirnov, see Appendix 1. Maslov (1891–1938) held managerial positions in the textile industry, and was assistant to the commissar of post and telecommunications, a job he held until his death in the purges. Orekhov (1887–1951), a lathe operator from a working-class Tula family and a Red army veteran, went on to work in city and national industrial management and from 1923 on the CCC. Stefashkin (1883–1940) came from a poor peasant family, moved to Moscow and trained as a lathe operator; joined the Bolsheviks in 1905; worked in administrative posts in the Moscow garrison and district soviets in the 1920s and 1930s. Fonchenko (1887–1966) was born into a railway worker's family in Briansk; started work at the age of ten; joined the Bolsheviks in 1914; and spent his life in the rail industry, from the 1930s as a party official. Lidak (1880–1937) was born into an agricultural labourer's family in Latvia and worked in a metal works; joined the Bolsheviks in 1905 while on military service; a leading Red guard in 1917; then a full-time party official and from 1925 a factory director.
68 RGASPI, 5/2/134.
69 Bubnov (1883–1938) joined the social democrats in 1903, served on the CC in 1918–19 and again from 1924; participated in the Left Communist group and the DCs; signed the opposition Platform of the 46 in 1923, but then switched to support Stalin and was appointed head of the Red army political administration to replace the oppositionist Anton Antonov-Ovseenko.

But they were themselves divided as to how far the rank-and-file oppositionists should be permitted to go: while Rafail twice served on commissions set up to investigate the Baumanites, and twice urged tolerance rather than expulsions and suspensions, Bubnov joined in demands for such measures.[70]

While in early 1919 the Ignatov group had been close to the DCs, in 1920 it was considered, as was the Bauman group, part of the generic 'workers' opposition'. But the links between these groups and the WO group organized nationally by Aleksandr Shliapnikov and S.P. Medvedev were informal and tenuous. The national WO, which only became a defined grouping during the trade union discussion in December 1920, comprised union and industry officials: the signatories to the WO platform on that issue included nine national union executive members, two Moscow union executive members, three heads of *glavki* and six members of other national industrial administration bodies. There were tensions between these officials, who were above all alarmed at the centralization of power in the VSNKh, and the rank-and-file oppositionists. It is indicative that in May 1921, a public complaint from the heavy artillery works, the Bauman group's stronghold, about the Central Authority for Artillery Factories' 'negligent attitude' to workers' problems, was directed specifically against two signatories of the WO platform, Genrikh Bruno and A. Tolokontsev.[71]

The battle for Moscow

The ninth party congress in March 1920 had opened with protests by the DCs against the party leadership's refusal to implement the decentralizing decisions of the party and soviet gatherings in December 1919, and the congress left the issue unresolved.[72] The wave of protest at material privileges over the summer of 1920, in Moscow and elsewhere, compelled the party leadership to acknowledge the scale of the 'tops and ranks' problem and to put it at the top of the agenda for the forthcoming ninth party conference. In the run-up to this event, the Bauman group organized an invitation-only meeting to plan its assault on the district party committee; the MC bureau reacted to this 'conspiracy' on 3 September by ordering key activists out of Bauman; but this only exposed the MC's weakness, as Kutuzov and Korzinov refused to go.[73] The next day a CC circular acknowledged

70 TsAOPIM, 3/2/18/12, 15, 18; 3/1a/6/29ob; 3/1a/7/55; 63/1/7/16.
71 TsAOPIM, 465/1/4/37.
72 *Deviatyi s"ezd*, pp. 12–86; Daniels, op. cit., p. 114.
73 The oppositionists had complained about the use of administrative postings to separate them from their supporters at the ninth party congress in March 1920: the DC Konstantin Iurenev referred to 'the system of exile, of sending [dissident communists] away on various pretexts'. Zinoviev told the ninth conference in September 1920 that the CC secretariat had a file of 500 complaints about measures taken to silence dissidents. *Deviatyi s"ezd*, p. 47; *Deviataia konferentsiia*, p. 149. See also G. Gill, *The Origins of the Stalinist Political System*, Cambridge: Cambridge University Press, 1990, p. 50.

that the 'tops and ranks' problem was a 'burning' one. On 16 September, there was a pre-conference clash between Bukharin and the oppositionists at an MC meeting. Bukharin blamed 'inevitable material inequality' on 'parasitic elements', and insisted that 'centralized military-proletarian dictatorship' was the only way forward over a 'long period [until] the final victory of the international proletariat'. The DC Bubnov, speaking for the opposition coalition, insisted that the party's defects, including inequalities, were largely the result of 'bureaucratic centralism'. The meeting put the onus for change on 'responsible party workers' at the top: they had to do regular stints at the workbench, as the eighth congress had decided; those in the Moscow commissariats had to return to the localities; and their rations had to be equal to the ranks' (although there was a get-out clause for those who worked 'unlimited hours').[74] At the national conference on 21 September, Zinoviev retreated further than Bukharin had been prepared to. He acknowledged the opposition's main criticisms: the causes of the 'ranks and tops' problem were accumulation of power in the *glavki*; the negative consequences of militarism, which had imbued some communists with arrogant, authoritarian methods; the integration of some communists into the circles of *spetsy* with whom they worked and consequent corrupt relations; and the party's failure to counter these tendencies. Kutuzov suggested sarcastically that if the speech had been made a week earlier in a Moscow district, Zinoviev would have been expelled. The measures proposed by the MC were incorporated into a conference resolution.[75]

The Moscow dissidents, having helped force these concessions from the party leadership, now turned on the MC, hoping to take control of it at the regional party conference in November. As the MC retreated, voting down a proposal to expel the Bauman 'conspirators', the Bauman dissidents advanced, and in October supported a demand by Boguslavskii that the MC disband.[76] When the conference opened on 20 November, Bukharin, on behalf of the CC, said the party had to cure the Moscow organization of its propensity to 'ridiculous squabbling'. Angarskii, responding on the oppositions' behalf, extended the medical metaphor popular at the time: 'Bukharin says the answer to the illness is just to cut off the patient's head. Better to find out what the ailment is first.' In 1917, the working class had 'imbued the revolution's slogans with its own most cherished content' and now had high expectations that clashed with 'tremendous inequality and tremendous bureaucratism'. The opposition coalition caucused jointly in support of Ignatov's resolution on 'party building'; this was voted down by 154 votes

---

74 TsAOPIM, 3/1a/7/35, 51; 3/1a/6/22–23. *Kommunisticheskii trud*, 17 September 1920; *Izvestiia TsK*, no. 21, 4 September 1920, pp. 1–3.
75 *Deviataia konferentsiia*, pp. 31, 139–56 and 186; Daniels, op. cit., pp. 115–17.
76 TsAOPIM, 63/1/7/17, 19; and 3/1a/6/29ob.

to 124 in favour of a text by Kamenev, based on that adopted by the national party conference.[77] The MC elections at the end of the conference brought the Moscow organization close to a split. The two sides presented alternative lists, and the conference recessed as an attempt was made to negotiate a unified list. But the CC loyalists – whose prominent spokesmen included Lenin and Fedor Artem, who had been brought back from Bashkiriia to head the MC – opted for a showdown. Of the four leading oppositionists that Ignatov proposed for the joint list of 39, Lenin and his supporters accepted only one, Boguslavskii. They rejected proposals for proportional representation, and used their slim majority to install an unrepresentative MC. The oppositionists were dumbfounded at these heavy-handed methods: Ignatov and 114 other delegates, evidently surprised, declared that the opposition 'henceforth absolved itself of responsibility for the work of the Moscow committee'. This in turn spurred a group of 70 loyalists to urge disciplinary action against them.[78]

The trade union debate

Into the cauldron heated from below by the 'ranks and tops' dispute there was now hurled, from above, the trade union debate, which began on the CC on 8 November 1920 and continued until the tenth congress in March 1921.[79] Rank and file reactions, discussed here, were often related to the discussions on centralization and privilege. There was widespread aversion to the compulsion inherent in Trotsky's proposals and, on the left, support for the WO's arguments for giving the unions greater political power. The DCs and others saw the debate as an irrelevant diversion from the issues of centralization and privilege. And indeed the tenth congress (see Chapter 3) spent far more time on those questions – which were discussed, together with the party's crisis in its relations with workers and peasants, in a mammoth

---

77 *Pravda*, 16 November 1920. TsAOPIM 3/1a/2/34, 88–91; 8654/1/309/127; *Des'iatyi s"ezd*, p. 869.
78 TsAOPIM, 3/1a/2/41–42, 98–105; RGASPI, 17/84/73; Z.P. Korshunova (eds), *Ocherki istorii Moskovskoi organizatsii KPSS, kn. II, noiabr' 1917–1945*, Moscow: Moskovskii rabochii, 1983, p. 179; V.I. Lenin, *Polnoe sobranie sochinenii (izd. 5-ogo)*, Moscow, Gospolitizdat, 1958–65, vol. 42, pp. 17–40.
79 For accounts of the debate, see Daniels, op. cit., pp. 119–36; Y. Tsuji, 'The Debate on the Trade Unions, 1920–21', *Revolutionary Russia* 2: 1, 1989: 31–100; L. Holmes, *For The Revolution Redeemed: The Workers Opposition in the Bolshevik Party 1919–1921*, Carl Beck Papers no. 802, Pittsburgh: University of Pittsburgh, 1990; Sakwa, op. cit., pp. 247–53; W.G. Rosenberg, 'The Social Background to Tsektran', in D.P. Koenker, W.G. Rosenberg and R.G. Suny (eds), *Party, State and Society in the Russian Civil War: Explorations in Social History*, Bloomington: Indiana University Press, 1989, pp. 349–73. Documents in *Diskussiia o profsoiuzakh: materialy i dokumenty 1920–21gg.*, Moscow/Leningrad, 1927, and *Des'iatyi s"ezd*, pp. 633–90.

session on 'party building' – than on the trade union debate, suggesting that its importance had already receded.[80]

The immediate cause of the debate was Trotsky's drastic plan to pull the transport system out of ruin. His, and his supporters', efforts to implement elements of labour compulsion – and specifically, to compel the water transport union to accept supervision by party commissars that had already been imposed on the railways – met resistance by trade union activists. Trotsky responded by arguing that compulsion should be developed into a general system, covering all industries. This implied new forms of industrial administration and decision-making, based on a merger of unions with industrial administration bodies. Much has been made subsequently of Trotsky's enthusiasm for this 'statization' of the unions, but until the discussion began, that had been accepted as the natural order of things under 'war communism'. But Lenin, Zinoviev and the CC majority, while agreed that labour compulsion would remain a key element of economic policy, now envisaged a partnership of the unions, whose role would be auxiliary, educational and propagandistic, and existing industrial administration bodies under the VSNKh. The WO urged that the unions should manage the economy, the soviets control the state apparatus, and the party guide both. Although subsequent generations of Soviet propagandists depicted the trade union debate as a clash of principle between Lenin and Trotsky, the differences between them should not be overstated. Many points of principle were indeed touched upon. But the limited character of their disagreements – about what to do with the unions under circumstances of state monopoly and suppression of the market – became evident when they were swept away, along with many shared presumptions about economic policy, by NEP.

The discussion about the 'tops and ranks' fed into rank-and-file reactions to the trade union debate, in the shape of concerns about the damage Trotsky's proposals would do to workers' democracy. The evidence of hostility to Trotsky needs to be treated with care. Some of it emanated from the CC apparatus and press, which the Lenin-Zinoviev group enthusiastically mobilized for factional ends. When district party organizations voted on the platforms, the Lenin-Zinoviev group's supporters contrived to retake votes that didn't go their way (in Sokol'niki and Zamoskvorech'e against Trotsky and in Gorodskoi against Ignatov). Nevertheless, rank-and-file fears about anti-democratic elements of Trotsky's proposals seem to have played a role. In Sokol'niki, where Vasilii Kotov headed a concentration of Trotsky supporters in the railway depots, Zinoviev played heavily on these fears at a meeting of several thousand party members which reversed the district's

---

80 The discussion on 'party building', the longest at the congress, took up three sessions and included four reports and 17 speakers. The trade union discussion was wrapped up in a single session with three reports and seven speakers.

previous pro-Trotsky stand.⁸¹ Significantly, the Bauman district organization and the heavy artillery works cell, both controlled by the Bauman oppositionists, supported the Lenin-Zinoviev platform. At a district delegate meeting to debate the issues, a local activist, Zheltov, complained: 'We have seen the merging of [the chief political administration for transport] Glavpolitput and [the transport union] Tsektran⁸² in practice. We can't get into [the organization of] production because we've been chucked out by all these *glavki*'.⁸³

While in that instance the Lenin-Zinoviev platform was seen as the best means of increasing rank-and-file participation in decision-making, activists in the metalworkers' union gave support to the WO for similar reasons. The WO advocated 'putting production unions in charge of the branches of industry' as the first step to 'the desired end, when trade unions will concentrate [all] industry in their hands', as Shliapnikov told a Moscow metalworkers' delegate meeting in December 1920. He was supported by both party members and non-party workers. The AMO communist Gavrilin complained that the unions, by concentrating on pay and social welfare, had become 'nursemaids [*nian'ki*]', while their decision-making power was 'eaten up' by other organizations.⁸⁴ Sadovnikov, a non-party delegate, called for 'a third revolution in production' to follow the 'two political revolutions' made in 1917. Non-party speakers at the metalworkers' meeting of February 1921 made some of the most consistent calls for rank-and-file democracy heard in the trade union discussion. The meeting demanded 're-election of all trade union bodies on a strictly democratic basis', participation by representatives elected at general factory meetings in all management bodies, and inspection of, and participation in, *glavki* by trade union delegates. One speaker, Tikhomirov, warned that unions taking charge of production would be ruinous, because they were organizationally ill-equipped. But most speakers were concerned that the attempt should be made. Korfilin favoured a 'shake up' of the unions 'from the roots … on the basis of free elections'. The unions were not doing their job because they were 'subordinate to the government'. Written proposals from the floor argued for the reconstruction of the metalworkers' union 'by applying the elective principle strictly, from top to bottom … without pressure from the party cells' and for 'equally weighted secret votes'.⁸⁵

81 *Pravda*, 26 January 1921. Kotov (189?-1937) was a metal worker; joined the Bolsheviks in 1915; from 1919 a full-time party official in Moscow; in 1928 supported the right opposition; a CC member from 1930.
82 It was this merger, pushed through by Trotsky, that ignited the differences on the CC in November 1920.
83 TsAOPIM, 63/1/44, 2–5; 465/1/1/1.
84 The platform comprised an article by Shliapnikov, *The Workers' Unions*, written in December 1920. *Diskussia o profsoiuzakh*, pp. 175–87. TsGAMO, 186/1/460/36ob-38ob. On the place of 'nursemaids' in Bolshevik discourse, see note 36 to Chapter 4, p. 105.
85 TsGAMO, ibid, 38ob-39; 180/1/236/45–48, 63; 180/1/237/114, 146.

An additional important trend in the party believed that the whole trade union discussion was a diversion from the real problems. This was the essence of the DCs' platform on the issue, which stated that the Lenin-Trotsky division was between 'two tendencies of former militarizers of the economy' and the unions' crisis 'only one part of the general crisis of the soviet apparatus'. In January 1921, the Lenin-Zinoviev group tried to raise the temperature and turn the debate into a loyalty test, by accusing Trotsky of endangering the revolution and calling for tenth congress delegates to be elected according to their stance on the trade union question. The MC opposed this procedure, and it was the DCs who reacted with particular vehemence. At the Moscow regional party conference in February, Rafail rounded on Kamenev, who supported the Lenin-Zinoviev group, for failing to implement earlier decisions on party democracy and then 'mounting an all-Russian talking shop about the trade unions on festival days, so as to leave everything else unchanged'.[86]

The DCs' scepticism about the trade union debate's relevance to the party's most pressing problems was widely shared, and not just by oppositionists. Many Moscow factory cells did not even put the issue on the agenda, preferring to discuss immediate production and supply problems, and an apocryphal story circulated, that Lenin was 'bored to death' by the debate.[87] In the *Pravda* offices, scepticism was sufficient to allow publication of an article warning that workers who 'love the revolution', and had joined the party in 1919–20, were leaving, because corruption and authoritarianism were spreading while the leaders continued the impenetrable trade union discussion. *Pravda* quoted a worker, Evstigneev, who had joined the party in 1919, and told his Moscow factory cell that he now knew less than ever about who was taking the decisions, and where. Of the trade union debate he asked: 'Do any of you understand it? Don't lie to me.' Evstigneev understood only that the party leaders were at each others' throats, but nothing of the substance of the disagreement – and knew, also, that Zinoviev had promised the party conference to confront 'the commissars' outrageous behaviour', but that nothing had been done.[88]

The trade union debate highlighted contradictions in the party's industrial management strategy, helped clarify attitudes to labour compulsion, and laid to rest the WO's aspirations to union participation in management. In the party's transition from a political-military organization towards an authoritarian tool of administration, the factional excesses of the Lenin-Zinoviev group were a

---

86 TsAOPIM, 3/2/2/67; TsAOPIM, 3/2/23/5–13.
87 Of the five relatively complete sets of factory cell minutes for 1920–21 that I have read, only two (at Goznak and the heavy artillery works) recorded an agenda item, both brief, on the trade union discussion. By contrast, at AMO there were three substantial, fully minuted discussions on party building. On Lenin, P. Avrich, *Kronstadt 1921*, Princeton: Princeton University Press, 1970, p. 177.
88 *Pravda*, 25 January 1921.

notable step. Nevertheless, the DCs surely had a point in seeing the debate as a diversion, and insisting that the question of the unions was part of the larger issue of who wielded power, and how. The problems at the front of their minds – centralization, apparatus and privilege – were clearly of greater long-term consequence than the differences over the unions. That is not to claim that the DCs, still less the Baumanites or frustrated departees such as Evstigneev, had developed any strategy to prevent the state's degeneration. The central role that that state played in reproducing and reinforcing hierarchical social relations, and the exploitative nature of those relations in the economy, were only rarely alluded to by any of the participants in the discussions of 1920–21. Soon, the tenth congress would silence what discussion there had been, and strengthen the authoritarian tendencies that the dissidents of 1920, albeit partially or incoherently, tried to resist.

3 The revolution that wasn't
Workers and the party in January–March 1921

The early spring of 1921 was a turning point for the Soviet state. The grain requisitioning system used during the civil war had aggravated the crisis in the countryside. Everywhere, the peasantry responded by reducing the area of land sown for crops; peasant revolts, the most organized of which was in Tambov, spread across European Russia, the Urals and Siberia.[1] The transport breakdown disrupted the supply of food to Moscow, Petrograd and other urban centres, provoking worker protests. The crisis culminated in early March in the uprising at the Kronshtadt naval base, which the Bolshevik leadership perceived as a threat to its survival. In the discussion of worker protests in Moscow that follows, the heterogeneous character of this movement is emphasized. Many workers were exasperated that, although the civil war was behind them, supply problems seemed more intractable than ever. But there were political strands in the movement, too. Opposition to the Bolshevik monopolization of political power was widespread and the demand for renewal of the soviets was popular. On the other hand advocates of a 'third revolution', or any challenge to the soviet system as such, were in a tiny minority. Very few even spoke of an alternative government. The movement's uneven character, and the lack of unity between Kronshtadt and the other main urban centres, cast doubt on claims that a revolutionary challenge was made to Bolshevik rule. The movement helped to force the party's hand towards the fundamental policy shift that would soon be named NEP, though. The tenth congress, held in the first week of March while the Kronshtadt revolt was being put down, decided to replace grain requisitioning with a tax in kind. It also banned factions in the party and approved the further centralization of the apparatus; this, together with the suppression of Kronshtadt and the invasion of Georgia, confirmed the authoritarian, apparatus-centred direction that the Soviet state was to take.

1 Recent work on these movements includes V.N. Brovkin, *Behind the Front Lines of the Civil War: Political Parties and Social Movements in Russia 1918–1922*, Princeton: Princeton University Press, 1994; S.A. Pavliuchenkov, *Krestianskii Brest, ili predystoriia bol'shevistskogo NEPa*, Moscow: Russkoe knigoizdatel'skoe izdatel'stvo, 1996, especially pp. 250–58; and I. Narskii, *Zhizn' v katastrofe: budni naseleniia Urala v 1917–1922 gg.*, Moscow: Rosspen, 2001, pp. 271–327.

The transport and supply problems had started multiplying through the winter. In Moscow, the closure of the Sukharevka market and the Cheka clampdown on small traders had choked off many sources of food on which workers relied to supplement rations. Distribution of bread rations fell into arrears; by mid January, those from the Moscow soviet were 51 days behind. Rations had been increased as winter set in, and the Moscow party leadership put off cutting them back again as long as it could. But by early January it was clear that, since the transport crisis was stopping supplies getting to the capital, things could only get worse. The Moscow soviet presidium, and the committee that oversaw supplies to the Moscow and Petrograd workers, raised the alarm with the government, and on 20 January jointly decided to reduce the level of rations. A second cut was made on 1 February.[2] On 31 January a 'bread commission' was set up, headed by Lenin, but it could do little. The food was on its way, but could not move much faster. There were 1266 trains en route to Moscow carrying food supplies, but because of fuel shortages they were moving at only 80–100 km a day. Emergency measures were taken on the railways, including the closure of some lines to speed up the movement of supply trains on others, and the assignment to supply duties of trains used by the party apparatus. By the end of February food was pouring into Moscow – but it was too late to contain workers' dissatisfaction.[3]

The Moscow soviet, struggling to make up political ground, belatedly acknowledged the principle of 'equal rations' for which workers had argued. It took measures to reduce inequalities: some academic rations, and 'shock' rations for workplaces not properly entitled to them, were cancelled. In mid-February the soviet met with Sovnarkom to demand the abolition of all privileged rations, and Sovnarkom scrapped most, but not all, of these. But this policy shift came too late. A wave of strikes over rationing and pay issues, longer in duration and more widespread than any in late 1920, spread across Moscow in late January and February. In Zamskvorech'e, workers at the Gustav List engineering works staged a nine-day sit-down strike, from 18 January, the cause of which Cheka agents recorded as 'the distribution of unequal rations'. A sit-down stoppage at the machine-building

---

2 As a result of the cuts made on 20 January, bread rations went down to 1.5 funt for group A (workers doing heavy industrial work), 1 funt for group B (most other workers and *sluzhashchie*), and 0.5 funt for group C (workers under 18, and non-working citizens). The 1 February cuts reduced rations for groups A and B by a further half-funt. A funt is 409.5 grammes. N.M. Aleshchenko, *Moskovskii sovet v 1917–1941 gg.*, Moscow: Nauka, 1976, p. 298; B.M. Patenaude, *Bolshevism in Retreat: the Transition to NEP 1920–22* (PhD diss., Stanford University, 1987), p. 128; TsGAMO, 66/12/879/206–107; *Kommunisticheskii trud*, 14 January and 23 March 1921.

3 *Pravda*, 22 January 1921; Pavliuchenkov, op. cit., pp. 259–60; *Shirokaia konferentsiia fab-zavkomov g. Moskvy 29 okt. 1921*, Moscow, 1921, p. 55; Aleshchenko, op. cit., pp. 297–99; Patenaude, op. cit., pp. 118–29; E.B. Genkina, *Gosudarstvennaia deiatelnost' V.I. Lenina 1921–1923 gg*, Moscow, 'Nauka', 1969, p. 62.

factory no.5 was attributed to 'the absence of rations'. The Bromlei works struck in the last week of January, and the nearby Russkaia mashina (former Mikhel'son) factory came out in solidarity. In Khamovniki, sit-down strikes at the 1st state drinks factory and the saddle factory were both attributed to pay issues. In Rogozhsko-Simonovskii, Cheka agents reported a 'strike wave' over pay, including a sit-down strike at the cable factory, and brief stoppages at the Kursk railway workshops and the Merkurii shoe factory. A two-day stoppage on 1–2 February at the Bari boiler factory spread to the Trudestkozh leather industry offices and some nearby workshops.[4] The Socialist Revolutionaries' (SR) influence among the strikers was occasionally evident, for example in a resolution sent by a group of workers in Khamovniki to the president of the republic, Mikhail Kalinin, demanding the convocation of a legislative assembly, restoration of free trade and a change in economic policy to stop 'provoking' the European powers. But this was primarily a movement about food supply: it was the call for equalization of rations that 'ran like a red thread through all the resolutions and speeches by non-party speakers at any workers' meeting', as the Bolshevik trade union leader Solomon Lozovskii told the tenth congress. 'During the civil war we created a ration system that – before we even mention the privileges of the "tops" – comprised among workers themselves no less than 13 categories: extra-shock, half-shock, and so on. [Once the war ended] this issue made itself felt.'[5]

The metalworkers' conference

The closest thing the workers' movement had to a political programme was the decisions of the Moscow metalworkers' conference on 2–4 February. With the soviet due for re-election and its plenary sessions lifeless, the conference was the city's most representative workers' gathering of the spring. Although it was subsequently dismissed in a leading article in *Pravda* as a 'notorious' 'non-party' gathering, the delegates were elected by normal metalworkers' union procedure. This industry, a Bolshevik bastion in 1917, had been least seriously affected by civil war closures, and had the most active factory organizations.[6] The party was alarmed by the level of hostility

4 GARF, 393/43a/1714/253; TsGAMO, 66/12/879/26; TsAOPIM, 412/1/5/3.
5 *Desiatyi s"ezd RKP(b): stenograficheskii otchet*, Moscow: Gos. izd. polit. literatury, 1963, p. 291; R. Sakwa, *Soviet Communists in Power: A Study of Moscow During the Civil War*, London: Macmillan, 1988, p. 222; J. Aves, *Workers Against Lenin*, London: Tauris, 1996, pp. 137–38.
6 There were about 1000 delegates at the meeting, one for every 50 members of the metalworkers' union. Minutes, TsGAMO, 180/1/236/6–66; 180/1/235; other materials, TsGAMO, 180/1/237. Resolutions, *Kommunisticheskii trud*, 8, 15 and 16 February 1921. See also *Pravda* 27 May 1921; Aves, op. cit., pp. 131–36; P. Avrich, *Kronstadt 1921*, Princeton: Princeton University Press, 1970, pp. 35–36; Patenaude, op. cit., pp. 129–40; L. Siegelbaum, *Soviet State and Society Between Revolutions, 1918–1929*, Cambridge: Cambridge University Press, 1992, p. 76.

expressed by workers it considered its strong supporters: a front-page article in *Pravda* by Andrei Vyshinskii, then a food supply commissariat official, said the meeting had revealed 'a complete break of the masses with the party and the union .... "We" against "you", "the bottom" against "the top" – that was the basic message'.[7] The conference called not only for the 'equalization of rations', but also, crucially, for the replacement of grain requisitioning by a tax in kind. It played a part in shifting party attitudes on the latter issue. Lenin attended the meeting, and, within a week, had drafted his notes on the abolition of requisitioning, which formed the basis for a Bolshevik party Central Committee (CC) resolution on the subject. While the meeting was in progress, Tsiurupa, the food commissar, acting on a decision of the Bolshevik CC, announced the suspension of grain requisitioning in 13 provinces of central Russia where there was a threat of famine.[8]

There were three loosely defined political tendencies represented: the Bolsheviks themselves; the SRs and their sympathizers, who moved the call to abolish grain requisitioning; and non-party socialists and workerists who had supported the Bolsheviks in 1917 but become distrustful of them. In the latter group were some who saw the industrial working class, acting without the help of and even against the *intelligentsia* and the socialist political parties, as the primary force for change. This approach had been theorized by Jan Machajski, who had been active in the pre-revolutionary workers' movement in Poland, in his book *The Thinking Worker* (*Umstvennyi rabochii*).[9] Although the Bolshevik leaders were fond of accusing the WO and other Bolshevik dissidents of 'makhaevism' (after the russianized version of Machajski's surname) and 'syndicalism', these terms would have been more appropriate to some non-party workers. Many of those who spoke at the metalworkers' meeting had supported the soviet seizure of power in October 1917, but subsequently become disillusioned, and urged that the centre of gravity return to the workers' movement, as opposed to the party. Kolyshkin of the Ustinskii works said that 'the very slogan of equality, which the communists brought to us in 1917, has simply rotted away' due to a supply policy that divided the tops from the ranks. Kuz'min of Elektrostal' said: 'For three years we've heard all the arguments. But all these "gains of the revolution" are reducing us to tears'. (The development of the non-party socialist movement is further discussed in Chapter 4.)

7 *Pravda*, 8 February 1921. Vyshinskii, a former Menshevik and the future prosecutor at the Moscow trials, was 'attached' to the party cell at the Bromlei works.
8 V.I. Lenin, *Polnoe sobranie sochinenii*, Moscow: Gospolitizdat, 1958–65, vol. 42, p. 333; V.A. Shishkin, *Vlast', politika, ekonomika: poslerevoliutsionnaia Rossiia (1917–1928 gg.)*, St Petersburg: 'Dmitrii Bulanin', 1997, p. 168; Pavliuchenkov, op. cit., pp. 270–71.
9 See J. Machajski, *Umstvennyi rabochii*, New York: Mezhdunarodnoe Literaturnoe Sodruzhestvo, 1968, and A. D'Agostino, *Marxism and the Russian Anarchists*, San Francisco: Germinal Press, 1977, pp. 115–38.

76 *The revolution that wasn't*

The non-party workers' sense of betrayal contributed to the meeting's angry tone. Bolshevik speakers were interrupted and sometimes shouted down. The delegates, Vyshinskii complained, 'did not trust anybody, not even the presidium they themselves had elected', and insisted that the drafting commission for resolutions be elected directly from the floor. Vyshinskii claimed that anti-semitic speeches were made, but this was sharply rebutted by the Bolshevik trade union leader Lozovskii, who was also present, and there is little evidence of it in the verbatim minutes.[10] As well as discussing the supply crisis, the conference decided, against Bolshevik recommendations, to hold a more wide-ranging discussion of relations with the peasantry. This resulted in the call to abolish requisitioning. Mel'nichanskii gave a report on supply issues, stressed the effect of the railway breakdown, and said he had seen food rotting in warehouses in Siberia because it could not be transported. Speakers including Khristoforov from the Presnia workshops and Portnov from the Motor factory replied that the problem lay with requisitioning methods rather than transport. Kazenkov from Dobrovykh-Navgolts, an SR sympathizer, argued that the forced-march economic policy had reached a dead end. Neither workers nor peasants could take it any more. 'How many crises have we suffered already? ... The sort of procurement being carried out at the moment can not be continued.' Matrosov of the Bari works, who had family links with the Tula countryside, referred to the peasantry in the first person: 'Everything has been taken from us. We peasants face the threat of death from starvation.' The decision by the eighth congress of soviets to set up sowing committees in the countryside came under fire. One of Kamenev's many hecklers said:

> You are not taking into consideration that this is a peasant country; the worker can not live without the peasant. You forgot that; you set up sowing committees, and that's a yoke around the peasant's neck.

Vasilii Kuraev of the land commissariat defended the soviet congress decisions, arguing that 'we can not renounce compulsion' in gathering supplies; without the bread monopoly the country could not feed itself. But speakers from the Il'in works, where the anarchists had influence, countered that the Bolsheviks were destroying the worker-peasant alliance. One of them, Solovev, said that the workers and peasants 'will perish together' if they permitted the sowing committees to go ahead. Begin from the Krepo-sklad warehouse

---

10 Vyshinskii named the perpetrator of anti-semitism as Petrov, an inn-keeper from Podol'sk, the engineering town near Moscow. Lozovskii wrote to *Pravda* stating that Vyshinskii had untruthfully libelled Petrov, who had an 18-year record of activity in the workers' movement. *Pravda*, 8 and 17 February 1921. In the minutes, the only anti-semitic remark I found was by Mosolov of the Ustinskii works, who spoke of the 'domination by Jews, in the main' in state institutions; 'their bulletins smell of jargon [pakhnet zhargonom] ... I am not against Jews, but [I want to know] who elected them to the union'.

complained about the suppression of an SR-inspired attempt to organize a peasant union in Moscow. Resolutions from the floor demanded that the right to organize be granted to 'our peasant brothers'. The resolution adopted stated that requisitioning was ruining agriculture, and was in the interests neither of peasants or of workers. It called for its replacement by a tax in kind, set 'with reference to local conditions' at a level that would allow agriculture to develop through the production of surpluses, and administered by local co-operatives. The SRs' strength at the conference, and on the drafting commission, is evident from the inclusion of calls for the organization of peasant unions and for the establishment of trade relations with western Europe to make possible imports of agricultural machinery.[11]

In the discussion on wages, SR influence was apparent in denunciations of labour compulsion. A proposal handed to the platform from the Elektroperedacha power station urged 'the emancipation of the workers: allow them to move to any factory at any time'.[12] But the main opposition to government policy came from workerists who wanted to curb the *glavki* and the specialists. Kireev from the AMO car factory criticized Gol'tsman's report on wages because 'it didn't mention the specialists' colossal pay rates, which are so many times higher than those of workers', and which were continuing to be paid, despite union decisions to the contrary. Kamenetskii from Metallo-khimik, touching on an issue that would recur in arguments over elite privileges in 1922–23 (see Chapter 7, pp. 188–9), complained that extras supposedly paid to specialists for their irreplaceable skills 'are also being paid to communists who have no special knowledge or training. I can name names'. Fedor Chukhanov, a leader of the AMO non-party group,[13] said that the system of extra payments for 'military orders' was being abused, citing the example of a 600 per cent bonus paid to workers to reupholster a car for Kamenev. He attacked payments to specialists – and theatrical performers – as excessive, and voiced support for the regulated bonus system advocated by the metalworkers' union. The problem lay with arbitrary changes to that system from on high, he said. Vasilii Nastias'ian, another representative of the AMO non-party group, stressed that, despite monetary devaluation, the differential in money payments between specialists and workers 'who work like horses' remained crucial, because money could be used to buy a range of otherwise unavailable goods on the black market. Dodonov, in a written proposal to 'abolish money', argued that 'for workers [money] is just a sham, a fiction that can not be put to use. It only benefits the specialists'. He advocated 'a system of complete payment in kind'.[14] The resolution adopted was a compromise

11 TsGAMO, 180/1/236/65–66.
12 TsGAMO, 180/1/236/77ob; and 180/1/237/136, 173.
13 On Chukhanov, see Appendix 1.
14 TsGAMO, ibid, 81.

between the workerists and the Bolsheviks: it recognized the need to retain 'divisions [of workers] into categories' as long as differences in skill levels remain, acknowledged the injustice of arbitrary rewards for specialists and said that 'all workers without exception, including specialists' must be paid according to trade union-sanctioned wage scales. Bonuses in kind should be 'distributed equally among all factories, in proportion to the number of workers employed' (i.e. without special provisions for 'shock' workplaces). While the resolution supported the principle of regulation against arbitrary arrangements made by the *glavki*, it also argued for the abolition of limits on bonuses paid to workers and advocated '*unlimited* piece-work bonuses' – in other words, it opposed those aspects of state regulation that cut across the metalworkers' sectional interests.

The strike movement

The strike wave in Moscow climaxed in three days of stoppages and meetings on 23–25 February. There were also strikes in Petrograd, starting on the 24th, and in other urban centres. On 28 February the first anti-Bolshevik resolution was passed on the battleship Petropavlovsk at the Kronshtadt naval base, precipitating the sailors' armed revolt. Together, these events posed serious dangers to the Bolshevik government, and gave it a final push towards NEP. But the strikes were not coordinated, and, by the time the Kronshtadt revolt got underway, the Moscow factories were back at work. There was also political disunity: while SRs, Mensheviks and others won a sympathetic hearing, and there were pockets of support for the political programme advanced at Kronshtadt, for a renewal of 1917-style soviet democracy, no mass movement developed on these issues. Even on the crucial issue of food supply, workers were divided: the largest strike in Moscow, at the Goznak printing works in Khamovniki, was in support of a demand for a ration supplement of the very type that undermined the 'equalization' principle. The Bolsheviks rode the storm by rectifying the worst supply problems, promising further improvements, and selectively but thoroughly silencing political opponents.

The Goznak works was one of Moscow's largest. Its workforce of 7000 was predominantly female, relatively young, and worked in poor conditions. *Pravda* had published an article complaining of 11-hour shifts (with an hour's break) in fume-filled, poorly ventilated workshops. Goznak's output included bank notes, which the government needed desperately, due to hyperinflation; perhaps because of this, the works had in 1920 been placed on 'shock' rations. But discontent began brewing in early January. The factory committee had received 'collective declarations' from various workshops with 'ultimatistic demands' and threats to walk off the job. When the Moscow soviet decided on 20 January to withdraw 'shock' status from less deserving workplaces, Goznak was among those affected. Most rations were cut by half a funt of bread. On 29 January workers downed tools; a mass meeting called for the reduction to be put off until 10 February; for prompt delivery of firewood; for families' rations to be exempted from cuts; for potatoes, cabbage and other vegetables to be provided; and for shop foremen to 'treat us like workers and not preach sermons at us'. The factory committee agreed to try to reverse the ration reduction, but met with a blank refusal from food supply officials. That was logical: the cuts had been made to meet the widespread demands for 'equalization', which implied resistance exactly to this sort of special pleading. On 23 February, Goznak struck; party members and some others who tried to work were forcibly picketed out. The main demands were 'economic', but calls were also made to 'free political prisoners, and there were even people shouting for the constituent assembly', a district party meeting was told later. A crowd of 3000 marched through the district to win support, but attempts to picket out workers at the Zempalatka, Givardovskii and Giunberg factories were unsuccessful. The Kauchuk rubber goods factory also declined to join the action. The local party organization tried to disperse the crowd by persuasion rather than force. But at the Khamovniki barracks, the demonstrators clashed with sentries who feared that 700 recently demobilized Red army men, reported by the Cheka to be 'of a clearly anti-soviet disposition', might join the protest.[15] In the confusion, a Komsomol member, Kuzmenko, was fatally wounded and a woman worker received a superficial injury.[16] On the evening of the 23rd, the strikers called an open meeting in Khamovniki, to which 5000 workers came. Stanislav Messing, head of the Moscow Cheka, reported that in two of three auditoria, where much of the audience was from other workplaces, resolutions were passed 'covering the strikers in shame'. In the third hall, where the crowd was almost entirely made up of Goznak workers, Kalinin successfully urged a return to work.

It is not surprising that other factories declined to support the Goznak workers. Their claim to 'shock' status undermined the very 'equalization of rations' most workers wanted. It is likely that assumptions about the

15 *Pravda*, 18 January 1921; TsAGM, 2626/1/70/10; 2626/1/77/9; TsAOPIM, 3/2/23/36; 1099/1/3/36, 40. RGASPI, 76/3/166/2–2ob; 76/3/166/3, published in V.P. Naumov and A.A. Kaskovskii, *Kronshtadt, 1921*, Moscow: Mezhdunarodnii fond Demokratiia, 1997, pp. 27–29; G. Maximoff, *The Guillotine At Work, vol.1. The Leninist Counter-Revolution*, Chicago: Cienfuegos press, 1979, p. 160. Aves, op. cit., p. 139.

16 Several historians, relying on the memoirs of the SR S.S. Maslov, wrote that troops were brought in and refused to fire on the workers, and that a special security detachment intervened, killing and wounding several people. Aves, op. cit., p. 139; Sakwa, op. cit., pp. 244–45. Archives now available, including those of Messing's correspondence with Dzerzhinskii, throw doubt on Maslov's claims. The incident in which Kuzmenko was shot so concerned Messing that he reported it in detail, and referred to it again twice subsequently. But he made no mention of other casualties. Messing referred to the demobilized soldiers' dangerous mood, but made no mention of them, or other troops, being ordered to shoot at the crowd or refusing to do so.

superiority of masculine labour also played a role. While metalworkers believed that extra payments to reward their own physical labour were justified, as mentioned in Chapter 1, they seemed less inclined to support similar rewards for a predominantly female workforce doing lighter work, no matter how arduous it was or how unhealthy the conditions. So no united strategy to address the rations crisis was advanced. On the other hand, frustration and impatience at the renewed threat of supply interruptions was universal. Cheka agents reported that a 'wave of mass meetings', with some strikes, washed over Moscow on 24 February, the day after the Goznak demonstration. The 3000 workers at the VSNKh warehouse in Zamoskvorech'e held 'endless meetings, all day'. A railway workers' meeting, influenced by the SRs, passed a resolution censuring the party for wasting time on the trade union debate. On 25 February, three leather factories in Zamoskvorech'e, where the Mensheviks were reportedly active, stayed out on strike after their meetings.[17] Messing reported: 'The general character of the movement is economic, and so far there are only isolated political actions'.

The wave of mass meetings hardly constituted a political movement, but did provide a platform for opposition political groups. At the Riazan'-Ural railway depot, the SRs Mikhailov[18] and Korolev debated Lunacharskii in front of 4000 workers, and won a majority for an anti-Bolshevik resolution calling for the liberation of arrested political activists, freedom of the press, independent trade unions, the replacement of commissars by 'popular power [*narodi vlasti*]', 'the expulsion of all communists from power' and a coalition government of 'all socialist parties except the communists'. The call for the Bolsheviks' removal was an exception. Other political resolutions urged a coalition, such as one from the Bogatyr works calling for 'unity of all socialist parties in struggle to counter the destruction of the economy'. At the Salmson and Manometr plants in Bauman, Bolshevik delegates to local soviets were recalled and replaced with a non-party representative and a Menshevik, respectively. At the auto repair plant, the Bolshevik soviet delegate was mandated to support Menshevik resolutions.[19] But these were minority voices. Most mass meetings expressed discontent, but not active political opposition. For example, Lunacharskii, who addressed a mass meeting at Dinamo, reported to Lenin that the mood was 'gloomy', but that workers had listened to him 'without protest'.[20]

---

17 RGASPI, 17/3/166/3, 6, published in Naumov and Kaskovskii, op. cit., pp. 29 and 34.
18 Mikhailov, an SR workers' leader who had also been active during the civil war, was arrested in May 1921.
19 RGASPI, ibid.; TsGAMO, 66/22/64/19; *Sotsialisticheskii vestnik* 1921, no. 4. Sakwa, op. cit., p. 245.
20 TsAGM, 100/5/5/16; Shcherbina et al. (eds), *V.I. Lenin i A.V. Lunacharskii. Perepiska, doklady, dokumenty*, Moscow: Nauka, 1971, pp. 253–54.

Dissident Bolshevik and non-party socialist tendencies – both of which would be of continued significance – were active in the movement, alongside anti-Bolshevik organizations. In Saratov, the leader of the rail workers who initiated the city-wide strike action was a former Bolshevik. In Moscow, a group of 30 ex-Bolsheviks at Goznak had 'stirred up the masses' and stood against their former comrades in elections to the factory committee. After the strike, the bureau of the factory's party cell discussed at length a proposal to sack these dissidents, but held back for fear that their friends and relatives would then agitate in their defence.[21] At the tenth congress, Shliapnikov spoke of the organization of non-party groups in the factories to push the Bolsheviks out of elected positions: 'The communists are now being thrown out of the factory committees. These committees, the bedrock of our unions, are becoming non-party.'[22]

The Bolshevik leadership was well prepared to deal with the strike movement. It responded positively to demands on supply, and organized a selective, but thorough, clampdown on its political opponents. On 13 February, 10 days before the Goznak strike, Cheka and military leaders based in Moscow had written to the CC warning that if the economic situation got worse, workers would be 'torn away' from the party's influence 'and may even taken action against soviet power'. Not all Bolshevik leaders were so sensitive to the tensions: on 20 February at the Moscow regional party conference, Kamenev insisted 'there is no crisis in the soviet state, and it is absolutely out of place to shout from the rooftops about such a crisis'; rather, the party's own 'illness' had to be cured.[23] But he was in a minority. When the crisis broke in Moscow, on 23 February, a joint session of the CC and Moscow committee (MC) of the Bolshevik party decided on a threefold approach. First, efforts to improve supplies and stamp out the worst abuses were redoubled: yet another commission to oversee supply to Moscow and Petrograd was established, this time headed by Lozovskii. As the commission juggled to contain discontent in the forthcoming weeks, exceptions to the 'equalization' principle soon began to be made again, for example, at Goznak. The workforce was back on the higher Red army ration by March, and 'special representation' was made to exempt it from subsequent reductions.[24] Second, the 23 February meeting

---

21 The leaders of the former Bolsheviks at Goznak included Solov'ev, a former delegate to the local soviet. The outflow of members did not halt after the strike and on 8 March a vocal participant in the cell's affairs, Miniuk, resigned, declaring that he had 'become disillusioned … it makes me sick to see all that has happened'. TsAOPIM, 1099/1/3/5/7–8, 41–45. On Saratov, D.J. Raleigh, *Experiencing Russia's Civil War: Politics, Society and Revolutionary Culture in Saratov, 1917–1922*, Princeton: Princeton University Press, 2002, p. 379.
22 *Desiatyi s"ezd*, p. 389.
23 RGASPI, 17/84/265/1–2, published in Naumov and Kaskovskii, op. cit., pp. 24–25. Kamenev, TsAOPIM, 3/2/2/39.
24 TsAGM, 2626/1/70/16–16ob.

ordered a review of the deployment of soldiers such as those at the Khamovniki barracks to civilian labour, and their dispersal where necessary, even at the cost of closing some factories. Third, a commission comprising Messing and the MC members Iakovleva and Isaak Zelenskii[25] was appointed to organize repression; it was instructed 'not on any account to arrest people of working-class origin or those connected to the factories', and concentrated on SR, Menshevik and anarchist activists. This was in line with the approach adopted by the Cheka nationally.[26] Caution about the detention of oppositionist industrial workers was again expressed on 3 March by Bolshevik trade union leaders, who resolved that any such arrests had to be sanctioned in advance by a special commission of party, trade union, soviet and Cheka representatives, and demanded that those arrested so far without such sanction be released.[27] Their decision appears to have taken immediate effect: two of the AMO non-party group, Nastas'ian and Vasilii Davydov, who had been detained at 2.00 am that day, were freed immediately. On 4 March, a mass meeting at the factory expressed 'grave concern' over the incident, which constituted a breach of the immunity to which the pair was entitled as delegates to the Moscow soviet.[28]

Moscow and Kronshtadt

By early March, the transport crisis had abated and Moscow workers' rations were restored, albeit at a reduced level for many. As usual, supply to the textile towns around Moscow lagged behind, and in several of them, there were long strikes over rations: 5000 workers at the Glukhovskaia mills in Bogorodskii district struck for five days; 1000 at the Belova and Shipkova factory nearby for two days; and 4000 workers at the Voskresenskaia mills in Narofominsk for six days.[29] Political tensions were raised, as newspaper reports confirmed rumours that the Kronshtadt sailors had risen in revolt and been violently suppressed. But the political uncertainties apparent during the February strikes persisted. Most workers were disgruntled, but not actively opposed to Bolshevik rule. Only a minority were prepared to express solidarity with the demands for wider soviet democracy that dominated the

---

25 On Zelenskii, see Appendix 1.
26 RGASPI, 17/2/57/1–2, published in V.K. Vinogradov, V.P. Kozlov, M.A. Antifeeva and I.I. Kudriavtsev (eds), *Kronshtadtskaia tragediia 1921 goda: dokumenty v dvukh knigakh,* Moscow: Rosspen, 1999, vol. 2, pp. 364–65; RGASPI, 76/3/167/24, published in Kudriavtsev et al., op. cit., vol. 1, p. 105; RGASPI, 76/3/166, published in Naumov and Kaskovskii, op. cit., pp. 28–29; Maximoff, op. cit., p. 160; B. Dvinov, *Moskovskii Sovet Rabochykh Deputatov, 1917–1922: vospominaniia,* New York: Inter-university project on the history of the Menshevik movement, 1961, p. 100.
27 RGASPI, 95/1/22/44ob.
28 TsAGM, 415/16/262/14; 415/16/317/41.
29 GARF, 393/43a/1714/257.

Kronshtadt rebels' programme.³⁰ The majority's unease was reported by party speakers who toured factories, and found workers 'psychologically inclined to a major anarchist deviation' – but not in active opposition. The Cheka judged workers' moods to be 'exacerbated, due to the reduction in rations', and their attitude to soviet power 'satisfactory, albeit with ... complaints'. Only 'less conscious' elements believed 'absurd rumours' about the imminent collapse of soviet power.³¹ Industry-based Bolsheviks feared that a planned 'trade union week' would backfire and provide a platform for protest. The Moscow metalworkers' leadership warned that the event could produce 'completely undesirable results' and the Bolshevik fraction of the Moscow regional concil of trade unions (Moskovskii gubernskii sovet professional'nykh soiuzov — MGSPS) advised cancelling it completely. But the Moscow party leadership only postponed it, from mid February to late March. Supporters of the arrested anarcho-syndicalist bakers' leader, Pavlov, used it to demand his release.³² There was a brief strike on the SR-influenced Riazan'-Ural railway, but the Bolshevik leaders Tul'iakov and Viktor Nogin convinced the workers to return.³³

The high point of pro-Kronshtadt protest in Moscow was the adoption by the Bromlei factory workers on 25 March of a resolution supporting the rebels. The party responded by having them sacked en masse; they demonstrated through Zamoskvorech'e and inspired some brief solidarity strikes. Left SRs and anarchists initiated the action; former and current Bolshevik party members expressed sympathy with it.³⁴ The Bromlei workforce included many recent in-migrants from, and workers with family ties to, nearby rural districts, particularly Mozhaisk. The factory, which during the civil war produced and repaired machinery for the armed forces, maintained production throughout 1920. Political opposition was headed by I. Ivanov, a left SR toolmaker, and Kruglov, an anarchist who worked in the diesel

---

30 The main programmatic document from Kronshtadt was a resolution passed on the battleship Petropavlovsk, where the rebellion began. It demanded re-election of the soviets by secret ballot with free agitation beforehand; freedom of speech for workers and peasants, and for anarchists and left socialist parties; freedom of assembly for trade unions and peasant organizations; the convening of a non-party conference in Petrograd region; liberation of political prisoners; election of a commission to review cases of those in prisons; and abolition of political departments. It demanded 'full freedom of action in regard to the land' for peasants, legalization of private handicraft production and equalization of rations. Avrich, op. cit., pp. 72–76 and 157–92.
31 GARF, 393/43a/1714/257, 259.
32 *Pravda*, 19 January 1921; GARF, 5469/5/29/126; TsAOPIM, 3/2/28/37; TsGAMO, 201/1/266/1; S.V. Shedrov (ed.), *Profsoiuzy Moskvy: Ocherki istorii*, Moscow: Profizdat, 1975, p. 146.
33 TsAOPIM, 8654/1/1131/4–5.
34 GARF, 393/43a/1714/259–259ob; 7952/3/95/141; 7952/3/96/14–15; 7952/3/98/1ob-4ob, 5; TsAOPIM, 412/1/5/6–8; TsGAMO, 66/22/64/30–31; 186/1/585; Maximoff, op. cit., p. 185.

assembly shop. Both the left SR leader O.L. Chizhikov and the anarchist-universalist activist Vladimir Barmash[35] addressed mass meetings. There were also non-party socialists active at the works. Anikeev, who was sacked for his part in the pro-Kronshtadt protest, recalled that one veteran activist who 'commanded colossal respect', and had usually acted as a 'buffer' between SRs and Bolsheviks, swung against the government on the issue of grain requisitioning. Anikeev recalled a repeating pattern of industrial conflict in the months prior to March 1921: discussions would be held in the diesel assembly shop; sometimes there would be brief strikes that would spread through the factory; negotiations with district or sometimes city union officials would produce a compromise; and things would go quiet again. On 25 March, opposition moved from economic to political: a mass meeting was called to discuss an unconfirmed rumour that Kaliaev, a worker dissident, had been arrested. It adopted a resolution that 'demagogically blackened the name of the [Bolsheviks] and the soviet power, and voiced greetings to the Kronshtadt rebels', according to a Cheka agent. Ivanov, who had moved the resolution, advised the workers to 'play a waiting game'. The Moscow party leadership took the offensive: a meeting of party, soviet, Cheka, trade unions and metal industry management representatives decided to arrest those who had initiated the resolution, and to sack and selectively re-employ the entire workforce. The decision to close the plant was announced in notices posted on the gates: although the party often sent speakers to Bromlei to negotiate on rations and production issues, it had no wish to discuss politics with workers. A delegation of workers appealed to the metalworkers' union, which had helped to organize the mass sacking, but got no response.[36] The next day, the workers marched through Zamoskvorech'e to picket out other factories. More than 3000 workers, mainly at small factories, struck in solidarity, and about 1000 of these joined the flying picket. The Sytin printers, who had a record of independent political activity, were locked in by managers, and the pickets could not reach them.[37] In the days after the demonstration, most workers were soon re-employed. They worked hard to defend the political activists in their midst, staging two strikes and two mass meetings to demand the release of arrested activists, and concealing Ivanov from Cheka search units for several weeks. They remained buoyant on supply issues, too, striking again in May, July and August.[38]

35 Chizhikov was a member of the left SR party's central organizing bureau; 1920–22 edited its journal *Znamia* together with Shteinberg; developed left SRs' economic policy; a Moscow soviet delegate; arrested in 1923 (see Chapter 8, p. 198). Barmash was an intellectual, prominent in the Moscow federation of anarchists and the Black Guard in 1917–18; in 1921 a Moscow soviet delegate; arrested in November 1921 during the raids on anarchist organizations (see Chapter 4, p. 107); freed shortly afterwards; rearrested in 1929.
36 TsGAMO, 186/1/585/9; GARF, 5469/5/29/131.
37 GARF, 7952/3/98/30ob.
38 TsAOPIM, 412/1/5/19; *Sotsialisticheskii vestnik* 1922, no. 9, p. 12.

By supporting the Kronshtadt mutineers' democratic demands, the Bromlei workers split the factory's Bolshevik cell down the middle. The Bolshevik-dominated factory committee opposed the mass dismissal. The cell secretary, E.N. Sashilin, recalled that 'very few' party members had agreed with the sackings. At least one communist participated in the workers' demonstration and spoke in support of its demands; one, Koliadov, was expelled from the cell for venting his disagreements 'in an open forum'. There are other instances of such support by rank-and-file Bolsheviks for the Kronshtadt rebels: at Kronshtadt itself, Trotsky and Smilga had estimated that 30 per cent of party members supported the rising and 40 per cent stayed neutral.[39] And although in Moscow most party members supported the action against the Kronshtadt rebels unambiguously, they could easily be thrown off balance by the defiant minority. In late March, a dissident party member at the Kauchuk factory, Viktorov, expressed sympathy with the workers' movement at a mass meeting, and proposed – 'in the name of the non-party workers', significantly – a resolution 'of the most anarchist character'. The cell decided to expel him, but had to note vacillation by other communists, who 'failed to judge, and reject [Viktorov's resolution] in a categorical manner'.[40] In Khamovniki's sub-district no. 3 party organization, in which the Kauchuk cell was one of the largest, uncertainty was expressed by a district party official, Sazonov, who despaired at the decision to retreat from the forced-march economic policies, while simultaneously acknowledging that calls for wider soviet democracy were legitimate.[41] He told a sub-district meeting on 19 March that the tax in kind 'has taken the communist ground from under our feet, and I don't know how to explain that to workers. We have made a great leap all right – into the abyss'. Such concessions were a bow of respect to world capital, Sazonov added. At the sub-district's next meeting a week later, the Kronshtadt rebels' platform was read out in full, an implicit acknowledgement of its validity. Sazonov then delivered standard Bolshevik arguments – that the Kronshtadt garrison had been flooded by peasant elements, that its leaders were counter-revolutionaries, etc. – but also pointed out: 'There are points [in the Kronshtadt resolution] against which one can not object, such as the re-election of soviet delegates and the convening of non-party conferences'.[42] Sazonov's hesitation did not save the dissident Viktorov, though: a commission comprising Sazonov, Anna Kaspirovich[43] and Timofei Emel'ianov recommended to the Kauchuk cell that Viktorov be expelled from the party and dismissed from his job.

39 *Des'iaty s"ezd*, p. 253; Avrich, op. cit., pp. 69, 183–86.
40 TsAOPIM, 475/1/2/3–5, 33–34.
41 TsAOPIM, 88/1/65/6–6ob.
42 TsAOPIM, 88/1/65/3.
43 Kaspirovich (1896–?) started work at the Kauchuk factory in Riga aged 14; moved with the factory to Moscow; 1917, joined the Bolshevik party and became cell secretary, a position she held with some interruptions in the late 1920s; 1923, supported the opposition.

Some historians have merged the February strike waves with the Kronshtadt revolt, and presented the aggregate total as a revolutionary uprising. Orlando Figes suggests that 'the Bolsheviks were facing a revolutionary situation. ... Whereas earlier strikes had been a means of bargaining with the regime, those of 1921 were a last desperate bid to overthrow it'. Richard Pipes acknowledges that the political aims of Kronshtadt were not necessarily shared by strikers elsewhere, but, along with Figes, draws exaggerated parallels with the outbreak of the February 1917 revolution. Pipes wrote that Lenin, when confronted with worker defiance, 'reacted exactly as had Nicholas II' and 'turned to the military', but whereas Nicholas 'soon caved in', Lenin was prepared to 'go to any length to stay in power'.[44] Certainly the upsurge of working-class dissatisfaction, combined with the widespread peasant revolts, by early 1921 appeared threatening to the Bolsheviks. But it is also clear that, in contrast to February 1917, (i) the participants in these movements were not united to overthrow the government nor convinced that it should be overthrown; and (ii) the government was not so paralysed that it was unable to work out a change of policy (i.e. NEP) to ensure its survival. Without these ingredients, the contention that there was a 'revolutionary situation' appears shaky at least.

In Moscow, there were scattered expressions of anger at the attacks on democracy, but no organized presentation of demands for reform of the soviet system. In mid March there were the strikes by textile workers, mentioned above, and in mid April a scattering of short strikes in the city of Moscow. But the Cheka agents who surveilled these strikes, super-sensitive to any signs of politicization, insisted that they only concerned late or short rations. The strikes in Petrograd were longer than those in Moscow, and involved larger numbers of workers, especially in a three-week period from about 14 February. The Petrograd workers also presented a clearer political challenge than those in Moscow had: in addition to demands to abolish food requisitioning and for 'equalization of rations', several large workplaces called for free soviet elections by secret ballot, and for political rights for the other socialist parties.[45] In Saratov, as Donald Raleigh has described, in the first few days of March workers elected a popular assembly, free of Bolshevik control, which demanded new soviet elections, the liberation of political prisoners, independent unions and freedom of speech, the press and assembly. This was accompanied by a 'near general' strike in the city

---

44 O. Figes, *A People's Tragedy: the Russian Revolution 1891–1924*, London: Jonathan Cape, 1996, pp. 758–59; R. Pipes, *Russia Under the Bolshevik Regime*, London: Harvill, 1994, p. 380.
45 S.V. Iarov, *Gorozhanin kak politik: revoliutsiia, voennyi kommunizm i NEP glazami petrogradtsev*, St Petersburg: 'Dmitrii Bulagin', 1999, pp. 63–78; M. McAuley, *Bread and Justice: State and Society in Petrograd 1917–1922*, Oxford: Clarendon, 1991, pp. 403–11.

that was quelled only by means of several hundred arrests.[46] But even these movements, which were more coherent than the Moscow strikes, did not constitute an organized challenge to the government, and, although they were almost contemporaneous, they were obviously uncoordinated. Indeed, when the Kronshtadt uprising began, a few days after the Petrograd and Moscow strike movements had passed their peaks, it inspired scarcely any active support in the two capitals – a disjuncture that, as Mary McAuley notes, dismayed the Kronshtadt sailors, and, as Sergei Iarov argues, threw into sharp relief the workers' movement's political weakness. The unwillingness of the two capitals' workers to act in support of Kronshtadt assured the Bolshevik government's survival. In Moscow, many workers sympathized with Kronshtadt's demands, but did not feel themselves to be part of a national political revolt. They applauded pro-Kronshtadt speakers at mass meetings, but this did not translate into action. Even at Bromlei, things went no further than the adoption of a resolution; the demonstration there resulted from the mass dismissal. In Petrograd, as in Moscow, the movement was ended by a combination of repression and concessions.[47]

The strike movement was political in places, but not politically united. The anarcho-syndicalist leader Grigorii Maksimov[48] claimed that it sought 'a change in the general policies of the government, putting a stop to persecutions and terror, the restoration of freedom and free Soviet elections'.[49] But in Moscow such issues were raised only sporadically. The main slogans at Kronshtadt and Petrograd, for soviet democracy and political rights for non-Bolshevik parties, implicitly challenged the Bolsheviks' form of rule. But many workers hoped that such changes could be achieved by means of an accommodation between the Bolsheviks, the other socialist parties and workers' organizations. In Moscow, the Riazan'-Ural rail workers alone called for the Bolsheviks to be removed all together. Much more widespread were hopes that a compromise could be reached between workers' parties. The metalworkers' meeting, which sounded the clearest warning to the government on food requisitioning and rationing, gave the floor to speakers who demanded political freedoms and democratic reform of the soviets. But it did not adopt the sort of resolutions on these issues that were passed at Kronshtadt. In Moscow the drive to revive soviet democracy was pursued not through armed revolt but subsequently, by electoral methods – participation in the April-May soviet election campaign – and negotiation with the Bolsheviks. This, too, speaks against the interpretation of the spring events as a 'revolutionary situation'.

46 Raleigh, op. cit., pp. 387–89.
47 Iarov, op. cit., p. 78; McAuley, op. cit., p. 410.
48 Maksimov (1893–1950) joined the revolutionary movement in 1915 as a student and spent the rest of his life as an anarcho-syndicalist organizer and writer; 1925, went into exile via Paris to Chicago.
49 Maximoff, op. cit., p. 160.

The tenth congress

The tenth party congress – which opened on 8 March, when most workers' protests had barely subsided and special detachments were on their way to Kronshtadt – was seen by all trends within Bolshevism as a key turning point. Trotsky much later wrote that it 'brought the heroic history of Bolshevism to an end and made way for its bureaucratic degeneration'.[50] Its two most notable decisions were the endorsement of the tax in kind to replace grain requisitioning, which set the course towards NEP, and the ban on factions inside the party, which confirmed the trend towards authoritarian political rule. But this latter decision – taken after the briefest of discussions, at a closed session held after many delegates had already left – did not, by itself, accomplish the huge about-turn in party life for which the congress was remembered. It was part of a broader shift, evident in the main discussion on 'party building', away from the democratism espoused by the ninth party conference in September 1920, towards an insistence on strengthening centralism after the civil war. This turn marked a defeat for the DCs and their federalist vision of limited soviet democracy, and strengthened the position of those who identified socialism with a strong state, guided by a large, centralized apparatus. This helped remove obstructions to the advance of the party elite.

Bukharin's report on 'party building' articulated the leadership's abandonment of the democratic slogans it had embraced under rank-and-file pressure at the ninth conference. The 'greatest danger' to arise from Kronshtadt was not that from the counter-revolutionary general Kozlovskii, he said, but the strikes in Petrograd, and workers' resolutions calling for free trade. In response, the party had to close ranks, to make itself a 'single party, with a single psychology and a single ideology'. During the civil war, the party had 'split into different parts, with differing psychologies and differing deviations'; now such clashes had to end, the erstwhile leader of left communism declared. The party had 'again and again to turn ... towards greater centralization and militarization of the apparatus'. Bukharin called the DCs' proposals on party democracy – which had been incorporated into earlier congress resolutions and formally speaking constituted party policy – an unacceptable expression of 'SR labouring-people's-power politics [*eserovskoe trudovlastie*]'.[51]

50 L.D. Trotsky, *Writings of Leon Trotsky (1935–36)*, New York: Pathfinder, 1977, pp. 185–86.
51 The CC's move away from its positions of 1920 began before the Kronshtadt events. Its draft resolution for the tenth congress on 'party building', in contrast to that of the DCs, made no reference to previous congress decisions. It argued that bureaucratization was a negative consequence of militarization and in no sense caused by the failure of party attempts to combat it. While repeating that wider inner-party democracy was needed, the CC stressed that the *main* task was not to combat bureaucratism or inequality, but to combat the political inadequacy of the party membership, i.e. to 'raise the level [of political consciousness] of party members and at the same time bring them actively into party life'. Resolution adopted, *Desiatyi s"ezd*, pp. 217–31 and 559–71.

The revolution that wasn't 89

Bukharin's call for 'greater centralization and militarization of the apparatus' made nonsense of the references to inner-party democracy and equality that had been written into the CC's draft resolution. These were perhaps a sop to the DCs and other oppositionists, while the practical measures pushed by the CC at the congress were in line with demands made by a group of 40 delegates, avowed centralizers, who lobbied from the other side. This group was led by Ivar Smilga, head of the Red army political department, who after the congress was appointed deputy head of VSNKh, and Karl Danishevskii, head of the party's Siberian bureau.[52] It claimed to speak with 'the voice of the borderlands' where soviet power was insecure. It opposed the ninth conference decisions, on the grounds that they were unrealizable, and called for those democratic slogans the conference had adopted to be removed from the tenth congress resolution. Public pronouncements by the oppositions were 'intolerable' and Bukharin's 'liberal-pink policy' of accommodating them had to end, Smilga told the congress. In what the DC spokesman Vladimir Maksimovskii described as 'a policeman's analysis', Smilga proposed scrapping entirely the elective principle the oppositionists sought to widen. He attacked frontally those who criticized the 'tops', and demanded an end to the ranks' 'intolerable attitude' to party members working as commissars and in other official posts. Significantly, in view of subsequent bitter conflicts between communist industrial managers and factory cell members, such as those described in Chapter 7, Smilga urged the deletion of a paragraph in the congress resolution that gave factory cells the right to challenge decisions taken by communist managers. The positions taken by Smilga's supporters provide insight into the thinking of a particularly authoritarian section of the party elite. Murakhin argued that the party dissidents' 'fractionalism and discussion' only produced events like Kronshtadt, and Mashatov said the congress should 'give all these polemicists their final clip round the ear'.[53] Maksimovskii, in the DCs' counter-report to Bukharin's, had warned that to expand democracy and reverse bureaucratization, the party would have to 'overcome the resistance of ... inveterate bureaucrats', both military and civilian, within its own ranks. The Moscow-based DC Rafail identified Smilga as 'the clearest and most typical representative of bureaucratism'; thus the congress's 'most important' speech had been Smilga's. When Lenin moved the resolution that imposed the ban on factions, empowered the CC to discipline members who participated in factional activity, and enshrined in policy the characterization of the oppositions as an 'anarchosyndicalist deviation', he was carrying into practice exactly the type of authoritarian centralization for which Smilga had campaigned.[54]

52 On Danishevskii, see Appendix 1.
53 *Des'iatyi s"ezd*, pp. 252–61, 301–3 and 306–9; I. Smilga, *Na povorote: zametki k X-mu s"ezdu partii*, Moscow: Gos. izdatel'stvo, 1921, pp. 6–7 and 14–25; G.L. Olekh, *Povorot, kotorogo ne bylo: bor'ba za vnutripartiinuiu demokratiu 1919–1924 gg.*, Novosibirsk: izd. Novosibirskogo universiteta, 1992, p. 62.
54 *Des'iatyi s"ezd*, pp. 251–52, 274–75; R.V. Daniels, *The Conscience of the Revolution: Communist Opposition in Soviet Russia*, Cambridge, MA: Harvard University Press, 1960, pp. 150–52.

4 The NEP and non-partyism
Workers in 1921

The end of the civil war, the retreat from grain requisitioning, and the revival of legal trade with the countryside paved the way for economic revival. Straight after the tenth congress, closed factories began to reopen and industrial output began to recover. As the party looked forward to peacetime construction, it also remoulded its political relationship with the working class. A social contract evolved, under which workers would maintain discipline and improve labour productivity, and cede real decision-making power to the party – which in return would ensure a consistent improvement in living standards. This required a redefinition of politics, both in the broad sense (societal/state politics) and in the workplace. In societal/state politics, mass participation in decision-making had to be severely restricted, and this restricted participation presented as working-class power. The aspirations of 1917 to collective, participatory democracy were abandoned, and the fora for working-class political activity, the soviets and unions, allocated restricted functions that involved implementing, rather than making, decisions. At the same time, workers were encouraged to participate in public displays of support for the new order – and indeed many of them supported the Bolsheviks as an alternative to the pre-1917 regime. But politically active workers who did not accept this social contract, such as the non-party group on the Moscow soviet discussed below, were marginalized. Those who actively resisted, including opposition socialists, anarchists, and dissident Bolsheviks, were silenced by repression.[1]

In the workplaces, a new system of labour relations developed. The civil-war-time experiments with labour compulsion and militarization were

---

1 Linda Cook and others have used the term 'social contract' with reference to the Brezhnev period, as an arrangement under which 'in return for ... comprehensive provision of social and economic security, Soviet workers gave the regime their political compliance and quiescence'. Although there are superficial similarities between this and the arrangement of the mid 1920s, the differences – between the class make-up of Soviet society in the two periods, the social and political balances of forces, etc. – are more significant. I therefore do not attempt any comparison. L. Cook, 'Brezhnev's "social contract" and Gorbachev's reforms', *Soviet Studies* 44: 1, 1992: 37–56.

abandoned. But the product of workers' labour remained under the state's control; the label 'workers' state' masked the alienated character of that labour. This 'workers' state' imposed labour discipline, with the help of the party, union officials and factory leaders who owed it allegiance; material rewards were freely used to raise productivity; residual strivings towards working-class participation in management were extinguished; and 'workers' democracy' confined to secondary questions. The industrial managers, notwithstanding real tensions between them and other sections of the party, were afforded political and institutional support. The majority of workers accepted, and to some extent welcomed, a set-up that provided the hope of better living standards. The combination of state-imposed labour discipline and political exhortation at the heart of the social contract was a step in the direction of the mature Stalinist system that, as Michael Burawoy described it, 'revolv[ed] around the use of "extra-economic" force in the reproduction of relations in production and relations of exploitation', which was distinctive in the way that 'the organs of state politics directly enter the regulation of production'.[2]

The subordinate position to which the party assigned the working class was reflected in the changing meaning of the word *samodeiatel'nost'* (self-activity). In 1917 it had embraced the creative political activity of the working class in its mass organizations and in the workplaces. In the first years after the revolution, it was thrown in the Bolshevik leaders' faces by their left critics, as a principle they had abandoned. Jan Machajski, the Polish socialist-workerist, complained in 1918 that 'self-management, self-activity, elective and federal bases are deemed [by the Bolsheviks] to be very often undesirable and responsible for general chaos – and are replaced by their opposite, the dictatorial principle'. The DC leader Timofei Sapronov, protesting at the dominance of executive committees over soviets and one-man management over collegiality, asked the ninth party congress in March 1920: 'Why talk about the proletarian dictatorship or workers' self-activity?

---

2 Burawoy argues that 'the harnessing of the party and trade union structures to the managerial function', as he observed it in Hungary and the USSR in the post-war period, is 'distinctive to the politics of bureaucratic despotism', as opposed to the 'market despotism' of capitalism. M. Burawoy, *The Politics of Production: Factory Regimes Under Capitalism and Socialism*, London: Verso, 1985, p. 181. On labour relations under NEP, see D. Filtzer, *Soviet Workers and Stalinist Industrialization: the Formation of Modern Soviet Production Relations 1928–1941*, London: Pluto, 1986, pp. 15–29. Some historians describe these relationships in terms of 'labour motivation', e.g. W.J. Chase, *Workers, Society and the Soviet State: Labour and Life in Moscow 1918–1929*, Urbana: University of Illinois Press, 1990, pp. 35–38 and pp. 214–55; A. Markevich and A. Sokolov, '*Magnitka bliz Sadovogo kol'tsa*': *stimula k rabote na Moskovskom zavode 'Serp i molot', 1883–2001 gg.*, Moscow: Rosspen, 2005; and several contributors to A.V. Buzgalin, D.O. Churakov and P. Shul'tse (eds), *Rabochii klass v protsessakh modernizatsii Rossii: istoricheskii opyt*, Moscow: 'Ekonomicheskaia demokratiia', 2001.

There's no self-activity here!'³ In the party's own discourse, though, *samodeiatel'nost'* was narrowed down to mean voluntary worker participation in the tasks of economic construction – tasks that workers had no role in setting. This is the sense suggested by the resolution on trade union work passed by the tenth congress.⁴ It was 'workers' energetic self-activity' that had overcome the economic chaos of 1920, declared one party newspaper; another proclaimed as an ideal example of self-activity the decision by Podol'sk engineering workers to march en masse to the forest to cut firewood to restart the boilers.⁵ In this view, the party not only points the way, but also prescribes organizational forms. The social contract produced further changes in the meaning of *samodeiatel'nost'*. James von Geldern, in his study of Bolshevik festivals, noted that *samodeiatel'nost'* became 'a contradictory notion', because participation in displays of support for the government was courted, but efforts made to 'limit mass initiative'. And *samodeiatel'nost'* became bureaucratic parody when the trade union leader Mel'nichanskii declared in 1922 that its realization required the granting by the national trade union federation to regional executives, and by regional executives to district executives, 'the right independently to manage their own affairs and the right to have their own rubber stamp [?!], their own publications, their own funds, their own headed paper'.⁶ As *samodeiatel'nost'* acquired this anti-meaning, the adverb *samovol'no* (self-willed or wilful) was attributed to workers' activity that contradicted the party line, for example a meeting called by Orekhovo-Zuevo weavers in response to a unilateral announcement of their collective expulsion by their trade union.⁷

The social contract began to take shape, in part, in response to the resurgence of political activism by non-party workers after the tenth congress, which is the main subject of this chapter. This centred on the soviet elections in April-May 1921 when non-party groups successfully challenged the Bolsheviks, winning the mandates of most of Moscow's large factories. The account that follows challenges the assumption by some historians that the non-party candidates were usually former or undercover Mensheviks and Socialist Revolutionaries (SRs), and describes the much wider political base on which the non-party groups rested. The non-party groups' offers of

3 J. Machajski, *Umstvennyi rabochii*, New York: Mezhdunarodnoe Literaturnoe Sodruzhestvo, 1968, p. 401; *Deviatyi s"ezd RKP(b): stenograficheskii otchet*, Moscow: Gos. izd. polit. literatury, 1960, p. 52.
4 *Desiatyi s"ezd RKP(b): stenograficheskii otchet*, Moscow: Gos. izd. polit. literatury, 1963, p. 664.
5 *Pravda*, 6 February 1921; *Kommunisticheskii trud*, 6 March 1921.
6 MGSPS, *Otchet o deiatel'nosti Moskovskogo gubprofsoveta 1921–22*, Moscow, 1922, p. 9; TsAOPIM, f3 op3 d5, ll. 51–52; J. von Geldern, *Bolshevik Festivals, 1917–1920*, Berkeley: University of California Press, 1993, p. 209.
7 TsAOPIM, 3/3/34/225ob. The meeting, called of necessity without sanction by the trade union, which had just expelled the workers en masse, was described in a Cheka report as a 'wilfully organized [*samovolno-ustroennoe*] mass meeting'. This strike is discussed in Chapter 6, p. 157.

collaboration were rejected by the Bolsheviks, who thereby shut the door on an opportunity to revive the participatory democracy that had begun to develop in 1917. This, combined with the renewal of Cheka repression against SRs, Mensheviks and anarchists, and its use against dissident Bolsheviks who left the party in early 1921, amounted to a decisive renunciation of alternatives to one-party rule. This narrowing of the political space for the workers' movement took place against the background of the first steps of economic recovery, which are discussed in the last section of this chapter.

Non-partyism

The workers' groups which in 1921 described themselves as *non-partyist* included workerists and others who had supported the Bolsheviks in October 1917, some of whom eschewed party politics in principle; former Bolsheviks; and workers with loose Menshevik and SR sympathies. The terms non-partyist (*bezpartiinyi*) and non-partyism (*bezpartiinost'*) will be used here in this sense. Their meanings went through some subtle shifts during and after the Russian revolution. Several historians have noted the importance in 1917 of the basic striving for unity felt by workers entering political struggle for the first time, which was the progenitor of non-partyism. It was strong in workers' movements against tsarism and arguably at its height in the February 1917 revolution. Between March and November 1917, soviet elections generally moved from their initial form – direct, unmediated elections from bodies of workers, soldiers and peasants – to systems of competing party lists. Israel Getzler concluded that the advance of partisanship 'encroached on and weakened the participatory democracy of the rank-and-file workers and soldiers'. On the other hand Timothy McDaniel argues that the 'unresolved tension between unity and partisanship' was rooted in two basic conditions of the workers' movement: its need for solidarity and its need for political direction. In a small minority of soviets, for example at Helsingfors, non-partyism was expressed by a ban on election by party list. But in any case, as partisanship took hold – faster in the main centres than in the provinces, and faster among workers than among soldiers – there grew together with it what Getzler described as a 'self-consciously non-party fraction'.[8] In Kronshtadt, one of the most politically developed soviets, the non-partyists were the largest fraction active in the 'Kronshtadt republic' in May 1917, and jointly largest with the Bolsheviks from elections

---

8 I. Getzler, 'Soviets as Agents of Democratization', in E.R. Frankel, J. Frankel and B. Knei-Paz (eds), *Revolution in Russia: Reassessments of 1917*, Cambridge: Cambridge University Press, 1992, pp. 17–33; T. McDaniel, *Autocracy, Capitalism and Revolution in Russia*, Berkeley: University of California Press, 1988, pp. 373–77; A.Ya. Grunt, *Moskva 1917-y. Revoliutsiia i kontrrevoliutsiia*, Moscow: 'Nauka', 1976, p. 226.

in August. Soon afterwards, they declared themselves SR maximalists. In Moscow in 1917, the striving for unity, and lack of understanding of parties' differences, meant that until the summer there was no party fraction system in the soviet. Even after it was adopted in June, and the party differences became much clearer as a result of the July Days, non-partyism persisted. Diane Koenker points, for example, to donations to the Municipal Fund (a political fund shared between all workers' parties), which in August-September continued to dwarf donations to separate parties.[9] Another influence on non-partyism was that of traditions of peasant self-organization. Nikolai Mikhailov argues that, in the pre-revolutionary period, the organization of Councils of Representatives (*Sovety Upol'nomochennykh*) in the factories amounted to a continuation of forms derived from the peasant commune. In 1921 at the Bogatyr works, where non-partyism was strong, such a council was elected to oversee the work of the factory committee.[10]

In the autumn and winter of 1917, the circumstances that produced the huge wave of working-class support for Bolshevism – workers' loss of confidence in the provisional government, the Kornilov events and the split in the SR party – also undermined a key assumption of non-partyism, that differences among workers' parties were secondary. Many workers who earlier in the year had been non-partisan, as well as those who supported the Menshevik-SR alliance, moved in October-November to support the Bolshevik stance on soviet power. Nevertheless, non-partyism emerged in a new form in the first significant workers' movement under the Bolshevik government, i.e. the unrest triggered by the breakdown of supply in Petrograd in the spring of 1918. The protests began with the formation of the Emergency Assembly of Factory Representatives and ended with the shooting of strikers at Kolpino and arrests of opposition socialists. Sergei Iarov considers that politically, they were coloured on one hand by disillusionment in the soviets, which had ceased to be representative, and on the other by 'the strengthening of "non-party" moods that are usual among workers, but that had now ... taken on a strong anti-Bolshevik colouring'. The Mensheviks and SRs, many of whom quit the soviets in late 1917 and some of whom were now subject to repression, were keen to influence non-soviet work-

---

9 I. Getzler, *Kronstadt 1917–1921: The Fate of a Soviet Democracy*, Cambridge: Cambridge University Press, 1983, pp. 37–38, 55–56, 66 and 134–42; A.F. Zhukov, *Ideino-politicheskii krakh eserovskogo maksimalizma*, Leningrad: izd. Leningradskogo universiteta, 1979, pp. 48–49; D.P. Koenker, *Moscow Workers and the 1917 Revolution*, Princeton: Princeton University Press, 1981, pp. 189–92 and 290–91; Kh.M. Astrakhan, *Bol'sheviki i ikh politicheskie protivniki v 1917-m godu*, Leningrad: Lenizdat, 1973, pp. 364–70.
10 N.V. Mikhailov, 'The Collective Psychology of Russian Workers and Workplace Self-Organization in the Early Twentieth Century', in M. Melancon and A.K. Pate (eds), *New Labor History: Worker Identity and Experience in Russia, 1840–1918*, Bloomington: Slavica, 2002, pp. 77–93; TsAGM, 337/2/39.

ers' bodies such as the Emergency Assembly, and this poses a question that comes up again in 1921: was the label 'non-party' simply a cover for opposition socialist activity? Iarov considers that the Mensheviks and SRs had the initiative, and met 'the most active sympathy' among other workers. Vladimir Brovkin writes that the movement expressed not so much support for the SRs and Mensheviks as 'painful disappointment' in the hopes raised by the Bolshevik seizure of power.[11]

A group with non-partyist traits, the United Workers party, participated in the Petrograd protest movements. This group, led by two Putilov workers who sat on the Emergency Assembly's leading bodies, Nikolai Glebov and Aleksandr Rozenshtein,[12] sought liberation from the 'yoke of partyism'. At the Emergency Assembly's first meeting Glebov, quoting the Communist Manifesto's insistence that the liberation of the working class 'is the task of the working class itself', attacked 'the Bolshevik and Menshevik party bureaucrats alike'. At the Putilov works, non-partyist declarations appeared in resolutions that supported soviet power; at the Obukhov works, where Glebov's group was also active, non-partyism was linked to demands for the reconvocation of the Constituent Assembly. A resolution, drafted by Glebov and adopted by a mass meeting of Putilov workers at the height of the 1919 strike wave, called – vaguely, without mentioning organizational forms – for a 'united socialist front and the mobilization for socialist construction of all in the revolutionary democracy who are able to work'.[13]

---

11 S.V. Iarov, *Gorozhanin kak politik: revoliutsiia, voennyi kommunizm i NEP glazami petrogradtsev*, St Petersburg: 'Dmitrii Bulagin', 1999, p. 24; V.N. Brovkin, *The Mensheviks After October: Socialist Opposition and the Rise of the Bolshevik Dictatorship*, London: Cornell University Press, 1987, pp. 165–66. See also M. McAuley, *Bread and Justice: State and Society in Petrograd 1917–1922*, Oxford: Clarendon, 1991, pp. 94–99; D. Mandel, *The Petrograd Workers and the Soviet Seizure of Power: from the July Days 1917 to July 1918*, London: Macmillan, 1984, pp. 379–83 and 390–413; and W.G. Rosenberg, 'Russian Labor and Bolshevik Power After October', *Slavic Review* 44: 2, 1985, pp. 213–38, and polemic with Moshe Lewin and Vladimir Brovkin, ibid., pp. 239–56. Documents in V.Iu. Cherniaev and E.I. Makarov (eds), *Piterskie rabochie i 'Diktatura Proletariata'. Oktiabr' 1917–1929: ekonomicheskie konflikty i politichestkii protest*, St Petersburg: Russko-baltiiskii informatsionnyi tsentr BLITs, 2000, pp. 55–113.
12 Glebov, a metalworker who joined the Social Democratic party in 1901, was a delegate to the 1905 St Petersburg soviet and a collaborator of G. Plekhanov's in exile from 1906. He returned to Petrograd after the February revolution in 1917 and took a job at the Putilov works. He joined the Bolshevik party in 1920, and remained in it until his death in the purges. Rozenshtein, a member of the Putilov factory committee and, in mid 1917, of the Menshevik fraction on the Petrograd soviet, was arrested in 1918 by his brother Mikhail Rozenshtein, a Bolshevik Putilov worker. V.Iu. Cherniaev and E.I. Makarov (eds.), *Piterskie rabochie*, p. 66 and p. 71.
13 Brovkin, op. cit., p. 167; Iarov, op. cit., pp. 28–29 and 38–39, M.S. Bernshtam, *Narodnoe soprotivlenie kommunizmu v Rossii: nezavisimoe rabochee dvizhenie v 1918 godu*, Paris: YMCA Press, 1981; Cherniaev et al. (eds.), op. cit., pp. 113–15.

The Petrograd movements also helped into being what would become one of the Bolsheviks' most effective means of mediating their relationship with workers, the non-party conferences. Such meetings were first called in early 1918 by opposition socialists, but soon adopted by the Bolsheviks.[14] During the civil war, some such conferences became battlegrounds between the Bolsheviks and groups of workers and peasants who tried to reclaim the 'non-party' title for themselves, for example by nominating presidia against those proposed by the Bolsheviks.[15] After 1921, as the political space for workers narrowed, the opposition socialist parties were silenced and organized non-partyism declined, the character of these gatherings changed. Convening them became a standard task for party workplace organizations and they became passive sounding-board for non-party workers' views. The meaning of 'non-partyism' thereby changed again: in line with the Bolsheviks' view that theirs was the only legitimate, pro-soviet party, all workers outside the Bolshevik party were defined as non-party.

The soviet elections

In 1918–20, assaults on soviet democracy (including closure of soviets dominated by opposition parties and arrests of delegates)[16] and on workplace democracy (limitations of factory committee power and replacement of collegial management with one-man management)[17] were usually attributed to, or justified in terms of, military exigencies. Both non-Bolshevik socialists and many Bolsheviks held out hopes that the trend to dictatorship would be reversed after the civil war. The test came in the spring of 1921, in elections to soviets and other workers' organizations. Non-party candidates came to the fore, presenting a new challenge to Bolshevik hegemony. Their strong showing in Moscow, discussed below, was part of a national trend.

14 Iarov, op. cit., p. 24.
15 M.M. Helgesen, *The Origins of the Party-State Monolith in Soviet Russia: Relations Between the Soviets and Party Committees in the Central Provinces, October 1917 – March 1921* (PhD diss., State University of New York at Stony Brook, 1980), pp. 370–74; M. Baker, 'Establishing Soviet Power in the Countryside: Kharkov Province 1918–21' (paper presented at the AAASS convention, Boston, December 2004).
16 In June 1918 the Bolshevik-dominated central executive committee excluded all Menshevik and right SR delegates and instructed local soviets to do likewise. In July 1918, after the attempted left SR rising, most left SRs were banned from the soviets. The extent to which the anarchists, SR maximalists and other smaller groups were tolerated by the Bolsheviks often depended on local factors. Brovkin, op. cit., pp. 126–60 and 220–93; O. Anweiler, *The Soviets: the Russian Workers', Peasants and Soldiers Councils, 1905–1921*, New York: Pantheon Books, 1974, pp. 218–44; G. Gill, *The Origins of the Stalinist Political System*, Cambridge: Cambridge University Press, 1990, p. 23.
17 S.A. Smith, *Red Petrograd*, Cambridge: Cambridge University Press, 1983, pp. 230–52; Mandel, op. cit., pp. 379–413.

In Petrograd, a non-party assembly, summoned on the Bolsheviks' initiative, turned into a political battleground between the party, opposition socialists and non-partyists. In Ukraine, non-party groups won a majority at city workers' conferences in Rostov in January and Kharkov in February, and the majority of industrial workers' mandates to the Kiev soviet in April, according to a Menshevik correspondent. In Smolensk, the Menshevik newspaper reported that soviet elections held in February returned an absolute majority of non-party delegates from industrial workers' constituencies.[18]

The political content of non-partyism had changed: this time the impetus came neither from the striving for unity (as it had in 1917) or its breakdown (as in 1918), but from hopes for a revival of participatory democracy on one hand and the active repression of the opposition socialist parties on the other. The non-partyist groups in 1921 were loose coalitions, embracing workers who had supported Bolshevism in October but become disillusioned; workerists, including those whose hostility to parties and to the intelligentsia reflected strains of makhaevism; former SRs (particularly lefts), and, along with them, some less clearly defined narodnik influences; and former Mensheviks. These former SRs and Mensheviks were usually workplace militants whose political life was lived among their colleagues, and who had little or no contact with those parties' Moscow organizations, which had borne the brunt of Cheka repression. The non-partyists operated in a political space from which the opposition socialists had been driven, and as a result the Bolsheviks regularly claimed that they were undercover Mensheviks and SRs. Some historians agree. D.B. Pavlov argues that the threat of repression dissuaded workers from voting for Menshevik-SR candidates or resolutions, and that non-partyism was essentially a cover. But there is strong evidence to the contrary. First, Cheka repression was not comprehensive, and there were places where opposition parties continued to operate openly (for example the Mensheviks among chemical workers, and the anarchists and left SRs among bakers). Second, in Moscow the Mensheviks on principle retained the maximum possible legality until 1922, and valued their identity as distinct from the non-partyists. Boris Dvinov, a Menshevik delegate to the soviet, wrote that the non-partyists on the soviet held the separate Menshevik group in high regard, but were not hidden Mensheviks: 'If they had been [Mensheviks] we would have been overjoyed. Unfortunately it wasn't like that.' The left SRs and anarchists also had their own, albeit tiny, fractions. When the Mensheviks' Moscow organization risked repression to organize a series of lectures in the spring of 1921, one of them was entitled 'Why mustn't one be non-party?'. The Menshevik trade union activist D. Chizhevskii defined non-partyism as 'a new

---

18 Iarov, op. cit., pp. 79–82 and 86–88; *Sotsialisticheskii Vestnik* 5, 1921, p. 15 and 17, 1921, p. 9.

obstruction' to rebuilding of the workers' movement, 'one more illusion' to be overcome.[19]

The Moscow soviet elections in April 1921 provided the first opportunity for political activity after Kronshtadt, and the non-partyists reaped the benefits. Although their fraction on the soviet comprised only about one-quarter of the delegates, these included the representatives of most of the big factories. The Bolsheviks' Moscow leadership considered this a disaster. Of the 2115 soviet delegates, 1543 were communists, 533 non-party, 28 members of other parties (6 left SRs, 4 SR maximalists, 12 Mensheviks, 2 anarchists, 2 anarcho-universalists, 2 anarcho-syndicalists and 1 right SR) and 11 unidentified. When the Moscow committee (MC) of the Bolshevik party met to review the results, Zelenskii, who took over as Moscow party secretary in April 1921, said that 'in some industries the party was so weak that it failed to attain a majority ... Some groups that are of no interest to us ... gave us the majority'. That was a reference to the *sluzhashchie*. Boguslavskii, then deputy chairman of the soviet, noted sarcastically that the *sluzhashchie* had all suddenly become 'arch-communists'.[20] This analysis accords with the figures: provided the Bolsheviks had retained some support among *sluzhashchie*, they could easily have won the majority they did (73 per cent of soviet delegates) while their support among industrial workers collapsed.

At the pre-election mass meetings, the Bolsheviks lost most heavily in the largest enterprises, the Cheka reported. Zelenskii observed that they suffered greater setbacks among male industrial workers, who tended to abstain, than among women. In Zamoskvorech'e, the Bolsheviks were

19 D.B. Pavlov, *Bol'shevistskaia diktatura protiv sotsialistov i anarkhistov 1917-seredina 1950-kh godov*, Moscow: Rosspen, 1999, pp. 59–60; B. Dvinov, *Ot legal'nosti k podpol'iu 1921–22*, Stanford: Hoover Institution, 1968, p. 47; *Sotsialisticheskii vestnik* 2, 1921, p. 15, and 17, 1921, pp. 9–10.
20 The voting system gave equal weight to workers, *sluzhashchie* and soldiers, who had one representative per 500 or part thereof above 100; some other groups, including pensioners and domestic workers, were entitled to one representative per 500 voters; and trades unions sent one delegate per 5000 members, giving unionized workers an extra 10 per cent weighting. There were 671,927 eligible voters, and 340,061 (50.5 per cent) voted. Census figures for late 1920 show that there were 205,427 workers and 233,375 *sluzhashchie* in Moscow, and along with garrison soldiers they made up the vast majority of the electoral college. The election setback so candidly acknowledged by Zelenskii is a 'black spot' of party history: two official histories of the soviet (*Moskovskii sovet rabochykh, krestianskikh i krasnoarmeiskikh deputatov 1917–27*, Moscow: izd. Moskovskogo soveta, 1927, and N.M. Aleshchenko, *Moskovskii sovet v 1917–1941 gg.*, Moscow: Nauka, 1976), and one of the Moscow party (Z.P. Korshunova et al. (eds), *Ocherki istorii Moskovskoi organizatsii KPSS, kn. II, noiabr' 1917–1945*, Moscow: Moskovskii rabochii, 1983) make no mention of it. TsGAMO, 66/12/814/82; TsAOPIM, 3/2/23/51–53; Aleshchenko, op. cit., pp. 248–49; Chase, op. cit., p. 311.

Cell and district party activists. Top: members of the Moscow institute of prosthetics cell in front of a banner hailing "the international Red army" (1922), and, above, activists in the Rogozhsko-Simonovskii district (1920).

defeated in all the big factories, where there was sympathy for other parties, the Cheka reported; in the small factories there was an 'inclination to non-partyism'; 'our majority consists of delegates from small enterprises and associations'. At the Sytin print works, both Bolsheviks and Mensheviks, for whom this was reputedly a stronghold, were beaten by non-partyists 'whose motto was, we are tired of these parties and their constant bickering; the workers must take power themselves', and who advocated 'workerization' of soviets and trade union control of industry. In Krasnopresnia, the communists won 83 per cent of Moscow soviet mandates and 67 per cent for the local soviets, but large workforces turned against them. The Cheka reported that the elections were 'ruined twice' at Gustav List engineering works, at the Il'in motor works three anarchists were elected, and at the Presnenskii tram depot 'the communist list was rejected and three non-party loudmouths elected'. The Cheka reported from Bauman that 42 per cent of metalworkers', 71 per cent of leatherworkers' and 66 per cent of food workers' delegates were non-party; only textile workers and the military garrison produced Bolshevik majorities. Chemical workers who had previously supported the Mensheviks voted 50 per cent communist. In Rogozhsko-Simonovskii, the Bolsheviks won an absolute majority, but not among the biggest concentrations of workers, including the Kursk railway repair depot, long a left SR stronghold, the Dinamo works, the Guzhon steel works and the AMO car factory.[21] The non-partyists' level of organization varied widely. The group at AMO held meetings and issued leaflets; in February 1921, it convinced a mass meeting at the factory to reject a list of candidates for the soviet proposed by Dorofeev, then Bolshevik district organizer, and to hold a secret ballot. Four non-partyists were elected, against a Bolshevik list, by 277 votes to 136: Davydov and Nastas'ian, who had been briefly arrested in the aftermath of Kronshtadt (see Chapter 3), and Chukhanov and Kireev. Elsewhere, non-partyism was spontaneous. From Zamoskvorech'e the Cheka reported a rush to find any non-communist prepared to join the soviet: small enterprises that took no part in previous elections banded together to organize hustings, and at 'practically every elective gathering' the restriction of candidates to those registered 24 hours beforehand with the district electoral commission was ignored.[22]

Clearly the non-partyists received some votes that might otherwise have gone to the opposition parties. This was effectively the Bolshevik leadership's doing, as it had rejected arguments for a free election. On 11 April the DC Vardin wrote to the Bolshevik CC, arguing that it was 'expedient' to permit opposition parties who had not taken up arms against soviet power to stand candidates and publish newspapers. 'I do not

21 Dvinov, *Ot legal'nosti*, p. 42; TsAOPIM, 3/2/48/15ob-18; TsAOPIM, 432/1/7/27; *Sotsialisticheskii vestnik* 9, 1921, p. 5.
22 TsGAMO, 186/1/598/3ob and 10; TsAGM, 415/16/318/9.

understand what danger we would face from [the Menshevik journal] *Sotsialisticheskii Vestnik*, if it was published in Moscow and not in Berlin', he wrote. The CC secretariat, on Lenin's recommendation, rejected Vardin's proposal. On the MC, David Riazanov opposed arresting Mensheviks during the elections: 'this just gave them a martyr's halo'. Riazanov said the arrests were part of an approach that insulted voters' intelligence: 'Of course we need to put people in prison, but we don't need excessive brutality, heartlessness and stupidity.' He also complained about the 'unacceptable tactic' employed by some Bolshevik workplace cells, of holding up wages payments for long periods and handing several months' pay to workers just before the poll.[23]

But none of this indicates that the non-partyists, or their voters, were mainly would-be Mensheviks and SRs. On the contrary, the election results seem to have reflected a striving for a socialism made by workers that eschewed party divisions. Zelenskii told the MC that, while there had been some limited electoral freedoms,

> [T]he overwhelming majority of the Mensheviks were sitting in Butyrka [prison]. There simply was no anarchist press. In comparison with other parties, we had much better conditions. But then we witnessed a high level of activity by the masses and *a striving to be in power themselves*. [My emphasis, SP.] ... The workers do not trust the Mensheviks and SRs, but they have stopped voting for communists.

Boguslavskii reported:

> There were calls for non-party soviets. ... The worn-out workers did not consider that slogan counter-revolutionary. They didn't vote for popular communists, loyal communists or even their favourite communists. They voted for non-party people 'on a trial basis'. ... Along with the decline of our influence, faith in the other parties has been completely exhausted.

Several MC members blamed the defeat partly on the parlous state of the factory cells. Lozovskii complained about cell members who 'think that they are God's representatives on earth' and never listen to workers. Tul'iakov said that many communist cells (*komiacheiki*) had 'turned into "*komishcheiki*" and lost their authority'. The evocative slang term *komishcheiki* adds the prefix *kom-* (i.e. communist) to *ishcheika*, a sniffer dog used by police forces.[24] So deeply did the Moscow party feel its isolation that it collectively gave up convening non-party conferences. Three months after the election,

23 Pavlov, *Bol'shevistskaia diktatura*, pp. 195–97; TsAOPIM 3/2/23/52.
24 TsAOPIM, 3/2/23/51–53.

on 21 July, P.S. Zaslavskii told the MC bureau that such conferences were needed, to explain NEP to workers 'tortured with rumours' about it – but faced a storm of opposition led by the MC official Isaak Minkov, who argued that the party membership was itself too confused about NEP to explain it to non-party workers.[25]

The party leadership was not seriously deterred by this disorientation of middle- and lower-level Bolsheviks. It had decided not to share political power with other workers, and to divide non-party activists into those who would help implement Bolshevik-inspired policies, and those who would be frozen out of the soviet system. Only non-party representatives that supported the party (?!) could be tolerated in soviet executive bodies, the MC decided. Its bureau ordered a ban on non-partyist fractional activity on the soviet.[26] This clampdown on political activity was combined with a campaign to involve non-party activists in 'soviet work' as doers, not deciders: 300 'honest non-party workers' were invited to apply for administrative jobs, mainly in the fields of production and welfare. This approach was a matter of national party policy: the CC had published instructions to 'feel out the most valuable non-party people' to do soviet work, and to avoid non-party assemblies being 'used for counter-revolutionary SR-Menshevik ends'.[27]

The newly elected Moscow soviet convened for the first time on 13 May. Non-partyist delegates tried to turn the disillusionment with Bolshevism expressed at the polls into a constructive opposition in the soviet's executive bodies, but ran into a brick wall. The non-partyist fraction met before the plenary session. Dvinov described how this gathering greeted former Mensheviks (perceived as having abandoned their party in the face of adversity) with disdain, and former Bolsheviks (who had eschewed the easy option) with applause. No *current* member of any party was admitted. The non-partyists elected as their spokesman the metalworker Sergei Mikhailov, the Bogatyr factory committee chairman, who had 'never' been in a party.[28] The soviet met in the Bolshoi theatre where 2000 non-party people were present, the soviet delegates being supported by observers from district soviets and factory committees.[29] Once Kamenev, as chairman, had opened the meeting, the non-partyists supported challenges by the tiny Menshevik

25 Zaslavskii related the episode in an alarmed letter to the CC secretary, Viacheslav Molotov. Zaslavskii, a party member from 1905, was then secretary of the Gorodskoi district organization in central Moscow. A.V. Kvashonkin et al. (eds), *Bol'shevistskoe rukovodstvo. Perepiska. 1912–1927*, Moscow: Rosspen, 1996, pp. 207–8.
26 TsAOPIM, ibid.; TsGAMO, 3/2/28/38, 46.
27 *Pravda*, 7 May 1921; TsAOPIM, 3/2/23/51–53.
28 On Mikhailov, see Appendix 1. *Kommunisticheskii trud*, 13 May 1921; Dvinov, *Ot legal'nosti*, pp. 42–43.
29 TsGAMO, 66/12/814/4–5. See also B. Dvinov, *Moskovskii Sovet Rabochykh Deputatov, 1917–1922: vospominaniia*. New York: Inter-university project on the history of the Menshevik movement, 1961, p. 104.

fraction to Bolshevik attacks on democratic procedure. During a dispute about the authenticity of some delegates' mandates, Menshevik speakers said the mandate commission should review the 'general atmosphere of intimidation' in which the elections were held. When the Bolshevik majority started to shout them down, Mikhailov scorned the Bolsheviks for denouncing anyone they disagreed with, and said the mandate commission should consider the Mensheviks' allegations. He continued:

> We came here not to jabber and yell, but to work together fraternally. ... You don't have to try to silence everyone who tries to express his opinion. ... We should declare freedom of speech for all members of the soviet.

Next, the Mensheviks proposed an agenda item on the assault on political prisoners in Butyrka jail on 25–26 April. The Bolshevik majority voted for the matter to be investigated by the (all-Bolshevik) presidium. Kamenev allowed Bolshevik hecklers to shout down minority speakers. The non-partyist Ozerov – who described himself as 'an old activist, long a party member, now non-party' – declared his 'deepest contempt' for Kamenev's 'shameful behaviour'. The non-partyists, Mensheviks and left SRs also made common cause against the Bolsheviks' attempt to conduct soviet plenary sessions in the style of a public meeting. In contrast to procedures typical in 1917, when gatherings would discuss a report, elect a drafting commission to synthesize a resolution that the larger assembly would amend and finally approve, the Bolsheviks had Leonid Krasin give a lengthy report on the 'domestic and international situation' and propose pre-prepared declarations to the Russian and international proletariat. The first was passed unanimously. When the second was put, a non-party speaker said he had 'absolutely no objection' to the declaration by the communists, for whom he was 'filled with the greatest respect', but wanted to know 'how can you ask us to vote for this resolution when you, comrades, shut us up and don't allow us even to say who we are?' The left SR leader Isaak Shteinberg derided Krasin's 'pedantic, unnecessary, schoolroom report', and proposed, unsuccessfully, a more participatory procedure.[30]

The conflict between non-partyists and Bolsheviks came to a head over elections to the soviet executive. The two sides had agreed prior to the plenary session that the Bolshevik fraction would elect 20 non-party people to the executive, to work with the Bolshevik majority. The non-party fraction meeting had approved a list of 20 non-partyists by 339 votes to 20, but this was rejected by Bolshevik representatives who claimed it was full of 'artists and lawyers' rather than workers. This was hotly disputed on the non-party fraction's behalf by a building worker. After an almighty row, the Bolshevik majority threw out the non-party fraction's list and elected 17

---

30 On Shteinberg, see Appendix 1. TsGAMO, 66/12/814/40–44.

Bolshevik-approved non-party people instead. Kamenev made clear that the Bolsheviks would no more accept non-partyism as a soviet tendency than Menshevism or anarchism. He challenged Mikhailov's right to speak as the non-partyists' representative, on the grounds that non-party people could not take collective political positions; 'they are brought together exactly by the fact that they do not have a worked-out programme and do not answer for each other'.

There were further clashes about democratic procedure at the second and third plenary sessions, on 31 May and 20 June, respectively. At the second session, the non-partyist Bretan[31] joined Shteinberg and the recently expelled Bolshevik Paniushkin to demand that delegates be given immunity from arrest unless it was sanctioned by a plenary session of the soviet. This was watered down by the Bolshevik majority, to allow for the arrest of delegates provided the soviet presidium was notified, and sought post-facto approval from a plenary session. Immediately afterwards, Paniushkin and the anarcho-syndicalist Pavlov were detained.[32] Bretan also proposed that delegates' 'freedom of speech' include immunity from administrative or judicial punishment 'on account of anything they said at soviet sessions or workers' meetings', and the right of 'any number of delegates' to meet and discuss their work as they chose. That was for the non-partyists, he explained:

> They are abused for being disorganized, but at the same time not permitted to integrate themselves, to set up some sort of apparatus, or, perhaps, a party (laughter), so that we can disassociate ourselves from SRs or Mensheviks in disguise – and from communists in disguise, of which there are plenty.

The non-partyists' demands for wider soviet democracy struck a chord not only with the Mensheviks and left SRs, but also with dissidents now quitting the Bolshevik party. (The latter are discussed more fully in Chapter 5.) During the election campaign, a group of 'active revolutionary workers of Moscow' issued a leaflet[33] calling on voters not to support the Menshevik, SR, anarchist or 'bankrupt communist plutocrats' (i.e. Bolshevik) parties, and to elect only 'genuinely revolutionary workers, who are not in any of these parties, who have not dirtied themselves by betraying the workers' cause and have not forgotten October's great legacy'. The reference to October, and the scorn evinced in the text for the constituent assembly of 1918, was clearly Bolshevik in origin – although the group denounced the

---

31 The only subsequent information on Bretan was a report in the Mensheviks' newspaper of January 1922, stating that he was imprisoned in a detention camp in Arkhangel'sk and that the soviet executive had failed to question his arrest. *Sotsialisticheskii vestnik* 1, 1922, p. 14.
32 TsGAMO, 66/12/815/42–50; RGASPI, 564/1/13/3.
33 TsAOPIM, 3/4/49/50; *Pravda*, 17 April 1921.

Bolsheviks as 'the petty-bourgeois face of state capitalism'. But the voting advice was distinctly workerist. This group, or another close to it, issued proclamations at several factories, signed 'Moscow workers', and calling for a vote for 'honest worker-communists, who have seen the whole outrage and left the party'.[34] They specifically warned workers against voting for *any* Bolshevik party members, however honest, since once on the soviet they would be compelled to follow the CC line.

An appeal was addressed to the non-partyist group on the soviet by the best organized group of ex-Bolshevik dissidents, Paniushkin's Workers and Peasants Socialist Party (Rabochaia-krestianskaia sotsialisticheskaia partiia, RKSP). The group's declared aims were to combat the ideological and organizational degeneration of Bolshevism 'under the sway of elements alien to the workers' and to establish genuine rule by soviets. Its appeal to soviet delegates[35] decried the transformation of the soviet from a body that 'transmits and expresses the proletariat's will' to 'a screen for, a blind weapon of, the party of nanny-communists'.[36] It argued that during the election campaign everything the proletariat had fought for was cynically 'trampled on by these nannies'. It was no wonder that there were so few genuine workers' representatives in the soviet, which had degenerated into 'executive-committee-ism' (*ispolkovshchina*) and needed to be resurrected in its 1917 form. The appeal proposed that the chairman of the soviet and of the executive be different individuals, to ensure a division between decision-making and executive functions and prevent behind-the-scenes interference. It also demanded political rights for pro-soviet, anti-Bolshevik parties that 'have not betrayed the working class' – which, judging by Paniushkin's speech quoted above, meant the left SRs, left Mensheviks, anarchists, non-partyists, and ex-Bolsheviks like himself. The appeal called for the liberation of imprisoned members of those parties and extensive limitations on the death penalty. The RKSP also carried its campaign for reform of the soviets into workplaces. At a mass meeting of *sluzhashchie* at the housing authority, Moskomgosor, RKSP members successfully moved a resolution denouncing Kamenev's 'shameful behaviour' towards the non-partyists.[37]

34 TsGAMO, 66/22/64/67.
35 TsAOPIM, 3/2/18/ 2–3.
36 The phrase '*opekuny-kommunisty*' is used. An *opekun* is a guardian appointed to safeguard the interests of minors or incompetents; the sense here was that the communist 'tops' treated workers as incapable children. This was a common theme for oppositionists. For example Efim Ignatov called on party leaders at the tenth congress to 'cut out the petty nannying [otbrosit' melochnuiu opeku]'. *Desiatyi s"ezd*, p. 238. The Tatar communist S.G. Said-Galiev (not to be confused with his more well-known comrade Mirsaid Sultan-Galiev) wrote to Lenin protesting at Russian communists playing 'pedagogues and nursemaids' ('pedagogov i nianek') to Tatar workers. V.I. Lenin, *Polnoe sobranie sochinenii (izd. 5-ogo)*, Moscow: Gospolitizdat, 1958–65, vol. 36, p. 661.
37 TsAOPIM, 3/2/48/36ob.

Such protests fell on deaf ears. By the end of 1921 the soviet was hardly even pretending to be a forum for participatory decision-making. Political decisions were taken by party bodies and the soviet was being turned into a supervisory body for municipal administration. Even many party delegates stopped showing up to the plenary sessions. 'The Moscow soviet died of boredom,' wrote Dvinov. 'Politics was driven off the agenda, and so-called "business-like issues" were discussed, most of which were neither interesting nor comprehensible.'[38] A Cheka agent in Krasnopresnia reported rumours that the soviets would be wound up entirely and a president elected for the republic. And indeed the ninth congress of soviets in December 1921 decided that soviet elections would henceforth be held only annually. The left SRs argued that this would more firmly entrench the 'ruling bureaucratic caste'. The Bolshevik MC had a more practical problem: it warned the party's national leadership that in Moscow elections were unpostponable, because a 'significant proportion' of delegates had quit, and 200 of the 1543-strong Bolshevik fraction had been excluded during the 1921 purge. A new poll was held in January 1922. Few seats were contested; the number of non-party delegates was cut by more than half, to 251, plus three Mensheviks and one left SR.[39]

While the non-partyists were worn down on the soviet, the opposition socialist parties faced now relentless pursuit by the Cheka. By the end of 1921 they could make virtually no impact on working-class political life. Time and again, workers who had elected or otherwise supported members of non-Bolshevik parties had to choose between taking strike action to defend them, and courting instant dismissal, or lying low. On the Riazan'-Ural railway, the SR Mikhailov was arrested along with other activists in early May; workers who struck briefly to demand their release were sacked en masse and selectively rehired. Leaflets protesting about these arrests were distributed at the Gustav List factory, where a strike was in progress over rations, but attempts to organize solidarity strikes there, and at Bromlei, failed. Menshevik activists at the 1886 power station advised workers to protest against the arrests *without* striking, to avoid mass dismissals.[40] The Mensheviks' Moscow organization ground to a halt due to constant arrests; its last significant action was a hunger strike in January 1922 by 44 of its members imprisoned at Butyrka.[41] The left SRs' Moscow organization, into which the SR maximalist group had merged, had only a mite more legality. Shteinberg and Chizhikov continued to address factory meetings. But by late 1921, 65 of its members were in prison, of whom 42 staged a hunger

38 Dvinov, *Moskovskii Sovet*, p. 107.
39 Dvinov, ibid.; TsAOPIM, 3/2/48/244; 3/3/5/1; RGASPI, 564/1/13/31; *Sotsialisticheskii vestnik*, 1922, no.7, p. 8.
40 TsAOPIM, 3/2/48/27–27ob.
41 Dvinov, *Ot legal'nosti*, especially pp. 67–97; TsAOPIM, 3/3/33/15; 3/3/34/7; Pavlov, *Bol'shevistskaia diktatura*, pp. 64–72.

strike in March 1922.⁴² The anarchist groups in the city were hit hard by arrests, too, such as that of Pavlov (see Chapter 3). Even 'soviet anarchists' who had worked in soviet institutions during the civil war were not spared: in November 1921 the Cheka arrested members of the anarcho-universalist group led by Aleksandr Shapiro and German Askarov, while the anarcho-communist group led by Appolon Karelin managed to persist with legal activity until late 1922.⁴³

Non-partyist politics

In the Introduction, attention was drawn to the peculiar form of working-class formation in early Soviet Russia: it proceeded in relation to a state that claimed to express working-class interests. The working class had to articulate its interests in the face of that state. The experience of the non-partyists in 1921 was a microcosm through which this broader problem was reflected. They tried to articulate workers' strivings for a more democratic politics, which meant confronting the Bolsheviks, while at the same time working with them to rebuild the economy. They tried to be both for and against their statist alter ego simultaneously. This led them into compromises that the Mensheviks regarded as unacceptable, but in the end they were defeated anyway, due to the intolerance of the 'workers' state' for working-class politics. The non-partyist Bretan told the soviet that it should 'unite non-party people and communists, so that all the labouring people shall wield power, and all those who wield power shall labour'.⁴⁴ The formulation, with its reference to 'the labouring people' (*trudiashchikhsiia*) echoed narodnism. But the aspiration to a common wielding of power was one with which both Marx and Chernyshevskii could have agreed. The Bolsheviks could not, though.

Non-partyist/Bolshevik dynamics at workplace level are reflected in the records of the AMO car factory, where a strong non-party group controlled

---

42 RGASPI, 17/84/296/10–11; 17/84/454/39–40; 564/1/13/6, 16–17, 22; TsGAMO, 186/1/598/37; TsAOPIM, 3/2/48/19; D. Pavlov (ed.), *Soiuz Eserov-Maksimalistov. Dokumenty, publitsistika. 1906–1924 gg.*, Moscow: Rosspen, 2002, pp. 342–62; *Kreml' za reshetkoi (podpol'naia Rossiia)*, Berlin: izd. 'Skify', 1922, pp. 199–204.

43 TsAOPIM, 3/2/48/36ob, 87; 3/3/34/214ob; Pavlov, *Bol'shevistskaia diktatura*, p. 67. Askarov's anarcho-universalist group and Karelin's All-Russian Federation of Anarchist-Communists were both described as 'soviet anarchist', since they had collaborated closely with the Bolsheviks during the civil war. Both men had served on the VSNKh, and Askarov on the Moscow soviet. Karelin's group survived until his death in 1926, although most active members had been arrested and exiled. Shapiro was a member of the anarcho-syndicalist group Golos Truda; in 1920, he had worked at the foreign affairs commissariat, under Chicherin, where he read and translated dispatches.

44 TsGAMO, 66/12/815/46.

108 The NEP and non-partyism

the workers' organizations for most of 1921.[45] AMO was then being revived as the centre of Russian car production. Management positions were shared between party cell leaders who returned from the front, such as Semen Smirnov, Nikolai Korobitsyn, Lidak and Gavrilin, and a group of American communist car workers led by A. Adams, some from Russian émigré families, who moved to, or back to, Russia, to help rebuild the car industry.[46] In March 1921, the Soviet government struck an agreement with the American group, under which the latter joined the AMO workforce with a view to introducing mass production techniques learned in the US.

The non-partyist group took shape in late 1920, and between February and April 1921 swept the board in elections to the factory committee, the Moscow soviet and the Rogozhsko-Simonovskii district soviet. Most of its members were older skilled workers. One of them, Ivan Volodin, had a younger brother in the Bolshevik party. Several of the non-partyists had been among workers who arrived at the factory in 1920 from Nizhnii Novgorod in search of work, and the non-partyists were sometimes described as the *nizhegorodtsy*. These included Nastas'ian and two others who shared his SR sympathies, Vasilii Davydov and Sivkov. The latter, one of his comrades recalled, argued for 'all land to the peasants, distributed equally'. Another important figure, Kuznetsov, had been an active SR party member before and during the First World War. The non-partyist group was an alliance between these SR sympathizers, Menshevik sympathizers such as Vasilii Tikhonov, and workerists including Chukhanov, Kireev and Afanasii Lysenkov.[47] Chukhanov, the AMO factory committee chairman from 1920

---

45 As well as trade union and cell records I have consulted interviews conducted by the 'history of factories' project, especially TsAGM, 415/16/20, 39, 47, 110, 148, 167, 171, 171a, 217, 262, 657.
46 Adams was appointed manager of AMO in May 1921; in March 1923, having got caught up in a conflict between the AMO cell and the auto industry trust, was moved to a desk job at the VSNKh; in June 1924, despite having abandoned the relatively stable life of an American car worker to participate in Soviet construction, was excluded from the party as a 'hanger-on'; the AMO cell supported his appeal against the decision. The group, comprising 165 workers who arrived in 1920 and 47 who arrived in 1922, was organized by L.K. Martens, a Russian socialist who lived in exile in the US and from 1919 acted as the Soviet republic's unofficial representative. A.P. Churiaev, N.V. Adfel'dt and D.A. Baevskii (eds), *Istoriia Moskovskogo avtozavoda im. I.A. Likhacheva*, Moscow, izd. 'Mysl'', 1966, p. 96; F. Sviatenko, *Zavod 'AMO'*, Moscow: Gos. izd., 1929, pp. 13–14. The AMO group was among an estimated 20,000 workers who emigrated or returned to Russia from other industrial countries in the 20 years after 1917, often motivated by sympathy for socialism. See S.V. Zhuravlev, *'Malenkie liudi' i 'bol'shaia istoriia'. Inostrantsy moskovskogo Elektrozavoda v sovetskom obshchestve 1920-kh – 1930-kh gg*, Moscow: Rosspen, 2000, especially pp. 29–35.
47 On Kuznetsov, Chukhanov and Lysenkov, see Appendix 1. Information on 13 members of the non-party group who held soviet or factory committee positions shows these political sympathies: 3, SR centrist; 2, left SR; 1, Menshevik; 4, non-partyist on principle; 3, no information.

until 1922, was an experienced trade union leader nicknamed '*valerianka*' (after the sedative, valerian) for his ability to calm angry mass meetings. He recalled how Davydov had approached him to join the non-partyist group and they had agreed to challenge the Bolsheviks for control of the factory committee. They celebrated the decision at 'a party where we drank and sang'. Chukhanov came from Petrograd and worked until 1918 at the Obukhov factory, where it is likely he knew of Glebov's United Workers party. Although later he described himself as having 'democratic, Menshevik opinions', his speeches to the February 1921 metalworkers' conference contained elements of workerism and of Bolshevism. He said there that the Russian economic crisis was due to the failure of western European workers to follow the Bolsheviks' revolutionary path, and expressed support for the fight inside the Bolshevik party against 'bourgeois elements'. In the latter category he included even the American car worker Adams, who 'came almost out of the ranks of the nobility'.

The group's mixture of narodnism and workerism is reflected in the minutes of an 'assembly of skilled workers' at the factory in April 1921, which called for free movement of labour as the precondition for improving productivity, and for 'healthy criticism' of the *glavki*. Lysenkov, recalling the group's motivation in 1932, used terms far removed from the standard statist discourse of that time: the workers had 'lived through those difficult times', and gone through 'an enormous emotional experience', in order 'the better to realise a free, independent life', a life 'independent from oppression and authority of any kind'.[48] Talking about a 'free' (*svobodnaia*) life in the 1930s was hardly unusual, but to describe it as 'independent' (*nezavismaia*) was; that jarred with Bolshevik ideology, which stressed the class character of any oppression and regarded anything 'independent' with some suspicion.

Once elected to the factory committee, the non-partyists took the same responsibilities for economic construction as party members: Chukhanov was responsible for labour discipline and Sivkov for food procurement trips.[49] But the AMO cell's actions were dictated by the party's ideologized refusal to co-operate with non-partyists, and it set out to dislodge them from the factory committee. The first attempt, at elections in August 1921, was unsuccessful, but the result was annulled by the Bolshevik-dominated metalworkers' regional committee and the cell won the second time around. More party cell members returned from the front, while a round of redundancies in November was used as an opportunity to sack some of the non-partyist activists. By January 1922 most of the non-partyists had gone from their elected positions; only Chukhanov hung on, as factory committee chairman, until September.[50]

---

48 TsAGM, 415/16/171a/2–3.
49 TsGAMO, 186/1/598/3ob; TsAGM, 415/16/110/9 and 415/16/167/59–60.
50 TsGAMO, 186/1/598/33, 40; TsAGM, 415/16/167/95–96; 415/16/262, 25–27; 415/16/590/98, 105.

The non-partyists' readiness to co-operate with the Bolsheviks on economic construction drew criticism from the Mensheviks. Their newspaper reported that at a Moscow municipal workers' conference in April 1921, non-partyists and Bolsheviks on a drafting commission had agreed simply to leave politics out of the main resolution. The Mensheviks' own delegate had won nearly half the votes for a political resolution, and narrowly escaped arrest. Another example that pained the Mensheviks was that of the Sytin print works. On the eve of the January 1922 soviet elections, the Bolsheviks, fearing defeat in a three-cornered contest with non-partyists and Mensheviks, twisted the non-partyists' arms to bloc with them. The non-partyist V. Fedotov – who had expressed principled opposition to the Mensheviks, reminding a mass meeting how they had supported repression of the workers' movement under Kerensky – agreed, under protest. The bloc defeated the Mensheviks by a narrow margin. But this political climb-down did not save Fedotov, or his non-partyist comrade Nikolai Amelin, from being sacked in March 1922 during a conflict over redundancies. This dispute began when the factory committee, fearing that the lay-offs would be used as an opportunity to get rid of workers the Bolshevik management did not like, demanded that it be consulted over selection procedures for redundancy. A 'stormy' mass meeting, a strike, the instant dismissal of all strikers and an effective 10-day lock-out followed in rapid succession. Both Mensheviks and non-partyists were among those not re-employed.[51]

Such events epitomized the non-partyists' dilemma. They wanted to co-operate in building the economy, but the democracy to which they aspired was incompatible with Bolshevik one-party rule. The Bolsheviks forced them to choose, and this broke the non-partyist movement. On the Moscow soviet, when the Bolsheviks moved acceptance of a report that whitewashed the beatings of political detainees in Butyrka, Bretan challenged it – but other non-party delegates failed to support him.[52] For Bretan, and for the Mensheviks, that was a compromise too far. For some who made it, a factor would surely have been the unwillingness to challenge the Bolsheviks displayed by most workers during the crisis of spring 1921. And as standards of living improved – to the point where, in many cases for the first time in seven or eight years, workers could go beyond a daily battle to keep themselves and their families alive – this unwillingness became more pronounced. Along with repression, it naturally drained energy and activism from workers' organizations. This was an important element of the social contract.

---

51 TsGAMO, 699/1/269/48, 49, 55, 72; TsAOPIM 3/3/33/67, 80; 3/3/34/60, 65, 67–68, 70, 73, 74; Dvinov, *Ot legal'nosti*, pp. 106–7. I thank Diane Koenker, who kindly shared some research notes with me. See also *Sotsialisticheskii Vestnik*, 1921 no. 7, p. 13, 1922 no. 4, p. 12; and 1922 no. 8, p. 11. The editors of *Sotsialisticheskii Vestnik* referred to Fedotov as 'Fedorov'.
52 TsGAMO, 66/12/816/31–48.

The economic recovery

The social contract was no cynical bribe. It was based on the recovery of the economy and, specifically, of manufacturing industry, in which both the party and workers had an interest. In the months after the tenth congress, the party made huge strides in restarting closed factories, grouping them into trusts, and starting the move from rationing to money wages.[53] The congress decision on replacing grain requisitioning with the tax in kind was implemented, and most restrictions on trade lifted, by the end of March 1921. From 28 March, the Moscow soviet sanctioned free buying and selling of agricultural produce in the region.[54] Most workers were still paid with rations, which continued to arrive late, but the easing of trade restrictions helped: workers could travel into the countryside to barter for foodstuffs, and the organization of collective procurement trips soon became a central concern. On 6–7 April, Sovnarkom abolished many restrictions on the movement of labour, scrapped limits on bonuses and piece-work payments, and provided for the establishment of workers' co-operatives. It also formalized the *naturpremiia* system, under which enterprises put part of their output into a special stockpile to be traded, thus sanctioning the widespread practice of bartering manufactured products for food and consumer goods.[55]

Industrial relations continued to revolve around supply. In mid May, as workers returned from their spring holidays, bread deliveries rations were delayed, and food supply officials temporarily cut rations by one-third.[56] The most severe problems were, once again, in the textile towns: 'hunger' was reported in Bogorodskoe and Orekhovo-Zuevo, where the food commissariat's offices were besieged one morning by a crowd of 1000 children.[57] In the city of Moscow, workers reacted with a wave of strikes. Party officials reckoned that in a 24-day period in May there were stoppages at 66 large enterprises: between 9 and 14 May, there was a sit-down strike at the Guzhon plant, one of Moscow's largest; workers at engineering factories in

---

53 E.H. Carr, *The Bolshevik Revolution 1917–1923*, London: Macmillan, 1978, vol. II, pp. 280–359; I.B. Orlov, 'Vosstanovlenie promyshlennosti', in Pavliuchenkov, S.A. et al. (eds), *Rossiia nepovskaia*, Moscow: Novyi khronograf, 2002, pp. 121–49, especially pp. 121–31.
54 *Kommunisticheskii trud*, 30 March 1921; M. Gorinov, 'Moskva v 20-kh godakh', *Otechestvennaia istoriia* 5, 1996: 3–17, here 5.
55 *Kommunisticheskii trud*, 9 April 1921; Carr, op. cit., vol. II, pp. 280–83 and 318–20; A.A. Matiugin, *Rabochii klass SSSR v gody vosstanovleniia narodnogo khozaistva, 1921–1925*, Moscow: izd. Akademii nauk SSSR, 1962, pp. 128–29; P. Ashin, 'Wage Policy in the Transition to NEP', *Russian Review* 47, 1988: 293–313, here 297–98.
56 Khalatov reported to the Moscow soviet that on 10 May the basic workers' bread ration had been cut from 1 funt to two-thirds of a funt. TsGAMO, 66/12/815/23–34.
57 TsAOPIM, 3/2/48/28, 62.

Krasnopresnia followed suit, and Cheka agents reported 'dissent, culminating in strikes and occupations' in Bauman.[58]

There was a dramatic increase in the number of procurement trips. It seemed as though workers had taken the Sovnarkom decrees on free trade as a signal to get on the first available train to the countryside to find supplies. Workers from the Narofominsk textile mills, for example, upped and travelled 'to Kiev, and further', without waiting for permission, Cheka agents reported. Similar groups from the Moscow factories travelled to Kharkov and Belgorod, but were detained there by local authorities and prevented from going further. Speakers at the tenth party conference in May reported wholesale theft from the factories of consumer goods that could be traded for food. One Cheka agent described the procurement trips as factory workers' 'main source of hope'. Another claimed that 'dispiriting impressions' of bribery and corruption on the railways were the main cause of dissatisfaction. A third reported a horrifying example of 'how not to deal with supply': an expedition by 13,000 people in nine trains from Orekhovo-Zuevo district near Moscow to Tashkent in Uzbekistan, which failed to reach its destination and consumed most of the foodstuffs acquired on the return trip. Some participants died or fell seriously ill.[59] Disputes raged over how to organize procurement trips: in June, this became the *principal* cause of industrial disputes in Rogozhsko-Simonvskii district. Proposals worked out at the cable factory, to standardize distances, provide each participant with a standard amount of flour and compensate those whose trips were unsuccessful, became 'a sort of platform' that was taken up in nearby workplaces. Procurement trips, an exceptionally irrational form of exchange, began to fade out in 1922, when the food supply situation stabilized and monetary exchange replaced barter.

While the lifting of trade restrictions eased supply problems, the scrapping of some price controls produced a nasty shock. An increase in railway fares in June produced 'a stunning effect', Cheka agents reported, placing 'an almost insurmountable barrier' to procurement trips and triggering a three-to four-fold increase in prices on the free markets in Moscow. Workers were also uneasy about the imposition of rent and charges for public services. District party organizations reported fear among workers – into which they perhaps wrote their own concerns – of a return of elements of the old regime, expressed in questions such as 'will the state be able to maintain the workers', and 'will soviet power be able to block the revival of capitalism?'[60]

---

58 TsAOPIM, 3/2/9/34; 3/2/48/25–27, 33–33ob, 60, 76, 156, 160, 244; 63/1/44/40; TsGAMO, 186/1/585/39ob.
59 TsGAMO, 66/22/64/71; TsAOPIM, 3/2/48/18, 40, 46, 49, 128; RGASPI, 46/1/2/152, 186–87.
60 MGSPS, *Otchet o deiatel'nosti MGSPS, gubotdelov i uprofbiuro (mai-avgust 1921)*, Moscow: MGSPS, 1921, p. 5; TsAOPIM, 3/2/48/60, 76; RGASPI, 17/65/228/27, 38.

The reorganization of industry in Moscow was formally launched by the regional conference of soviets in June 1921. Workers' fears that NEP would lead to a return of the pre-revolutionary factory owners proved largely unfounded: the vast majority of enterprises remained in state hands. Most industrial enterprises were grouped into state-owned trusts.[61] To start with, a little more than two-thirds of these trusts' workers continued to receive wages guaranteed by the state, still mostly in the form of rations. The other one-third worked in enterprises subject to cost accounting, and this proportion rose gradually throughout 1922. Sovnarkom decrees provided for factories to be leased, mainly to foreign owners, and for enterprises with fewer than 20 employees to be privately owned. But these forms of ownership played no significant role in Moscow: at their height, in 1922, leased enterprises employed about one-twentieth of the city's workers and privately owned enterprises one-thirtieth.[62] The only proposed lease of a Moscow factory to provoke significant protests, that of the auto components plant in Zamoskvorech'e, was abandoned.[63]

Industrial recovery now took its first, timid steps; it would be another three years before the factories would approach pre-war production levels. For most Moscow factories, NEP meant in the first instance a revival of raw material supplies, and consequently of production. Straight away, heavy industry found itself lagging behind consumer goods industries; trusts dumped manufactured goods on the market as they struggled with market forces.[64] But by the end of 1921, most factories had reopened, albeit with output at low levels. In the textile industry, output multiplied five times over between the first half of 1921 and the second half. Workers began to return from the countryside, their ranks swelled by refugees from the famine-stricken Volga region, and the industrial workforce was estimated to have risen from 200,000 to 240,000 over the course of the year.[65] The wages system changed, too. Most workers continued to receive state supply

---

61 MK RKP(b), *K otchetu Moskovskoi gubernskoi konferentsii RKP (25–28 iiunia 1921) i III s"ezde sovetov*, Moscow: Gos. izdatel'stvo, 1921, pp. 10–11; *Moskovskaia gubernskaia konferentsiia profsoiuzov, 14–15 sent. 1921*, Moscow: MGSPS, 1921, p. 6; Aleshchenko, op. cit., p. 263; Matiugin, op. cit., pp. 101–6.

62 By September 1922, 640 enterprises with an aggregate workforce of 11,000 were leased out. In Moscow region in the financial year 1923/24, state industry accounted for 92.6 per cent of the workforce employed and 91.1 per cent of output; the remainder was shared by co-operatives, privately owned enterprises and leased enterprises. Aleshchenko, op. cit., pp. 263–65; Gorinov, op. cit., p. 5; Statisticheskii otdel Moskovskogo soveta, *Statisticheskii atlas gor. Moskvy i Moskovskoi gub. Vyp. 3. Promyshlennost' i torgovlia*, Moscow, 1925, p. 29.

63 *Otchet sed'moi Moskovskoi gubpartkonferentsii RKP 29–31 Oktiabria 1921 g.*, Moscow, 1921, pp. 14 and 16–17; TsAOPIM, 3/2/48/128; TsGAMO, 186/1/598/131–33; *Rabochaia Moskva*, 11 May 1922.

64 Carr, op. cit., vol. 2, pp. 309–15.

65 M.N. Korovina and T.F. Kogan, 'Bor'ba za uluchshenie blagosostoianiia rabochego klassa (1921–25gg.)', *Voprosy istorii* 9, 1961: 42–55.

directly. But there were also experiments with collective supply (i.e. the delivery of food supplies and money to a factory, the amounts linked to total output, and the director empowered to distribute them) and *naturpremiia* system, as well as limited privatization. The common theme in wages policy was material reward for higher productivity, and limits on bonuses and piece-work payments were abolished. Wages remained extremely low throughout 1921, reaching only about half their 1913 level by the end of the year. But qualitative improvements in living standards were in sight – and this was a factor, no less significant than the emasculation of the soviet, in determining how relations between the Bolsheviks and the workers would unfold.

5 Renegades, oppositionists, suicides and administrators

The party in 1921

Life in the Bolshevik ranks changed radically in the first year of the New Economic Policy (NEP). A significant minority of the civil war communists found themselves alienated from the party, often because they believed that it was deserting the working class and that the struggle against bureaucratism was being lost. Their attempts to articulate opposition thinking, whether inside or outside the party, met with repression. Others, who in 1920 had built up exaggerated hopes of rapid change, became disillusioned. But for most civil war communists, the economic recovery meant moving into administrative jobs in the Soviet state machine, for which they were often unprepared. By the end of 1921, such workers-turned-administrators, together with soldiers-turned-administrators and administrators-turned-Bolsheviks, formed a majority in the party. The new party elite began to build support in this milieu. As the party further consolidated its role in the state, its base among workers weakened. Its factory-based membership dwindled to a minority, and those who worked 'at the bench', rather than in management, to a minority of this minority. The discussions on alternative forms of political power and state organization that had raged in 1920 were sidelined. According to the predominant ideology, the root of the party's problems was the influence of petty bourgeois elements. This was to be tackled by training working-class members in the art of government and increasing the proportion of members of working-class origin. This thinking inspired the membership purge of late 1921. But its implementation manifested the lack of unanimity about the party's relationship with the state: some tried to use its anti-bureaucratic rhetoric as a weapon against apparatus privilege, while others saw it as an opportunity to silence dissent.

With the introduction of NEP, a cloud of political uncertainty settled over the party. Osinskii had toured Russia's central provinces in April-May 1921 and, on his return, reported to the Central Committee (CC) of the Bolshevik party that NEP had 'not been understood' by party members. On his proposal, a special party conference was called on 26–28 May.[1] The conference minutes, which were never published, reveal deep differences. Lenin's enthusiastic support for the free trade of surplus agricultural produce was challenged by food supply officials, who feared the consequences of letting market forces rip; these officials were in turn accused of carrying on grain requisitioning as if the decision to abolish it had never been taken; representatives of rural party organizations interpreted Lenin's call for local initiative as a signal to subordinate the food supply apparatus to themselves. City-based communists, including Muscovites, expressed fears that industry would be abandoned, and that the working class would lose out, if undue compromises were made with the peasantry. Larin, the journalist Lev Sosnovskii[2] and others warned that Lenin's proposed drive to revive small industry could, unless properly balanced, damage large-scale industry, and, by extension, the working class and the workers' state. The conference also heard reminders of the level of sheer incomprehension of NEP in the party ranks.[3] Confusion prevailed in the Moscow party organization, too. The changes in wages payment systems, the lease of factories to former owners and the failure thus far of the plan to revive large-scale industry had 'brought about chaos [in the party], which is aggravated by the [Volga provinces] famine', Zaslavskii reported to Molotov. 'Party members from the ranks, from the middle level and very often responsible officials are adopting an absolutely unacceptable tone in discussing the recent decrees [implementing NEP]'; members' meetings were exhibiting 'inopportune and oppositional features'; and, worse, there was no clear information from the central leadership.[4]

The alienation of the civil war communists

A steady stream of resignations, by valuable worker members among others, gathered pace in early 1921. In general, party membership was falling: the Moscow regional organization shrank from 52,254 in July 1920, to 50,836 in June 1921; 40,767 in September 1921, and 34,436 in February 1922 after the national re-registration.[5] Of those who resigned, rather than being excluded, most cited 'personal reasons', or gave no explanation. But a

---

1 A.V. Kvashonkin et al. (eds), *Bol'shevistskoe rukovodstvo. Perepiska. 1912–1927*, Moscow: Rosspen, 1996, pp. 204–5; S.V. Tsakunov, *V labirinte doktriny: iz opyta razrabotki ekonomicheskogo kursa strany v 1920-e gody*, Moscow: Rossiia molodaia, 1994, pp. 52–53.
2 Sosnovskii (1886–1937) joined the Social Democrats in 1905 and thereafter worked as a professional revolutionary and journalist on Bolshevik publications; 1918–24 wrote for *Pravda* and founded and edited *Bednota*; 1920 supported Trotsky in the trade union debate; participated in the oppositions of 1923 and 1927.
3 Lenin, *Polnoe sobranie sochinenii*, Moscow: Gospolitizdat, 1958–65, vol. 43, pp. 205–45; RGASPI 46/1/2, especially 61–81, 113–15, 118, 127–29, 140–45, 156–58, 160–62, 164–67, 180–86, 191–95.
4 Kvashonkin et al. (eds.), op. cit., pp. 207–8. Zaslavskii reported in this same letter that the MC had given up organizing non-party assemblies. See Chapter 4, pp. 101–2.
5 For membership statistics, see Appendix 4, p. 259.

minority quit for political reasons. CC secretary Molotov attributed these 'individual or group resignations' to 'vacillation' in the face of the policy turn made at the tenth congress.[6] But the process was deeper-going than that. The departures had begun before the congress, resulting in part from the unease over hierarchy and privilege. The Goznak cell accepted the resignation of six active members between November 1920 and March 1921. The AMO car factory cell had suffered a substantial outflow at the same time (see Chapter 1, pp. 40–41). Ignatov told the tenth congress that the departure of worker members 'en masse' proved that the party 'is ceasing to be linked' with the working class of which it was supposed to be the vanguard.[7] In April 1921 the resignations were related to rank-and-file concerns over 'bureaucratism' in a letter to Lenin from G. Lebedev, a party official in Gorodskoi district, who had signed the Ignatov manifesto in February 1921 but relinquished opposition activity after the congress.[8] Lebedev warned that 'not only individual workers, but whole worker cells, are leaving', and gave Lenin the example of the communist group at the print shop of Registupr, a soviet administrative department, whose collective resignation Lebedev had been sent to forestall.[9] He explained the position of the group's leader, Ermolaev, a compositor and a 'thoughtful, independently minded' communist, recently promoted to print shop manager. Ermolaev's reasons for quitting were 'the party's alienation from the proletarian masses', 'the exploitation of the ranks, and the proletariat as a whole, by the party tops', and the prevalence of 'nepotism, influence-peddling and deal-doing, but no brotherhood or equality'.[10] Ermolaev had felt much closer to the party when he joined, during the 'party week' in October 1919, than in April 1921. In those 18 months, the party had consistently moved further from the working class; it had 'long since ceased to be a worker's party' and, as a worker, Ermolaev did not want to give it credit as such by remaining in

---

6 RGASPI, 17/65/223/46, quoted by Tsakunov, op. cit., p. 52; *Spravochnik partiinogo rabotnika* 2, pp. 78–79, cited by T.H. Rigby, *Communist Party Membership in the USSR 1917–1967*, Princeton: Princeton University Press, 1968, p. 105; A. E. Gorsuch, *Youth in Revolutionary Russia: Enthusiasts, Bohemians, Delinquents*, Bloomington: Indiana University Press, 2000, pp. 81–88.
7 TsAGM, 415/16/590/50; TsAOPIM, 1099/1/2/38, 42; 1099/1/3/5, 7ob, 8, 41, 43; *Desiatyi s"ezd RKP(b): stenograficheskii otchet*, Moscow: Gos. izd. polit. literatury, 1963, pp. 236–38.
8 *Kommunisticheskii trud*, 16 February 1921; M.P. Mchedlov and A.M. Sovokin, *V.I. Lenin: biograficheskaia khronika, 1870–1924*, Moscow: izd. polit. literatury, 1985, vol. 10, p. 300.
9 RGASPI, 2/1/18135/1–3. The 11 communists in the Registupr print shop belonged to the 132-strong Registupr cell. I presume Registupr is an abbreviation of 'registration division' (*registratsionnoe upravlenie*).
10 The phrase used was '*kumovstvo, svatovstvo, no tol'ko ne bratstvo i ravenstvo*', literally 'godfather-ism, match-maker-ism, only no brotherhood or equality'. *Kumovstvo* and *svatovstvo* carry a sense of the fixing, deal-doing and family politicking that these roles entailed traditionally.

its ranks. Ermolaev had urged building 'the workers' own communist party', as distinct from the Bolsheviks. Lebedev told Lenin that these and other departees were staying in touch with each other, and confided his suspicion that 'there is being organized, right now, a parallel party'. This fear was justified.

The most successful attempt to build such a party was that of Paniushkin, who won support for the Workers and Peasants Socialist Party (Rabochaia-krestianskaia sotsialisticheskaia partiia – RKSP) among dissident communists in the Gorodskoi and Bauman districts.[11] The group's first manifesto decried the Bolshevik party's ideological and organizational corruption 'under the sway of elements alien to the workers', who had created an atmosphere of 'disasters, bacchanalia, hair-brained scheming, protectionism and sharp practices, and every imaginable type of *khlestakovshchina*'.[12] It was 'impossible to fight all this' by remaining inside the party. The introduction of NEP led Paniushkin to conclude that the party leadership had transferred the power won by workers in October 1917 'back to the bourgeoisie', and in March 1921, just before quitting the party, he denounced the Sovnarkom decrees on the tax in kind and freer trade as 'favour[ing] the capitalists, landowners and bourgeoisie'. But the RKSP was more than a knee-jerk reaction to NEP. In politics, it sought the restoration of 1917-style soviet democracy, as its appeal to the non-partyists on the soviet showed. In the economic sphere, it supported the 'production unions' that the Workers Opposition (WO) had advocated during the trade union discussion, and proposed that all administrative appointments be made through such unions, and that appointees be immune from veto by the Supreme Council of the Economy (Vysshii sovet narodnogo khoziaistva – VSNKh) or its affiliated bodies, and instantly recallable by the unions.[13] The RKSP gained support rapidly in its few weeks of active existence, between April and June 1921. It recruited 2–300 members and established a premises in the centre of Moscow, where it held members' meetings of about 80 people. It sent speakers to workplaces and organized larger assemblies with workers and soldiers, at which it sought to engage the Bolsheviks in discussion.[14] On 7 June the RKSP premises were raided. At least 18 people were arrested, and Paniushkin and others jailed or sent into administrative exile. Presumably since the targets were communists, albeit dissident ones, the Cheka felt compelled to justify its action on the grounds that the RKSP was 'trying' to bribe officials and 'preparing' to steal printing equipment. But at the Moscow committee (MC) of the

11 TsAOPIM, 3/2/48/43; 5/1/2572/52; 'O "Narodnoi sotsialisticheskoi rabochekrestianskoi partii"', leaflet archive, Library of Social and Political History in Moscow.
12 That is, fawning to bureaucratic superiors, from Gogol's character Khlestakov in *The Government Inspector*.
13 TsGAMO, 3/2/28/36ob; TsAOPIM, 3/2/18/2–3.

Bolshevik party, Zelenskii acknowledged that the aim was to 'put [Paniushkin's supporters] out of action'. Paniushkin was released on conditional bail in December 1921, met with Lenin, 'confessed his mistake', and was readmitted to the Bolshevik party.[15]

Another group of dissidents who broke with the party in 1921 were the 'revolutionary left communists', who condemned the Bolshevik leadership for 'returning to capital'. They urged a vote in the soviet elections for 'communists from the ranks, the trades unions, the workers' opposition and the left' rather than for those who have, 'under the influence of the "tops", abandoned and forgotten our interests'. This group complained that, for attempting to reform the Moscow party organization and challenge 'Kamenevite demagogy', its members had been 'driven underground'. It took up arguments being made by left communists internationally, denouncing the Comintern's 'united front' policy as damaging to the struggles of German and English workers.[16]

There is a distinction between these oppositionists, who left the party to pursue a political fight, and other communists who quit in disillusionment. For the Paniushkins and Ermolaevs of this world – as well as the oppositionists who remained inside the party – Marxism was a means of understanding the world and changing it, to be turned against the leaders of the party within which they had learned it. These dissidents accepted the need for the retreat implicit in NEP, but rejected the manner of its implementation and the form of political regime. For others, whose relationship to the party was founded more on emotions than on political considerations, and in particular on the adrenalin-fuelled optimism of the civil war, NEP was an unpalatable shock. For those who had seen 'war communism' as the highway to some sort of state socialism, NEP was the loss of much that they had fought for – whether or not they seriously envisaged any alternative to it. At AMO, the young communist Dvoretskii returned from Kronshtadt, where he was wounded

---

14 Pavliuchenkov has shown, from research in the Cheka archives, that Paniushkin held discussions with anti-government conspirators at the general staff academy in Moscow, who in turn had contact with a larger SR-inclined conspiracy, 'the insurgent army of the Don'. The conspirators had been attracted by Paniushkin's arguments, but he rejected as premature their proposal to form military cells of the RKSP. Pavliuchenkov, 'Ekonomicheskii liberalizm v predelakh politicheskogo monopolizma' in S.A. Pavliuchenkov et al., *Rossiia nepovskaia: issledovaniia*, Moscow: Novyi khronograf, 2002, pp. 15–57, pp. 23–24. See also TsAOPIM 3/2/48/36; *Documents of the 1923 Opposition*, London: New Park Publications, 1975, p. 19; Sol'ts, 'Partiia v bor'be s rabochei oppozitsii', *Bor'ba klassov* 5, 1935, p. 25; R. Sakwa, 'The Soviet State, Civil Society and Moscow Politics: Stability and Order in Early NEP 1921–24', in J. Cooper, M. Perrie and E.A. Rees (eds), *Soviet History, 1917–53*, Birmingham: Macmillan, 1995, pp. 42–77, here p. 47.
15 TsAOPIM, 3/2/18/4a; 3/2/48/23; *Sotsialisticheskii Vestnik* 14–15, 1921, p. 14.
16 RGASPI, 5/1/2572/73; 17/84/454/3; 17/84/455/8.

helping to suppress the rising, and resigned from the party straight away. 'I can't say exactly what he was dissatisfied with. I just saw that his mood had completely changed,' a comrade recalled. Another AMO memoir recounted how Vigant Zemliak, a Latvian communist who had participated in street fighting in 1917, quit the party in 1921. 'He came to the factory wearing his broken boots and cried: "what is it we were fighting for?"' Grislin, a 'good party man' who worked at the next bench, told him: 'We can't do everything at once. We need to bide our time.' Zemliak shouted back that leading cell members 'sat at home while my wife and I were out fighting' during the civil war. The honest Bolshevik, returning from the front and disillusioned by NEP, was very much a folk character of the time, and frequently appeared in literature. For example, Libedinskii's novel, *Kommissary*, features conversations that includes all the same elements as this one at AMO – poverty-stricken civil war heroes, party cell officials who stayed at home while others fought, and the doubts engendered by NEP. So the AMO memoirists, relating such incidents 10 years later, may have been influenced by things they had heard and read since. But the power of post-civil-war disillusion is reflected in other contemporaneous evidence.[17]

Disillusionment with NEP was eloquently expressed by some of Russia's foremost worker poets who left the party in 1921. Of the six worker poets elected to the proletkult central committee at its founding congress in September 1918, one (Fedor Kalinin) died in 1920 and four more – Mikhail Gerasimov and Il'ia Sadof'ev of Moscow, and Vladimir Kirillov and Aleksei Mashirov of Petrograd – quit the party in 1921.[18] Of the Moscow-based poets who, together with Gerasimov, formed the Kuznitsa group in 1920, Vasilii Aleksandrovskii (probably) and Sergei Obradovich (certainly) also quit the party in 1921, while Grigorii Sannikov and Vasilii Kazin remained within it.[19] Gerasimov's poetic outcry of 1921, 'Chernaia pena' ('Black foam'), has an anti-NEP word-play (pena/NEPa) in the title.[20] The poet contrasts a 'leaden-faced', shivering victim of hunger, languishing under a bridge, with the 'white lumps of sov-bourzh [i.e. soviet bourgeois, an NEP colloquialism] ladies' in the parterre of the theatre, 'piled up' in their sparkling silks. Infuriated by these ladies' finery, Gerasimov writes:

---

17 TsAGM, 415/16/170/7; 415/16/657/8; Iu. Libedinskii, *Nedelia: Kommissary: Povesti*, Moscow: Voennoe izd., 1968, pp. 200–203.
18 The eight-member CC comprised the five poets mentioned, plus the poet Karl Ozel-Prednek, the actor Vasilii Ignatov and the trade union official Vladimir Kossior. L. Mally, *Culture of the Future: the Proletkult Movement in Revolutionary Russia*, Berkeley: California University Press, 1990, pp. 41–50 and 96.
19 On the formation of Kuznitsa, see note 9 to Chapter 2, p. 48. For biographical sketches, see M.D. Steinberg, *Proletarian Imagination: Self, Modernity and the Sacred in Russia, 1910–1925*, Ithaca: Cornell University Press, 2002, 287–312.
20 *Kuznitsa* 9, 1922, pp. 6–8.

> Blue-collared and vulgar I cry
> With teeth chattering and my veins twisted tighter:
> 'Bind your carmine lips!'
> They, scumbag sores,
> Ooze out the past!

Gerasimov stood in a tradition, well established by male communists and workers in their denunciations of privilege, of demonizing the wives of communist officials. There are many examples. Vlasov's letter to Lenin, cited in Chapter 2, denounced party leaders' wives who 'ride to their dachas, sporting huge hats with bird-of-paradise feathers'. During the discussion on 'the tops and the ranks', a cell on the Moscow-Nizhny Novgorod railway, having urged that the party be 'purged of hangers-on masquerading under the communist flag', added angrily that 'while a rank-and-file communist self-sacrificingly gives up his life and watches his children dying of hunger, others [i.e. women] are not prepared to give up even their gold jewels'.[21] The privileged official's wife later secured a place in literature: for example in 1930 she appeared, as 'comrade Pashkin's lady wife', in Andrei Platonov's bleak parody of forced collectivization, *Kotlovan*.

The sexist manner of these complaints, and the male-dominated culture of the workers' movement that they reflected, does not mean they were never valid. Moreover, in the context of Gerasimov's outpourings, they expressed the social and political impotence that some communist civil war heroes felt as they came down from the high of the civil war. Certainly in 'Chernaia pena', symbols that during the civil war had signified the vitality of proletarian revolution are spoiled. 'The shining force is draining into the Moscow swamp.' The bright sun in the May air – which just a year before had for one of Gerasimov's comrades, Vasilii Kazin, been 'raising to the summit the fire burning in [our] shoulders'[22] – is 'waning'.

The subject of 'Budni' ('Weekdays'), written in June 1921 by Vasilii Aleksandrovskii,[23] is the gulf between apparatchiks and the rank-and-file communists. Morals are a 'new acquaintance' for the apparatus men, he says sarcastically. They imagine they can deal with division and alienation in soviet society by a Sovnarkom decree, but this corrupted life 'crawls into the management, into the local committee, hanging on to the hems of the rouge-faced madames'. The main target of his wrath is 'that scum behind the table' in a typical soviet department; 'his office hour is "from 3 to 4" / And how dare you turn up without a report'; at 4 he gets in his car while the visitor stands there 'struck dumb with fright'. Aleksandrovskii contrasts the apparatchik with the genuine communist activists:

---

21 A. Vlasov, 'My vse vidim i vse znaem: krik dushi krasnogo komandira', *Istochnik* 1, 1998: 85–88; TsAOPIM, 80/1/37/6–7.
22 Kazin, 'Slitsia solntse maia', *Kuznitsa* 1, 1920, p. 4.
23 *Kuznitsa* 9, 1922, pp. 8–9.

> I know there's another life, other people,
>   Creating their life's work: a great dream,
>   Their breasts gnawed by consumption,
>   Like sentries on guard.
>   There are people with great patience;
>   Not for them the thieving, the Sukharevka and the rations,
>   They are convinced of their own transformation
>   And they won't be taken from the rusting lathe.

The turnaround in the proletarian poets' beliefs in the transformative power of their own activity is striking. During the civil war they had swept all before them, but in mid 1921 were acutely aware of their own powerlessness. In 'Chernaia pena', Gerasimov imagines his lone raging in the theatre to be effective somehow. 'It's me – the blue-collar trade unionist / I shout from the gallery / And who would silence my iron cry?' That cry that makes the white sov-bourzh lady lumps 'fall into a black chasm'. But out on the street again, as a 'vile brand' is burned into people's foreheads, the worker poets are 'crucified on the lamp-posts'. There the poem ends. And this is the same Gerasimov whose exaggerated claims for the transformative power of his craft had a year earlier won acclaim throughout the proletkult movement. Loyal party members were mellowing, too. Semen Rodov, in his short poem 'Songs' ('Pesn'ia')[24] is walking along at night, singing a revolutionary song, on his own.

> There were times – not long ago
>   – Where have they gone?–
>   When we walked in solid ranks
>   Linked together,
>   A million hearts
>   Like one,
>   And half the sky
>   Was shaken by our song.

But now his 'lonely song' was not helping to rally those who had weakened. Anton Prishelets, a junior contributor to Kuznitsa, lamented the humdrum character of a job in an editorial office – typical NEP-period employment for an aspiring writer – in his poem 'Poet'.[25]

> On the walls – Zinoviev, Trotsky, Lenin,
>   On the floor – fag ends, dust and empty packets.

A far cry from the world-conquering declamations of the civil war.

Mark Steinberg, in his study of the proletarian writers, has emphasized that 'doubt, ambivalence, and unresolved ambiguity play large parts in this history'.[26] He shows that, even during the revolution and civil war, worker

24 *Gorn* 7, 1922, p. 9.
25 *Kuznitsa* 8, 1921, p. 11.
26 Steinberg, op. cit., pp. 19–20.

writers sometimes voiced doubts about the revolution, the collective, technical development, and about the city and modernity – even while simultaneously expressing strong beliefs built on these modernist themes. These doubts and question marks were certainly present, even during the civil war: these were people who took ideas and feelings seriously and tried to think through their consequences. Nevertheless, during the civil war a mood of collective strength was predominant; in 1921 it was rapidly deflated.

The disillusionment of 1921–22 also formed the background to a wave of suicides by communists. There are too few statistics to determine the scale of this phenomenon – but it existed, especially in the universities and the Red army. The largest wave of communist suicides was still to come, in 1924–26. But in early 1922 M. Reisner had already written:

> It's hardest of all for the revolutionary romantics. The vision of a golden age unfolded so close to them. Their hearts burned out. ... And sad stories are circulating. Here, one of our war heroes went home and shot himself. He couldn't stand vile little squabbles any longer. One drop and the cup overflowed. ... And there, they talk about the early death of a young worker, a member of the Komsomol. Also as a result of trifles. There are more than a few such incidents.[27]

27 M. Reisner, 'Staroe i novoe', *Krasnaia Nov'* 2, 1922, p. 284. It is difficult to separate historical reality from the discourse around the tragic image of romantic civil-war communists, committing suicide in dismay at the retreat implied by NEP. In Soviet times efforts were made to hide or destroy information on the subject. Viktoriia Tiazhel'nikova concluded from research on suicides among communists that the largest wave was in 1924–26. In 1925, recorded suicides in the population as a whole peaked, at more than double the level of 1922. The incidence of suicide was seven times the average among communists, and 15 times the average among communists in the Red army. But the wave of NEP-related communist suicides began in 1921, as Reisner indicated. One high-profile Bolshevik suicide in 1922 was Petr Belousov, a senior party member in Ukraine. A case reported by *Pravda* was that of Berdonosov, a worker at the textile mill in Serpukhov rural district outside Moscow, who was so 'deeply ashamed' of his expulsion from the party for drunkenness that he cut his throat with a razor. The motivation for suicide was as difficult to determine among communists as elsewhere. For example, I.I. Litvinov, in the diary quoted, gives an account of the suicide in 1922, following chronic depression, of his room-mate Mesezhnikov, who left a letter stating that he had 'no more strength to keep pulling the load'. Litvinov, who had been one of Mesezhnikov's few friends, said that the latter had manifested 'a nervous condition, ... hypochondria, lack of belief in his abilities'. In the mid 1920s there were some apparently politically motivated suicides by communist oppositionists, including Iurii Lutovinov and Evgeniia Bosh. V. Serge, *Memoirs of a Revolutionary*, New York: Writers & Readers, 1977, pp. 193–95; V.S. Tiazhel'nikova, 'Samoubiistvo kommunistov v 1920-e gody', *Otechestvennaia istoriia* 6, 1998: 158–73; K. Pinnow, *Making Suicide Soviet: Medicine, Moral Statistics and the Politics of Social Science in Soviet Russia, 1920–1930* (PhD diss., Columbia University, 1988); S. Pirani, *The Changing Political Relationship Between Moscow Workers and the Bolsheviks, 1920–24* (PhD diss., University of Essex, 2006), pp. 361–63.

Opposition inside the party

The tenth congress brought sharp changes for those oppositionists who fought on inside the party. Lenin's assurances that the ban on factions would not impede free discussion proved to be worthless. Lenin's collaborators (Molotov, Iaroslavskii and V.M. Mikhailov) replaced Trotsky's supporters (Krestinskii and Serebriakov) and Preobrazhenskii in the CC secretariat, and in May 1921 this secretariat stamped its authority on the Bolshevik trade union fractions.[28] It imposed a new leadership on the metalworkers' union, until then the WO's heartland, and removed the moderate Bolshevik leaders of the All-Russian Central Council of Trade Unions (Vserossiiskii tsentral'nyi sovet profsoiuzov – VTsSPS), Tomskii, Riazanov and Rudzutak, for defying an arcane instruction about the wording of a congress resolution.[29] While the DCs, a relatively close-knit pressure group, could retreat into semi-secrecy, the WO, which had won considerable rank-and-file support, had to choose: fight and face expulsion, or submit. These alternatives were discussed at meetings in February 1922. Among the participants were Moscow trade unionists and industrialists, including Genrikh Bruno, F.D. Budniak and Mikhail Mikhailov, who held leading positions in the artillery, auto and aviation trusts, respectively, and Grigorii Deulenkov, a metalworkers' union official who had risen through the ranks at Dinamo. Some WO supporters urged taking the offensive, and making the group an organizing centre against the petty-bourgeois tendencies enlivened by NEP. That would probably have meant a break with the party, and most of the group hesitated at such a prospect. Efforts were focused, instead, on an appeal by Shliapnikov, Medvedev and other WO leaders to the Comintern against the disciplinary measures imposed by the Bolshevik leadership. The appeal failed, the party's eleventh congress tightened these measures, and the opposition was pushed irreversibly onto the defensive.[30]

The opposition groups in Moscow, which had given the city's party organization a reputation for dissidence, faced the same dilemma. Ignatov's group formally dissolved itself. But the Bauman group took the offensive: it argued against aspects of NEP it considered damaging to the working class and urged implementation of the tenth congress resolutions that provided

---

28 R.V. Daniels, *The Conscience of the Revolution: Communist Opposition in Soviet Russia*, Cambridge, MA: Harvard University Press, 1960, pp. 149–51.

29 RGASPI, 17/65/224/205–8; 17/84/219/4–7; Daniels, op. cit., pp. 157–58; 'The Evolution of Communist Party Control Over the Trade Unions', *Revolutionary Russia*, 15: 2, 2002: 72–105.

30 A letter from a former oppositionist, most likely Ivan Perepechko, declared that the CC's offensive in the unions had compelled some former WO members 'to consider seriously whether or not to remain in the party' and others 'to practice self-flagellation'. RGASPI, 17/71/77. See also B. Allen, 'Alexander Shliapnikov and the Letter of the Twenty Two: A Critical Episode in the Russian Communist Party's Internal Debate over Criticism and Party Discipline' (paper presented at the mid-Atlantic Slavic conference, March 2003).

for inner-party democracy. In July 1921, Shliapnikov addressed a meeting in the district and argued that the soviet government had failed to use wealth expropriated from the bourgeoisie to strengthen the proletarian dictatorship or improve the workers' situation. 'It has distributed that wealth freely even among groups who have given nothing in return.' Sovetov put a resolution that accepted NEP in principle, but urged policies that would 'strengthen the proletariat' and use its 'forces of collective creativity', for example leasing enterprises to workers' collectives rather than to 'entrepreneurial, speculative lessees'.[31] The Bauman group's arguments on inner-party democracy were presented in a letter to delegates at the Moscow party regional conference in October 1921. It called on the MC to 'break decisively with the practice of appointism [i.e. *naznachenstvo*, the appointment, rather than election, of office-holders] in party bodies at all levels' and 'break with the unaccountability and absence of report-backs that inevitably produces servility and toadying, that produces a special type of cadres imbued with special trust from the party tops and executive careerists'. Genuine unity and the collective elaboration of party decisions could be achieved only if questions were discussed 'with full freedom of internal party criticism'. The letter protested against the by-now-standard practice of 'endlessly moving party activists from one industry to another and from one area to another'.[32]

The Bauman group's arguments remained potent, since apparatus privilege and encroachments on inner-party democracy continued to stir communists' emotions. In June, the regional party conference had noted that implementation of 'the drive to equalize the material conditions of party members, agreed on by the tenth congress', had been poor, and called for 'real measures' in this regard. The Kauchuk cell, which had not supported the 1920 opposition, warned that the party's moral authority depended on some members ceasing to exercise 'special privileges associated with their administrative responsibilities'. The issue of privilege at the Kremlin, so explosive in 1920, came up again: in November 1921 the MC bureau decided to close the co-operative shop in the Kremlin, to demand answers from the CC about 'exclusive rights of appropriation' that the Kremlin co-op enjoyed, and to transfer administration of the Kremlin's food supply to the local organizations that served the rest of the population.[33] The MC's anger at the Kremlin residents' comparative comfort was surely real enough. But so was its belief that such outspoken critics as the Baumanites had to be silenced, and it turned against them the full panoply of disciplinary methods – the redirection of cadres, 'exile' of undesirables out of Moscow, and the packing of meetings. In August-September the district was reorganized, the loyalist numbers raised by importing young full-timers from elsewhere, and

---

31 TsAOPIM, 63/1/44/28.
32 TsAOPIM, 3/2/18/18.
33 *K otchetu Moskovskoi gubernskoi konferentsii RKP* (25–28 iuniia 1921g.), Moscow, 1921, p. 8; TsAOPIM, 3/2/28/161ob; 475/1/2/24.

the dissidents thrown off the district committee. Next came punitive measures. Sovetov, who had returned from the civil war with tuberculosis and suffered a relapse in September 1921, was repeatedly ordered to the countryside for food procurement duty. The MC granted his first appeal against this order to commit suicide, but the second time around, in December, his plea that the mobilizations were 'a way of settling of scores with me, for daring to have my own opinions' fell on deaf ears. The MC bureau upheld his expulsion.[34] Kuranova and Berzina were sent out of the district, and at the heavy artillery workshops, Burdakov was expelled for 'disagreeing with NEP'.[35] The leaders of the defunct Ignatov group were also targeted: Ignatov was sent to head the party organization in Vitebsk, which in the context was a form of exile and Angarskii was sent to work in the Soviet trade mission in Berlin.[36]

Dissident ideas found a receptive audience in the higher education institutions established to lay the foundations for a new 'red intelligentsia'. No sooner did large numbers of civil-war recruits gather at these institutions – in Moscow, the Sverdlov Communist University, which provided tertiary education for worker communists; the Institute of Red Professors, an analogous postgraduate school; and workers' faculties (*rabfaky*) of other universities – than they became breeding grounds for opposition.[37] The clandestine Workers Truth group, which depicted the party leadership as representative of a 'technical intelligentsia' overseeing the restoration of capitalism, had its main base in the 'red' academy. Two of its prominent organizers, Polina Lass-Kozlova and Fania Shutskever, were communist students.[38] The group's platform argues that NEP amounted to 're-establishment of

34 Sovetov was not the only dissident Bolshevik to be sent on food procurement duty despite his unsuitability. When a group of communists clashed with the manager at Kauchuk in 1922 (see Chapter 7), they alleged that one of their supporters, Bentsel', a veteran Latvian communist who spoke Russian very poorly, was sent to do grain collection duties, where he had to 'work among [Russian] peasants, who, as is well known, distrust those who don't speak Russian'. TsAOPIM, 3/2/28/177–177ob, 182; *Rabochaia Moskva*, 28 May 1922.
35 TsAOPIM, 465/1/4/18; 3/2/18/2; 467/1/5/32.
36 A.V. Lunacharskii, L. Trotsky and K. Radek, *Siluety: politicheskiie portrety*, Moscow: izd. politicheskoi literatury, 1991, p. 431; TsAOPIM, 3/2/28/88.
37 TsAOPIM, f685 op1 d23. See also M. David-Fox, *Revolution of the Mind: Higher Learning Among the Bolsheviks 1918–1929*, Ithaca: Cornell University Press, 1997, pp. 42–52, 57–62 and 113–14.
38 On Lass-Kotlova and Shutskever, see Appendix 1. The Workers Truth platform, distributed in typewritten copies and published in 1922 in the Menshevik newspaper, is the only document of the group that I have found. Two numbers of its newspaper, *Rabochaia Pravda*, were published and distributed by post to factory committees in Moscow. See RGASPI, 17/71/81; V.Iu. Cherniaev and E.I. Makarov (eds), *Piterskie rabochie i 'Diktatura Proletariata'. Oktiabr'1917–1929: ekonomicheskie konflikti i politichestkii protest*, St Petersburg: Russko-baltiiskii informatsionnyi tsentr BLITs, 2000, pp. 305–12; *Sotsialisticheskii vestnik* 3, 1923, pp. 12–13. See also TsAOPIM, 3/3/34/329, 364, 365; E. Iaroslavskii, '*Rabochaia oppozitsiia*', '*Rabochaia gruppa*', '*Rabochaia pravda*', Moscow: Molodaia gvardiia, 1927, pp. 56–80; *Sotsialisticheskii vestnik* 19, 1923, pp. 3–4.

typical capitalist relations'. The October revolution had been 'the most heroic event in the history of the Russian proletariat's struggles' – but, in breaking the power of the landowners, parasitic tsarist bureaucracy and bourgeoisie, had only opened the way to Russia's 'rapid transformation to an advanced capitalist country'. After the revolution and civil war, the bourgeoisie was divided against itself and the working class was 'not prepared for the organization of society on a new basis'. A 'technical organizing intelligentsia' was coming to the fore; a new bourgeoisie would be formed as this group merged with elements of the old bourgeoisie. The Bolshevik party, which had been a workers' party in 1917, had become the party of this organizing intelligentsia, divided by an ever-deeper chasm from workers. 'Class activity' among 'vanguard non-party workers and the class-conscious elements in the [Bolshevik] party' was the basis on which a new 'party of the Russian proletariat' should be built; such a party would stand for closer links with the US and Germany and 'for a boycott of reactionary France'; it would struggle for democratic goals of 'freedom of speech and assembly for the revolutionary elements of the proletariat', oppose 'administrative arbitrariness' and combat the fetish of reserving the right to vote for the labouring classes.

The diary of Iosif Litvinov,[39] who studied at the Institute of Red Professors after Red army service, and knew Shutskever, paints a vivid picture of the milieu in which the Workers Truth group operated. Litvinov saw the corruption of the new communist elite, and the stifling of internal party discussion, driving many of the communist students, who lived in considerable poverty, to despair. In January 1922 he recorded a conversation with Shutskever about the 'cruel jokes of fate' being played on the party and its ideals. While Russia suffered a famine and an 'infestation' of speculators, the communists had degenerated, they agreed.

> People who declare they aim to change the world must themselves be bold, revolutionary and fearless in deeds, words and thoughts. And so the Bolsheviks were, at one time. And now? ... A herd of sheep, bereft of its own judgement, out to please those with influence, terrified of taking a single independent step. The communists have worked out their own caste prejudices, their rules, their catechism.

The 'stench of bureaucracy [*kazenshchina*], spiritual stagnation, the catechism and the small-mindedness' was everywhere. The WO leaders' appeal to the Comintern provoked 'huge discussions' and won 'great sympathy'. But many of the students felt powerless, and that led to resignations from

---

39 I.I. Litvinov, '"Ptitsegontsvo nadoelo do smerti". Iz dnevnika I.I. Litvinova', in *Neizvestnaia Rossiia* IV, 1993: 81–139, citing RGASPI, 589/3/1509/16–52. Litvinov (1896–?), who headed the Jewish section of the Latvian Social Democratic party during the civil war, and worked in industrial and economic management throughout the 1920s and 1930s, defected to the UK in 1933.

the party. In March 1922 Litvinov recorded: 'The outflow from the party has recently become an epidemic. The most honest proletarian elements are leaving. If this goes on for long, it will soon be hard to find a single rank-and-file proletarian communist'.

Historians working before the opening of the Soviet archives assumed that the Workers Truth group were followers of Aleksandr Bogdanov, the theoretician of 'proletarian culture' and pre-revolutionary factional opponent of Lenin's. Certainly there was common ground: Workers Truth saw culture as a central battlefield with the 'organizing intelligentsia', which had 'imprisoned' workers with bourgeois ideology, and it urged 'the sharpest delimitation from official soviet literature and art' and support for proletarian cultural organizations.[40] But it was another opposition group, the Collectivists, who explicitly embraced Bogdanov's theories and sought to adapt them to NEP conditions. Their manifesto, distributed at the proletkult congress in Moscow in November 1921, denounced the 'religious-abstract' Marxism of Plekhanov and Lenin and declared Bogdanov the leader of their theoretical school. Lenin urged that a response be drafted, but apparently none was.[41]

The manifesto is more philosophical than political. It sets out a view of 'collective consciousness' that echoes Bogdanov's pre-revolutionary writings: ideology in general, and science and art in particular, comprise 'the experience of collective labour – gathered, put into order and organized', which is a weapon both to strengthen the collective and to organize collective labour. Only once the Collectivists have deemed the struggle for the 'class purity of proletarian culture' primary, and politics an indissoluble part of culture, and declared their dedication to freeing proletarian ideology from 'authoritarian-religious and individualist-abstract elements', do they address political issues. Having supported the WO in 1920, they had witnessed the party's transformation from a proletarian to a worker-intelligentsia party. They believed a split to be inevitable, but pledged to stay and fight within. They considered the soviet state a worker-peasant dictatorship with a 'state capitalist' economy; to move to 'genuine communism, or, more accurately, collectivism', and forestall the rise of a 'technical-bureaucratic intelligentsia, i.e. a new bourgeoisie', a new, political, revolution was necessary. This was a general aim, though, not a current political slogan. The immediate tasks were 'resuscitation of industry'; the scientific organization of labour; and, to develop proletarian culture, 'resuscitation of the proletkults', purged of non-proletarian elements. (Unfortunately no information has yet come to light about the manifesto's supporters or of any subsequent activity.)

40 Z.A. Sochor, *Revolution and Culture: The Bogdanov-Lenin Controversy*, Ithaca: Cornell University Press, 1988, pp. 179–80; Daniels, op. cit., pp. 159–61. See also N.S. Antonova and N.V. Drozdova (eds), *Neizvestnyi Bogdanov v 3-kh knigakh*, Moscow: AIRO, 1995, kn. 1, pp. 204–22; and N. Karev, 'O gruppe "Rabochaia pravda"', *Bol'shevik* nos. 7–8, 1924: 27–43.
41 RGASPI, 17/60/43/20–28. See also Sochor, op. cit., pp. 179–80; Lenin, op. cit., vol. 44, p. 266.

The oppositions, which in November 1920 had come so close to winning a majority in the Moscow party, were a year later divided and defeated. Their supporters had left the party, been expelled, retreated into silence, been pushed back or driven into clandestinity by disciplinary measures, or politically reconciled themselves with suspending criticism while implementing the tenth congress decisions.

Out of the factories, into the apparatus

Oppositionists' fears that the party was deserting the working class ideologically were reinforced by the sight of it deserting the working class physically. Its worker members were moving off the shop floor into management and soviet administrative posts. Those returning from the Red army were more likely to go to government offices than to factories. The party leadership was in a bind: it wanted to put communists, and especially worker communists, in charge of branches of the state and industrial apparatus that it felt it did not control, but needed those same people to mediate its relationship with workers and, even more desperately, with the peasants. It had dismissed all proposals to reform the soviet state politically: that in turn hobbled the discussion on how to tackle the state apparatus. The party's own apparatus had to be used to control the state apparatus, while simultaneously maintaining, or repairing, its relations with the population. This approach put a premium on the party members, who were alone deemed fit to fill the most important administrative and political positions. A huge amount of attention was paid, and energy spent, on ordering them from one post to another. Countless committees' first response to problems was to shift personnel. So appeared the phenomena of transfer (*perebroska*) and movement of members (*dvizheniie chlenov*), precursors of the cadre distribution system established in the mid 1920s. In 1922, the first year for which there are records, about 40 per cent of the Moscow membership moved from one district to another, to say nothing of those who switched jobs within districts.[42]

In Moscow, a tug of war developed between the MC, for whom effective functioning of industrial cells was a priority, and the administrative institutions – of which Moscow, as the capital, had more than its fair share. From February 1921, office-based communists were 'mobilized' into the factories by both the MC and the national leadership, leading many to resist or complain.[43] In October, Zelenskii reported to the regional party conference that the 'vast majority' of Moscow communists were working in soviet institutions. Of the region's 30,000-plus communists, he said, 15,000 worked

---

42 Pirani, op. cit., p. 355.
43 *Pravda*, 4 May and 10 May 1921; Z.P. Korshunova (ed.), *Ocherki istorii Moskovskoi organizatsii KPSS, kn. II, noiabr' 1917–1945*, Moscow: Moskovskii rabochii, 1983, pp. 207–9; O.I. Shkaratan, *Problemy sotsial'noi struktury rabochego klassa SSSR*, Moscow: 'Mysl'', 1970, p. 240.

in administrative institutions and 6500 in the Red army (including many in office jobs at headquarters). There were only 2000 in transport and 4000 in the factories – and, as discussed below, most of these were in management posts. Since September 1920, the numbers in administrative institutions may have risen by up to 50 per cent, while those in the factories were cut in half. In its four years in power, the party had 'acted as a pump, sucking in members and pumping them into the soviet institutions', Zelenskii declared despairingly. 'As soon as a worker communist becomes fully-fledged, stands up and flies out to battle, he instantly gets landed into soviet work. ... It's no wonder we have started to lose influence among workers.' In the factories, 'there is no yeast to ferment, to grow, to produce activists and strengthen them'. Zelenskii demanded that 'the pump be put into reverse' to send members back to the factories, and denounced those who considered factory postings beneath them as '*chinovnichii*' (an adjective from *chinovnik*, a member of the ranked tsarist bureaucracy and symbol of snobbish high-handedness).[44] By March 1922, when the next Moscow regional conference was held, the situation had improved slightly. Zelenskii reported that, of about 26,000 party members in the city, 6000 were in industry while 'the rest are on military service, or in administration or economic management, or studying'.[45] But attempts to mobilize communist *sluzhashchie* into the factories had failed. In the four months since the October conference had called for the mobilization, district organizations had asked for 1300 members to go into specific factory jobs and 850 were actually assigned. But after a process of appeals, only 250 were transferred. Zelenskii concluded that many white-collar members were 'ballast ... who are just not accustomed to factory life'. Only by easing recruitment conditions for workers could the factory cells be strengthened.[46]

In the soviet institutions' cells that contained most Moscow members, the workers-turned-administrators and peasant-soldiers-turned-administrators rubbed shoulders with party members who had been state officials or students before the revolution.[47] There were frictions. Petr Korotkov, a *sluzhashchie*

---

44 *Otchet sed'moi Moskovskoi gubpartkonferentsii RKP 29–31 oktiabria 1921 g.*, Moscow, 1921, pp. 24–25.
45 *Vos'maia gubernaskaia konferentsiia Moskovskoi organizatsii RKP (23–25 marta 1922 g.)*, Moscow: MK RKP, 1922, p. 39.
46 *Vos'maia Moskovskaia konferentsiia*, p. 41. *Izvestiia MK RKP(b)* 1, 1922, pp. 22–23.
47 The latter category, of those who had worked in the tsarist bureaucracy and joined the party after 1917, is difficult to define. A group of Soviet political scientists analyzed results of a 1922 survey of *sluzhashchie*, and showed that those party members in senior administrative jobs mostly described themselves as having been 'technical personnel', 'students', 'free professionals' or 'military service' before the revolution. Fewer than one-tenth could find a pretext on which to put themselves in the most politically desirable category, i.e. 'workers'. V.I. Vasiaev, V.Z. Drobizhev, L.B. Zaks, B.I. Pivovor, V.A. Ustinov and T.A. Ushakova, *Dannie perepisi sluzhashchikh 1922g. o sostave kadrov narkomatov RSFSR*, Moscow: izd. Moskovskovskogo universiteta, 1972, pp. 148–52; Pirani, op. cit., p. 160.

at a trading organization in Moscow, resigned from candidate party membership in March 1921, complaining that the cell was divided between 'sons' and 'stepsons'. The 'sons' were workers who had come into administration since 1917, 'leaders, big or small, of endless regional and district collegia', who had sources of additional income. The 'stepsons' were 'old professional *sluzhashchie*', who were discriminated against materially and politically.[48] In contrast to the upwardly mobile worker communists, who wore their proletarian status as a badge of superiority, some worker communists felt unprepared for the responsibilities thrust upon them. M.A. Matekhin, a worker from Sokol'niki, who had done one administrative job after another since February 1917, begged in 1921 not to be put in charge of a rural district soviet executive because 'I, like many of my comrades, came directly from the factory. We have no education', he wrote. The state apparatus was 'becoming more complex' and 'a definite level of knowledge' is needed to work in it. He asked to return to his factory or to work in the metalworkers' union.[49]

Those modest enough to ask to return to the factories, and those who resisted leaving as a matter of principle, mentioned in Chapter 2, were small minorities, though. Zelenskii calculated in October 1921 that while the Moscow factory cells had an average of 14 members each, 24 cells in the central administrative offices had 5400 members between them. Moreover, most communists in industry were administrators: a report compiled by the CC in early 1922 found that, of the 5424 communists in Moscow industry, only 1819 were 'at the bench' and 3605 were in other, mainly administrative, roles. The Bromlei cell seems to have been typical: 26 members remained after the 1921 purge, of which 15 were semi-skilled or skilled metalworkers – but only 10 of these still worked at their trade, and at least 12 cell members worked in administrative posts at, or away from, the factory. Across the party nationally, of the 10.5 per cent of members in factory cells and 7.1 per cent in transport cells, more than half were in managerial posts. A survey of the 14,750 communists in industrial cells across Russia's 22 most industrialized regions showed that only 4255 of these were actually 'at the bench'; the rest, i.e. 71 per cent, were in administration or seconded to other work such as trade union or co-op organization.[50]

The party purge

The context for the purge of late 1921, in which one-fifth of the national party membership was excluded, was the development of the one-party

48 TsAOPIM, 63/1/62/43–44.
49 Postings to rural areas were especially unpopular, and Matekhin may have been hoping to be kept in Moscow – but that does not mean his fears about lack of training were not genuine. The issue is further discussed in Chapter 7, p. 186. TsAOPIM, 3/2/28/176.
50 TsAOPIM, 412/1/14; TsK RKP(b), *Itogi partiinoi raboty za god 1922–23*, Moscow: Krasnaia nov', 1923, pp. 146–47.

political system. Having junked the DCs' schemes for broader soviet structures, snubbed the non-partyists' overtures of co-operation, and appropriated all political decision-making power, not only at national level but also in local and industrial bodies, the party was more than ever reliant on its members to wield that power responsibly. The greater the power concentrated in the party's hands, the greater the members' moral responsibility. Sol'ts, explaining the policy of exclusions, stated that the party 'can establish ... the mode, the norm by which society must live. We are the ruling class here, in our country, and life will be constructed according to us'.[51] From the moral imperatives flowed organizational aims. One task was to rid the party of elements deemed to be corrupt. Another was to pursue the fight against 'bureaucratism' (in the one-dimensional sense, of authoritarianism and inefficiency in the soviet institutions, separate from any discussion of the party's assumptions about its exercise of political power). Honest, proletarian party members were declared to be the guarantor of good government, while dishonest and/or petty-bourgeois members were seen as the source of 'bureaucratism'. Enthusiasm for the purge was broadly shared by the party leadership and those who had been in opposition in 1920. But within this 'anti-bureaucratic' discourse, the left targeted the privileges of the 'tops', while the Leninist, or Smilga-ist, opponents of workerist dissent tried to use the purge to silence the oppositionists.

The CC's initial announcement of the purge states the case against individual members from non-proletarian backgrounds: in the years since the revolution, it said, when the proletariat had attracted the peasantry and urban middle-class layers to its side, representatives of these alien classes had entered an otherwise proletarian party, bringing with them bureaucratism and corruption. These now had to be excluded. The Moscow regional purge commission declared as its main target 'gentlemen, whose aim is not the struggle for communism, but simply their own self-seeking, mercenary motives: to get a responsible posting, or rather a warm, comfy little number'. These communists-in-quotation-marks 'practice the old ways of the tsarist official bureaucrats', and drive workers from, and discredit, the party.[52] The purge commissions often invited non-party workers to give their views on communists' suitability for party membership, and workers took the opportunity to express misgivings about factory managers. At one military unit stationed in Moscow, 400 non-party soldiers threw 36 party members out of such a meeting and decided themselves who should be purged (!), although their rulings were later nullified by the purge commission.[53]

---

51 A. Sol'ts, 'Communist Ethics', in Rosenberg, W.G. (ed.), *Bolshevik Visions: First Phase of the Cultural Revolution in Soviet Russia*, Michigan: University of Michigan Press, 1990. Part 1, p. 31.
52 *Pravda*, 16 August 1921; *Izvestiia TsK RKP(b)* 33, 1921, pp. 38–41.
53 *Izvestiia MK RKP (b)* 1, 1922, p. 6.

The purge was launched in August 1921; in Moscow it got underway in earnest in November. In total, 7270 members of the regional organization were expelled. The largest groups, accounting for nearly one-third of the total between them, were expelled for being 'alien elements' and for 'passive membership'.[54] An instruction that the purge was not to be used to settle scores with dissidents was sometimes overlooked. Although only 10 members were expelled for 'disagreement with NEP', there were catch-all clauses such as 'refusal to carry out party directives' or 'unreliable or vacillating element', that were used against dissidents and other awkward cases, and accounted together for more than 1300 expulsions. The purge was followed by a national re-registration of membership in February 1922, on the basis of which official figures on the party's social composition were issued.

The emphasis placed on party members' social origins, and the need to increase the proportion of members of proletarian origin, put a premium on proving one's proletarian roots – and exaggeration and falsification to that end became widespread. The re-registration statistics showed that nationally the party was 44.4 per cent proletarian, with the remainder divided almost evenly between *sluzhashchie* and peasants. The Moscow organization was 49.1 per cent proletarian, 35.5 per cent *sluzhashchie*, and the remainder divided between peasants and 'other'.[55] But the figures must be treated with caution. In the central purge commission's report to the eleventh congress, M.F. Shkiriatov explained: 'We hear that a person is a worker, but sometimes ... it is 20 years since he picked up a hammer, and sometimes it's even worse: he's never picked up a hammer, but he puts himself in the category "worker" because his grandfather was a worker.' Antipov, the chairman of the Moscow purge commission, reported that 27 former tsarist policemen had been expelled, but only after being caught 'counting themselves as workers and thereby attempted to hide their criminal past'.[56]

---

54 The categories under which people were expelled, with number of expulsions, were: Alien element 1340; Passive membership 976; Voluntarily left and automatically excluded 906; Refusal to implement party discipline 706; Unreliable and vacillating elements 607; Careerism and self-seeking 600; Discredited the party 374; Drunkenness or vulgar behaviour 364; Party ballast 361; Carrying out religious practices 179; Abuse of powers 159; Doubtful elements 104; Theft and misappropriation 123; Failure to understand party programme 121; Avoidance of military duty 95; Speculation 62; On trial for criminal offences 59; Bribe-taking 45; Avoidance of labour mobilization 30; Former police officers 30; Extortion and blackmail 22; Playing cards 19; Agitation against soviet power 15; Failure to provide recommendation 15; Bourgeois life style 11; Disagreement with NEP 10; Entered the party with counter-revolutionary aims 4; Anti-semitism 3. *Izvestiia MK RKP(b)* 1, 1922, pp. 5–18.

55 *Vserossiiskaia perepis' chlenov RKP 1922 goda*, Moscow: izd. otdel TsK RKP, 1922, pp. 20–21. See also S. Ivanovich, *VKP: desiat' let kommunisticheskoi monopolii*, Paris: bib. demokraticheskogo sotsializma, 1928, p. 65; Rigby, op. cit., p. 85.

56 *Odinnadtsatyi s"ezd RKP(b): stenograficheskii otchet*, Moscow: Gos. izd. politicheskoi literatury, 1961, p. 376; TsAOPIM, 3/2/18/39.

Presumably other impostors were not caught. And the problem was exacerbated after the congress, as proletarianization became a prescribed task for all party bodies and they were tempted to massage figures on members' social origins.

The way that the purge reflected the party's unresolved political disputes, and its divided attitudes to the apparatus, is illustrated by comparing the work of the purge commissions in Khamovniki and Bauman. The former descended like an avenging horde upon the soviet and military office cells in the district and tried to expel two senior Bolshevik leaders for corruption and anti-worker behaviour, while the latter trod gingerly around the apparatus cells, and tried – in defiance of a clear directive that people should not be purged for political dissidence – to expel a leading member of the opposition Bauman group. The Khamovniki commission was chaired by Shubin, a former supporter of the WO. Its other members were Kochetkov, another WO sympathizer who had joined the Bolsheviks in 1913; Nikolai Mizikin, who had a strong workerist streak; Gurvich; and Grigorii Belen'kii, a leadership loyalist.[57] The commission regarded the purge as an opportunity to reach into the top of the apparatus, and took literally the public rhetoric that provided for stringency against former workers who 'have justly been called "commissarized"' or 'dignitaries' who had 'acquired all the negative characteristics of bureaucrats'.[58] Among those expelled by the Khamovniki commission were two senior Bolsheviks: Danishevskii, a civil-war-time member of the revolutionary war council and Smilga's main supporter at the tenth congress; and Trifon Enukidze, a close collaborator of Stalin's and brother of the CC member Avel' Enukidze.[59] They were both reinstated later, in circumstances that remain unclear.

Danishevskii, now head of the forestry chief committee Severoglavles, stood accused by the purge commission of sacking a woman worker who had complained about the Severoglavles bosses' 'scandalous rolling in luxury'. When trade union leaders demanded the woman's reinstatement, Danishevskii allegedly called in Cheka agents to arrest two union activists. He had also commandeered a luxury house, and engaged in a lengthy intrigue to subvert decisions, by bodies up to and including the Sovnarkom,

---

57 TsAOPIM, 88/1/101/46; TsAOPIM, 685/1/36, especially 261. Belen'kii (1885–1938) joined the revolutionary movement at the age of 14 and was in the Bolshevik fraction from its inception in 1903; sat on the MC 1917–25; was expelled for supporting the united opposition in 1927. Mizikin (1886–1958) was born into a family of landless peasants and moved to Moscow aged 11 to start work as a warehouseman; joined the Bolsheviks in 1911; a civil war veteran. In a discussion about revolutionary legality in 1918 was reported to have said: 'Why all these questions? I would go into the kitchen and look in the pot. If they have meat: enemies of the people! Up against the wall!' L. Sosnovskii, *Dela i Liudi*, kn. 1, Moscow, 1924, pp. 53–54.

58 *Izvestiia TsK RKP(b)* 33 (1921), pp. 38–40.

59 On Danishevskii and Enukidze, see Appendix 1.

that he return it to state property. He had appropriated other state property (an estate, two cars, luxury foodstuffs, and so on) for his family's use.⁶⁰ Enukidze, manager of the Goznak printing works, was accused of treating party and union organizations with 'contempt'. The purge commission found that he had spurned conciliatory efforts and declared that factory committees were 'a sore on the body of soviet power', and claimed that he was so unpopular that workers 'whistled and swore' when he appeared on the factory floor. There was undoubtedly a measure of anti-*spets* prejudice at the works that may have worked against Enukidze. For example Ivan Bogdanov, a Goznak delegate to the district soviet, concluded a report on the clashes with Enukidze by stating: 'The ninth congress gave all the power to the *spetsy*. We need to make the revolution of 25 October all over again, to take power from them.' Nevertheless, the charges that Enukidze lorded it over the cell and factory committee are substantiated in their records. Hostilities continued in 1922, when workers and union officials complained that a large cash bonus fund was being distributed among managers; a Moscow-level arbitration commission found in the union's favour, but a national arbitration commission reversed that decision.⁶¹

The Khamovniki purge commission defied the Moscow garrison leadership, which had tried to prevent local commissions purging Red army communists, and ripped in to 10 cells of military command office staff, denouncing 'nepotism and toadying' there, and recommending that they be reorganized.⁶² The commission further provoked opposition from the Khamovniki district party leadership, by severely criticizing the cell made up of officials working for the local soviet and ruling that the 'old Bolshevik' Boris Breslav and two other district committee officials spend time in industrial cells. The district party secretary Aleksandr Mandel'shtam flatly refused to implement these measures; in the row that followed, he accused Kochetkov of being a 'criminal type'.⁶³

The Bauman purge commission's secretary, Gans Lemberg, was a collaborator of Stalin's who saw himself as an agent of the party's central apparatus. The other commission members were Ivan Kamkov, a worker member of the party from 1902 who worked in supply organizations; Georgii Blagonravov, a party member from 1917 and Cheka officer from

60 TsAOPIM, 685/1/36/95–95ob.
61 TsAOPIM, 3/2/28/135; 3/3/34/178; 1099/1/2/35; RGASPI, 17/84/151/15, 21ob; 17/84/378/15–16. On a further clash between Enukidze and the party cell, see Chapter 7, p. 189.
62 *Izvestiia MK RKP(b)* 1 (1922), p. 6; TsAOPIM, 685/1/36/256.
63 TsAOPIM, 685/1/36/251–61; 88/1/101/2, 50. Breslav (1882–1938) was born into a family of labourers near Vitebsk, trained as a cobbler; 1899, joined the Social Democrats; repeatedly arrested and exiled; 1918, served briefly as MC secretary; a civil war veteran; 1923, one of the first three signatories of the Platform of the 46. Mandel'shtam (1878–1929) was a native Muscovite; 1902, joined the Bolsheviks; member of the Bolshevik MC in 1905 and subsequently; repeatedly arrested and exiled; from 1917, worked in numerous party and administrative posts.

1918; and Gadarein.[64] Its fire was concentrated in the opposite direction from its Khamovniki counterparts, i.e. away from the party elite and towards its most vigorous opponents. Two leaders of the district's 1920 opposition group, Maria Berzina and Sergei Maslennikov, complained of its bias against that group's supporters. The commission singled out for expulsion a factory-based activist of the very type the party was short of, Baranov, for 'insufficient discipline in undertaking his party duties'. His appeal, on the grounds that he was being victimized for supporting the opposition, was upheld.[65] On the other hand the Bauman commission eschewed the type of criticism of apparatus cells made by its counterparts in Khamovniki. It was lenient towards former members of other parties in those cells, against which official directives required the harshest line. It reported that 30 of the 154 members of the cell at Tsektran were former members of other parties, but excluded none of them. Apparently the Bauman commission shared Lenin's belief that, notwithstanding the public rhetoric, former members of other parties in the apparatus were doing valuable work for the economy and should not be undermined.[66]

The purge and re-registration had aimed to make the party more proletarian by social composition. Once the results had been reported, and the difficulties of doing so made clear, a dispute broke out in the party leadership about the way forward. Lenin, convinced that members from non-proletarian backgrounds were the main source of reactionary social pressure on the party, urged that recruitment criteria be tightened. Crucially, he wanted to limit the intake of factory workers from 'petty bourgeois' backgrounds, i.e., in the first place, first-generation migrants from the countryside who made up a significant proportion of many factories' workforces. Lenin proposed to the politburo *greater* restrictions on working class recruits with less than 10 years in industry, whom 'we are always counting as workers' despite their not having had 'the least bit of serious schooling in heavy industry'. Many party leaders shared Lenin's political distrust of the working class, but believed it impractical to tighten the recruitment criteria. Kalinin and others pleaded with Lenin to water down his proposals. The CC drafted theses that provided for workers and Red army men from proletarian and peasant backgrounds to join

---

64 TsAOPIM, 685/1/2. On Lemberg, see Appendix 1.
65 TsAOPIM, 3/2/13/150; 63/1/50/6; 685/1/2/133. On Berzina, see Appendix 1. Maslennikov was born into the family of a clerk and furniture trader in Tver', joined the revolutionary movement at technical school in 1906; did underground trade union organizing; joined the Bolsheviks in 1911; a civil war veteran; member of the Moscow soviet 1917–24.
66 Lenin had called publicly in September 1921 for the expulsion of '99 out of every hundred Mensheviks who joined the party after 1918' – but then joined other senior party members to plead with the Moscow purge commission for leniency in the case of specific former Mensheviks, such as L.G. Shapiro, on the basis that their skills were badly needed in industry. Lenin, op. cit., vol. 44, pp. 122–24 and vol. 54, pp. 52–55. On Tsektran, TsAOPIM, 685/1/2/63.

the party, with a six-month candidacy, on the recommendation of three party members of three years' standing. Conditions for other workers, peasants and Red army men would be slightly tougher. *Sluzhashchie* and others needed five recommendations from members of more than five years' standing, and had to remain candidates for two years. The CC pulled back from Lenin's most extreme proposal, that the fast-track six-month candidacy should apply only to workers with 10 years 'at the bench'.[67] The leaders of the Moscow organization, who were daily dealing with the factory cells' weakness and trying to cover the gaps left by communists who went into administration, opposed Lenin's plans. The Moscow regional conference, held in March in the run-up to the eleventh congress, deemed the CC's proposals an obstruction to recruiting workers 'who are outside the party, but who support the party in practice and carry out the party line'. Moscow's alternative theses advocated a concerted effort to recruit into the factory cells, using existing criteria. Zelenskii, introducing the theses, said that average party membership in the largest industries was below 4 per cent of the workforce. He knew from experience that the only real alternative to casting the net wider among factory workers was to transfer junior members working in administration to the factories – and this had been tried, and failed. Members from the apparatus cells would have no 'authority among workers', and their transfer to the factories would just leave the state apparatus in the hands of 'former tsarist officials'. Zelenskii pointed to Bogorodskii rural district in Moscow region: it had 45,000 textile workers, and of its 490 party members, only 150 could be spared from the district administration to work in industry.[68]

At the eleventh congress, the CC theses were introduced by Zinoviev, who spoke, in a similar vein to Lenin, of the danger that the party would be overcome by an influx of 'the young, petty-minded philistine, the urban proprietor, the declassed worker'. Richard Pikel', the former Comintern official and future left oppositionist, countered that even if Zinoviev's claim that the working class was '90 per cent declassed' was accepted, that still left 10 per cent – and only 1 per cent of workers were currently members. The CC's proposals were adopted by the congress, with a minor concession to Zelenskii – a passage acknowledging that quality, not quantity, should be considered in the transfer of members from administrative cells to industrial ones.[69] In the city of Moscow, recruitment to the factory cells remained painfully slow until the end of 1922; in the region as a whole, and the rest of Russia, these cells only grew substantially in 1924, when all Lenin's restrictions were scrapped and workers were drafted into them *en masse*.

---

67 *Odinnadtsatyi s"ezd*, pp. 10–44, 554, 680–87 and 734–35; Kvashonkin et al. (eds), op. cit., p. 239.
68 *Izvestiia MK RKP(b)* 1, 1922, pp. 56–61; *Vos'maia gubernskaia konferentsiia*, p. 41.
69 *Odinnadtsatyi s"ezd*, pp. 380–410, especially p. 392, pp. 442–45, 453–56 and 545–54.

6 Mass mobilization versus mass participation

Workers in 1922

The political expropriation of the working class was not a simple act of theft. The Bolsheviks' rivals in the workers' movement – the non-partyists, other socialist parties and communist dissidents – had by early 1922 been silenced or isolated. It remained for the party to fashion new methods to mediate its relationship with the majority of the working class. Forms of mass mobilization – including big public campaigns against the church and the Socialist Revolutionaries (SRs) party – were used to subvert and replace the forms of democratic mass participation that had begun to take shape in 1917. The fora in which participatory democracy might have developed, the soviets and unions, were assigned limited functions that involved implementing decisions made by the party – and, increasingly, the elite that was now bringing the party under its control. Mechanisms for isolating leaders of both political and economic strikes, usually by expulsion from unions, were refined. The rapid upturn in the economy in 1922 made possible an improvement in workers' living standards, which provided the basis for most workers to accept such arrangements. The unemployed, who could not be included in the social contract, were pushed to the political margins.

Living standards improve

The economic recovery was important not only for the stability it brought immediately, but for the improved living standards it promised. It had started in late 1921, notwithstanding interruptions and imbalances such as the weakness of heavy industry and the collapse of industrial prices. In 1922 the results were already evident. In Moscow, industrial output roughly doubled, year-on-year. It was still only about one-third of the 1913 level – but the slump had been reversed.[1] And workers' material conditions began to

---

1 The aggregate output of enterprises overseen by MSNKh, in gold rubles, against a figure of 1069 billion for 1913, was 167.6 billion in 1921, 319.7 billion in 1922 and 420.4 billion in 1923. Output surpassed the 1913 level in 1926. Statisticheskii otdel Moskovskogo soveta, *Statisticheskii atlas gor. Moskvy i Moskovskoi gub. Vyp. 3. Promyshlennost' i torgovlia*, Moscow, 1925, pp. 21–23, 29.

change. In mid 1921, it was only barter trade that kept at bay the threat of starvation. But in 1922 workers began to be paid regularly, usually in cash that had definite worth. Thenceforth, wages rose in each of the first five years of the industrial relations system put in place after the eleventh party congress (mid 1922 to mid 1927).[2] Unemployment and wild leaps of inflation threatened, but the industrial recovery boosted confidence, and workers often resorted to industrial action to defend what had been gained. Important, too, were workers' high expectations – justified, as it turned out – that the improvements would continue.

The increase in wage levels is striking. In the Moscow region, industrial workers' aggregate monthly pay (including wages and food rations) rose from an estimated 2.4 rubles in January 1920 to 3–3.5 rubles in January 1921, 11.5 rubles in January 1922 and 14 rubles in May-June 1922.[3] So from mid 1922, when it became possible to count one's wages in a meaningful fashion, they were several times higher than in the civil war, and rising. Payment in kind was disappearing: in Moscow, the non-money content of wages fell from more than 75 per cent in January 1922 to 13.6 per cent in December 1922 and 3 per cent in February 1923. Nationally, the non-money content of wages fell from 86.2 per cent in 1921 to 21.7 per cent in January 1923. In late 1922 the party urged a wage freeze for the best-paid workers, but this was combined with public acknowledgements by government and union leaders that wages should rise to, and beyond, 1913 levels, with which statistical comparisons were constantly made. Moscow achieved the 1913 level sooner than the rest of Russia: average industrial workers' wages in the city reached 67 per cent of their 1913 level in the last quarter of 1922, and 83.4 per cent in the third quarter of 1923. By then, printers had passed the 1913 mark and metalworkers and garment workers were approaching it, while textile workers, mostly women, were trailing behind.[4]

The eight-hour day, considered a key gain of the 1917 revolution, was retained almost everywhere; the Menshevik David Dalin, a harsh critic of Bolshevik labour policy, regarded this as so significant that in 1923 he cited it as proof that Russia was not a 'bourgeois' state.[5] At the Goznak works, management attempts to retain a longer working day were fiercely contested and the issue of whether the lunch break would be 30 or 60 minutes disputed at length. Even shorter hours for workers could be negotiated for

---

2 A.G. Rashin, *Zarabotnaia plata za vosstanovitel'nyi period khoziaistva SSSR 1922/23–1926/27 gg.*, Moscow: Gosizdat, 1928, p. 6.
3 Wages statistics are set out in Appendix 3, p. 257.
4 A.A. Matiugin, *Rabochii klass SSSR v gody vosstanovleniia narodnogo khozaistva, 1921–1925*, Moscow: izd. Akademii nauk SSSR, 1962, p. 164; M.N. Korovina and T.F. Kogan, 'Bor'ba za uluchshenie blagosostoianiia rabochego klassa (1921–25gg.)', *Voprosy istorii* 9, 1961: 42–55, here 48; E.H. Carr, *The Interregnum 1923–1924*, London: Macmillan, 1978, p. 68.
5 *Sotsialisticheskii vestnik* 19, 1923, pp. 3–4.

workers working in bad conditions; at Serp i Molot, the wire-drawing shop workers went so far as to strike for a six-hour day.[6] (In 1927, a seven-hour day was introduced in soviet industry, but largely abandoned during the first five-year plan, and completely scrapped in 1940.)

Food consumption data, a key measure of real living standards, show that the calorie intake in working-class households in Moscow hit a nadir in early 1919 and then rose gradually until 1924. In early 1919 it was at 58 per cent of the 1924–25 level; between mid 1919 and early 1922 it hovered between 70 per cent and 80 per cent of that level, with one unexplained upward blip in early 1920; it rose to 91 per cent of that level in October 1922, 97 per cent in February 1923 and 100 per cent in October 1924. Consumption of meat and fat, which almost disappeared from working-class diets during the civil war, revived from insignificant levels in September 1921.[7] During 1922 the proportion of income spent on food fell sharply, reflecting the move from a weekly battle for survival to an expansion in the range of household purchases: until mid 1922, more than 95 per cent of income was spent on food; by December 1922 this proportion was under 50 per cent and falling.[8] Other indicators of living standards were improving, too: while workers' housing remained awful, essential services – including hospitals, water and sewage services, the electricity network, and public transport – were being extended to working-class suburbs.[9]

The changes in industry changed the character of industrial disputes. The move from payment in kind to money wages was heralded by the introduction in November 1921 of the 'goods ruble', a measuring standard based on a basket of 1913 prices, against which prices and wages counted in soviet rubles (including those paid in kind) were set. In March 1922 a new gold ruble was introduced, but industrial managers and unions, nervous about any measure that might undermine the value of real wages, continued to use the 'goods ruble'.[10] All eyes in the factories turned to the shifting exchange rates. A Cheka report to the Moscow committee (MC) of the Bolshevik party in January 1922 explained:

---

6 K. Murphy, *Revolution and Counterrevolution: Class Struggle in a Moscow Metal Factory*, Oxford: Berghahn Books, 2005, p. 97; TsAGM, 2626/1/70/10ob; 2626/1/77/5ob; TsAOPIM, 1099/1/4/19; 1099/1/5/37.
7 S. Wheatcroft, 'Famine and Food Consumption Records in Early Soviet History, 1917–25', in Geissler, C. and Oddy, D. (eds), *Food, Diet and Economic Change Past and Present*, Leicester: Leicester University Press, 1993, pp. 151–74.
8 W.J. Chase, *Workers, Society and the Soviet State: Labour and Life in Moscow 1918–1929*, Urbana: University of Illinois Press, 1990, pp. 178–79.
9 N.M. Aleshchenko, *Moskovskii sovet v 1917–1941 gg.*, Moscow: Nauka, 1976, p. 293 and pp. 311–14; Chase, op. cit., pp. 184–85 and 188–89; T.J. Colton, *Moscow: Governing the Socialist Metropolis*, Cambridge, MA: Harvard University Press, 1995, pp. 164–71 and 796.
10 On changes to the Soviet currency, see Appendix 3, p. 257.

Enterprises ... are suffering desperately from a lack of money in circulation, and that means payment of wages is being delayed. With consumer prices going up, not by the day but by the hour, this impacts strongly on workers' lives, and the [officially-set] minimum subsistence level has no force.[11]

Supply problems had by no means disappeared. In January the Moscow soviet executive bought extra grain supplies abroad and reduced rations for *sluzhashchie*, after stockpiles were depleted by the drought, failed harvest and the Volga famine of 1921.[12] Late distribution of rations remained a problem, too. But most attention focused on the timing of wage payments and the exchange rate used. These caused 95 per cent of strikes in the first half of 1922. And workers constantly upped the ante: demands were made not only for prompt payment, but also for the guilt of those responsible for delays to be ascertained, or for extravagant increases or early payments to pre-empt management delay.[13] By the second half of the year, the substance of workers' concerns had shifted again. More enterprises had moved on to cost accounting; currency stabilization measures were having some effect; and the unions had begun to negotiate collective agreements. These signs of improvement stimulated more ambitious demands. When 10,000 workers struck for higher wages at the Glukhovskaia textile mill at Bogorodskoe (see below, p. 157), *Pravda* reported: 'They admit that they live much better this year than last year. And, all the same, they want to live better still.' The Goznak party cell bureau, discussing demands by workers for a 100 per cent pay rise and the abolition of differentials, minuted its collective opinion that 'the relative improvement in workers' material conditions', brought about by 'the move to economic construction on the basis of New Economic Policy (NEP), and the great wealth of products available in the markets and shops' had 'raised the level of demands, and the striving to achieve a better-off, even a well-fed, life style'.[14]

Mass mobilization versus mass participation

Having dealt with their political opponents in the soviets, the Bolsheviks now developed mass mobilization techniques as an alternative to mass participation in making decisions. In the history of socialist ideas, the participatory democracy that flourished imperfectly in 1917 was favoured by the 'socialism-from-below' tradition, represented, in Hal Draper's description, by Thomas Munzer against Thomas More, Marx against the nineteenth-century

11 TsAOPIM, 3/3/33/13.
12 Aleshchenko, op. cit., pp. 303–4.
13 VK, 'Godovoi opyt professional'noi raboty v novykh uslovyakh', *Vestnik truda* 2–3, 1923: 3–24, here 7; S. Pirani, *The Changing Political Relationship Between Moscow Workers and the Bolsheviks, 1920–24* (PhD diss., University of Essex, 2006), pp. 321–26.
14 TsAOPIM, 1099/1/5/70; *Pravda*, 14 June 1922.

state socialists and William Morris against Sidney Webb.[15] Mass mobilization, in which the party defines the parameters and aims of a campaign, calls on the mass of people to support it, and judges mass consciousness by levels of participation, stands clearly in the 'socialism-from-above' tradition. It fences off the mass from decision-making, and assigns it a limited role, undertaking activity guided by decision-makers in the party. This aspect of it was pinpointed by the Workers Group manifesto, published in early 1923 and centred on the demand to revive workplace soviets, which asked:

> What are we being told [by the Bolshevik leadership]? 'You sit quiet, go out and demonstrate when you're invited, sing the Internationale – when required – and the rest will be done without you, by first-class people who are almost the same sort of workers as you, only cleverer.' ... But what we need is a practice based on the self-activity of the working class, not on the party's fear of it.[16]

Historians who have written about Bolshevik mass mobilization techniques have stressed its relationship with state-building, from Robert Tucker – who described the Bolsheviks' state as a 'movement-regime' owing something to Mazzini's Young Italy movement: a 'revolutionary mass-movement regime under single-party auspices' – to Thomas Remington and David Priestland, whose work was discussed in the Introduction, and Lewis Siegelbaum, in his work on Stakhanovism.[17] Priestland and Wendy Goldman have also written about the use of mobilization techniques during the purges.[18] Other studies of mass mobilization focused on China, where mass mobilization was used to mediate a relationship from which the working class and its traditions of organization and participatory democracy were largely absent, in the first instance that between the Maoist party/army and the peasant populations in the Kiangsi soviet republic (1931–34) and the Yenan period (1940–45).[19] In contrast to Priestland, who treats mobilization above all as a product of ideology, the account that follows situates the use of mobilization

---

15 H. Draper, 'The Two Souls of Socialism', *New Politics* 5: 1, Winter 1966: 57–84; H. Draper, *Karl Marx's Theory of Revolution. Volume II: The Politics of Social Classes*, New York: Monthly Review Press, 1978, vol. II, pp. 147–65.
16 RGASPI, 17/71/4/71.
17 R.C. Tucker, 'Towards a Comparative Politics of Movement-Regimes', *American Political Science Review*, 55: 2, 1961: 281–89; L. Siegelbaum, *Stakhanovism and the Politics of Productivity*, Cambridge: Cambridge University Press, 1988.
18 D. Priestland, *Stalinism and the Politics of Mobilization: Ideas, Power and Terror in Inter-War Russia*, New York: Oxford University Press, 2007, pp. 304–403; W. Goldman, 'Stalinist Terror and Democracy: the 1937 Union Campaign', *American Historical Review* 110: 5, 2005: 1427–53.
19 G. Bennett, *Yundong: Mass Campaigns in Chinese Communist Leadership*, Berkeley: Centre for Chinese Studies, 1976, especially pp. 20–32; C.P. Cell, *Revolution at Work: Mobilization Campaigns in China*, New York: Academic Press, 1977, especially pp. 8–21, 38–40 and 44–46. See also discussion by Priestland, op. cit., pp. 416–29.

techniques, alongside the assault on participatory democracy, in the context of the class relations that were taking shape in early Soviet Russia.

The erosion of participatory democracy and the use of mass mobilization techniques had both begun soon after the Bolsheviks took power. Contemporaneous with the decline of the soviets, the campaign of *subbotniki* (Saturday work) began on the Moscow railways in April 1919 and became a national event on 1 May 1920. There were military mobilizations, for example the 'party week' of October 1919 in which thousands of workers were recruited to the party and sent to the front; the 'defence week' that immediately followed, when people were mobilized to build barricades; and the 'collection week' in September 1920 to support the Polish offensive. The despatch of factory-based food procurement squads into the countryside, borne of necessity during and straight after the civil war, took on some characteristics of mobilization campaigns. In 1920 there were mobilizations of factory workers to cut peat for fuel, to heat buildings, to restore the railways and to clean up after the spring thaw, and even a sanitation week (some people called it 'bath week') to tackle hygiene problems and disease.[20] While these civil-war-time mobilizations were given a political rationale, they were directed at specific practical goals associated with defeating the Whites and building the economy. The campaigns of 1922 were, on the other hand, largely symbolic public actions, designed to demonstrate worker support for the Bolsheviks and raise public antipathy to the party's main political enemies, i.e. the church and the SRs.

The campaign to confiscate church valuables

During 1921, while the party in the urban centres was preoccupied with restarting production and implementing NEP, a famine crisis was developing on the Volga and in some other rural areas.[21] Towards the end of the year, the campaign to aid famine victims was given increasing prominence in the party press. In January 1922 a proposal by Trotsky, to turn the campaign against the church, was accepted by the Bolshevik leadership. Articles in party publications condemned the church for retaining its valuables while people were starving, and on 23 February the CEC ordered the confiscation of all church valuables to aid famine victims. The head of the Russian Orthodox Church, Patriarch Tikhon, responded with a declaration that all

---

20 Aleshchenko, op. cit., pp. 137–40 and 169–71; A.I. Mazaev, *Prazdnik kak sotsial'no-khudozhestvennoe iavlenie*, Moscow: 'Nauka', 1968, pp. 301–4; A.M. Sinitsyn et al. (eds), *Istoriia rabochykh Moskvy 1917–1945 gg.*, Moscow: 'Nauka', 1983, pp. 63 and 98–99; Iu.A. Poliakov, *Moskovskie trudiashchiesia v oborone sovetskoi stolitsy v 1919 godu*, Moscow: izd. Akademii nauk SSSR, 1958, p. 137; *Otchet sed'moi Moskovskoi gubpartkonferentsii RKP 29–31 Oktiabria 1921 g.*, Moscow, 1921, p. 19; TsAOPIM, 3/2/48/18, 40, 46, 49, 128; M. Borrero, *Hungry Moscow: Scarcity and Urban Society in the Russian Civil War, 1917–1921*, New York: Peter Lang, 2003, pp. 89–99.

non-sacred valuables should be contributed to famine relief, but that confiscations were sacrilegious.[22] The Bolsheviks departed from the approach they had adopted after the decree of January 1918 separating church from state, the implementation of which was accompanied by anti-religious propaganda and education. The 1922 campaign amounted to an offensive underpinned by state repression.[23] In the countryside, violent conflicts between confiscation detachments and crowds of peasants led by priests culminated in the bloody clash at Shuia, a textile town in Ivanovo region; two major trials of priests; executions (which Lenin specifically advocated); and jailings. It was coordinated nationally and monitored by the party and the security police of the GPU (as the Cheka was renamed) in a way that no previous campaign had been. Party organizations presented standard resolutions to workers' meetings, district party leaders checked that they were doing so, and the results of such meetings were systematically surveyed by GPU agents.[24] This coordination and monitoring helped to empty the campaign of any participatory democratic element it might have had.

The campaign on church valuables was placed before a working class in which the nature of religious belief had changed substantially during urbanization. Belief, for many believers, had in many ways become more compatible with secular culture. Sergei Firsov concludes that in the decade up to 1917, many religious workers 'began to view religion and the official church through the prism of the idea of social justice clearly wrapped in a socialist "package"'. While many workers remained 'traditional' believers, the

21 The famine, a large-scale tragedy that affected areas with a population of more than 30 million, and claimed up to 5 million lives, is one of the key events of the post-civil-war period. It awaits much more historical research. C. Edmondson, 'The Politics of Hunger: the Soviet Response to Famine, 1921', *Soviet Studies* 29: 4, 1977: 506–18, assesses the Bolshevik response. Recent historiographical discussion has been clouded by cold-war-style assertions that the Bolsheviks caused the famine and kept it secret as long as they could, especially in R. Pipes, *Russia Under the Bolshevik Regime*, London: Harvill, 1994, pp. 410–19. B. Patenaude, *The Big Show in Bololand: The American Relief Expedition to Soviet Russia in the Famine of 1921*, Stanford: Stanford University Press, 2002, concentrates on the US relief effort.
22 W.B. Husband, *'Godless Communists': Atheism and Society in Soviet Russia 1917–1937*, DeKalb: Northern Illinois University Press, 2000, pp. 54–59; A. Luukkanen, *The Party of Unbelief: the Religious Policy of the Bolshevik Party 1917–1929*, Helsinki: SHS, 1994, pp. 107–17; O.Iu. Vasil'eva, 'Russkaiia pravoslavnaia tserkov' i sovetskaia vlast' v 1917–27 godakh', *Voprosy Istorii* 8, 1993: 40–54; J. Meijer (ed.), *The Trotsky Papers 1917–1922*, The Hague: Mouton, 1964, vol. II, pp. 670–72; N.N. Pokrovskii and S.G. Petrov (eds), *Arkhiv Kremlia: Politbiuro i tserkov' 1922–1925 gg.*, Moscow: Rosspen, 1997, kn. 1, pp. 113–15.
23 Husband, op. cit., pp. 47–54; Luukkanen, op. cit., p. 100.
24 J. Daly, '"Storming the Last Citadel": The Bolshevik Assault on the Church, 1922', in V. Brovkin (ed.), *The Bolsheviks in Russian Society: the Revolution and Civil Wars*, New Haven: Yale University Press, 1997, pp. 252–59; Husband, op. cit., pp. 57–58; Pokrovskii and Petrov (eds), op. cit., kn. 1, pp. 42–54 and kn. 2, pp. 45–50.

church viewed them as the least religious section of society.²⁵ On the other hand urban religious workers clung determinedly to their right to celebrate religious holidays, and in the post-civil-war years this caused numerous labour disputes. Workers threatened to strike if prevented from marking the holidays, demanded extra produce for their celebrations, and negotiated with managers to take religious holidays instead of communist ones, or to make up the time in other ways.²⁶ When the issue of famine relief was raised, many believers were ready to support it – but not in the way the Bolsheviks wanted. An example is provided by the Trekhgornaia textile mill in Krasnopresnia, where both religion and narodnism continued to exercise influence on a predominantly female workforce that had a large proportion of recent migrants from the countryside. In February 1922, before the confiscations campaign got underway, a mass meeting at the mill heard a report from a food procurement expedition to Chuvashiia, where grain was held in stores and not distributed to the famine-stricken population. The meeting instructed the factory committee chairman to protest to the All-Russian Aid Committee (Pomgol).²⁷

The confiscations campaign properly started in March, with factory meetings, meetings of believers, and film screenings, followed by confiscations of valuables, carried out by special detachments and Red army units. The available evidence indicates that most Moscow workers supported the campaign, but passively. The MC's agit-prop commission reported 550 workplace meetings, at about 10 per cent of which opposition or hesitation was expressed.²⁸ Even when fear of repression, exaggerations of success in activists' reports, and the fact that most opposition was at larger-than-average workplaces, are factored in, there is still a headcount in favour. The party organized gatherings of believers at churches to win support for the campaign. These would often resolve to hand over some valuables, but not the most important, for example sacred vessels and crosses, and sometimes elect representatives to negotiate with the confiscation commissions. When the confiscations began, crowds gathered at some Moscow churches. There

---

25 S. Firsov, 'Workers and the Orthodox Church in Early Twentieth-Century Russia', in M. Melancon and A.K. Pate (eds), *New Labor History: Worker Identity and Experience in Russia, 1840–1918*, Bloomington: Slavica, 2002, pp. 65–76. See also P. Herrlinger, 'Orthodoxy and the Experience of Factory Life', in Melancon and Pate (eds), op. cit., pp. 35–64; and E. Kabo, *Ocherki rabochego byta: opyt monograficheskogo issledovaniia domashnego rabochego byta*, Moscow: VTsSPS, 1928, pp. 199–201.
26 TsAOPIM, 3/3/34/46, 98, 100; 3/2/48/17ob; 3/1a/11/57ob; GARF, 393/43a/1714/255, 261, 263ob. See also D.J. Raleigh, *Experiencing Russia's Civil War: Politics, Society and Revolutionary Culture in Saratov, 1917–1922*, Princeton: Princeton University Press, 2002, p. 217; and Murphy, op. cit., p. 137.
27 TsAGM, 425/1/100/1; S. Lapitskaia, *Byt' rabochikh trekhgornoi manufaktury*, Moscow: OGIZ, 1935, pp. 128, 137–40.
28 RGASPI, 17/60/336/74–82, reproduced in Pokrovskii and Petrov, op. cit., kn. 2, pp. 207–16.

were some violent clashes with the confiscation commissions, but nowhere on the scale reached in the countryside.[29]

Desire to aid the famine victims again combined with distrust for the Bolsheviks at factory meetings, where both believers and non-believers would have been present. Opposition to the Bolsheviks' campaigning methods was expressed by socialist, i.e. non-religious, activists. At the AMO car factory, the non-party group argued for 'popular control' of the famine relief campaign 'to ensure that the valuables really are disposed of as they should be'. A representative, Solov'ev, was elected to check. Vasilii Tikhonov, a non-partyist, told a mass meeting that the confiscation should have begun earlier, and supported Solov'ev's election by referring to reports of 'incorrect confiscations' – presumably, those that breached regulations against 'excesses' and needless confrontation – in Tambov. At other workplaces where non-Bolshevik socialists remained active, Bolshevik resolutions on the confiscation of church valuables were not opposed but amended: at the 1886 power station, a meeting chaired by Epifanov decided to contribute 500 pud (8.2 tonnes) of excess grain from the station's own stores, supplemented by voluntary donations. At a bakery in Gorodskoi district, Mensheviks raised 'the need for control' over confiscations, linking this to the issue of free speech. The confiscation committee in Krasnopresnia was told by a speaker at one meeting:

> Many people don't trust [you]. Will what is collected reach the starving? It would be good if we knew exactly to whom it is given, for example by linking a particular village to a workplace here, and how many people the aid is feeding, the region, district, village.[30]

Meetings on the confiscation of church valuables were used by some workers to re-raise the issue of elite privileges. A heckler in Krasnopresnia shouted:

> Comrades, have we really got to the point when we have to take the decorations from the churches? ... It would be better for you to give the surplus wealth that you've made under soviet rule. Let's take off that bourgeois coat, that was taken from the bourgeoisie, and share it with the starving children. ... Let the idealistic communists' wives work for the starving.[31]

---

29 TsAOPIM, 3/3/34/53, 58ob, 60ob, 76ob, 78, 78ob, 79; TsGAMO, 66/22/71/9, 14, 15, 45; Pokrovskii and Petrov, op. cit., kn. 2, p. 135.
30 TsAOPIM, 3/3/34/85, 85ob; 433/1/14/10; TsAGM, 415/16/318/37; Pokrovskii and Petrov, op. cit., kn. 2, p. 210; GARF, 1235/140/59/68ob, reproduced in Pokrovskii and Petrov, op. cit., kn. 2, pp. 110–13.
31 On the significance of the complaint against Bolsheviks' wives, see Chapter 5, p. 121. The heckler is one of several similar quoted by Vinogradov, in Pokrovskii and Petrov, op. cit., kn. 2, p. 210.

Similar points were written into resolutions at the Kosa metallurgical works, a stronghold of non-partyist organization, which voted to support the CEC decree on confiscation 'with an addendum: to confiscate all valuables from citizens of the Soviet republic', and the Varts Makgill foundry, which voted to 'confiscate gold first from the communists, their wives, and traders, and then from the church'.[32] Perhaps these workers were unaware that the Moscow party leaders had themselves, in the summer of 1921, called on party members to surrender valuables to aid the famine victims,[33] or perhaps that decision had not been implemented. Some workers protested at Bolshevik appropriation of decision-making by refusing to give post-facto approval to a decision in which they had not participated. At the Geo-fizika factory in Sokol'niki, only 18 votes could be mustered for a resolution supporting confiscation; a representative of the majority called out: 'you've published the decree, now implement it; there's nothing to ask us about'. At Miusskii tram park in Krasnopresnia, and three workplaces in Zamoskvorech'e – the Sytin print works, the Gulutvinskaia textile works and the artificial limb factory – the workforce refused to vote on resolutions supporting confiscation for the same reason.[34] The campaign to confiscate church valuables is agreed by historians to have contributed little to the relief effort.[35] But it shifted the emphasis of Bolshevik anti-religious work from propaganda to offensive campaigning action, coordinated by party and state bodies and backed by state repression. These methods were next employed against the party's secular rivals.

The trial of the SRs

In June 1922 a group of leaders of the SR party were put on trial in Moscow, for conspiring to organize terrorist acts against the Bolsheviks and related charges.[36] The second big mobilization campaign of the year was arranged to build public support for the trial. It involved a greater shift away from the traditions of 1917 than had the church valuables campaign, and faced greater opposition from politically active workers. During the church valuables mobilization, these workers, many of whom had become both literate and conscious of political issues during the process of urbanization and revolution, objected to the manner of the campaign rather than its substance. But the SR trial posed greater dilemmas. First, there was

32 TsAOPIM, 3/3/34/78ob, 80; A. Pospielovsky, 'Strikes During the NEP', *Revolutionary Russia* 10: 1, 1997: 1–34, here 14–15.
33 TsAOPIM, 3/2/28/92; 63/1/50/4.
34 Pokrovskii and Petrov, op. cit., kn. 2, p. 209; TsAOPIM, 3/3/3/70.
35 Daly, op. cit., p. 258; Husband, op. cit., pp. 56 and 58.
36 On the trial itself, see M. Jansen, *A Show Trial Under Lenin*, The Hague: Martinus Nijhoff, 1982; and S.A. Krasil'nikov, K.N. Morozov and I.V. Chubykin (eds), *Sudebnyi protsess nad sotsialistami-revoliutsionerami (iiun'-avgust 1922 g.). Podgotovka. Provedenie. Itogi. Sbornik dokumentov*, Moscow: Rosspen, 2002.

residual support for the SRs, who were seen as bearers of the narodnik tradition. Of course there was opposition to the SR leaders on the issue of soviet power, implicit in the majority the Bolsheviks won among politically active workers in late 1917. And the participation by many SR leaders in the Komuch government during the civil war finished them off in the eyes of many left-wing workers. But for others, that did not settle the issue. After the Komuch government collapsed, the SR party leadership split several ways, due to disagreements over whether to continue armed resistance to the Bolsheviks, and on whether to combat the Whites.[37] In Moscow, rank-and-file SRs remained active in the rail workshops and textile mills, and among telegraph and postal workers, and had posed as a socialist alternative to the Bolsheviks during the hardship of 1920–21. Another dilemma was presented to workers, whether they sympathized with the SRs or not, by the Bolsheviks' demand for the trial defendants to be executed. This involved renouncing opposition to the death penalty, a democratic principle of 1917 to which the Bolsheviks, on paper, still subscribed.[38]

The Central Committee (CC) of the Bolshevik party first decided to try the SR party leaders in December 1921 and announced this intention publicly in February 1922. The propaganda campaign began with a public dispute with the leaders of the Socialist International, during which Lenin initiated the call for the death penalty. In Moscow the MC supervised a campaign of resolutions at workplace meetings during May and June. This activity was coordinated with a 'technical troika' of GPU officers, headed by the anarchist-turned-Bolshevik Timofei Samsonov[39] who in April oversaw a crackdown on the Mensheviks' Moscow organization, and in late May moved on to arrest all known SR activists, starting with those on the

---

37 See, for example, Jansen, op. cit., pp. 1–21.
38 The Bolsheviks had throughout the civil war repeatedly expressed opposition in principle to the death penalty and insisted that extrajudicial executions by the Cheka were due to military exigencies. The widely distributed popularization of the party programme published in 1920 states: 'While the civil war continues, abolition of the death penalty is impossible. But a dispassionate comparison of proletarian justice with the justice of the bourgeois counter-revolution shows the marvellous leniency of the workers' courts in comparison with the executioners of bourgeois justice. The workers pass death sentences in extreme cases only'. N. Bukharin and E. Preobrazhenskii, *The ABC of Communism: a Popular Explanation of the Program of the Communist Party of Russia*, London: Communist Party of Great Britain, 1922, p. 232. This harked back to the position taken by the second congress of soviets in 1917, which as it endorsed the Bolshevik seizure of power also reversed the death penalty at the front imposed by the provisional government. A recent historian of the death penalty writes that this decision was in keeping with the predominant outlook of 1917 – that abolition of the death penalty, to quote a typical soviet resolution, was 'one of the most precious gains of our great Russian revolution'. S. Zhiltsov, *Smertnaia kazn' v istorii Rossii*, Moscow: Zertsalo-M, 2002, pp. 213–27. On the introduction of a new legal code prior to the trial, see G. Gill, *The Origins of the Stalinist Political System*, Cambridge: Cambridge University Press, 1990, p. 31 and p. 333.
39 On Samsonov, see Appendix 1.

Moscow railway network. The party and GPU bodies also coordinated the monitoring of workplace responses to the resolutions.[40] Street demonstrations started with one at the train station on 25 May to protest at the arrival of the Belgian social democrat Emile Vandervelde, a defence lawyer for the accused. They culminated on 20 June with an enormous demonstration on the fourth anniversary of the assassination of the Bolshevik leader Moisei Volodarskii.[41]

In the factories, the Bolsheviks initially found it more difficult to win support for the trial than they had for the mobilization against the church. A preliminary summary of working-class attitudes, compiled by the GPU on 1 June, suggested that three-fifths were supportive, more than one tenth had a 'definitely negative' attitude and the rest were 'doubtful' or 'passive'.[42] The fiercest opposition was provoked by the arrest of SR sympathizers at the Trekhgornaia textile mill. On 25 May, Lunacharskii addressed a meeting there, and a resolution was passed condemning the SR 'murderers and traitors to the working people' – with one vote against and five abstentions. The GPU resolved to quell this opposition, and on 4 June six weavers were arrested for 'suspected agitation about the SR trial'. On 6 June the weaving shop's 600 day-shift workers struck, demanding the release of the six detainees and a wage increase. The management threatened to close the shop and sack all its workers. This ended the strike, and work resumed on the night shift. On 19 June, the day before the big demonstration, another mass meeting was addressed by Lunacharskii, at which the demand to release the detainees was raised again.[43] Other workplaces where support for the SRs was expressed included the Alekseevskaia water works in Sokol'niki, where SRs and non-partyists had clashed with the Bolshevik cell on account of the latter's egregious *spets*-baiting (see Chapter 7, pp. 187–8). Bolshevik resolutions on the trial were also defeated at workplaces where the

---

40 Krasil'nikov and Morozov, 'Predislovie', in Krasil'nikov, Morozov, and Chubykin (eds.), op. cit., pp. 61–63.
41 Volodarskii was assassinated by Sergeev, a SR party member. The prosecution case at the trial referred both to the SRs' role in mounting armed resistance to the Bolsheviks during the civil war, but also to claims that leading SRs had conspired to order Volodarskii's assassination and other terrorist acts against the Bolsheviks. These latter claims relied in crucial respects on the unsafe evidence of informers. Legal procedure was routinely breached and the prosecutor, Nikolai Krylenko, made clear that the judgement should be a political one. The SR leaders denounced the court and repudiated all charges. The grandiose fabricated conspiracies and absurd confessions that were key features of future show trials were absent.
42 TsAOPIM, 3/3/33/71. The GPU's survey covered 31 workplace meetings attended by an aggregate total of 10,600 workers, of whom 6400 were counted as supportive of the trial, 1400 had a 'definitely negative attitude', 2300 were 'doubtful' and 500 'passive'.
43 TsAOPIM, 3/3/34/149, 150, 166ob; Krasil'nikov and Morozov, op. cit., pp. 64 and 67; Jansen, op. cit., pp. 147–48, citing *Golos Rossii*, 22 September 1922.

Demonstrations in Moscow marking, top, building workers' and their family members' graduation from a literacy course (mid 1920s) and, above, the fifth anniversary of the October revolution (1922).

Mensheviks and left SRs remained active, such as the 27th print works in Khamovniki and the Rusalkii tram depot.[44] The left SRs, most of whose leaders were already in exile abroad, renewed their public activity in Moscow, to protest against both the trial of the right SR leaders and a trial of some of their own activists. The left SR K.N. Prokopovich – who, along with the anarchists, had some support at the Il'in motor works – was expelled from the

Krasnopresnia soviet, to which he was a delegate, on 1 June after speaking against the Bolshevik campaign around the SR trial. At the factory, non-partyists and left SRs called on workers not to join the anti-SR demonstration.⁴⁵

Concerns among broader layers of workers, i.e. beyond those who somehow identified politically with the SRs, were provoked by the Bolshevik insistence on the death penalty. The GPU noted that workers who 'sympathized with, or felt sorry for' the defendants passed 'softened' resolutions, i.e. without calls for 'severe punishment'. On the 20 June demonstration, there were three groups of people carrying banners declaring opposition to the death penalty. At the Moscow higher technical school, a meeting on the trial had split three ways: one group supported a Bolshevik resolution, another (presumably sympathetic to the SRs) refused to vote on the trial 'since it is being conducted one-sidedly', and a middle group argued that 'given the present strength of the Russian soviet republic and the Russian Communist Party, there is no need to subject the SRs to severe punishment'.⁴⁶ Some workers challenged the mobilization on the grounds that it undermined judicial process. At the Tsutran factory in Bauman, a Bolshevik resolution was rejected after two workers argued that 'making decisions about a matter in front of the court is a job not for workers, but for the court itself'. A group of workers at the Podol'sk engineering works gave similar reasons for abstaining from voting. At a print shop in Bauman, and at the Shapov factory, there was 'dissatisfaction at the way that the defending counsel for the SRs, Vandervelde and co., had been greeted', suggesting that workers thought that the trial was damaging the soviet state's reputation in Europe.⁴⁷ At the central telegraph office, a non-party 'mechanics' group' led by Ikonnikov joined forces with a separate SR group and proposed deleting from a Bolshevik resolution a clause calling for the 'highest order of punishment' for the trial defendants; both these groups would continue to clash with the Bolshevik leaders of the works trade union committee throughout the year.⁴⁸

Working-class unease at the changing format of mass meetings, away from participatory democracy and towards the approval of standard resolutions, resulted in mass abstentions. Deprived by procedure of decision-making power, workers stayed silent and gave their views only when

---

44 TsAOPIM, 3/3/34/148; 3/3/33/81.
45 TsAOPIM, 3/3/34/147; Krasil'nikov and Morozov, op. cit., p. 65; *Pravda* 30 June 1922.
46 TsAOPIM, 3/3/34/166; Krasil'nikov and Morozov, op. cit. p. 66; *Sotsialisticheskii Vestnik* 15, 1922, pp. 7–9.
47 TsAOPIM, 3/3/34/147, 161; *Pravda* 23 June 1922.
48 Ikonnikov's group was separate from, and allied to, the SR group headed by Uvarov and two brothers Lavrent'ev. In September 1922 a member of the factory committee, perhaps associated with one of these groups, was arrested. TsAOPIM, 3/3/34/210, 213, 214, 217, 261, 264, 351.

pressed. So when a standard Bolshevik resolution was put to a 150-strong mass meeting at the Varts MakGill ironworks, it received 40 votes for and two abstentions, with a large majority declining even to register an abstention. Asked to explain his stance, one of the majority replied: 'why are we judging the SRs, and not those who shot at, beat and robbed the masses when we went for potatoes and bread [during the civil war]?' At a print shop in Bauman, a party resolution attracted 25 votes and more than 800 abstentions; at the Uvarov tram park in Khamovniki a party resolution was passed at a meeting of 100 workers by 35 to 18, with the rest abstaining. Another mass mobilization technique that provoked resistance was that of asking workers individually to sign resolutions supporting the death penalty. At the Miusskii tram park in Krasnopresnia, 600 workers voted for a resolution supporting the trial, but only 50 would sign it.[49]

There was opposition to the conduct of the campaign within the party, too. At the Sverdlov communist university, where the student body predominantly comprised rank-and-file Bolsheviks, a delegation had attended the demonstration against Vandervelde, but then the mood of 'hostility' to the SRs had been replaced by one of 'repentance', according to a GPU agent's report. The students had begun 'to take a judgmental view of their own demonstration' and, having read letters in the press from imprisoned SRs, become 'critical' of the campaign. At a Moscow regional party conference on 25–26 June the perennial dissident David Riazanov argued that the party should not have urged the death penalty against specific SR leaders. The Moscow party leader, Kamenev, responded with a tirade of abuse, and told Riazanov he had 'no right ... to defend or cultivate a mood against the death penalty'. The CC accepted Kamenev's proposal to 'take measures' against Riazanov, who was assigned to work abroad, on literary tasks only, for a year.[50]

20 June and other demonstrations

Notwithstanding all the forms of opposition mentioned above, a huge number of people – between 200,000 and 300,000 from a total city population of about 1.28 million – turned out on the 20 June demonstration.[51] This

---

49 TsAOPIM, 3/3/34/147ob, 161, 161ob; Krasil'nikov and Morozov, op. cit., p. 66.
50 TsAOPIM, 3/3/34/148; Krasil'nikov, Morozov, and Chubykin (eds), op. cit., pp. 494–99; RGASPI 17/3/1394/1–2, quoted in Krasil'nikov, Morozov, and Chubykin (eds), op. cit., pp. 756–57; Ia. Rokitianskii and R. Muller, *Krasnyi dissident: akademik Riazanov – opponent Lenina, zhertva Stalina*, Moscow: Academia, 1996, pp. 202–4.
51 As a proportion of the city's population, the number is comparable to that on the big demonstration in February 2003 in London against the imminent invasion of Iraq (1.5 million from a population of 7.6 million), the city's largest in modern times. *Pravda* 22 June 1922; Jansen, op. cit., pp. 146 and 208.

was a triumph of mass mobilization over participatory democracy, and in that sense the Menshevik Boris Dvinov was right that the spectacle of workers marching under red banners calling for the death penalty was 'a turning point' for the Russian revolution. Dvinov argued that 'fear of death from [unemployment, and the resulting] hunger moved the hand of the worker, when he voted for the party cell's resolution and when he signed a petition for punishment, and brought him willy-nilly to the demonstration'.[52] This, though, seems an insufficient explanation for the large turn-out. The nadir in terms of shortages had been passed in the spring of 1921. Dismissal might have brought the imminent prospect of death from hunger in 1919–20, but by 1922, the possibility of return to the countryside and the rudimentary welfare benefits system ensured survival. One of the SR trial defendants, Mikhail Gendel'man, referred in court to the arrests at the Trekhgornaia mill and claimed that the demonstrators had been driven onto the streets by GPU threats.[53] This is also difficult to accept: very small numbers were arrested, and while fears of repression, and of a return to the horrors of the civil war, may have been aroused by the assault on the SRs, these cannot alone explain such a huge mobilization. Nor, to be sure, can the formulaic, set-piece speeches by worker delegates to the revolutionary tribunal. In *Pravda*'s report, among the alarming calls for the defendants to be executed, only two moments of reality stand out. The first is a denunciation of the SRs by a mother of three children as the murderers of her husband, who was killed at the front. The second is a speech by a representative of the Moscow post and telegraph offices, where SR influence remained strong, who said that he had switched allegiance to the Bolsheviks for the most prosaic and materialistic of reasons: 'Soviet power gives us everything that it can. ... It has given us the Vysotskii mansion [for workers' families to live in]. ... If Gots and co. were in power, I am sure they would drive us out of there.' Between those at one end of the scale moved by fear or apprehension, and those at the other end who genuinely saw the SRs as enemies of the revolution and its gains, many more were probably taking the line of least resistance. Here was a chance to leave the factory for half a day on a sunny summer's afternoon, most likely with the management's permission and with no reduction in pay.[54]

The 20 June demonstration exemplified the social contract. Some politically conscious workers were suspicious or sceptical of, or downright hostile to, a

---

52 B. Dvinov, *Ot legal'nosti k podpol'iu 1921–22*, Stanford: Hoover Institution, 1968, pp. 136–37.
53 *Pravda*, 24 June 1922; Jansen, op. cit., p. 147.
54 Workplace contingents assembled in the districts at 2.00 pm, in fine weather. The single detailed description of a factory delegation said it was 'headed by management'. Given that communist managers would have to attend, it is reasonable to assume that that was widespread. *Pravda*, 22 June 1922. Kevin Murphy found that Serp i Molot workers participated in the demonstration 'with normal wage rates paid to participants'. Murphy, op. cit., p. 162.

'socialism' that demanded mass approval for the death penalty to deal with its political enemies. But the price paid in terms of repression for expressing such opposition was rising. And most workers were focused on the aim of returning their families to pre-war living standards, and aware that the Bolsheviks could deliver it. The justice of handing over the Vysotskii mansion to former slum dwellers was very real. Many workers associated the Bolsheviks with the destruction of the old exploiting classes, and saw the industrial revival as their own. Moreover, they could see the limitations being imposed on forms of working-class organization, and had little faith in the political opposition. Soviet and workplace democracy was limited; the possibilities of industrial growth seemed not to be. In November 1922, MC secretary Zelenskii, never one to overstate the party's achievements, said that fences were being mended with non-party workers because 'living standards have improved. Gone is the horrible worry about where to get a crust of bread today or tomorrow, the need to trick and speculate; and now workers' interest in politics has increased'.[55]

The 20 June demonstration may also be placed in the context of the systematization in the Bolshevik propaganda programme of public events marking May Day, the anniversary of the October revolution, and other similar occasions. Several historians have observed that these events, notable for spontaneity and inventiveness during the civil war, became official and formulaic. Before 1922, they were not 'subordinated to a strict structure', but thereafter 'the canon was put in place' and remained unchanged for decades afterwards (V. Glebkin); in the factories, the celebrations were marked in a 'social, family' spirit, but later stifled by officialdom (Viktoriia Tiazhel'nikova); revolutionary content was replaced by 'heavy instrumentalism' (Richard Stites).[56] The relative weight in achieving large turnouts on such occasions of threats, paternalistic arm-twisting, the distribution of extra rations, worker sympathy with the regime, and hopes of upholding the traditions of 1917, could be further researched. Certainly, the celebrations were already being more tightly directed by the fifth anniversary of the October revolution in 1922. There was a high turnout (more than 250,000), and at a frank, behind-closed-doors meeting in Krasnopresnia, Bolshevik organizers referred to workers' high spirits: so elevated, as one organizer, Shapiro, put it, 'that even the late payment of wages did not stop people

---

55 *Izvestiia MK RKP(b)* 3, 1922, pp. 5–13.
56 V.V. Glebkin, *Ritual v sovetskom kul'ture*, Moscow: Inus-K, 1998, pp. 98–99; R. Stites, *Revolutionary Dreams: Utopian Vision and Experimental Life in the Russian Revolution*, Oxford: Oxford University Press, 1989, p. 50; V. Tiazhel'nikova, 'Povsednevnost'' i revoliutsionnie preobrazovaniia sovetskoi vlasti', in G.N. Sevost'ianov (ed.), *Rossiia v XX veke: Reforma i revoliutsiia*, Moskva: 'Nauka', 2002, vol. 2, pp. 84–100, here 89–94. See also J. von Geldern, *Bolshevik Festivals, 1917–1920*, Berkeley: University of California Press, 1993, pp. 208–19; C. Lane, *The Rites of Rulers: Ritual in Industrial Society – the Soviet Case*, Cambridge: Cambridge University Press, 1981, pp. 162–69.

turning out'. Likhachev made the telling remark that 'this time, the demonstration was not officially contrived', implicitly acknowledging that others had been.[57] A key element in cementing the workers' position as passive followers of an exalted vanguard was the iconization of Bolshevik leaders. On the fifth anniversary of the revolution, factories were renamed in honour not only of senior figures such as Lenin and Trotsky, but also of less remarkable 'old Bolsheviks', e.g. Viktor Taratuta and Ian Rudzutak.[58] In December 1922 Lunacharskii, who had long advocated a secular 'religion', spoke in reverent tones about Lenin to a mass meeting at the Trekhgornaia mill, that outpost of peasant religiosity a few hundred metres from the Kremlin. The meeting sent greetings to Lenin, addressing him as 'thou, great leader of the working class'.[59]

Soviets and unions

The more sophisticated the party's mass mobilization machinery became, the more powers were stripped from the soviets and trade unions, i.e. fora in which working-class collective *political* activity might develop. The Moscow soviet plenum's transformation from a participatory body to a lifeless lecture theatre reaped a harvest in 1922 in the form of worker apathy. At election times, workers either attended meetings in silence and declined to vote, as they had during the anti-SR campaign, or did not turn up at all. During soviet elections held in December 1922, a leaflet issued by the virtually underground left SR-maximalist group pointed out that unanimous support for Bolshevik candidates often came from meetings at which there was not a word of discussion: 'First prize ... should probably go to the workers of the Moscow Consumer Association [a retail trading house]', 2500 of whom listened for an hour to a report on the domestic and international situation and voted 'without a murmur' for a list of candidates headed by Lenin. The leaflet argued that, given the level of GPU surveillance, the obligatory use of open voting rather than secret ballots usurped democracy. Examples it gave of mass abstentions include that of the Guzhon steelworks, where a list of Bolshevik candidates was elected to the soviet by 100 votes against 2 with about 1900 abstentions.[60]

Just as the soviet was redefined as an organ of municipal administration, so the unions were allocated a new, subordinate role, implementing industrial

---

57 TsAOPIM, 69/1/93/130.
58 Workplaces were also named after Bukharin, Chicherin, Kalinin and Kamenev, as well as the then-deceased Sverdlov, Volodarskii and Uritskii. Trotsky encouraged this trend, urging the Moscow soviet after May Day 1922 that factories be renamed 'in a soviet manner'. RGASPI, 17/84/347/38.
59 *Pravda*, 15 December 1922; N.I. Rodionova, *Gody napriazhennogo truda: iz istorii Moskovskoi partiinoi organizatsii 1921–1925 gg.*, Moscow: Moskovskii rabochii, 1963, p. 68.
60 TsAOPIM, 3/11/76.

policies elaborated and supervised by party bodies. The tenth congress had made the unions responsible for mobilizing workers for production tasks; in practice this amounted mainly to campaigning for labour discipline. The eleventh party congress in March-April 1922 passed a resolution, based on a draft by Lenin, that once and for all quashed any suggestion that unions might participate in industrial administration. The resolution defined the unions' role as to 'defend workers' interests', this being hedged with important qualifications for the state-owned enterprises, where care had to be taken 'not to prejudice the ... development of the workers' state as a whole'. It permitted only such industrial action as 'corrects blunders and excesses [in state-owned industry] resulting from the bureaucratic distortions of the state apparatus', and in the next breath specified that the unions had to 'act as mediators' between workers and industrial administrators.[61] When the draft was discussed in the party leadership, it was the Bolshevik union leaders Andrei Andreev and Aleksandr Dogadov who opposed suggestions that the resolution might sanction strikes in state enterprises. In Moscow, this put the lower-level Bolshevik trade union officials – and they were all Bolsheviks, since after the removal in November 1921 of the Menshevik leadership of the chemical workers' union, the non-Bolshevik parties were active only at enterprise level – in an impossible position. As the Moscow union leader Mel'nichanskii explained to the MC, officials such as himself were 'bound hand and foot' by their belief in their responsibilities to the soviet system; they saw strikes and the threat of strikes as 'politically inexpedient' and were therefore *de facto* if not *de jure* entirely dependent on the party' to resolve conflicts.[62] Negotiations were conducted between Bolsheviks assigned to represent workers and Bolsheviks assigned to industrial management, who both accepted that the prime task was to improve production, and discussed labour issues only from that standpoint.

The unions' political dependence on the party manifested itself in two linked respects: first, they helped to discipline workers who went outside the prescribed negotiating procedure and used the strike weapon to bargain; second, their apparatus became organizationally and financially more closely integrated with the state's. In industrial disputes, the unions almost always acted as, and were perceived by workers as, industrial managers' allies. Three disputes in the textile towns in the Moscow region provide examples. The first, at the Voskresenskaia mill in Narofominsk, flared in mid January 1922 among weavers, when an argument over time off to celebrate the Orthodox New Year merged with alarm triggered by an announcement that the mill was to be removed from the state rations system and put on cost accounting, with wages paid in cash. There was a

---

61 *Odinnadtsatyi s"ezd RKP(b): stenograficheskii otchet*, Moscow: Gos. izd. politicheskoi literatury, 1961, pp. 528–37; A.V. Kvashonkin et al. (eds), *Bol'shevistskoe rukovodstvo. Perepiska. 1912–1927*, Moscow: Rosspen, 1996, pp. 234–35.
62 TsAOPIM, 3/3/5/55–59.

brief strike. The weavers' anger was directed primarily at a particularly unpopular manager, Sergei Sel'diakov. He was supported unwaveringly by the district trade union bureau and, less consistently, by the factory committee. A week later, searches at the mill gates reignited the dispute; a mass meeting denounced the district trade union bureau's 'churlish attitude' and demanded that Sel'diakov be sacked. Trouble flared again in June, when Sel'diakov locked out the spinners, who responded by demanding a 50 per cent pay increase. The regional union leadership proposed that the entire mill be closed for two months, a suggestion at which the factory committee balked.[63] In March at the Glukhovskaia mill at Bogorodskoe, trade union officials' arrogance had escalated a pay dispute into a strike by all 10,000 workers, *Pravda* reported.[64] In August, workers again faced aggression by union officials during the Moscow region's largest recorded strike in 1922, at the Orekhovo-Zuevo textile mills. The strike, for a wage increase, lasted several days and had 19,000 participants at its height. The union responded by expelling the weavers who had initiated the action, while management said they would be permanently sacked and their bread rations stopped. When other workers joined the strike, they elected a rank-and-file delegation to negotiate with the union's regional leadership, who were assumed to be on the other side.[65] It became common practice in the early NEP period for workers in dispute to elect delegates to negotiate with 'their' unions, and even factory committees. The Moscow trades unions opposed not only the textile workers' pay campaign, but also those by tram workers (who sought, as they had in 1920, to strengthen inter-depot solidarity), and teachers (who organized strikes and mass meetings to protest at several months' delay in wages payments).[66]

The textile workers' union's decision to expel the Orekhovo-Zuevo weavers was also not exceptional. In March 1922, the Moscow regional teachers' union leadership urged the sacking of a district trade union leader, and the dissolution of a district trade union committee, for supporting pay demands. In June 1923, organizers of one of the largest strikes in Moscow that year, by 13,000 seasonal peat workers, were expelled from their union as well as being dismissed.[67] This ostracism of industrial militants did not significantly impact on workers' instincts for striking, though. A party journal, surveying strikes and conflicts in state enterprises in 1923, most of which concerned late payment of wages, found that 96.5 per cent of them were undertaken by workers 'without informing, and even in breach of the decisions of, their trade unions'.[68]

63 TsAOPIM, 3/3/34/12, 17, 147, 164ob, 165.
64 *Pravda*, 14 June 1922.
65 TsAOPIM, 3/3/34/218, 225ob, 226ob, 229ob, 230, 233ob, 242ob, 244; *Sotsialisticheskii Vestnik* 19, 1922, pp. 14–15.
66 Pirani, op. cit., pp. 328–32.
67 TsAOPIM, 3/3/33/74–75; 3/3/34/55, 56, 61; 3/4/49/99–101; *Trud*, 12 July 1923.
68 I.B. Orlov, 'Problemy edinoi ekonomiki', in S.A. Pavliuchenkov et al. (eds), *Rossiia nepovskaia*, Moscow: Novyi khronograf, 2002, pp. 150–65, here p. 156.

158 Mass mobilization versus mass participation

In financial and organizational terms, the unions made a half-hearted, and ultimately unsuccessful, attempt to reduce their dependence on the state, which had been established during the civil war. Until 1921, the unions were financed almost entirely via the labour commissariat. In 1922 their staff were subject to cutbacks, in line with cost accounting. In a drive to centralize and standardize structures, some unions were merged and others reorganized. Both before and after the cutbacks, the unions were staffed mainly by the ubiquitous party 'cadres' who moved freely to and from other branches of the state. And at all levels, unelected officials outnumbered elected ones: for example, only eight of the 33 senior officials of the Moscow regional council of trade unions (Moskovskii gubernskii sovet professional'nykh soiuzov – MGSPS) were elected. Direct state aid to unions' central committees was supposed to stop under cost accounting, but did not. Unions' regional departments also continued to receive such aid. At the end of 1922, the state still directly employed more than 40 per cent of the Moscow region's 1500 union officials, and provided free accommodation, electricity and food supplies to the whole union apparatus.[69]

Bolshevik trade unionists acknowledged the need for organizational independence from the state, and from industrial managers, but could not achieve it. Their difficulties were highlighted by the failure in 1922–23 of a campaign to move from the deduction of trade union subscriptions from workers' wages prior to payment (i.e. 'deduction at source', along with insurance contributions) to a system of voluntary payment of subscriptions to activists. The former was historically associated, in Russia as well as in Western Europe and North America, with dependent 'yellow' unions, and the latter with strong workplace organization. The eleventh party congress decided that all union members should be reregistered on a voluntary basis. At first, union officials had feared that voluntary membership would undermine the unions' ability to impose labour discipline. At a meeting in Moscow, Mel'nichanskii argued that workers should be assumed to be union members, and sanction given to managers to sack those that wished to opt out. Gud'kov, who argued that unions had to put the issue of voluntary membership in front of workforces 'whether it suits us or not', in order to promote genuine commitment from union members, found himself in a minority of one.[70] However, the congress decision on voluntary membership was motivated less by such considerations of workplace militancy, and more by the perceived need – with a view to resisting the dilution of the

---

69 S.V. Shedrov (ed.), *Profsoiuzy Moskvy: Ocherki istorii*, Moscow: Profizdat, 1975, pp. 148–49; MGSPS, *Rezoliutsii i postanovleniia IV-ogo Moskovskogo gubernskogo s"ezda profsoiuzov (5–8 sent. 1922)*, Moscow, 1922, p. 4; *Sotsialisticheskii vestnik* 19, 1922, p. 12; *Otchet o deiatel'nosti Moskovskogo gubprofsoveta 1921– 22*, Moscow, 1922, pp. 60–61; G. Mel'nichanskii, *Moskovskie professional'nye soiuzy*, Moscow: Glavlit, 1923, p. 14; *Perepis' sluzhashchikh sovetskikh uchrezhdenii g. Moskvy 1922 g.*, Moscow, 1922, p. 122.
70 TsAOPIM, 3/2/27/3–22.

working class by 'non proletarians' – to exclude from the unions 'semi-proletarian elements' such as handicraftsmen and seasonal workers, and those who had lost their jobs in the first round of NEP redundancies. The metalworkers' union resolved that those who supplemented their wages from a home workshop were ineligible for membership; one official argued that a skilled worker whose wife ran a market stall, or sold kvass (a soft drink) and paid a home help, were 'clear' candidates for expulsion.[71]

Re-registration was supposed to be followed by a move away from 'deduction at source' to subscription collection by activists, but this nexus of union dependence on industrial managers could not be broken. At the vast majority of enterprises, the transition to 'voluntary' payment was accomplished by means of a single collective decision at a mass meeting ... which was followed by the continued deduction of subscriptions at source. (The door to such a procedure had been opened by the wording of the eleventh congress resolution, which urged 'voluntary membership, whether in respect of individual or collective recruitment'.) The inadequacy of such decisions in terms of workplace activism, and the failure of the voluntary membership campaign to revitalize enterprise-level organization, was widely acknowledged in trade union journals, and, from 1923, largely unsuccessful attempts were made to increase the proportion of subscriptions collected independently of factory managements.[72] By November 1923, hardly any progress had been made: in Moscow industry, the proportion of workers paying individually, as opposed to by deduction at source, was 'not high, about 10 per cent'. Individual collection was least well received in large enterprises, and union officials complained that late payment of wages, and the use of large-denomination notes to pay them, made collection more difficult.[73] The unions' dependence, both political and organizational, had become an accomplished fact.

The unemployed

The contradictions in the party's view of the working class were reflected in its attitude to the unemployed, whose numbers soared in 1922–23, as renewed migration into Moscow swelled the workforce and cost accounting

---

71 As a result of the reregistration drive, the membership of the Moscow regional union organization fell from 728,906 to 653,274 between January and December 1922. On the metalworkers' union, *Metallist* 2, 1923, cols. 17–20.
72 M. Tomskii, 'Pervye rezul'taty novoi soiuznoi politiki', *Vestnik truda* 8–9, 1922: 3–11; TsAOPIM, 3/3/5/30; M. Briskin, 'Perekhod k individualnomu chlenstvu', *Vestnik truda* 1, 1923: 3–14; A. Gurevich, 'Dobrovol'noe chlenstvo v soiuzakh', *Vestnik truda* 2, 1922: 38–40; *Sotsialisticheskii vestnik* 11, 1922, pp. 10–11; 16, 1922, pp. 8–9; *Odinnadtsatyi s"ezd*, p. 531.
73 MGSPS, *Piatyi gubernskii s"ezd moskovskikh profsoiuzov. Itogi, rezoliutsiia, postanovleniia*, Moscow: Mosgublit, 1923, p. 13; TsGAMO, 609/1/183/46–49, 184; *Trud*, 4 September 1923; *Metallist* 8, 1923, cols. 47–48.

forced enterprises to shed labour and reduced hidden unemployment (i.e. workers going to the factories and having no work to do). Some Bolsheviks encouraged unemployed self-organization, but this clashed with prevalent party opinion, which held that many of the jobless – for example women, young workers, and recent migrants – were less proletarian than others, and that such organization was permissible only within strictly predetermined limits.

Officially registered unemployment rose in Moscow from a little more than 14,000 in January 1922 to more than 100,000 in mid 1923. As demobilized Red army men arrived in Moscow, and the influx of people from the countryside resumed, women, young workers and the unskilled tended to be pushed out of the workforce, giving way to male workers and particularly to those with skills. By mid 1922, just under three-quarters of Moscow's unemployed were women. Statistics compiled in 1922 and 1923 showed the largest group of registered jobless (more than one-third of the total) to be 'soviet employees', mostly *sluzhashchie*, rather than industrial workers. The second-largest group (one-fifth in 1922, more than a quarter in 1923) was unskilled workers. By 1923 there were also considerable contingents of unemployed clothing workers, leather workers and even metal workers, although labour shortages remained in some specific trades.[74]

Fault lines soon appeared in the party's attitude to organizing the unemployed. The Komsomol organized clubs for unemployed young workers, and the factory cells supported mutual benefit funds for unemployed union members.[75] But in the workplaces – Cheka reports from which started listing the threat of lay-offs among workers' concerns from September 1921 – there was a different emphasis.[76] Trade union officials, in particular, externalized the problem, claiming that its main victims were non-proletarian elements. One report to the Moscow regional trade union conference in 1922 emphasized that 'only a few per cent' of the unemployed were union members; most were *sluzhashchie* or unskilled; and 20–30 per cent, it claimed, were 'fake unemployed, who are traders or have some other income, and who didn't work in the enterprises previously'. Another report drafted by the MGSPS said that the unemployed were in the main 'a johnny-come-lately element who landed in the factories by chance [*prishlyi, sluchainy v proizvodstve element*]', who had 'strong links to the countryside, and to trade'.[77] The party sought, where possible, to protect its own members

---

74 Statistics from *Otchet MGSPS 1921–22*, p. 22 and Chase, op. cit., p. 139, compiled from a range of Soviet sources. See also Chase, op. cit., pp. 141–43 and 149–50; F.D. Markuzon (ed.), *Polozhenie truda v Moskovskoi gubernii v 1922–1923gg.: sbornik materialov biuro statistika truda*, Moscow: MGSPS, 1923, pp. 8, 18 and 38–40; Matiugin, op. cit., p. 195; *Pravda*, 4 November 1921.
75 TsAOPIM, 634/1/10/38; TsAGM, 415/16/318/71.
76 TsAOPIM, 3/2/48/156–58; 3/3/33/9.
77 MGSPS, *Piatyi s"ezd*, p. 38; MGSPS, *Otchet o deiatel'nosti 1921–22*, p. 5.

from redundancy – in August 1922 the MC bureau issued a specific directive to trade union fractions to this effect[78] – and it was widely perceived that unemployed communists were helped to the front of the queue for jobs. This caused resentment, and in early 1922 provided the Bolsheviks' political enemies with some of their few remaining chances to try to turn protest at economic hardship into political opposition.

Selection procedures for redundancies, and claims that they were used to target Mensheviks and other workers the management disliked, caused Moscow's most bitterly fought industrial dispute of the spring of 1922, at the Sytin print works (see Chapter 4, p. 110). In the bakers' union, the veteran SR maximalist Petr Kamyshev[79] aspired to leadership of the unemployed; in March 1922 he told 500 of them at a meeting that 'the workers themselves should take extraordinary measures to help the unemployed, since nothing could be expected from the state'. Kamyshev urged that the governing apparatus be cut back and parasitic functionaries 'who received great stockpiles [of supplies] at the workers' expense' be unloaded, a Cheka agent reported. The communist president of the food workers' union, Samuil Krol', was present, and moved a resolution that employed bakers should donate a day's pay per week to their unemployed colleagues.[80] The prospect of the unemployed organizing independently worried some Cheka agents. In June 1922 one reported from Zamoskvorech'e that the unemployed 'sit around near the enterprises' discussing the need to protest and 'struggle against the soviet power, in view of its alleged inability to carry through the revival of industry'.[81]

The hostility of most party officials to anything that smacked of working-class self-organization was nowhere more clearly expressed than during a dispute in early 1923 about the attitude the party's womens' sections should adopt to women driven out of the factories. Vera Golubeva, national deputy head of the womens' sections, advocated a new type of association to organize women hard-hit by NEP, which had not only caused the 'mass exit of women from the factories', but also ended state funding for nurseries, communal kitchens and other facilities designed to lift the burden of housework. Womens' section delegates' meetings, theoretically open to the unemployed and housewives, had in practice failed to sustain organization among 'those who, only yesterday working women, have today have gone into the swamp of everyday philistinism'. Special associations 'standing for the complete economic, legal and social emancipation of women' were needed, Golubeva argued. This attempt to encourage organization of those at the sharp end provoked a storm of opposition. One especially blunt respondent, Pavlovskaia, argued that the party had 'nothing to say' to

78 TsAOPIM, 3/2/28/90ob.
79 On Kamyshev, see Appendix 1.
80 TsAOPIM, 3/3/34/65.
81 TsAOPIM, 3/3/34/150. See also Chase, op. cit., p. 158.

unemployed women, and that organization had to centre on 'a small circle of women linked to production'. F. Niurina said that the party's task was not to 'submerge its tentacles still further into the depths of the backward female mass' in a vain attempt to find 'self-active [*samodeiatel'nykh*] women',[82] but to centre organization on workplace facilities such as factory-based clubs and co-operatives. Golubeva's proposals were forcefully rejected at a national meeting of womens' sections' leaders in April 1923, and she was lambasted from a high level. Clara Zetkin, the veteran German communist, joined the attack on her. Aleksandra Kollontai, who was by this time in a form of exile as the Soviet ambassador to Norway, and had intervened to support Golubeva, was also denounced.[83]

The working class, ideal and actual

The campaigns for the confiscation of church valuables, and around the SR trial, brought mass mobilization methods to the centre of political life in a form more deliberately directed and systematically monitored than ever before. These campaigns, together with the emasculation of the soviets and unions as organs of mass participation, were important steps in the Bolsheviks' political expropriation of the working class. And at the top, the party elite was evolving as the nucleus around which the new Soviet ruling class took shape, accumulating political power and material privileges. Whether the Russian workers could have offered substantial resistance to this process is a moot point. All hopes that the revolution might spread to Western Europe had long since been dashed; Russia had only just started out on the road to industrialization and urbanization. It has often been argued that, by prioritizing industrial development above all else, the Bolshevik leaders were simply acknowledging historical realities. But their vanguardism and contempt for participatory democracy, married to their monopoly of political power, killed off the potential of the working class to develop as a creative historical force that had shown itself in 1917.

The party's position as master of the state impacted on its ideology. The tenth congress had effectively anathematized dissent. By the eleventh congress, the justifications for the Bolshevik monopoly of political power during NEP were being elaborated. The 'workers' state', however imperfect, was the means by which industrialization and modernization would be undertaken. Its 'proletarian' character was ensured by the party, whose own 'proletarian' credentials were based on the position it had taken in 1917. The working class itself was by contrast very un-proletarian, 'diluted' by

---

82 The adjective '*samodeiatel'nyi*' has the same root as '*samodeiatelnost*', the meaning of which was discussed in Chapter 4.
83 E. Wood, *The Baba and the Comrade: Gender and Politics in Revolutionary Russia*, Bloomington: Indiana University Press, 1997, pp. 188–91 and pp. 261–62; *Pravda* 1 February, 9, 10 and 20 March, and 5 and 14 April 1923.

women, recent arrivals from the countryside, and others. Politics was not about bringing workers into the process of making decisions, but about ensuring that as far as possible they understood the decisions made on their behalf by the party, and that they improved productivity and observed labour discipline.

The travesty of socialist ideas implicit in this thinking was clear to many, both inside and outside the party. This is clear from the reaction to the party leadership's argument, spelled out by Lenin in his well-known speech to the eleventh congress, that the economic 'retreat' implied by NEP had to be accompanied by a political offensive, in the form of repression of political opponents and harsh measures against Bolshevik dissidents. In a section of the speech that deserves more attention, Lenin specifically ruled out a possible revival, in post-civil-war conditions, of mass working-class participation in politics. He reiterated his belief that party membership had to be restricted more tightly, to prevent the entry of petty-bourgeois elements. He rebuked those who claimed that economic recovery, and the consequent return of many workers to the factories, provided a new reservoir of working-class activists, and opportunities for a renaissance of working-class consciousness, of which the party should make use. Lenin argued that the Russian working class could not be regarded as properly proletarian. 'Often when people say "workers", they think that that means the factory proletariat. It certainly doesn't,' he said. The working class that Marx had written about did not exist in Russia, Lenin claimed. 'Wherever you look, those in the factories are not the proletariat, but casual elements of all kinds.'[84] The practical consequence of this was that political decision-making had to be concentrated in the party, and it had to explain its superiority over its political enemies to the working class. The place of the campaigns on the church and the SRs in this thinking is clear.

The former WO leader Shliapnikov considered Lenin's redefinition of the working class as a more serious threat to socialist ideology than any of the arguments used against the WO the previous year. The 1920 discussion had concerned 'tactical' issues, but Lenin's rejection of the now-reurbanizing working class 'threatens us with the manifestations of a principled difference', Shliapnikov told the congress. Party leaders were deceiving themselves, for example by blaming on 'monarchists' strikes that were triggered by economic hardship. Kamenev had claimed that even the advanced Moscow workers 'express the interest of peasant proprietors'. Shliapnikov feared that

> By painting the proletariat in false colours, comrades are seeking justification for political manoeuvres and their search for support in other social forces [which with hindsight may be seen as those being drawn

84 *Odinnadtsatyi s'ezd*, pp. 10–44.

together by the new party elite]. Remember, once and for all, that we will never have a different or 'better' working class, and we need to be satisfied with the one we have.[85]

Shliapnikov's alarm was shared by other oppositionists. The 'anonymous platform' of late 1922 warned of the 'extremely dangerous features' of this passage in Lenin's speech. I.N. Smirnov, who stood on the left wing of the 1923 opposition, returned to this theme during the party discussion of 1923-24. Zinoviev had asserted that it had been impossible to implement the tenth congress decisions on internal party democracy, because of 'objective conditions' and the dissolution of the working class. In response, Smirnov pointed to the 'giant increase in our economic potential' in 1921-22. It was a parody, he argued to blame the lack of party democracy on the dissolution of the working class, when it was precisely after the tenth congress that workers had flooded back to the cities.[86]

The impact of the Bolsheviks' vanguardism-in-power was also clear to those politically active non-party workers marginalized by it. In January 1923, at an open meeting (i.e. one to which non-members were welcome) of the party cell at the Krasnyi proletarii works (as Bromlei had been renamed),[87] discussion of this issue was ignited when Stolentsev, a party member, was criticized for insufficiently conscientious educational work among non-party workers. In self-defence he blurted out: 'All these workers are conscious. They were at the front during the civil war. There is no [educational] work I can do among them. I don't understand any more than they do.' That contradicted standard Bolshevik assumptions that consciousness was determined above all by one's relationship with the party – and Velichenko, a non-party communist, developed the theme. He said that the party disparaged workers' intelligence, and ruminated with some irony on the non-party workers' abstentionism.

> Comrade Velichenko (non party): It's pointless calling those present 'non party'. We are [just] politically lazy; we spend our time on domestic trifles and are too lazy to attend meetings. If there are Whites to be fought, we'll all go to the front. ... we are all communists at heart, but politically lazy by nature, and therefore not in the party.

Beliakov, apparently a left SR sympathizer, snapped back that Velichenko was wrong to say that conscious workers were politically lazy. The problem was the Bolsheviks' false policy:

---

85 Ibid., pp. 101-9.
86 RGASPI, 324/1/35/164; TsAOPIM, 3/4/36/61-62.
87 GARF, 7952/3/76/177-83.

> Comrade Beliakov: The Communist party is a usurper of the socialist parties and of workers' freedoms. ... It's our country's shame that, even now, socialists are sitting in prison.
>
> Comrade Velichenko [implying that the SR and Menshevik leaders were bourgeois, SP.]: And smoking cigars.
>
> Comrade Beliakov: The communists took power, and wield it without taking any notice of workers.

Another non-party worker, Aleksandrov, argued that the Bolsheviks could not have taken and held on to power without the support of the working class. Beliakov replied that in 1917 workers had had no idea what the communists wanted.

> Comrade Beliakov: ... Every day we slide further and further from what we gained in October. In Russia there's no communism. The communists aren't even in power: they sign the decrees, but non-communists write them. The decrees are aimed against workers.

Bolshevik policy marginalized, and then silenced, this type of discussion among worker socialists, which could only have helped to revive the democratic and socialist elements of the revolution.

7 The party elite, industrial managers and the cells

The party in 1922

The tiny elite against which the rank-and-file communists' anger had been directed in 1920 expanded in the first years of the New Economic Policy (NEP), and its privileges swelled rapidly from their meagre starting-point. As the state consolidated, the elite accumulated greater political power. As the economy recovered, considerable wealth was also there for the taking. The retreat of the revolution played out in changes in class relations: industry and factory management structures took shape around the imposition of labour discipline; antagonisms evolved between workers on one side and industrial managers, technical specialists (*spetsy*) and party cells on the other. Notwithstanding the tensions between these groups that would merge into a new Soviet ruling class, the party elite, through the party apparatus, supported all of them against workers. The account that follows considers the acquiescence of the Bolshevik party as a whole in the elite's advance, the appearance of communist industrial managers and their role in disciplining workers, and the relationships between these managers, the technical specialists, and the party's workplace cells. In western historiography, the role of politics in the formation of the Soviet bureaucratic class has previously been examined by Graeme Gill. He described the advance of an 'oligarchy' of senior party leaders, on whom those at lower levels of the apparatus were dependent. Gill built on the work of T.H. Rigby, one of whose contributions was to identify the role of personal networks and cliques in the party elite. Gerald Easter's research on regional leaders also developed that theme. A sociological definition of the new bureaucratic class has been given by Stephen Sternheimer. Don Rowney defined the bureaucratic class as a 'technocracy', whose advance was driven above all by the need for technical skills – an approach that in my view puts too far into the background the class relations between the workers and the state bureaucracy.[1]

Socialist theory has experienced many difficulties in establishing a framework for understanding the Soviet bureaucratic class. Marx elaborated no theory of bureaucracy. But in discussions of the issue he asserted that abolition of bureaucratic hierarchy and the introduction of officials paid a skilled workman's wages – which he believed, perhaps erroneously, had been undertaken by the Paris Commune – would be integral to 'the political form of ... social emancipation'.[2] In Bolshevism, this aspect of Marx's thought was almost completely obliterated. In the party's endless discussions about the need to control the state apparatus and to tackle bureaucratism (in the narrow sense, i.e. officials' authoritarianism, corruption and inefficiency), these were considered only as defects of a workers' state. Marx's aims of abolishing bureaucratic hierarchy, and the payment of a skilled worker's wages to officials, were, at best, postponed to the distant future. Those who attempted to analyse the bureaucracy as exploitative, or as a class, and those who attributed to the party elite an exploitative role in the Soviet economy, were silenced in the way described in previous chapters. The 1923 left opposition condemned the suppression of inner-party democracy because, among other things, it constrained criticism of the bureaucracy (see Chapter 9) – but did not question the assumption that the party and its elite were instruments, however faulty, of 'proletarian dictatorship'. In the late 1920s, Stalin's most prominent Bolshevik opponents continued, from exile, to analyse the bureaucracy as a hostile organism within a fundamentally progressive workers' state. Even Christian Rakovsky – who acknowledged that the bureaucracy had 'not only objectively but subjectively, not only materially but also morally' ceased to be part of the working class – saw it as no more than a wayward 'agent' of a temporarily quiescent proletariat-in-power. The most influential socialist analysis of the USSR, Trotsky's, saw the bureaucracy as 'parasitic' on the proletarian state and denied it the possibility of an independent historical role. His account of the bureaucracy's origins relied heavily on the Bolsheviks' old discourse about 'alien class elements', and excluded from examination the party's political expropriation of the working class.[3] Means to overcome these contradictions were

1 G. Gill, *The Origins of the Stalinist Political System*, Cambridge: Cambridge University Press, 1990, especially pp. 51–112; T. Rigby, 'The Soviet Political Elite', *British Journal of Political Science* I: 4, 1971: 415–36, and 'Early Provincial Cliques and the Rise of Stalin', *Soviet Studies* 33, 1981: 3–28; G. Easter, *Reconstructing the State: Personal Networks and Elite Identity in Soviet Russia*, Cambridge: Cambridge University Press, 2000; S. Sternheimer, 'Administration for Development: the Emerging Bureaucratic Elite, 1920–30', in W. Pintner and D. K. Rowney (eds), *Russian Officialdom: the Bureaucratization of Russian Society from the Seventeenth to the Twentieth Century*, London: Macmillan, 1980, pp. 316–54; G.K. Rowney, *Transition to Technocracy: the Structural Origins of the Soviet Administrative State*, Ithaca: Cornell University Press, 1989. See also M. Lupher, *Power Restructuring in Russia and China*, Oxford: Westview Press, 1996.
2 K. Marx, *Critique of Hegel's 'Philosophy of Right'*, Cambridge: Cambridge University Press, 1970, pp. 45–54 and 131–42; K. Marx, 'First Draft of the Civil War in France' and 'The Civil War in France', in *The First International and After*, London: Penguin, 1974, pp. 136–68 and 187–235.
3 Kh. Rakovsky, 'The Professional Dangers of Power', in *Selected Writings on Opposition in the USSR 1923–1930*, London: Allison & Busby, 1980, pp. 124–36. Trotsky's theory is set out most comprehensively in 'The Class Nature of the Soviet State', in *Writings of Leon Trotsky (1933–34)*, New York: Pathfinder, 1972, pp. 102–22, and L. Trotsky, *The Revolution Betrayed: What is the Soviet Union and Where is it Going*, London: New Park, 1973.

suggested by Cornelius Castoriadis, who attributed to the bureaucracy the ability to 'substitute ... itself for the bourgeoisie as the social stratum that carries out the tasks of primitive accumulation' and to accomplish such functions as 'manager of centralized capital'. Castoriadis made central to the bureaucracy's rise the Bolshevik party's reduction of the working class to 'enthusiastic and passive citizens'. From this starting point, Claude Lefort developed an analysis according to which the Soviet bureaucratic class became dominant not, as the bourgeoisie does, 'by virtue of a professional activity which endows them with private power', but 'through dependence on state power which grounds and maintains the social hierarchy'. From a reading of Weber, Lefort argued that the 'class unity' of the bureaucracy, which develops in a range of state and non-state institutions, 'does not prevail "naturally"; it requires a constant activity of unification'. Furthermore: 'The rivalry of bureaucratic apparatuses reinforced by the struggle of inter-bureaucratic clans is brought under control only by the intervention, at every level and in all sectors of social life, of a principle which is properly political'.[4] In the account that follows, the party elite is seen as the agent of this principle, and the driving force for this 'constant activity of unification', both during the civil war when it was laying the foundations of the Soviet state, and during the economic revival of early NEP.

The rise of the party elite

The party's elite-in-embryo of 1920 comprised, in Moscow, a few thousand high-ranking Bolsheviks, attempting to control unwieldy commissariats, and often succumbing to bureaucratic vices. Across vast swathes of Russian territory, party officials were trying to lay firmer foundations for soviet rule. The party elite controlled the economy, but that economy was impoverished. Elite privileges were meagre – a dacha or motor car or two, good food, comfortable living quarters – and provoked communist rank-and-file anger not because of their scale, but because they represented, amidst poverty, a visible abuse of the principles for which people believed the revolution had been fought. In 1921–23, with one-party rule firmly assured, political power, and, in particular, the ability to direct the administrative machinery of the state, was rapidly concentrated in the hands of the party elite. In exercizing

4 C. Castoriadis, 'The Role of Bolshevik Ideology in the Birth of the Bureaucracy' (1964) < http://www.geocities.com/cordobakaf/castbolsh.html >; Castoriadis, 'On the Content of Socialism', in D.A. Curtis (ed. and trans.), *The Castoriadis Reader*, Oxford: Blackwell, 1997, pp. 40–105, and C. Castoriadis, 'The Social Regime in Russia', in Curtis, op. cit., pp. 218–38; C. Lefort, *The Political Forms of Modern Society: Bureaucracy, Democracy, Totalitarianism*, Cambridge: Polity Press, 1986, especially pp. 89–120; M. Weber, *Essays in Sociology*, London: Routledge and Kegan Paul, 1970, pp. 196–244. For socialist views of the Soviet elite, see also Farber, *Before Stalinism: the Rise and Fall of Soviet Democracy*, Oxford: Polity Press, 1990, and A.M. Podshchekoldin, 'The Origins of the Stalinist Bureaucracy – Some New Historical Facts' < http://www.revolutionary-history.co.uk/supplem/podsheld.htm >.

this power, the elite accumulated and legitimized its own material privileges, and those of other groupings that joined the bureaucratic class, including the industrial managers and technical specialists. The contours of this process were sketched in western historiography in the 1950s and 1960s; Russian historians, initially in the context of Gorbachev-era discussions about the breakdown of the USSR, have researched many aspects of it in greater detail.[5]

Attention has been concentrated on the growth, under the secretariat of the Bolshevik party Central Committee (CC), of a centralized system of party functionaries effectively appointed by, and beholden to, that secretariat and its apparatus. This system expropriated power not only from the soviet bodies to which it constitutionally belonged, but also from local party bodies.[6] The CC secretariat, in which Stalin played a key role after his

---

5 The notable Russian monographs and articles of the last 20 years include, in order of publication: V.S. Lel'chuk (ed.), *Istoriki sporiat: trinadtsat' besed*, Moscow: izd. polit. literatury, 1988; Iu.A. Poliakov '20-e gody: nastroenie partiinogo avangarda', *Voprosy istorii KPSS* 10, 1989: 25–38; S.V. Kuleshov, O.V. Volobuev and E.I. Pivovar (eds), *Nashe otechestvo: opyt politicheskoi istorii*, Moscow: Terra, 1991; N.S. Simonov, 'Reforma politicheskogo stroiia: zamysly i real'nost' (1921–23 gg.)', *Voprosy istorii KPSS* 1, 1991: 42–45; I.V. Pavlova, *Stalinizm: stanovlenie mekhanizma vlasti*, Novosibirsk: Sibirskii khronograf, 1993; T. P. Korzhikhina and Iu.Iu. Fignater, 'Sovetskaia nomenklatura: stanovlenie, mekhanizmy, deistviia', *Voprosy istorii* 7, 1993: 25–38; G.A. Trukan, *Put' k totalitarizmu, 1917–1929 gg.*, Moscow: 'Nauka', 1994; E.G. Gimpel'son, *Formirovanie sovetskoi politicheskoi sistemy 1917–1923 gg.*, Moscow: 'Nauka', 1995; V.V. Zhuravlev et al. (eds), *Vlast' i oppozitsiia: Rossiskii politicheskii protsess XX stoletiia*, Moscow: Rosspen, 1995; V.A. Shishkin, *Vlast', politika, ekonomika: poslerevoliutsionnaia Rossiia (1917–1928 gg.)*, St Petersburg: 'Dmitrii Bulanin', 1997; S.V. Leonov, *Rozhdenie sovetskoi imperii: gosudarstvo i ideologiia 1917–1922 gg.*, Moscow: Dialog-MGU, 1997; E.G. Gimpelson, *Sovetskie upravlentsy 1917–1920 gg.*, Moscow: Institut istorii RAN, 1998; A.B. Nenin, *Sovnarkom i Novaia Ekonomicheskaia Politika (1921–23 gg.)*, Nizhnii Novgorod: izd. Volgo-Viatskoi akademii gosudarstvennoi sluzhby, 1999; E.G. Gimpel'son, *Novaia ekonomicheskaia politika i politicheskaia sistema 20-e gody*, Moscow: Institut istorii RAN, 2000; I.V. Pavlova, *Mekhanizm vlasti i stroitel'stvo staliniskogo sotsializma*, Novosibirsk: izd. SO RAN, 2001.

6 This account is based on S. Pirani, 'The Party Elite, the Industrial Managers and the Cells: Early Stages in the Formation of the Soviet Ruling Class in Moscow, 1922–23', *Revolutionary Russia* 19: 2, 2006: 197–228; Gimpel'son, *NEP i politicheskaia sistema*, pp. 124–25, 131 and 160, 348–50; R.V. Daniels, *The Conscience of the Revolution: Communist Opposition in Soviet Russia*, Cambridge, MA: Harvard University Press, 1960, pp. 166–67; Pavlova, *Stalinizm*, pp. 66–67, 70–73, 75, 85–93; S.A. Pavliuchenkov, '"Novyi klass" i stanovlenie sistemy gosudarstvennogo absoliutizma', in Pavliuchenkov et al. (eds), *Rossiia nepovskaia: issledovaniia*, Moscow: Novyi khronograf, 2002, pp. 169–207, p. 174. See also *Odinnadtsatyi s"ezd RKP(b): stenograficheskii otchet*, Moscow: Gos. izd. politicheskoi literatury, 1961, pp. 46–47; *Izvestiia TsK RKP(b)* 3, 1922, pp. 27–28 and 3, 1923, pp. 39–40; RKP(b), *Uchet i raspredeleniia rabotnikov (k soveshchaniiu sekretarei i zaveduiushchikh orgotdelami gubkomov)*, Moscow: izd. otdelenie TsK RKP, 1923, pp. 3–6; *Otchet o rabote MK RKP(b) za 1922–23 g.*, Moscow: MK RKP(b), 1923, pp. 31–33.

appointment as party general secretary in April 1922, gathered together separate strands of party organization. The bodies that directed local officialdom, the record and assignment department and organization and instruction department, were subordinated to it. Even before the eleventh congress in March–April 1922, there were 7000 national- and regional-level officials reporting directly to the CC secretariat's record and assignment department; by the congress, the department had collated lists of 33,000 officials, and set about taking charge of them. In 1922–23 the appointment of officials was systematized; in late 1923 the first lists (*nomenklatury*) of party and state appointments that required central approval were drawn up; in 1924, record and assignment departments, responsible to their central parent body, were established in all the main branches of the state apparatus. The Moscow regional party's record and assignment department was set up in July 1922, together with corresponding departments at district level; in its first seven months, it appointed 5863 party members (i.e. about one-fifth of the Moscow membership) to positions, mostly in central or local party or soviet bodies. The 'appointism' (*naznachenstvo*) that had begun during the civil war expanded, and soon predominated. The tenth congress, in response to the discussions of 1920, had condemned it, but in the years that followed, it spread, becoming comprehensive in 1924–25. A key turning-point was the twelfth party conference in August 1922, which adopted an amendment to the party statutes, proposed by a commission headed by Molotov, that regional party secretaries had to be pre-1917 members and to have their elections 'confirmed' at national level, i.e. appointment in all but name. In the three-year period after the tenth congress, the party apparatus reinforced its control over the party, and thence over the state apparatus, in a myriad of other ways: it used channels of appointment and command to determine the election of delegates to party congresses; it established tight control over the distribution not only of information about the political and economic situation, but also of full information about its own instructions and policies; it systematized the upward flow of information to the secretariat; and it achieved a degree of immunity from legal proceedings for party members, and for officials in particular.

Irina Pavlova has argued that the acceleration of these processes in mid 1922 amounted to a 'secret state-political reform'.[7] Alongside the centralization of cadres that it controlled, the party elite in that year pushed forward its appropriation of responsibility for the day-to-day functioning of the state and industrial apparatus. Notwithstanding regular warnings by party leaders about 'the party organization growing into the soviet apparatus, and the swallowing of party work by soviet work',[8] the party apparatus penetrated inexorably into all fields of state activity. The twelfth party congress in April 1923 once again reiterated the principle that state bodies should function separately from party bodies, with only political guidance

7 Pavlova, *Stalinizma*, pp. 66–95.

Not so far apart. Delegates to the Moscow congresses of, top, the chemical workers' union (1923) and, above, the union of soviet employees (i.e. *sluzhashchie*) (mid 1920s).

172 *The party elite, industrial managers and the cells*

from the latter; a year later, Zinoviev reported proudly that 'our politburo is a basic organ of the state'.[9] Control over the GPU security police and military apparatus evolved differently, but by 1923 the GPU had reasserted the status the Cheka had had during the civil war, as a structure directly answerable only to the highest party bodies, and free of supervision by the justice ministry or courts.[10] At regional and district level, the Moscow committee of the Russian Communist Party (MC) and party district committees assumed the pervasive control over soviets, trade unions and industrial management bodies that the CC had at national level.

In defining the party elite sociologically, I began in Chapter 2 with its 'responsible officials' in 1920, and the same method will be applied here to 1922–23. Information on the officials' social background has to be gathered from scattered sources. Close to the summit of the elite, among 101 secretaries of regional party organizations, there was a strong contingent of civil war communists (35 who joined the party between March 1917 and December 1919), and a larger group of pre-revolutionary veterans (10 pre-1905 recruits and 53 1905–17 recruits); 14 had university education and another 35, secondary education. But this pre-revolutionary 'old guard' was already under attack from Stalin's CC secretariat. The 1922 CC report on cadre distribution in which this information appeared also contains a harangue against such 'old boys' (*stariki*), and argued that civil war and even post-civil-war recruits were malleable and therefore preferable: 'The young, active worker, elected at some all-Russian congress, meeting or conference, having attended and got the hang of things there, already has a great advantage over an authoritative, respected old cadre.'[11] The place in the elite's development of the culture of unthinking obedience reflected in this report, and of the contempt for old Bolsheviks whose independence of mind brought them into conflict with Stalin, often referred to in memoirs, deserves further research. There is abundant evidence that Stalin's secretariat sought to take control, over the heads of the 'old boys', of the 33,000 'responsible officials' polled at the eleventh congress. These were mostly former workers and Red army men. But nearer the top was a layer that was less proletarian. Statistics covering party members working as senior *sluz-*

---

8 The words quoted are from the CC's report to the eleventh congress in March 1922. The congress passed a resolution urging that party organizations not interfere with the day-to-day functioning of soviet and economic bodies. The separation was not implemented, though. The communist fraction at the tenth congress of soviets in 1922 called on the CC to work out concrete measures to do so, but the CC decided not to discuss the matter. Simonov, op. cit., p. 47.

9 *Trinadtsatyi s"ezd RKP(b), mai 1924 goda: stenograficheskii otchet*, Moscow: Gos. izd-vo politicheskoi literatury, 1963, p. 73.

10 S.A. Pavliuchenkov, 'Ekonomicheskii liberalizm', in Pavliuchenkov et al. (eds), *Rossiia nepovskaia*, p. 53; Leonov, op. cit., p. 297; G.L. Olekh, *Krovnye uzy: RKP(b) i ChK/GPU v pervoi polovine 1920-kh godov: mekhanizm vsaimootnoshenii*, Novosibirsk: Novosibirskaia gosudarstevennaia akademiia vodnogo transporta, 1999.

11 RKP(b), *Uchet i raspredelenie*, p. 40.

hashchie in the people's commissariats in 1922 show that former workers were a small minority (12.3 per cent), and that others came from a wide variety of middle-class backgrounds; their pre-1917 occupations were given as students (17.3 per cent), on military service (16.7 per cent), in the 'free professions' (12.9 per cent), technical personnel (12.3 per cent), or *sluzhashchie* for the old regime (11.2 per cent).[12]

As the elite centralized its political power, it also sought to legitimize its material privileges in a way that broke with Bolshevik tradition and paved the way for the development of the bureaucratic ruling class as a whole. The door was opened by the eleventh party congress, which ordered the CC to examine 'the material conditions of active comrades [i.e. full-timers]' and 'at all costs [ensure them] tolerable living conditions'.[13] A CC commission, headed by Molotov, came back to the twelfth party conference in August 1922 with a resolution providing for 15,325 party officials to receive (i) salaries equivalent to middle and senior management grades (twelfth to seventeenth grades), plus 50 per cent; (ii) guaranteed housing and medical support; and (iii) child care and education for their children. The draft resolution had stated that party members receiving more than one-and-a-half times the seventeenth grade should pay part of the surplus into the party's mutual support fund, but this paragraph, which already contained a get-out clause allowing the CC to suspend this requirement, was deleted entirely. The conference, most of whose delegates would have qualified for the benefits, also voted for Komsomol officials to receive them, at slightly lower rates, and called on the CC to work out a similar system for some categories of party officials (those in rural sub-districts) who had not been included.[14]

Only a year earlier, the 'old Bolshevik' Ivan Skvortsov-Stepanov, after visiting party organizations in the Volga and Urals regions, had appealed to the CC to endorse the principle that 'responsible officials" living standards not be allowed to fall *lower* than those of skilled workers, no matter how desperate things were. At that time, Moscow communists who were 'literally collapsing where they stood' were being sent on procurement trips to the countryside to feed their families.[15] But with the industrial recovery underway, members of the party elite holding office in soviet and industrial institutions, where senior managers' pay levels were rising in leaps and

12 These high-up people of 1922 contrasted with, for example the communist 'technical *sluzhashchie*' of 1922, amongst whom there was a much larger group of former soldiers (43.8 per cent), a similarly modest group of former technical personnel (9.7 per cent) and hardly any former *sluzhashchie* (3.6 per cent) or former workers (3 per cent). V.I. Vasiaev, V.Z. Drobizhev, L.B. Zaks, B.I. Pivovor, V.A. Ustinov and T.A. Ushakova, *Dannie perepisi sluzhashchikh 1922g. o sostave kadrov narkomatov RSFSR*, Moscow: izd. Moskovskovskogo universiteta, 1972, pp. 148–52.
13 *Odinnadtsatyi s"ezd*, pp. 551–52 and pp. 685–86; *Vserossiiskaia konferentsiia RKP (bol'shevikov) 4–7 avgusta 1922 g.*, Moscow: izd. MK RKP(b), 1922, pp. 98–99.
14 *Vserosiiskaia konferentsiia*, pp. 98–102 and 136–39; Pavlova, *Stalinizm*, p. 68.
15 RGASPI, 17/65/228/12; *Otchet sed'moi Moskovskoi gubpartkonferentsii RKP 29–31 Oktiabria 1921 g.*, Moscow, 1921, p. 19.

bounds, could now legally receive salaries dozens of times greater than those of workers – a far cry from the hardships on the Volga a year before. Even so, the privileges agreed at the twelfth conference were modest in some respects: they would perhaps have brought party officials up to living standards comparable with, say, those of local government officials in Western Europe. But the decision to entitle them to supplements on account of the positions they held was an open assault on the principle of equality among communists. It sent a moral signal that party officials could share in the wealth NEP had begun to generate. In 1919, at the height of the dispute about extra payments for specialists, the trade unions had established an official ratio of 1:5 between the lowest and highest pay, and in 1922 this had been amended to allow for some salaries to be paid at eight times the minimum. These limits were now overridden, both by the party conference decision and by a decision of the Council of Labour and Defence (STO) that sanctioned the payment of 'personal' salaries to specialists and 'tantiemes' (bonuses) to some industrial managers. In December 1922, official minimum and maximum salaries began to be published in the form of decrees; in that month the differential was 1:80, and it fell to 1:40 by June 1923.[16] In 1924, M. Vovsi, a statistician for the trade union of *sluzhashchie*, was scandalized by his discovery that 13.8 per cent of *sluzhashchie* surveyed admitted to earning more than eight times, and some more than 30 times, the minimum wage. He wrote: 'At the start of 1922, when the principle of equal payment of labour still predominated, rates higher than five times the minimum could not be found', but within a year, notwithstanding the official loosening of the ratio, widespread breaches of the rules were evident. Vovsi found that in soviet, industrial, trade, banking and co-operative institutions, more than 80,000 people were earning more than eight times the minimum; of these, 15,400 were earning between 15 and 30 times the minimum and about 1500, more than 30 times the minimum. Without question, many of these people were members of the party elite, and their associates, rewarded for their position, not their skills. In late 1923, when the trade unions were protesting vociferously about industrial managers being overpaid, they pointed to the 'dubious "specialists"' who benefited.[17] Party members in industrial management were also foremost among those guilty of egregious *sovmestitel'stvo*, a commission of the CC secretariat complained to Stalin in 1923.[18] Excessive pay was not confined to industrial

16 On minimum and maximum, the trade union leader A. Andreev stated that most enterprises paid the lowest-paid workers twice the minimum rate, in which case the differentials would have been 40:1 falling to 20:1. See Dewar, *Labour Policy in the USSR, 1917–1928*, London: Royal Institute of International Affairs, 1956, p. 94; E.H. Carr, *The Interregnum 1923–1924*, London: Macmillan, 1978, pp. 41–42.
17 M. Vovsi (ed.), *Polozhenie truda sluzhashchikh, ob"ediniaemykh profsoiuzom administrativno-sovetskikh, obshchestvennykh i torgovykh rabotnikov v 1923/24 g. (Statisticheskii sbornik.) Vyp 3-i.*, Moscow: TsK VSASOTR, 1924, pp. 97–98; *Trud*, 1 December 1923.

management, though: a survey of members' earnings at the Krasnyi proletarii factory in October 1923 showed that the highest earners were political officials 'attached' to the cell: the metalworkers' union national official Aleksei Gurevich, who received at least 12 times the minimum, and the Hungarian communist Bela Kun, living in exile in Moscow, who received at least 25 times the minimum.[19] Naturally none of these figures take account of illegal income, of such non-cash benefits as the housing, education and health care stipulated by the twelfth party conference, or of, for example, gold watches presented to party members in industrial management, about which a provincial party official complained to Stalin.[20]

How the party acquiesced

The issue of material privilege may be used as a measure not only of the party elite's advance, but also of the whole party's acquiescence before it. The ranks, who in 1920 reacted so angrily to the 'tops'' fairly meagre privileges, were comparatively cautious in 1922. The yawning gap between members paid above the seventeenth grade and those who were unemployed was discussed at the Moscow regional party conference in March 1922. It decided to establish a mutual assistance fund; that members on salaries above the seventeenth grade should donate the excess; that the great disparities in communists' income 'must decidedly come to an end'; and that ways had to be found to provide 'help for communists in need, invalids, demobilized, etc, those who have lost their health and strength in working for the party and the revolution'. Later that month, Bubnov told the eleventh congress: 'the problem of material inequality ... is posed in a far more threatening form than it was [in 1920]'. But he was swimming against the tide: the resolution adopted incorporated Moscow's proposal for mutual assistance funds, but made contributing to them voluntary. And four months later, the twelfth conference sanctioned the inequalities that caused the problem.[21] The voluntary appeals for mutual aid were not especially effective. In September 1922, a meeting of communist *sluzhashchie* and industrial managers in Krasnopresnia heard a report that a sack factory had been opened to employ 620 unemployed communists, but was short of equipment and had no roof. Sokolov, the reporter, complained that only nine of the district's several dozen cells were passing on contributions to the mutual assistance fund from highly paid 'responsible workers'.[22]

---

18 RGASPI, 17/84/480/20–21.
19 TsAOPIM, 412/1/14/3–4, 9.
20 A.V. Kvashonkin et al. (eds), *Bol'shevistskoe rukovodstvo. Perepiska. 1912–1927*, Moscow: Rosspen, 1996, p. 285.
21 TsAOPIM, 3/3/2/141; *Vos'maia gubernaskaia konferentsiia Moskovskoi organizatsii RKP (23–25 marta 1922 g.)*, Moscow: MK RKP, 1922, p. 53; *Odinnadtsatyi s"ezd*, pp. 434–35, p. 459 and p. 552.

The shifting mood was reflected in a report by the MC secretary, Zelenskii, in February 1923, which listed among the regional organization's main ills the 'search for worldly comforts' by lower-level party officials. This resulted in 'careerism, intrigues against others, and a striving to move forward at the expense of one's comrades or, even more frequently, of non-party members'.[23]

There remained some civil war communists to whom inequality in the party presented a serious moral dilemma, for example Vladimir Petrzhek, a member of the AMO car factory cell who presented his resignation in June 1922 in a document asking 'what is communism?'. It was absent from the party, he argued. At a special meeting of party members from AMO and nearby factories,[24] Petrzhek acknowledged that Soviet Russia's poverty made impossible the implementation of egalitarian principles in society as a whole, but contended – as many Bolsheviks had in 1920 – that members of a truly communist party could and should strive for equality *among themselves*. Petrzhek rejected the proposition that inequality between communists was an objective reality that the party was powerless to change. 'In the communist party [Petrzhek] had hoped to find the realization of his dream of communism. But he did not find communism. He learned only that among communists there were strongly-developed private proprietorial instincts.' When leading cell members replied that objective circumstances were to blame, Petrzhek responded that 'he was not disillusioned with the idea of communism itself – he understood that communism was in general a long way off – but for him the lack of solidarity and equality among communists themselves was too hard to bear'. Lide and Korobytsin accused Petrzhek of utopianism. It was wrong, Lide said, to assume 'that communism must be established among 500,000 party members': the party was not a 'sect or a commune' and the members were not 'ascetics'; communism was a social form that could be realized only on the scale of 'a whole state' or indeed worldwide, but not in an isolated community. N.M. Talaiko, who himself remained in the party, supported Petrzhek, stating that 'one [party member] goes barefoot while the other travels about in a carriage'. The meeting ended with an unusually gracious acceptance of Petrzhek's resignation, rather than the standard condemnation of departure as desertion. Cell leaders had suggested that Petrzhek – a civil war hero whose wife's sudden death in 1918 had left him as a single parent, but had 'selflessly' gone to the front anyway, and then joined the party in April 1919 – was simply worn out. But he insisted that he was quitting for ideological reasons. Petrzhek and Talaiko had returned to issues hinted at by some of the 1920 oppositionists: given that, in the transition to socialism, inequality was inevitable, a communist party holding state power had a special responsibility to combat

22 TsAOPIM, 69/1/93/134.
23 TsAOPIM, 3/11/90/201–2.
24 TsAOPIM, 433/1/14/11–12.

inequality in its own ranks; the party could not lead society towards overcoming class divisions without creating an inner solidarity based on renunciation of privilege; its failure to address this question made it an active agent of inequality. This was a rudimentary, but important, challenge to the dogma of 'proletarian dictatorship' as a justification of inequality and authoritarian rule, which was polished and perfected only in the mid-1920s, but the outlines of which were visible in the cell leaders' attempts to justify the status quo.

Such considerations were being driven to the margins of party discussion, though. As the wealth of party and state officials grew, the opposition to it dwindled to timorous complaints. At the Moscow party conference of April 1923, a party district official, Gurov, mentioned the 'great disproportion' between some officials' material circumstances and those of most communists as 'a small point' at the end of his speech. 'Maybe it's not worth talking about this here', he added apologetically.[25] Party leaders occasionally railed against 'excesses': for example, a circular issued in October 1923 by Molotov on 'the struggle against excesses and the criminal use of posts' highlighted the evil of party members' wives wearing jewellery.[26] But such declarations appear demagogic in the context of the legalization of party and state officials' privileges. That point was made in a letter to Stalin from Boris Magidov, district party secretary in Poltava, Ukraine: on the basis of Molotov's circular, he warned, it would be 'entirely natural if [wider] questions about the "tops" and the "ranks", about "specialists", and about high salaries and all kinds of bonuses and tantiemes were raised'.[27]

The industrial managers

The communist managers[28] who rose to prominence in the immediate post-civil-war period were among the main groupings through which the party elite's relationship with the working class was mediated. Historians including E.H. Carr and Diane Koenker have noted the industrial managers' rapid rise, the way that raising production and productivity were made their overriding goals, the ease with which they slipped into anti-worker practices, and the opposition they provoked from party members who regarded their behaviour as anti-socialist.[29] Moreover, the directors' mandate had a

---

25 TsAOPIM, 3/4/1/61.
26 RGASPI, 17/84/467/58. On communists' wives, see Chapter 5, p. 121.
27 Magidov in Kvashonkin et al. (eds.), op. cit., pp. 282–86.
28 I avoid using the term 'red directors', which referred sometimes to communist managers specifically, and sometimes to all managers, emphasizing their duties to the Soviet state.
29 Carr, op. cit., pp. 40–46; D.P. Koenker, 'Factory Tales: Narratives of Industrial Relations in the Transition to NEP', *The Russian Review* 55: 3, 1996: 384–411; K. E. Bailes, *Technology and Society under Lenin and Stalin: Origins of the Soviet Technical Intelligentsia 1917–1941*, Princeton: Princeton University Press, 1978, pp. 63–64; M.R. Beissinger, *Scientific Management, Socialist Discipline and Soviet Power*, London: Tauris, 1988, pp. 45–49.

political aspect. In practice the party endorsed their authoritarian responses to independent workers' organization, for reasons that were broadly political, i.e. that had little direct bearing on production. In politically crucial cases in which communist directors were perceived to have breached fundamental principles of the workers' movement, they had far better chances of winning the support of workplace, district and national party organizations than did those workers, including worker communists, who opposed them. Communist managers, like other party officials, helped lay down the ground rules of the social contract with workers, under which there could be limited bargaining on workplace conditions, but no trespass by workers on the political sphere and no challenge to the directors' right to make policy decisions. Publicly, the party required managers to be sensitive to workers' interests, and those who were not sometimes faced challenges[30] – but institutional mechanisms buttressed the directors against worker opponents, and reinforced their right to make anti-worker decisions. Managers' responsibility to respect workers' rights was couched in terms of their relationships with 'workers' organizations', i.e. party cells, factory committees and other trade union bodies, and often these organizations' office-bearers were party members who understood their responsibilities to the working class as subordinate to their allegiance to the state. In the example discussed below, that of the Moscow rubber goods trust, party institutions rallied behind anti-worker communist managers. Although it is difficult to say that this is typical, it does appear that providing such support was party institutions' 'default position'. Such was the complaint of Gusev, a delegate to the Bauman district party conference in January 1924. If a director gets a worker expelled from the party, he said, 'they appoint a commission, and from the district committee they put two more directors on [to the commission]. They have no wish to hear how workers view the situation'. On the other hand a proposal to expel a director would get no hearing.[31]

The communist managers were brought into industry, during and after the civil war, to strengthen the party's control and dilute the influence of old managers and *spetsy*. There is insufficient information on their social background, but many were former workers. There was a considerable number of pre-1917 Bolsheviks among them: a survey in one Moscow district in mid 1922 found that communist factory directors had on average been in the party since 1915, their average age was 32, and six out of every seven were former workers.[32] By mid 1922, just one year into the industrial recovery,

30 For example in the discussion in the party press surveyed by Koenker, op. cit.
31 TsAOPIM, 63/1/144/78.
32 *Pravda*, 25 June 1922. In 1923, Zinoviev stated that among communist managers nationally, 28–30 per cent were pre-revolution Bolsheviks and 68–70 per cent were civil war Bolsheviks, and that 12 per cent had higher education, 10 per cent secondary education and the remainder elementary education. J.R. Azrael, *Managerial Power and Soviet Politics*, Cambridge, MA: Harvard University Press, 1966, p. 67, citing *Trinadtsadtyi s"ezd*, p. 243.

The party elite, industrial managers and the cells 179

there was not only a deepening rift between these managers and worker communists, but also concern about the managers' undue influence on party organizations. At the Moscow regional party conference in June 1922, Zelenskii warned not only of 'very deep, very serious conflicts' between communist managers and communist trade unionists, in which the managers 'relied on methods just like those of the old industrialists – on lockouts', but also of those managers' efforts 'to grab control of local party organs for themselves', for example by seeking election to party cell bureaus, leading to a 'curious merging of cell and management'.[33] (Zelenskii did not draw the obvious conclusion, that such developments cast serious doubt on the party's ideologically driven assumptions that the apparatus's anti-working-class characteristics were a function of the petty-bourgeois social origins of some of its members.)

The Menshevik journalist G. Shvarts argued that by mid 1922 the 'crystallization of a new social layer, the "red industrialists"', was complete, and that members of this social group took senior positions in the trusts and overshadowed the pre-revolutionary managers categorized as *spetsy*.[34] Carr suggests that between 1922 and 1923 a large number of non-worker managers, previously non-communists, joined the party, and this would have changed the overall composition of the group, but more research is needed to clarify this issue.[35] The managers, who were treated by themselves and others as a distinct group, began to organize politically; Smilga was actively involved. In September 1922 they set up a 'temporary bureau' for the 'coordination of simultaneous political action'. In December this became a permanent council of congresses of industrialists and a journal was published. In 1923 a Moscow 'club of red directors' was established as part of the national grouping, with 146 members; it argued for bolder use of market mechanisms, declaring that the industrial trusts' superficial and 'primitive' implementation of cost-accounting policies was partly to blame for the 1923 'scissors' crisis.[36]

33 Zelenskii, *Deviataia konferentsiia Moskovskoi organizatsii RKP*, Moscow: MK RKP, 1922, pp. 80–82.
34 *Sotsialisticheskii vestnik* 3, 1922, pp. 8–10.
35 Carr quotes statistics from the main trusts and syndicates, showing that the proportion of industrial managers who gave their social background as non-worker rose from 35 per cent in 1922 to 64 per cent in 1923. Of these non-workers, one-seventh were party members in 1922 and nearly half were party members in 1923. Carr concludes that 'the management of industry was passing back into the hands of former bourgeois managers and specialists, and a higher proportion of these were acquiring the dignity and security of party membership'. This conclusion needs to be further tested. For example Bailes, quoting the Soviet historian Fediukin, states that in 1922, 70 per cent of managers in the central industrial region around Moscow were *spetsy*, and that from 1923 this proportion began to decline rapidly; this suggests a countervailing tendency. At the twelfth congress it was reported that only 23–29 per cent of members of trusts' management boards were party members, which throws doubt on Carr's assertion that the *spetsy* were joining the party. Carr, op. cit., p. 40; Bailes, op. cit., p. 65; Azrael, op. cit., p. 46.
36 *Predpriiatie* 3, 1923, p. 7; 4–5, 1923, pp. 3–4; 1, 1924, p. 106; *Ekonomicheskaia zhizn'*, 2 August 1923; Carr, op. cit., pp. 40–46.

Intrigue at the rubber goods trust

One communist manager who acquired an exceptionally authoritarian reputation was Valerian Miurat,[37] who was brought from the Red army soon after the tenth congress to take charge of Bogatyr, then Russia's largest rubber goods factory. He was proclaimed an industrious battler against old *spetsy* and managers, and against the Mensheviks and non-partyists, whose control of the Moscow chemical workers' union he was instrumental in breaking. But in 1922, with the political opposition defeated and Miurat promoted to lead the newly formed rubber goods trust, his dictatorial methods provoked opposition not only from ordinary workers, but also from communists in the factory cells and the union. In these clashes, the party's institutional mechanisms worked in Miurat's favour. Only in late 1923 did he suddenly, and with little public explanation, fall from grace. The reasons Miurat received this institutional support need to be considered together with those for his downfall. The main cause of the latter was probably the campaign by the party's ruling clique to discredit industrial managers and, by association with them, the 1923 opposition.

At the end of the civil war, the rubber goods industry had almost ground to a halt due to a lack of raw material inputs. Glavrezin, the industry's chief committee, was dominated by old-regime managers and *spetsy*, who were difficult to replace because of the need for a high level of specialist technical training. In 1920, the party leadership singled out Glavrezin for savage criticism: Nikolai Krylenko, one of the most senior Bolsheviks, directed a public tirade against party members there, accusing them of being hopelessly compromised with the *spetsy*. In the spring of 1921 a new team was installed at Glavrezin, including Miurat as director of Bogatyr. Glavrezin's main factories – Treugol'nik in Petrograd, the Bogatyr, Kauchuk and Provodnik works in Moscow and two others in Moscow and Iaroslavl' regions – had been geared to military requirements during the First World War and civil war: Bogatyr produced tyre covers and other parts for military vehicles, and waterproofs and footwear for the army. All raw rubber, the industry's main input, had to be imported, and by 1920 these imports had stopped and production fell to a fraction of capacity. The first aim of the new management team, boosted substantially by the renewal of rubber imports in August, was to restart production of the industry's main peacetime product, galoshes.[38] The newcomers were based in Moscow and received political support from Sosnovskii; some of the old Glavrezin

37 On Miurat, see Appendix 1.
38 E. Dune, *Notes of a Red Guard*, Urbana: Illinois University Press, 1993, pp. 5–6; A.M. Panfilova, *Istoriia zavoda 'Krasny Bogatyr'*, Moscow: izd. Moskovskogo universiteta, 1958, pp. 74–75; M.Ia. Proletarskii, *Zavod 'Krasnyi bogatyr" (1887–1932)*, Moscow: gos. khim-tekh izd., 1933, pp. 39–43; V.P. Kravets (ed.), *Rezinovaia promyshlennost'. kn. 2.*, Moscow/Leningrad: tsentr upr. pochati VSNKh SSSR, 1926, pp. 5–6; G.M. Davydov and E.Ia. Knop, *Zavod na Usachevke*, Moscow: Moskovskii rabochii, 1980, pp. 30, 32. N.V. Krylenko, 'Proizvodstvennaia demokratiia v tsifrakh i faktakh', in *Na Strazhe (biulleten' osobmezhkoma i ekonomicheskogo upravleniia)* 1–2, 1921: 22–35.

leadership, based in Petrograd, including the Treugol'nik factory director, Shevchenko, were sponsored by Zinoviev. The new team was hailed by Sosnovskii as 'military communists, men from the front, who have learned to work with specialists and fight with much stronger enemies'; Miurat was 'a military cadre', who is 'business-like' and 'combative', although he had no previous experience of economic management. Sosnovskii's articles about the industry cast the frictions in its leadership as political (dynamic new communists against *spetsy* and old regime types), although they also clearly reflected competition for scarce resources, and investment, between the Moscow and Petrograd factories.[39]

Miurat set about restoring production at Bogatyr with undoubted energy. Machinery was brought over from the Provodnik factory, which was largely stood down; he tightened discipline, introduced measures against theft and ordered 300 redundancies. His most significant achievement, though, was political: he drove out of the factory committee its chairman Sergei Mikhailov, leader of the non-party group on the Moscow soviet, and mobilized the factory's Bolsheviks against the Mensheviks in the chemical workers' union. Before Miurat's arrival, the factory committee had challenged, and humiliated, the Bolshevik cell in a dispute about the transparency of a bonus system. But the tables began to turn straight after Miurat arrived. In factory committee elections in June 1921, Mikhailov was replaced as chairman by Aleksandr Titov, a Bolshevik. A mass meeting on 4 August 1921 adopted a resolution proposed by Miurat, denouncing the Menshevik-controlled Moscow chemical workers' union for failing to defend workers' interests. At a second meeting on 16 August, Miurat – supported by Sosnovskii, who attended as an invited speaker – accused some factory committee members of participating in organized theft, and Mikhailov personally of being a 'thief, double-dealer and speculator'. (The archival evidence is thin, but suggests that the charges were baseless.) Mikhailov was made redundant, despite being the factory's delegate to the Moscow and Sokol'niki district soviets; within three months, he had lost those positions. Miurat's offensive at Bogatyr was part of a campaign, coordinated by the Moscow party leadership, to dislodge the Mensheviks and non-partyists from the chemical workers' union. That aim was achieved at a regional union conference on 4 October. The Mensheviks and non-partyists jointly formed a narrow majority at the conference and on the newly elected executive; this was dissolved by the Moscow trade union federation and replaced by a 'red' chemical workers' union headed by Bolshevik appointees.[40]

During 1922, Miurat's dictatorial style led him into conflicts with many Bolshevik party members. The first challenge came from the Bogatyr cell. In January 1922, the rubber goods industry was reorganized, cost accounting introduced, and Glavrezin replaced by a rubber industry trust, Rezinotrest.

39 *Pravda*, 6, 7 and 26 August 1921, 24 June 1922 and 30 January 1923.

182 The party elite, industrial managers and the cells

Miurat was proposed as president of the new body. Zorina, a full-time communist official and secretary of the Bogatyr factory committee, and Ivanov, a communist who had quit the party, went to see Petr Bogdanov, president of VSNKh, to argue against putting Miurat in charge. Miurat's supporters in the cell confronted Zorina and Ivanov at a mass meeting and accused them of disloyalty. Ivanov responded: 'When asked [by Bogdanov] how Miurat gets on with the workers' organizations at the factory [I] replied that the factory committee is in Miurat's hands, completely subordinate to him, and that the Council of Delegates has no voice'. Miurat's supporters, apparently working as part of a concerted inter-institutional campaign, successfully moved a resolution supporting his appointment. Zorina was deemed to have 'breached party discipline' by sharing her concerns with Bogdanov, and was thrown out of the Bogatyr cell and removed from the factory committee and the Moscow soviet. In his new post at the trust, Miurat clashed with the Bolsheviks who had been installed in the Moscow chemical workers' union leadership; both the MC and the Moscow control commission tried to adjudicate. One cause of tension was Miurat's confrontational method of dealing with strikes. For example he took the most aggressive possible stance against a spontaneous walkout about piece-work rates in the varnishing shop at Bogatyr in June 1922, at the height of the propaganda campaign around the trial of the Socialist Revolutionaries (SRs). At a mass meeting on 1 July, after the adoption of a standard Bolshevik resolution calling for the 'sternest punishment' of the SR trial defendants, he announced that the varnishers' action was a 'strange Menshevik conspiracy' that would have 'very serious consequences'. It was decided, by several hundred votes against five, to expel the varnishers from the chemical workers' union. Korchagin, chairman of the union's Moscow region, argued in vain for a conciliatory approach. Miurat was becoming notorious for such anti-worker behaviour. The Mensheviks claimed he had told a mass meeting at the Provodnik factory that he was the 'new, red Riabushinksii'.[41] And the trust's contempt for trade union agreements angered the party cell at Kauchuk, Moscow's second rubber goods factory.[42]

---

40 Pirani, op. cit., 205–6; J. Hatch, 'Working-class Politics in Moscow During the Early NEP: Mensheviks and Workers' Organizations, 1921–22', *Soviet Studies* 34: 4, 1987: 556–74, especially 563–66; Panfilova, op. cit., pp. 101–2; Proletarskii, op. cit., pp. 40–41. See also TsAGM, 337/2/39/24–30, 99, 116, 125, 170ob, 187; TsAOPIM, 36/11/36; *Pravda*, 26 August and 5 and 9 October 1921; *Sotsialisticheskii Vestnik* 18, 1921, pp. 12–13; 22, 1921, p. 12; and , 1922, p. 16; *Moskovskaia gubernskaia konferentsiia profsoiuzov, 14–15 sent. 1921*, Moscow: MGSPS, 1921, p. 10.
41 The reference was to Pavel Riabushinskii, a leading Moscow industrialist, who in 1917 famously threatened that soviets would be dealt with by 'the bony hand of hunger'. *Sotsialisticheskii vestnik* 13–14, 1922, p. 16.
42 Pirani, op. cit., pp. 206–7; TsGAMO, 609/1/107/7, 69–70, 73ob, 80; TsAOPIM, 1300/1/1/1–3; 2867/1/4/41, 95; 3/3/6/57; 475/1/4/25; 475/1/7/9–9ob.

In 1923, the rubber goods industry was one of the first to feel the impact of the 'scissors' trading crisis, which is further discussed in Chapter 8. Sales were poor and Rezinotrest built up huge stockpiles, particularly of galoshes. In April, it was agreed to lay off 1000 workers at Krasnyi Bogatyr (as Bogatyr was renamed) and Kauchuk, and in August discussions began about the possible closure of the Provodnik works. At the beginning of the year, Miurat was riding high. He was combative in the face of worker opposition to the redundancy programme; he had been appointed to a VSNKh commission on workers' conditions and to the management board of the industrial bank; and his support bases within the party hierarchy continued to function. At Krasnyi Bogatyr, fears of redundancy were aggravated by resentment at the imperious behaviour of Miurat's successor as director, Sorokin, who did not allow workers to enter his office and, according to a GPU report, made them stand up and take their hats off when he entered the shops. And when party members at the factory clashed with Sorokin and the trust, the MC supported the latter. In January 1923 an MC commission dealt with 'abnormal' relations by means of expulsions, motions of censure and sackings. In the autumn, though, Miurat's fortunes reversed dramatically. The immediate authors of his downfall were, apparently, the Moscow chemical workers' union leaders. In September his contemptuous attitude towards the Provodnik workers had caused concern among party officials in Bauman; on 9 October they discussed his 'intolerable attitude' to the Provodnik party cell; and on 2 November the chemical workers' union complained formally to the MC about this. On 6 November Miurat attended a mass meeting at Provodnik where he abused those present as 'scroungers and parasites'. While previous accusations of similar behaviour had been stonewalled, this time a complaint received immediate attention from the MC bureau and was published in *Pravda*, in a letter over the name of 'the factory's workers'. Miurat had told the Provodnik workers that 'it's in his power to sack or not sack them, and that he would "flay the workers' hides"'. As a result, the letter continued, dozens of condemnatory notices had been posted on the factory's wall newspaper, stating, for example: 'The workers in a socialist state are not a grey herd, who can be insulted any old how. Obviously comrade Miurat has forgotten that there is workers' power in our republic.' The workforce, supported by the party cell and party-dominated factory committee, demanded Miurat's dismissal. On 20 November this demand was taken up by the Moscow chemical workers' union presidium; *Pravda* suddenly found space for adulatory reports of the work of Miurat's old enemy Shevchenko in Petrograd;[43] rumours began to fly around that Miurat was not even a party member; and, shortly afterwards, he was gone.

43 Pirani, op. cit., pp. 207–9; TsAOPIM, 3/11/86/30–32; 3/11/91/17; TsGAMO 609/1/183/5–18, 55, 141, 157ob; 609/1/168/143, 182; RGASPI, 17/84/468/67; *Pravda* 11 and 30 November and 6 December 1923; *Sotsialisticheskii vestnik* 4, 1923, p. 12 and 21–22, 1923, p. 19.

It would be comforting to think that this shows that authoritarian anti-worker communist managers got their just deserts – but too simple. Why did the MC leadership take seriously the complaints against Miurat, instead of victimizing the complainants as had been done before? And why did claims emanate from the party leadership – and end up being published by the central control commission (CCC) – that Miurat was not even a party member?[44] Suggestions had been made, by the communist dissident Miasnikov, that before 1917 Miurat had been a tsarist police provocateur. But these were, and remain, unsubstantiated.[45] A more coherent explanation for Miurat's transformation from a hero of industrial policy to a non-person is that, by endorsing his sacking, the ruling clique in the Bolshevik CC (Stalin, Zinoviev, Kamenev et al.) could make valuable political capital for its struggle with the opposition led by Trotsky, Preobrazhenskii and Sapronov. Showing readiness to curb the industrial managers' power was a leitmotif of the ruling group's tactics. Miurat's dismissal might not only have won approval in the party ranks, but also reflected badly on Sosnovskii, a leading opposition spokesman. Members of the Kauchuk cell – who had clashed with Miurat when he was strong, and who in their majority supported the 1923 opposition – suspected that the party leadership's volte-face was not wholly principled. At a cell meeting in December 1923, Kaspirovich, in a speech protesting at the lack of inner-party democracy, said: 'The most foul rumours started circulating about Miurat, and no-one could tell us anything. [After the cell criticized him,] suddenly it turns out that he's not a party member!' Solov'ev, another Kauchuk communist, told the Khamovniki district party conference in January 1924: 'When I went to one responsible comrade, and asked him what the score was with Miurat, he said: "You know it, you keep your mouth shut. There are other people to do the thinking about that one"'. Skvortsov-Stepanov, who supported the Zinoviev-Stalin group, responded: 'The MC and the chemical workers' union had several times proposed to dismiss Miurat, but you know who defended him – Sosnovskii. And he's a formidable opponent.'[46] The CCC, in its announcement claiming Miurat had never been a party member, also took the opportunity to mention Sosnovskii several times, in connection with supposed failed attempts to recruit his friend.

There are other examples of factory cells and district party organizations, as well as regional and national bodies, giving institutional support to the industrial managers in conflicts with workers. Even the Kauchuk cell, whose comparatively outspoken leadership had challenged Miurat's bullying, fell in – albeit after hesitation, and under pressure from district officials – behind Pokrovskii, the factory's manager, when he witch-hunted a dissident

---

44 Although Miurat had been universally accepted as a party member, a CCC declaration on his case suggested that he had never been one. *Pravda*, 13 January 1924.
45 RGASPI, 17/71/4; *Sotsialisticheskii vestnik* 21–22, 1923, p. 19.
46 TsAOPIM, 475/1/7/44–45; 88/1/169/14–19.

Kauchuk worker communist in 1922. Fedor Sorokin had publicly accused Pokrovskii of corruption and inefficiency, and the party cell of covering up for him. Sorokin said he had spoken out, in a letter published by the Moscow party newspaper, 'to make the management feel that, in Soviet Russia, the worker is not a frightened slave of cunning little people with their old [tsarist] mind-set, but a bold, conscious revolutionary, fighting against the masked careerists'. When Sorokin turned up at a cell meeting to justify his claims, Pokrovskii had him removed by armed guards. The cell condemned this use of force against a communist as 'shameful' – but backed down when the Khamovniki district party leadership intervened to support Pokrovskii. Sorokin was excluded from the party on an administrative pretext; he, and two other members who had spoken in his support, were sacked; and Angarskii, who was 'attached' to the cell and expressed some sympathy, treated to a derisory dressing-down by the district secretary, Mandel'shtam. Although shortly afterwards Pokrovskii was removed by district officials in an apparently unrelated dispute, Sorokin's numerous appeals against his victimization failed.[47]

Cell leaders, managers and *spetsy*

In the party's factory cells, a bottom layer of the party-state hierarchy was taking shape. The cells were changing their modus operandi, drawing closer to, and in some respects merging with, factory managements. Just as, at national level, party bodies encroached on soviet functions, so in the factories, the cells became increasingly involved in administrative details. Their meetings not only considered political issues, and agitation and propaganda around these, but also more regularly discussed production, technical, supply, maintenance, employment and financial questions. Decision-making power moved from plenary meetings to the increasingly important cell bureaus. Initially, the cells' weakness, discussed at the eleventh congress (see Chapter 5, p. 137), could not be overcome by fresh recruitment as the MC had hoped. Significant numbers of recruits started arriving in the Moscow factories only in late 1922 and 1923, and in the party nationally in the Lenin enrolment of 1924 (see Chapter 9, p. 228). In the meantime, the cells were reinforced by a new drive to transfer communists into them from the soviet apparatus.[48] The new arrivals tended to go into management; many more kept their office jobs and had 'attached' status.[49] And the cells became more disciplined, Zelenskii reported in November 1922: although there were still

47 Pirani, op. cit., pp. 209–10; TsAOPIM, 88/1/101/21–21ob; 88/1/169/91; 475/1/2/14; 475/1/4/12–17, l. 23; TsGAMO, 609/1/207/100; *Rabochaia Moskva*, 28 May 1922.
48 *Vosmaia gubernskaia konferentsiia*, pp. 40–41; *Deviataia konferentsiia*, p. 70.
49 On the 'attached' system, see Chapter 2, p. 61. In the 1923 discussion an oppositionist delivering a report at Kauchuk, Kivirkianov, complained about 'cells with three workers and 18 attached members, and a bureau entirely made up of attached members'. TsAOPIM, 475/1/7/42.

occasions when factory communists behaved 'neutrally' towards, or even supported, worker protests, most cells had undergone a 'process of self-purging' and shed 'disruptive elements'.[50]

The diffidence with which many worker communists took on administrative responsibilities has been mentioned in Chapter 5, p. 131. Here it is suggested that this bottom layer of the hierarchy was also a milieu in which *spets*-baiting (*spetseedstvo*) was strong. In western historiography, discussions of the motivation for *spets*-baiting in early Soviet Russia usually stress workers' lack of culture and anti-intellectualism, while the orchestration from the top of hostility to *spetsy* is associated with the 'great break' of 1928–30.[51] This account suggests that some of the most aggressive *spets*-baiters were not any old workers, but those workers who, through becoming party office holders, were being pulled into the lowest levels of the party elite. In some cases, cited below, their harassment of *spetsy* caused ordinary workers to protest in the specialists' defence; in others, party officials compelled *spetsy* to implement unpopular measures, e.g. new piece-work arrangements, and take the blame from workers.[52] These middle-ranking party members sometimes had problems adapting their civil war experience to NEP conditions; they also had to overcome nervousness and insecurity about asserting their authority. The specialists' superior knowledge may have seemed threatening in one way; their associations, however tenuous, with the pre-revolutionary regime, in another.

Spets-baiting has been linked in the historiography to the oppositions' workerism, but this deserves reconsideration. Accusations of anti-*spets* prejudice, and even insinuations of anti-semitism, were made against the oppositionists by leading party members in the course of heated polemics, and need to be treated with great caution.[53] While some rank-and-file dissidents certainly entertained crude workerist prejudices against specialists and the intelligentsia, the leaders of the Workers Opposition (WO) in general did not. They supported the use of specialists, while opposing Lenin's principle of material rewards for them. In 1922–23, the former WO member F.D. Budniak, president of the motor industry trust, in the course of a long quarrel with a group of leading cell members at the AMO factory, was accused of backing *spetsy* such as the factory's chief engineer V.I. Tsipulin against the cell; he in turn accused his opponents of *spets*-baiting.[54] And of course the Democratic Centralists (DCs), who were allied with the WO in the 1920 opposition, emphatically supported the use of specialists.

50 *Izvestiia MK RKP(b)* 3, 1922, pp. 5–13.
51 For example, Moshe Lewin states that *spets*-baiting under NEP had 'much to do with the very low cultural and living standard of the workers', while he writes that in the late 1920s it was encouraged by party officials. M. Lewin, *The Making of the Soviet System: Essays in the Social History of Interwar Russia*, New York: The New Press, 1994, pp. 231–33 and p. 248.
52 N.V. Valentinov, *Novaia ekonomicheskaia politika i krizis partii posle smerti Lenina: gody raboty v VSNKh vo vremia NEP*, Moscow: Sovremennik, 1991, p. 182.

Moscow's highest-profile *spets*-baiting case during early NEP was that of V. V. Oldenborger, chief engineer at the Alekseevskaia water works in Sokol'niki district. He committed suicide on 30 November 1921 after prolonged persecution by low-level representatives of the party elite, whose actions were held in contempt by non-party workers. The party leadership, on Lenin's insistence, made a public example of the *spets*-baiters: Elagin and Merkulov, two leaders of the works' party cell; Sedel'nikov, a local full-time official; and Semenov, an official of the Workers and Peasants Inspectorate. In March 1922 they were arraigned before the Supreme Revolutionary Tribunal, in a case conducted personally by the state prosecutor, Krylenko, and convicted of creating conditions that helped drive Oldenborger to suicide and thereby of bringing the party into disrepute.[55] The Tribunal heard how the *spets*-baiters tried unsuccessfully to use their apparatus connections to get Oldenborger sacked and engaged in petty intrigues against him. Oldenborger, who took pride in having run the water works since 1898 and

---

53 The oppositionists are mentioned in discussions of hostility to *spetsy* by S. Fitzpatrick, 'The Civil War as Formative Experience', in A. Gleason, P. Kenez and R. Stites (eds), *Bolshevik Culture: Experiment and Order in the Russian Revolution*, Bloomington: Indiana University Press, 1985, pp. 58–76; W.J. Chase, *Workers, Society and the Soviet State: Labour and Life in Moscow 1918–1929*, Urbana: University of Illinois Press, 1990, p. 45; and Bailes, op. cit., p. 59. However I have seen no primary source material where oppositionists express anti-*spets* prejudice, as distinct from their political arguments against additional payments for *spetsy*. On anti-semitism, Fitzpatrick states that 'attacks on the intelligentsia leadership by members of the WO appeared to have anti-semitic overtones' ('The Civil War as Formative Experience', 72). She cites Iaroslavskii, who complained to the tenth congress that the WO's proposed 'general attack' on party members of bourgeois origin could be understood by members in the provinces as a call to 'beat up the intelligentsiia', and Rafail, who compared the WO's position to that of workers and peasants who 'used to think that everything stemmed from the fact that there were a lot of "yids" everywhere'. But other speakers, with typical Bolshevik hyperbole, compared the WO to the Mensheviks, anarchists, syndicalists and to Machajski; obviously such accusations are not a serious guide to WO politics, and nor are Iaroslavskii's and Rafail's. In fact both of them fell short of accusing their party comrades of anti-semitism, instead making an argument that seems legitimate, if harsh, that the WO's position on the intelligentsia could *encourage* anti-intelligentsia prejudice in other workers. See also Chapter 3, note 10 on p. 76, on anti-semitism.
54 Pirani, op. cit., p. 213.
55 Sedel'nikov received a two-year prison sentence, reduced to one under a general amnesty; the other defendants were publicly censured and banned from responsible posts for three years. This account is drawn from N.V. Krylenko, *Za Piat' Let 1918–1922 gg. Obvinitel'nye rechi*, Moscow: Gosizdat, 1923, pp. 431–59, and *Izvestiia*, 9, 12 and 14 March 1922. Solzhenitsyn contrasted the lenient sentences handed down in the Oldenborger case to the severity of those in the trial of the Glavtop specialists. A. Solzhenitsyn, *Arkhipelag Gulag*, Paris: YMCA Press, 1973, vol. 1, pp. 336–41. See also *Odinnadtsatyi s"ezd*, pp. 730–31 and Lenin, *Polnoe sobranie sochinenii (izd. 5-ogo)*, Moscow: Gospolitizdat, 1958–65, vol. 44, pp. 354–55.

was depicted at the hearing as an introvert workaholic, killed himself after Semenov stymied an urgent repair by blocking an equipment delivery. The *spets*-baiters were not simply a wayward clique: they had access to national industrial decision-makers through V.A. Avanesov, a member of the VSNKh presidium, and, even after being convicted, were supported by party leaders at Sokol'niki district, although not Moscow regional, level.[56] They bullied Oldenborger in the course of inept and unsuccessful attempts to establish their authority over a politically active workforce that included non-partyist and SR sympathizers. Like many Moscow workers, those at the water works had been sympathetic to Bolshevism in 1917, but by 1921 had lost faith, if not with the government, then certainly with the workplace cell, which was defeated at factory committee elections by non-partyists and SR sympathizers.[57] In the soviet election campaign of April 1921, Oldenborger stood against the party candidate with some organized support from non-party workers. Cell members acknowledged to the Supreme Tribunal that their candidate had been 'a loser', fighting a 'hopeless' campaign, given Oldenborger's 'authority' among workers. Even so, the cell had during the hustings accused Oldenborger of 'sabotage' – an assertion howled down with shouts of 'lies' at a mass meeting. Oldenborger's death further damaged the cell's relationship with the workforce, and the intriguers' trial did not repair it. In March 1922 a non-party workers' slate again defeated the Bolsheviks in factory committee elections. In June, as the campaign around the SR trial reached a climax, the Alekseevskaia cell's resolution on the subject was voted down at a poorly attended mass meeting by 35 to 17. A GPU agent reported gloomily that 'distrust towards the [party] cell' was strong because 'workers put the principal blame for the murder [sic] of Oldenborger on the communists'.[58] Lenin's condemnation of the Alekseevskaia *spets*-baiters is well established in the historiography, but the context – that the campaign against Oldenborger was conducted not by a workforce gripped by anti-intellectualism, but by members of a budding party elite consolidating its position against both workers and specialists – requires consideration. At the Supreme Tribunal, Krylenko had accused the Bolshevik intriguers of 'petty tyranny' towards not only Oldenborger but the whole workforce ... but steered clear of the fact that such authoritarian behaviour was common. When a defence witness argued that the water workers were 'infected with petty-bourgeois psychology', Krylenko derided this as 'empty words' – sidestepping the fact that this was a standard, endlessly repeated Bolshevik explanation for the party's loss of support.

While some unqualified party officials jealously manoeuvred against *spetsy* in this manner, others masqueraded as *spetsy* in order to improve their own incomes. These middle- and lower-level communist officials who

---

56 TsAOPIM, 3/3/6/19.
57 Krylenko, op. cit., p. 437.
58 TsAOPIM, 3/3/33/64 and 3/3/34/165, 214.

took specialists' salary rates without having the technical skills to justify doing so became known as false specialists (*lzhespetsy*). At the Goznak printing works, the manager of the card-printing shop, Sergievskii, was sacked in October 1923 at the party cell's insistence – on the grounds that he was 'not a specialist, but a careerist', as a cell leader, Vinukurov, put it. The works' communist manager, Trifon Enukidze, who was constantly in conflict with the cell and trade union officials (see Chapter 5, p. 135), tried to defend Sergievskii and only sacked him after having 'dragged his feet' for three months.[59] In late 1923, when trade union leaders and others renewed their protests against managers' excessive salaries, anger was directed against the proliferation of fake specialists: an article in *Pravda* complained that 'special rates [of between 1 and 50 per cent above the norm] are being paid to those who are not specialists'. The union leaders' protests about the 'bacchanalia of "rates for specialists"', and demands for pay cuts, forced concessions from the labour commissariat in an agreement signed in November.[60] At a meeting of Moscow party activists in December 1923, Andeichin said workers were angry about pay differentials in general, and the 'unrestrained increases in the pay of soviet *sluzhashchie* and an assortment of yobs [*raznykh parshivtsev*] who call themselves specialists and help themselves to tantiemes that the state chooses to distribute freely to our enemies' in particular.[61]

Notwithstanding the suspicion and jealousy towards specialists by some lower-level party officials, there were many circumstances in which these two groups, plus the communist managers – all fragments of the future ruling class – worked together. Indeed in the industrial towns in the countryside around Moscow, visiting officials from the capital found that the heads of local political and economic institutions had begun to live as a discrete caste, separate from the rest of the population, and sometimes to form cliques with closer loyalties to each other than to the centre.[62] In the Zvenigorod district, a commission sent by the MC to investigate problems in the local administration in early 1923 found a close alliance between local party leaders and industrial managers, against both interference from the centre and disobedience from the ranks. In the local leadership there was 'isolation of some comrades from the communist ranks, which has created an unhealthy atmosphere' and 'unbusinesslike relations with *spetsy* by the majority of [party officials], ... expressed in the systematic arrangement of wine-fuelled

---

59 There is no evidence on the basis of which to assess whether the accusations against Sergievskii were justified. A group of workers in Sergievskii's shop, led by a former party member, Fedorov, campaigned against his dismissal. TsAOPIM, 1099/1/7/31ob, 45, 49; 1099/1/8/46, 56, 61, 74.
60 *Pravda*, 10 November 1923. See also *Trud*, 10 and 17 October and 1 December 1923; Carr, op. cit., pp. 95–96.
61 TsAOPIM, 3/4/36/32.
62 Rigby, 'Early Provincial Cliques'; Gill, op. cit., pp. 124–26; and Easter, op. cit., especially pp. 9–69.

banquets where the drunkenness knew no bounds'.[63] The trend is not uniform: in Moskovskii rural district, for example, there was a running battle between party and industrial officials.[64] In other cases, the two sides sank their differences with a view to stealing from the state budget and other forms of corrupt self-enrichment.[65] In October-November 1922, a show trial was staged in the Moscow region's largest textile town, Orekhovo-Zuevo, of textile trust officials and traders who had conspired to defraud the trust, which ended with 13 death sentences. The word 'Orekhovozuevism' (*orekhovozuevshchina*) was coined to designate corruption in local elites. The trial proceedings showed that leading local party members, including M.P. Serebriakov, the young president of the party's district executive and a member of the Moscow Cheka's collegium, and Bogatov, a member of the trust management committee, had covered up for, and likely profited from, the fraud. In March 1923, a similar scheme arranged by senior officials of the Serpukhov textile trust was broken up by the GPU.[66]

The formation of the party elite was a political process and depended primarily on the centralization of political power, and the communist industrial managers were a separate group within, or in some senses adjacent to, the party elite. The vilification of some of them during the 1923 'party discussion', which will be discussed in Chapter 9, reflected real tensions, as well as having propaganda value for the party leadership – in the same way that campaigns against 'bureaucratism' and corruption served political purposes. Nevertheless, the unfolding class relationships grouped the industrial managers and the *spetsy* on the side of the party elite – and against the working class, which was being systematically deprived of political power and expression. At the lowest level, in the factories, many party officials were still poorly prepared for wielding that power, and this unpreparedness, and the insecurity it caused in individuals, was a cause of *spets*-baiting. There

---

63 TsAOPIM, 3/11/90/17.
64 Corruption among industrial managers in Moskovskii district became an issue in an industrial dispute there in the summer of 1923. TsAOPIM, 3/11/90/16, 128.
65 Some indication of the extent of corruption among party officials may be gleaned from a CCC report covering May-November 1923. During this six-month period alone, the CCC expelled 1182 members for 'crimes in the course of duties'. It noted with concern that members guilty of this offence were *less* likely to be expelled than if they were found to be 'alien elements' or participants in religious practices. The figures are the more striking, if it is borne in mind that normally in corrupt institutions, the most skilful and highest-placed offenders are less often caught. RGASPI, 323/2/23/11ob-14.
66 *Pravda*, 31 October and 2, 3 and 5 November 1922; *Sotsialisticheskii vestnik*, 5–6, 1923, pp. 11–12; L.V. Borisova, 'NEP v zerkale pokazatel'nykh protsessov po vziatochnichestvu i khoziaistvennym prestupleniiam', *Otechestvennaia istoriia* 1, 2006: 84–97. A GPU report of December 1922 distinguished a case of 'Orekhovozuevshchina' from one of sabotage. RGASPI, 17/84/296/81.

were other tensions between *spetsy*, managers and party officials. And there were party members who continued in 1922–23 – and for years afterwards – to side with workers on workplace issues. But those who challenged the *political* power of the elite and its allies already found themselves confronting a system of institutions that defended that power. Even in this period, when it would be hard to say that a bureaucratic ruling class had taken shape, hierarchical class relations were developing.

8 The social contract in practice
Workers in 1923

By 1923, the economic problems facing industrial workers in Russia bore a closer resemblance to those in capitalist countries than at any time since the revolution. The market mechanisms being used under the New Economic Policy (NEP) were taking effect, unemployment was rising rapidly, and real wages were threatened by inflation – phenomena that some industrial managers regarded as the necessary overheads of economic growth. Workers thought that 'NEP has got carried away with itself', and mass meetings cheered anyone who said that the party needs to 'clip [NEP]'s wings' or even 'suffocate it a little', the Moscow regional party conference in April heard.[1] Resentment culminated in a wave of industrial unrest in the summer, to which the Bolshevik government responded by renewing its commitment to raise workers' living standards. Working-class politics, as distinct from industrial relations, was further stultified. The 'workers' state' had put working-class political dissent beyond the pale. Attempts to defend dissident communist workers' leaders associated with the Workers Group won only limited support. Most workers retreated into abstention from politics, often declining either to respond to the Bolsheviks' appeals for financial contributions or even to vote in soviet elections.

For workers, the most unwelcome aspect of NEP was unemployment. Registered unemployment in the Moscow region rose from 55,353 in December 1922 to 102,123 in June 1923. By October it was 124,424, about 15 per cent of the working population. Workers were extremely sensitive to the prospect of redundancies: in May, the Dobrovykh-Navgolts works struck over the issue.[2] The mass lay-offs often used to deal with strikes became more effective: in 1920–21 those made redundant might expect to be re-employed within a few days or find work elsewhere, but now they faced the prospect of long-term hardship. Unemployment was a consequence of industrial restructuring and in-migration from the countryside, not of economic slowdown. Growth continued, and with it, workers' hopes

---

1 TsAOPIM, 3/4/1/60.
2 TsAOPIM, 3/4/49/91.

of raising wage levels. In the first three months of 1923, real wage rates were pushed up by 22 per cent,[3] by a combination of the burgeoning recovery, union and government efforts to simplify payment methods and standardize collective agreements, and worker militancy. But downward pressure on wages came from industrial managers, who were responsible for making the trusts profitable, and from the finance commissariat, which prioritized a stable currency. Guidelines for state sector wages were set by negotiations between the Supreme Council of the Economy (Vysshii sovet narodnogo khoziaistva — VSNKh) and the All-Russian Central Council of Trade Unions (Vserossiiskii tsentral'nyi sovet profsoiuzov — VTsSPS); in reality, the party leadership arbitrated. All sides agreed that (i) wages should be strictly regulated in line with the task of raising industrial output; (ii) wages could only return to 1913 levels after a substantial increase in productivity; and (iii) working-class action on wages outside this framework should be dealt with harshly. Piece work was favoured by both management and unions as an ideal means to raise productivity: in 1923, the proportion of industrial workers on piece rates nationally was four out of ten and rising.[4]

In December 1922, the VTsSPS plenum decided that the economic situation made a general rise in wages in industry 'objectively impossible'. Acting under instruction from the Bolshevik party Central Committee (CC), it assigned unions the tasks of holding wages at their current level, and striving for increases only in sectors that lagged behind the average, in particular transport.[5] But this was not enough for the industrial managers. One particularly inflammatory article in the VSNKh newspaper, *Ekonomicheskaia zhizn'*, argued that 'the cost of labour power ... in both absolute and relative terms is far too high'. This, and other attempts to pin the blame for inflation on workers' wages, provoked a response from Larin on behalf of the party leadership. The Moscow committee (MC) of the Bolshevik party also noted with concern 'the tendency in some economic bodies towards reductions in wages'. In March 1923 the debate culminated in a new agreement between the VSNKh and VTsSPS, which stated that any reduction in wages would be 'inadmissible', that in transport and heavy industry they should be raised, and that both sides' main task was to 'create economic conditions' that would justify a further increase. In April,

---

3 A.G. Rashin, *Zarabotnaia plata za vosstanovitel'nyi period khoziaistva SSSR 1922/23–1926/27 gg.*, Moscow: Gosizdat, 1928, pp. 12–13.
4 N.V. Valentinov, *Novaia ekonomicheskaia politika i krizis partii posle smerti Lenina*, Moscow: Sovremennik, 1991, p. 182; Rashin, op. cit., pp. 32–33; *Predpriatiie* 4–5, 1923, p. 115; MGSPS, *Piatyi gubernskii s"ezd moskovskikh profsoiuzov. Itogi, rezoliutsiia, postanovleniia*, Moscow: Mosgublit, 1923, pp. 64–65.
5 *Trud*, 25 February 1923; *Trinadtsatyi s"ezd RKP(b), mai 1924 goda: stenograficheskii otchet*, Moscow: Gos. izd-vo politicheskoi literatury, 1963, p. 84; E.H. Carr, *The Interregnum, 1923–1924*, London: Macmillan, 1978, p. 73.

this deal was endorsed by the twelfth party congress.[6] In May, the MC spelled out what this meant in the capital: 'consolidation' of levels achieved in late 1922 for textile and metal workers; increases for rail and communications workers only; and a wage freeze in the food and tobacco industries.[7] To maintain or increase the level of real wages, workers had to fight constantly for prompt payments and fair currency conversion rates, as they had done in 1922. Price inflation in Moscow averaged 25 per cent per month in January–March 1923, 36 per cent per month in April–June and 67 per cent per month in July–September. So even a day's delay in payment meant a wage cut – and managers continued to pay wages late 'systematically', as one GPU security police survey pointed out. Trusts also manipulated exchange rates, usually by recalculating the level of the 'goods ruble' to their own advantage.[8] Pay grades were another weapon in this war of attrition: managers tried to downgrade workers, while factory committees argued for groups of workers to be upgraded.[9]

Managers tried so hard to remove discussion of pay and conditions from the shop floor, and take it as high as possible up the party and state hierarchy, that Bolshevik trade union leaders complained bitterly. Mel'nichanskii reported to the Moscow regional council of trade unions (Moskovskii gubernskii sovet professional'nykh soiuzov — MGSPS) congress in November that union central committees were trying to sign agreements without even consulting regional union leaderships: the Moscow council had forced the VTsSPS to rule that agreements had to be discussed at all levels. Factory committees and mass meetings had even less chance of being consulted. 'Many comrades [argue] that there is no need to discuss collective agreements at delegates' meetings or mass meetings. We flatly insisted that the preliminary text of agreements had to be discussed, before they were signed,' Mel'nichanskii wrote. Not that a mass meeting was any guarantee of discussion and participation: they 'all too often take on the character of a rally [*mitingovy kharakter*], and only a very small number of participants get a chance to give their views', Mel'nichanskii complained in another context. It was a point made by workers, too. For example, in August workers at the Krasnaia Roza textile factory (formerly the Zhiro silk works)

---

6 *Ekonomicheskaia zhizn'*, 25 and 27 January, 2, 16 and 18 February 1923, *Trud*, 24 March 1923; *Pravda*, 5 April 1923; TsAOPIM, 3/4/5/6; Rashin, op. cit., p. 13; Carr, *The Interregnum*, pp. 73–75 and 85–89.
7 TsAOPIM, 3/4/5/20–21.
8 TsAOPIM, 3/4/49/91; F.D. Markuzon (ed.), *Polozhenie truda v Moskovskoi gubernii v 1922–1923gg.: sbornik materialov biuro statistika truda*, Moscow: MGSPS, 1923, pp. 46–47; Carr, *The Interregnum*, pp. 76–79.
9 At Kauchuk, for example, nearly two-thirds (195 out of 321) of cases brought to the conflict commission in the period October 1922 to April 1923 concerned grading; another 53 concerned piece rates. TsGAMO, 609/1/207/99–100.

in Khamovniki protested at the factory committee signing an agreement with the silk trust without consulting the workforce.[10]

The communist left

The extent to which working-class political protest was marginalized can be judged from the failure of the only significant challenge to the party among Moscow workers in 1923, by the Workers Group of communist dissidents. In May, the group's leaders in Moscow, former members of the 1920 Bauman opposition, were expelled from the party and the metalworkers' union. Factory mass meetings and party organizations made protests, exceptional acts of defiance at a time when political opposition automatically invited GPU repression. But this turned out to be the apex of the Workers Group's activity. Party leaders' fears that the industrial discontent of the summer would develop into political struggle, and provide a support base for the dissidents, were misplaced. Most workers, willing if not happy to accept the social contract, concentrated on winning improvements in living standards and shunned those who challenged the Bolshevik leadership politically. The Workers Group, along with the Workers Truth group, was to all intents and purposes destroyed by GPU arrests in September.[11]

Just after the twelfth party congress in April, the Workers Group published a manifesto,[12] the central theme of which was the resurrection of workers' democracy in the form of workplace-based soviets. It argued that, whereas during the civil war the emphasis had been on suppressing the exploiters, NEP required rebuilding such soviets as the 'basic cells' of state power. There could be no free speech for those who oppose revolution, 'from monarchists to SRs', and curtailing democracy during the civil war had been an unavoidable necessity. But under NEP 'a new approach' was needed, including free speech for all workers: 'there is no such thing in Russia as a communist working class, there is just the working class, with Bolsheviks, anarchists, SRs and Mensheviks in its ranks', among whom 'not compulsion, but persuasion' had to be used. This view of democracy was

10 *Piatyi gubernskii s"ezd*, pp. 22–23; G. Mel'nichanskii, *Moskovskie professional'nye soiuzy*, Moscow: Glavlit, 1923, p. 7; TsAOPIM, 3/4/49/70.
11 P. Avrich, 'Bolshevik Opposition to Lenin: G. Miasnikov and the Workers Group', *Russian Review* 43, 1984: 1–29. New information was published in Russia in the 1990s, including G. Miasnikov, 'Filosofiia ubiistva, ili pochemu i kak ia ubil Mikhaila Romanova', *Minuvshee* 18, 1995, pp. 7–191; '1921 god. Miasnikov, Lenin i diskussiia', *Svobodnaia mysl* 1, 1989: 62–75; V.V. Zhuravlev et al. (eds), *Vlast' i oppozitsiia: Rossiskii politicheskii protsess XX stoletiia*, Moscow: Rosspen, 1995; G.L. Olekh, *Povorot, kotorogo ne bylo: bor'ba za vnutripartiinuiu demokratiu 1919–1924 gg.*, Novosibirsk: izd. Novosibirskogo universiteta, 1992, pp. 106–7.
12 RGASPI, 17/71/4. For an abridged English translation, see International Communist Current, *The Russian Communist Left, 1918–30*, London: ICC, 2005, pp. 163–80.

class-based and conditional, in the Bolshevik tradition, but wider than that of the party leadership, and of the DCs, whose demands for inner-party democracy the manifesto criticized, because they 'skip over a little detail – the proletariat'. The manifesto lambasted the use of 'bureaucratic appointments that brush aside the direct participation of the working class' to run industry. These methods had produced the 'comedy of red directors', exemplified by the 'provocateur' Miurat. The manifesto warned of the 'great danger' that NEP would degenerate into the rule of the 'commanding tops': already trust managers were earning 200 rubles per month plus lavish extras, while workers earned 4 or 5 rubles. But the Workers Group was not opposed to NEP *per se*, and did not share the Workers Truth group's analysis that 'capitalist relations' had been restored by a ruling 'technical intelligentsia'. The economic policy retreat had been made necessary by the 'state of our country's productive forces'; such an approach was needed to 'strengthen individual peasant agricultural production and move from the plough to the tractor' – but it had to be implemented by workers and peasants, otherwise it could turn into the 'New Exploitation of the Proletariat'.[13] The manifesto also set out a leftist view of international revolution and criticized the Comintern's 'united front' tactic.

The Workers Group accepted the Bolshevik party's programme and statutes, but believed that the working class had to save it from degeneration. This required an organizationally separate 'communist workers' group' comprising members, applicants for membership and expelled members of the party. The Workers Group no doubt had in mind here communists such as the 300 at one large enterprise, who, the metalworkers' union complained in August, had 'intolerably' supported a strike call by non-party workers over late payment of wages.[14] It also surely looked to the growing number of politically active former communists in the factories. At the Mospoligraf 5th print shop, such dissidents had joined with a Menshevik sympathizer and a candidate party member to propose, successfully, a resolution at a mass meeting that made a 'sharp criticism of the trade unions and economic authorities' and demanded that wages in state trusts be brought up to the level of those in private industry. At the Krasnyi proletarii works, the party cell bureau resolved to meet a group of former members to dissuade them from 'harmful political work'.[15] The Workers Group probably recruited several hundred members at its peak. In Moscow it was strongest among

13 The exaggerated assertion that the Workers Group denounced NEP as the 'new exploitation of the proletariat' has entered the literature by way of the official witch-hunting denunciation, V. Sorin, *Rabochaia gruppa ('Miasnikovshchina')*, Moscow: MK RKP, 1924. In fact, each of the three times that the phrase 'new exploitation of the proletariat' is used in the Workers Group manifesto, it is conditional, i.e. it states that NEP would *become* 'exploitation' without the revival of the soviets.
14 RGASPI, 17/84/559/238–44.
15 RGASPI, 17/84/296/82ob; TsAOPIM, 3/11/86/215; GARF 7952/3/75/221.

the party and trade union officials who had been in the Bauman opposition in 1920. Its members included Demidov and Berzina, now chairman and secretary, respectively, of the heavy artillery works party cell; Baranov; Shavtovalova; and Il'in, a party full-timer. Other Moscow industrial or trade union officials who joined included the former Workers Opposition (WO) supporters Mikhail Mikhailov, now an official of the aerospace industry trust, A.I. Medvedev and G.V. Shokhanov, and the former Ignatov group member K.D. Radzivilov from Rogozhsko-Simonovskii.[16]

In May 1923, after the twelfth congress had highlighted the need for vigilance against dissidents, the MC went on the offensive against those in the heavy artillery works cell. A tug-of-war had been going on for some months: both the MC and the dissidents had tried to transfer party members sympathetic to their side into the cell. Its leaders had found various excuses for rejecting the MC's candidates, and the MC appointed a commission to investigate. At its 18 May meeting, having heard the commission's report, the MC expelled Demidov, Berzina and other cell members from the party; soon afterwards the Moscow metalworkers' union expelled them for six months. A wider clampdown followed. The Workers Group leader Gavriil Miasnikov, who was based in Perm' but had been visiting Moscow to meet with his supporters, was arrested on 24 May, and sent to work in the Soviet consulate in Germany a few days later. Later in the year he was rearrested and sent to a prison camp.[17] The GPU started building criminal cases against other dissidents. Several party cells were shut down: the 400-strong cell at the Moscow Union of Consumer Associations (MSPO) in Sokol'niki, where Il'in had built support; and the cells at the Russian-American instrument works, the Gosmoloko dairy and the Oktiabr' engineering factory in Bauman. A letter to the CC by a group of Moscow party members protested at the repressive measures, and complained that these cells' only crime had been to 'try to introduce amendments to the MC theses for the regional conference'. Mikhailov protested in similar terms at a Sokol'niki district party conference on 30 May.[18]

16 The party's witch-hunting expert on the Workers Group, Sorin, using material made available by the GPU, stated that the group had 200 members in Moscow at its height. He quoted from intercepted correspondence by Kuznetsov, in which he claimed there were more than 2200 members in Moscow and another 800 nationally; these figures seem grossly exaggerated. Sorin, op. cit., pp. 112–15. The founders of the Workers Group are named in several sources as Miasnikov; Nikolai Kuznetsov, a metalworkers' union official, a Bolshevik since 1904, active in the WO in 1920–21 and expelled from the party in 1922; and P.G. Moiseev. Sorin, op. cit., p. 113, lists 28 Workers Group members expelled or censured by the party.
17 G.L. Olekh, *Krovnye uzy: RKP(b) i ChK/GPU v pervoi polovine 1920-kh godov: mekhanizm vsaimootnoshenii*, Novosibirsk: Novosibirskaia gosudarstevennaia akademiia vodnogo transporta, 1999, pp. 105–6.
18 RGASPI, 589/3/9103/vol.3/27–28. I thank Barbara Allen, who kindly shared her research notes on this material with me. See also RGASPI, 17/84/455/22–28; TsAOPIM, 3/4/5/21, 52; *Sokol'nicheskaia raionnaia konferentsiia RKP(b). 30–31 maia 1923 goda. Otchet.*, Moscow, 1923, p. 54.

The scale of the internal party repression attracted non-party workers' attention. The protesters to the CC warned that the 'petty tyranny of the party hierarchy', exemplified by the expulsions, was 'bringing non-party workers into this business, since the state of affairs in the cells doesn't pass them by'. On 30 May a delegates' meeting at the heavy artillery works called on the union to reverse Demidov and Berzina's expulsion; a mass meeting the next day resolved to take up their cause at a forthcoming metalworkers' union conference; and a further mass meeting elected the victimized pair as delegates to the conference. The anger spread to two nearby aircraft factories, Ikar' and Amstro. The Amstro workers' delegate to the metalworkers' conference raised the case of Demidov and Berzina, together with those of an anarchist, Rodionov, and a Menshevik, Koshtiurov, who had been the victims of politically motivated sackings.[19] Ultimately, though, the Workers Group was unable to sustain or widen its base of support among non-party workers. A big test was the summer strike movement, discussed below, which both the Workers Group and Workers Truth group saw as an opportunity to win a hearing for their ideas. Both failed, perhaps not because their critiques of the Bolsheviks were unconvincing, but because most workers had decided to press economic demands without linking them to political issues.

It was against this background, of working-class retreat from political struggle, that the other socialist parties' Moscow organizations were broken up by the GPU. The Mensheviks had been declared illegal in December 1922 and suffered a wave of arrests in the spring of 1923. They issued a protest declaration about the arrests, but in 1923 were for the first time unable to publish an agitational leaflet on May Day. The GPU found no record of Menshevik activity during the strike movement, and by October, although Menshevik leaflets were occasionally found in the factories, the GPU believed that the Mensheviks' public activity had essentially stopped. The left SRs and maximalists underwent a brief revival in the spring, when their numbers were boosted by members returning from Siberian exile, and they organized regular meetings of 75–100 people. But on 15 June, after a meeting to mark the 100th birthday of the narodnik Petr Lavrov, the leading Moscow left SRs, Prokopovich and Chizhikov, were arrested, along with the anarchist-individualist Aleksei Borovoi and the maximalist G. Nestroev.[20] There is no further record of open activity. While the communist

19 TsGAMO, 19/1/62/134-43; TsAOPIM, 3/4/49/96; 467/1/7/2-3, 16ob.
20 TsAOPIM, 3/4/49/104, 115; RGASPI, 17/84/468/61; G.N. Sevost'ianov et al. (eds), *'Sovershenno sekretno': Lubianka-Stalinu o polozhenii v strane (1922–1934 gg.)*, Moscow: Institut rossiiskoi istorii RAN, 2001: vol. 1 (1922–23), part 2, p. 772, citing TsA FSB, 2/1/782/12-18; D.B. Pavlov, *Bol'shevistskaia diktatura protiv sotsialistov i anarkhistov 1917-seredina 1950-kh godov*, Moscow: Rosspen, 1999, pp. 80–82; Ia.V. Leont'ev and K.S. Iur'ev, 'Nezapechatlennyi trud: iz arkhiva V.N. Figner', in *Zven'ia: istoricheskii almanakh*, no. 2, St Petersburg: Feniks/Atheneum, 1992, pp. 424–88, here pp. 460–61.

dissidents were active during the strike wave, and the United Opposition organized public demonstrations in 1927, no non-communist political organization worked openly in Moscow again until the end of the Soviet period.

Industrial unrest

The industrial unrest in the summer of 1923 unfolded in the context of a crisis of economic growth, in contrast to previous crises of scarcity, such as that of 1920–21.[21] Warehouses were full and there were substantial harvest surpluses, but there was a 'failure to establish terms and methods of trade' between town and countryside, as Carr showed. In early 1923, this took the form of a disproportion between high industrial prices and low prices of agricultural goods, and a lack of effective trading mechanisms. As a result of the high industrial prices, the trusts piled up unsold goods in warehouses and revenues fell. Trotsky, discussing the problem at the twelfth party congress, coined the phrase 'scissors crisis' to describe it.[22] A related problem was that of establishing a strong currency. The party leadership had recognized the need for one, and introduced the chervonets in November 1922. But it circulated alongside the soviet ruble, unlimited volumes of which continued to pour off state printing presses. Inflationary pressure was exacerbated by the trusts, who sought bank credits to make up for poor revenues. The two problems climaxed in the summer. The harvest arrived, the mismatch between agricultural and industrial prices remained unresolved, and, in a panic, the government resorted to printing rubles to buy grain. While this effectively wrecked the drive for a stable currency, it did not boost trade and sales of goods in the way that had been expected. Trade dried up. Soviet historians estimated that in Moscow the volume of trade fell by two-thirds between June and November 1923. The crises of finance and trade fed back into industry. The disproportion of prices aggravated the shortage of raw cotton for the textile industry; in May, the MC bureau of the party discussed the resulting threat of lay-offs, and wrote to the CC, comparing the impact on the region with that of food supply shortages in 1918–20. Trusts including Mossukno (cloth), Mostekstil (textiles) and Rezinotrest (rubber goods) began shutting factories whose goods were unsold. In June, two big mills

---

21 This account is based on Carr, *The Interregnum*, pp. 92–148 and 'Problemy edinoi ekonomiki', in S.A. Pavliuchenkov et al. (eds), *Rossiia nepovskaia*, Moscow: Novyi khronograf, 2002, pp. 150–65. See also N.I. Rodionova, *Gody napriazhennogo truda: iz istorii Moskovskoi partiinoi organizatsii 1921–1925 gg.*, Moscow: Moskovskii rabochii, 1963, pp. 137–43; N.M. Aleshchenko, *Moskovskii sovet v 1917–1941 gg.*, Moscow: Nauka, 1976, pp. 274–83; A.M. Sinitsyn et al. (eds), *Istoriia rabochykh Moskvy 1917–1945 gg.*, Moscow: 'Nauka', 1983, pp. 120–25.
22 *Dvenadtsatyi s"ezd RKP(b): stenograficheskii otchet*, Moscow: izd-vo politicheskoi literatury, 1968, pp. 309–52; also Carr, *The Interregnum*, p. 87.

were closed in Moscow region's largest textile town, Orekhovo-Zuevo. Closures and lay-offs continued through the autumn. Some managers intensified back-door wage-cutting to cope with lack of revenues. Late payment of wages reappeared, producing an angry reaction by workers who had thought that that problem was largely behind them.[23]

The industrial unrest to a large extent grew out of the economic crisis, peaking in late August and early September. Action by Moscow workers on comparatively low pay who were demanding parity with metalworkers – two big textile workers' strikes and coordinated protest on the railways – coincided with stoppages at the Sormovo engineering works in Nizhnii Novgorod region and by Kostroma forestry workers. Such statistical evidence as there is suggests that the number of participants in the 1923 strike wave was lower than the number who went on strike in the spring of 1921, but greater than in any other movement since 1917.[24] And their stubbornness alarmed the party. In comparison with the 1921 strike wave, though, the 1923 strikes were politically and organizationally tame. In 1921, openly political demands were heard, albeit less clearly in Moscow than in Petrograd; in 1923, there were virtually none. In 1921, the 'equality of rations' slogan was advanced to unite the movement; the 1923 unrest was more like a collection of separate disputes, conscious of each other's progress but hesitant to articulate common slogans. In 1921, workers at Moscow's two big centres of strike action, Goznak and the Bromlei works, had organized flying pickets, albeit with limited success; in 1923, participants in longer, tougher strikes made no such attempt. Party leaders were extremely sensitive to the danger of generalized action, and on guard against anything resembling political resistance; hence their nervous reaction to the communist dissidents' activity. Workers, sensing this, adjusted their forms of protest. The party had defined a framework for industrial conflict: the exact terms of the social contract (i.e. living standards) could be haggled over, but the basis of it (workers' surrender of political power) could not. Within these boundaries, the relatively disaggregated strike movement of 1923 was a success. The party leadership responded by demanding from the industrial managers an end to late payment, and in practice dropped its stand against the increase of real wages, which began to rise again by the end of 1923.

23 TsAOPIM, 3/11/91/323; C. Ward, *Russia's Cotton Workers and the New Economic Policy: Shop-Floor Culture and State Policy 1921–1929*, Cambridge: Cambridge University Press, 1990, pp. 130–32; Sevast'ianov et al., op. cit., vol. 1, part 2, p. 886 and p. 910, citing TsA FSB, 2/1/794/114–36, 137–59; Aleshchenko, op. cit., pp. 275–77; Sinitsyn et al. (eds.), op. cit., pp. 120–22; *Piatyi s"ezd gubernskikh profsoiuzov*, pp. 29–30.
24 Soviet strike statistics are patchy up to 1922, and unsystematic up to the mid 1920s. For discussion, see S. Pirani, *The Changing Political Relationship Between Moscow Workers and the Bolsheviks, 1920–24* (PhD diss., University of Essex, 2006), pp. 335–39, and A. Pospielovsky, 'Strikes During the NEP', *Revolutionary Russia* 10: 1, 1997: 1–34.

In the Moscow region, the unrest over wages began in June among seasonal peat cutters, who were employed for three months from April by the Moscow fuel authority and the textile trusts to produce peat from bogs, to be used as fuel. The peat cutters, most of whom worked as peasant labourers for the rest of the year, were organized into teams and paid piece rates. They had staged some strikes in the spring of 1922, and the next year launched wider action, which GPU agents estimated embraced 13,185 workers in 13 peat bogs and led to a loss of about 42,000 working days. Moreover, these stoppages were part of a national movement that 'spread spontaneously to almost all peat workings', notably those in Ivanovo-Voznesensk and Tver', 'with the presentation of analogous demands: pay rises, 50–60 arshins [35–42 metres] of textiles, and prompter payment'. The employers had helped provoke action by deductions that ate up much of the season's first wage packet. The peat workers' union leaders supported the employers, sanctioning the dismissal of recalcitrant teams and expelling their members from the union.[25]

The involvement of these semi-peasant workers in action was one indication of the breadth of the unrest; another was a protest organized over the summer by disabled workers, who were not union members and fell outside the party's ideologically constrained definition of workers. The several thousand disabled, mostly injured in the world war, civil war or industrial accidents, met at municipal centres (*doma invalidov*); those that could work generally did so in private or municipal workshops. Cost accounting impacted on disabled people's benefits, and on 19 July the Moscow soviet proposed to abolish free tram travel for the disabled. This drew immediate protests from mass meetings of the disabled in five of Moscow's six districts. A threat to demonstrate outside the Moscow social welfare department's main offices quickly secured assurances that the measure, due to take effect on 1 August, would be reconsidered. But it was not. In the days before the deadline, a disabled 'initiative group' was formed. Its political colouring is unclear, but it may well have included rank-and-file communists, who had previously been active among the disabled. Its representatives visited dormitories and workshops. On 30 July, with the cancellation of free travel imminent, a 400-strong demonstration was held at the social welfare department. On 2 August, the 'initiative group' organized a meeting and made plans to convene an all-Russian conference of disabled people's delegates. On 8 August a further gathering demanded not only free tram transport and the replacement of individual benefits by collectively paid benefits, but also the convening of a soviet of disabled deputies and places for disabled delegates on the Moscow soviet.[26]

25 TsGAMO, 3/4/49/100–101; Sevost'ianov et al. (eds), op. cit., vol. 1, part 2, pp. 890–91, citing TsA FSB 2/1/794/114–36; *Sotsialisticheskii vestnik* 1923, no. 16, pp. 6–7; *Trud* 12 July 1923.

Protests by the Moscow rail workers – whose ability to disrupt transport, and intentions of coordinating outside union structures, alarmed party officials – won rapid concessions. At a mass meeting on 23 August at the former Mikhel'son factory, now a railway repair works, a proposal to replace an allowance-based pay system with piece work was voted down and a large group walked out. A week later, at a 1000-strong meeting of other northern railroad repair staff, a walk-out took place before the proposed changes to the pay system could even be discussed. A resolution was passed, though, demanding a 75 per cent supplement to August and September pay packets and, significantly, the convening of a Moscow-wide delegates' meeting 'to discuss payment in hard currency for the work done, i.e. equality with other trades unions' rates'. Such a conference should be composed of 'genuine workers' representatives', speakers demanded. That day, and the next, a meeting on the Kursk railway demanded equal pay with metalworkers and payment in hard rubles (i.e. not *sovznaky*); northern railroad workers declared solidarity with the repair staff's demands; the Mikhel'son workers staged a sit-down strike; and elsewhere, work stopped early for mass meetings on pay. Changes were made in the payment system that amounted to a partial satisfaction of the workers' demands.[27]

The largest strikes in Moscow were by textile workers, mostly women, demanding parity with metalworkers. Seven thousand workers at the Trekhgornaia mill, and 2150 at the Tsindel' works, struck. Dissatisfaction over pay, piece rates and redundancies was reported contemporaneously by GPU agents from more than a dozen other mills. Crass management played its part: the Trekhgornaia workers returned from their summer holidays to be told that holiday payments had been 11 per cent greater than collective agreements stipulated, and that the difference would be deducted forthwith.[28] The Tsindel' works struck first, on 28 August, in pursuit of across-the-board pay increases. A mass meeting elected a presidium of three, and a negotiating team of six, none of whom were on the factory committee. The strike ended the next day, after management threatened mass dismissals, but a workers' 'initiative group', outside the trade union structure, remained active. When the Trekhgornaia mill struck, two weeks later, the Tsindel' group circulated leaflets and sent messages of support.[29] The Trekhgornaia action began in the weaving shop on 11 September and rapidly spread throughout the mill. The shutdown of Moscow's

---

26 I have found no information about the disabled workers' movement dated later than 8 August. It may have been repressed, or have struck a deal with the Moscow soviet. TsGAMO, 19/1/62/176, 186, 188, 192; 66/111/5/62; Sevost'ianov et al. (eds), op. cit., vol. 1, part 2, p. 637; *Pravda*, 31 March 1923.
27 RGASPI, 17/84/468/45–47, 58; TsGAMO, 19/1/62/205, 210ob, 211ob, 213ob, 220ob.
28 TsGAMO, 19/1/62/192.
29 TsAOPIM, 3/4/49/70; TsGAMO, 19/1/62/209, 214ob, 223.

largest enterprise, a few hundred metres from the Kremlin, quickly forced genuine negotiations with the real decision-makers, represented by Kalinin, president of the republic. First, conditions for a mass meeting were set: the workers demanded that its chairman be one of them, and that he be given immunity from arrest. The anti-semitic tone of their demand that the chairman be 'of Russian origin' suggests that the strike leaders were workers with no socialist traditions, rather than from the SR party, which had maintained a foothold at the mill. The duly elected chairman, Lazarev, opened the meeting, on 14 September, by presenting demands for parity with metalworkers and payment in 'goods rubles' at the exchange rate of the day of payment; the sacking of a party member, Alekseev, for 'lack of tact in his approach to workers'; the freeing of arrested strikers; a guarantee that no strikers would be sacked; and payment for the time lost. Kalinin gave away little. He accepted the principle of payment in hard currency, only suggesting that chervontsy might be preferable to 'goods rubles', but argued that parity between textile and metalworkers' unions would 'hit other workers, such as those on the railways who are paid less than you, in the pocket'. He proposed other ways be found, with the help of the textile workers' union and the Moscow soviet, of improving the workers' living standards. He proposed that strike days be paid at 50 per cent, and suggested forming a commission, comprising Lazarev, plus representatives of the party cell and factory committee, to decide Alekseev's fate. He promised to do 'all he could' to ensure that no strikers were sacked or arrested, and to free those already detained, 'providing they have not committed criminal offences and are not members of any anti-soviet organization'.[30] This offer was accepted. The deal reflected the terms of the social contract: the party could give some ground on wages, restrain industrial managers and silently pass over gross expressions of nationalist prejudice – but 'anti-soviet' activity, i.e., in this context, SR activity, would be punished.

Perhaps the most interesting aspect of the party leadership's reaction to the summer strike wave was the extreme nervousness it displayed at the possibility of the communist dissidents winning working-class support – a prospect that, as it turns out, it grossly overestimated. The part played by the Workers Group in the strike movement was minimal. Its organizing bureau, elected at a conference in Moscow in June 1923, discussed plans to politicize the movement with demonstrations and leaflets. The group's organizer, Nikolai Kuznetsov, argued that a popular programme was needed to shift workers from the 'indifference, fear and inertia' they felt 'thanks to

28 TsGAMO, 19/1/62/192.
29 TsAOPIM, 3/4/49/70; TsGAMO, 19/1/62/209, 214ob, 223.
30 TsAOPIM, 19/1/62/222–24.
31 For the significance of the phrase 'aunties and nannies', see note 36 to Chapter 4, p. 105.

the huge crowd of aunties and nannies[31] they have to put up with … in the soviets, factory committees, party, unions, etc'.[32] Although the Workers Group had dismissed the WO as the voice of 'trade union officialdom', it hoped to convince some of its leaders to side with the workers' movement. Kuznetsov and others met with Aleksandra Kollontai and invited her to participate in a public demonstration, but she declined. As for the Workers Truth group, no record of any activity in the strike movement, or of GPU surveillance of it, has come to light. Despite the dissidents' apparent lack of success, during September the GPU arrested 22 Workers Group members including Kuznetsov, Demidov, Makh, Kachkov and Tiunov. Baranov was arrested subsequently. From the Workers Truth group, Lass-Kotlova, Shutskever, E. Shul'man, Khaikevich and others were rounded up. Even Aleksandr Bogdanov was briefly detained, because of the interest dissidents had shown in his ideas.[33] Valerian Kuibyshev, then a leading light on the Central Control Commission of the Bolshevik party (CCC), lobbied aggressively, but unsuccessfully, for action to be taken against Kollontai. Moving against a popular, high-profile figure was perhaps considered unwise; the more effective strategy elaborated by the CCC secretariat, and approved by the party leadership, combined repression of the dissidents with public campaigns to improve workers' living standards, and against corruption and bureaucratism.[34]

There is a distinction, though, between the restrained approach of the CCC and the politburo, and the excited attention paid to the dissidents when the Bolshevik leaders came to present the lessons of the economic crisis and the industrial unrest to the wider party. An enlarged plenum of the Bolshevik CC assembled on 25 September, i.e. after the strikes had fizzled out. Dzerzhinskii, who gave the main report, emphasized the seriousness of the crisis – of whose scope many of his audience had previously been unaware – and also exaggerated the dissidents' role in the strike movement. Specifically, he claimed that the Workers Group organized some of the big strikes, although the record of his measured assessment of their limited resources, presented to the politburo behind closed doors a week earlier, suggests he can hardly have believed this.[35] Dzerzhinskii's report was greeted with stunned silence – 'like a graveyard', Boguslavskii later recalled.[36] Even relatively senior party members at the meeting were being presented with a full picture, only parts of which they had seen previously. This was itself an indication of

32 RGASPI, 323/2/62/3; Avrich, op. cit., p. 22; Sorin, op. cit., p. 110.
33 RGASPI, 589/3/9103/vol.3/38. Again, I thank Barbara Allen, who kindly shared her research notes on this material. See also RGASPI, 323/2/62/2–11; TsAOPIM, 3/11/86/35; V.P. Vilkova et al., *RKP(b): vnutripartiinaia bor'ba v dvadtsatye gody. Dokumenty i materialy 1923 g.*, Moscow: Rosspen, 2004, pp. 51, 104–5 and 116–17; Sorin, op. cit., p. 112; and N.S. Antonova and N.V. Drozdova (eds), *Neizvestnyi Bogdanov v 3-kh knigakh*, Moscow: AIRO, 1995, kn. 1, pp. 34–57.
34 RGASPI, 323/2/62/3, 6–8; Vilkova et al., op. cit., pp. 103–4.
35 Vilkova et al., op. cit., pp. 48–52 and 99–101.
36 TsAOPIM, 63/1/144/68–69.

the extent to which the party had changed: the rapid stratification of the previous two years had resulted in systematic strictures on the flow of information internally. The contrast with the spring of 1921 is striking. Then, the mortal dangers perceived by the leadership were frankly discussed at all levels, and Lenin readily called in public for the arrest and punishment of opponents. Now, Dzerzhinskii – who during the civil war had calmly and diligently organized the repression of much stronger enemies – felt the need to exaggerate the dissidents' role for the benefit of middle-ranking officials. This was the first battle in which the party elite felt vulnerable not to its traditional political enemies (Mensheviks, SRs, etc.) but to internal dissent. Paradoxically, the party's position in the republic was already assured; there was no question of its survival as there had been in early 1921. What was not secure was the party elite's ability to make the party do its will. That would only be fastened down as a result of the 'party crisis' of 1923–24, which is discussed in Chapter 9.

Protest and abstention

On 22 September 1923, at the height of the industrial unrest, GPU agents found a leaflet at the Sokol'niki machine works calling on workers to 'join together against the Bolshevik dictatorship'. But this was a rare exception. So muted were political themes during the unrest that a national GPU survey of workers' moods in July-September – a type of report heavy on formal categorization, but free of the false optimism of published documents – stated that, notwithstanding the anger at late wages payment and bad managements, workers' 'general mood' was 'without doubt in favour of soviet power', as the growing attendance of non-party workers at party cell meetings showed. The 'enormous increase in workers' and peasants' sympathy with our party' was even making party organizers complacent, the report complained.[37] This could be taken to be half the truth. Workers understood that the regime was willing and able to raise their living standards further; in this sense they supported it. While some workers certainly went further, and felt a political affinity with the government, others did not like the Bolshevik expropriation of political power, and acquiesced grudgingly. And Bolshevik attempts to organize campaigns of positive support soon revealed the limits of workers' enthusiasm, for example when it sought, literally, to cash in on its support with the gold loan. At many large workplaces, Bolshevik resolutions calling for compulsory purchase of the bonds (i.e. payment of a proportion of wages with bonds), were voted down in favour of voluntary subscription.

35 Vilkova et al., op. cit., pp. 48–52 and 99–101.
36 TsAOPIM, 63/1/144/68–69.
37 TsGAMO, 19/1/62/232; RGASPI, 17/84/486/222–23.

The finance commissariat first announced its intention of raising the gold loan, of 100 million gold rubles, in October 1922, to 'prepare the way for currency stabilization'. It followed the successful sale of one grain loan, and was sold alongside another. Grigorii Sokol'nikov, the finance commissar, spoke at the tenth congress of soviets in December 1922 about citizens' 'moral obligation' to support the loan, but demand was poor. The bonds were traded on the free market at a heavy discount, and by mid 1923 the state bank was paying 60 per cent of the face value to unwilling holders.[38] In early 1923, party organizations began a campaign to raise voluntary subscriptions to the loan, but doing so without compulsion proved difficult. The Moscow soviet volunteered to sell 15 million gold rubles' worth of the bonds, and announced that part of the proceeds would go to economic reconstruction in the Moscow region. The MGSPS resolved to sell 1.8 million gold rubles' worth of the bonds per month, and introduced a guideline that workers should contribute an average of 10 per cent of their pay, depending on grade, every month for five months. Individual unions agreed to sell bonds to their members and party cells and trade union organizations tried to push through decisions along these lines.[39] Workers at such former SR and non-party strongholds as the Alekseevskaia water works, the head post office and the former Mikhel'son works refused to accept them. The economic crisis, and in particular the gap in the state budget created by the decision in July to limit the issue of *sovznaky*, forced the government's hand. The loan became, in practice, an enforced levy. The part-payment of wages and salaries with bonds became widespread during July, and on 4 September was sanctioned by decree. The GPU reported 'strong dissatisfaction': at 'a significant number of the large enterprises' in Moscow, resolutions approving payment of wages in bonds were at the first attempt overturned and party cells only prevailed at the second attempt; at others, only voluntary subscription was sanctioned. The decree had sanctioned payment of between 3 per cent and 20 per cent of wages in bonds, but on 7 September the MC, taken aback by workers' hostility, decided that such payments should not exceed 4 per cent.[40]

---

38 The grain loans were much smaller than the gold loan. The first consisted of bonds issued in June 1922 with the purpose of purchasing 10 million puds (163,800 tonnes) of rye; the second was issued in 1923 to purchase 30 million puds (491,400 tonnes) of rye, later raised to 100 million puds (1.64 million tonnes). *Pravda* 10, 11 and 24 June 1922; E.H. Carr, *The Bolshevik Revolution 1917–1923*, London: Macmillan, 1978, vol. II, pp. 355–56.
39 TsGAMO, 609/1/183/36–38; TsAGM, 415/16/318/94; *Pravda*, 17 January and 1 February 1923; *Metallist* 1923, no. 6, cols. 63–64.
40 RGASPI, 17/84/486/58; TsAOPIM, 3/4/5/148; and 3/11/86/29; *Trud*, 27 July and 1 September 1923; *Pravda*, 28 November 1923; *Predpriiatie* 4–5, 1923, p. 136; Sevost'ianov et al. (eds), op. cit., vol. 1 part 2, p. 612, p. 631 and p. 731; Carr, *The Interregnum*, pp. 99–100.

Once the government committed itself to compulsory subscription, the most articulate opposition came from a Bolshevik stronghold, the Kauchuk works, rather than from workplaces with SR, Menshevik or non-party traditions. At a mass meeting on 6 September, the Kauchuk workforce rejected compulsory sale of the bonds on the grounds of workers' 'difficult material circumstances', but expressed 'profound belief in the proletarians' consciousness to subscribe voluntarily and buy as many bonds as their strength will allow'. That last phrase may have been slightly ironic, but the point about proletarian consciousness was serious: this could not be measured simply by the degree of enthusiasm shown for the party's every call for sacrifice. The Kauchuk mass meeting also rejected a Bolshevik motion approving the Moscow soviet's 10 per cent guideline. A proposal giving management the right to pay between 3 per cent and 20 per cent of wages in bonds was not even put to the vote. The opposition to compulsory subscription was headed by two former party members, Gorodnichev and Lukashevich. Worryingly for the cell's leaders, more than 20 party members abstained or voted against the Bolshevik resolution, while 50 supported it. The cell regrouped, and at a second mass meeting on 15 September pushed through a resolution approving enforced payment at the MGSPS's recommended rates. But by then, workers at three other factories in Khamovniki had taken heart from Kauchuk and, again encouraged by former party members, voted down resolutions approving compulsory subscription.[41]

Management-imposed part-payment of wages with bonds provoked sharp protests. A mass meeting at Goznak on 15 September elected a delegate to the soviet mandated to oppose the practice, and a party-sponsored resolution approving it only passed at the second attempt. At the AMO car factory, the party cell forestalled outright opposition with a compromise proposal that provided for 10 per cent of the factory's wages fund to be paid in bonds, but for the factory committee and party cell to work out means to lighten the burden on lower-paid workers. At Krasnyi Bogatyr, where a petition on the issue attracted 214 signatures, it was decided to exempt the lowest paid workers entirely. The GPU reported 'agitation' against enforced payment at a string of other Moscow workplaces, and from the Orekhovo-Zuevo textile mills.[42] The campaign faltered. In November, Sokol'nikov reported that subscriptions of only 75 million gold rubles out of the projected 100 million had been raised.[43]

Any illusions among Bolshevik leaders about the nature of workers' support for the party would have been severely damaged by the November 1923

---

41 TsGAMO, 19/1/62/217, 224ob; 609/1/207/122–122ob; TsAOPIM, 2/11/86/215–16; 475/1/7/30, 33.
42 TsGAMO, 19/1/62/224ob, 230; TsAGM, 415/1/318/93–95; TsGAMO, 19/1/62/213ob, 236, 237, 241, 259–259ob, 266ob.
43 Carr, *The Interregnum*, p. 100.

soviet election campaign. Workers' refusal to vote in unfair elections had been noticeable in December 1922 (see Chapter 6, p. 155); a year later, abstention had become an epidemic. The GPU reported turnouts of between 10 per cent and 50 per cent in many Moscow factories. At the Trekhgornaia works, 3000 attended an election meeting and when the time came to vote for the party candidates, half walked out. In Orekhovo-Zuevo things were worse: the turnouts were all below 10 per cent and many elections were cancelled.[44] Non-party candidates stood against Bolsheviks at some workplaces – and prevailed, for example, at the All-Russian Union of Textile Workers factory in Zamoskvorech'e and the Baranov leather works in Bauman. Some of these were probably Mensheviks, who had largely moved to underground political work. There were occasional protests of other kinds: at the Mospoligraf print shop, workers added to the soviet delegates' mandate a clause stating that 'the workers' state should not conduct [police] searches of workers' homes'.[45] But abstention was the most widespread phenomenon. Party leaders including Zinoviev admitted that workers were effectively surrendering the soviets to the party, and focusing on getting their 'own' people elected to jobs where they could influence day-to-day workplace issues. At a meeting of party members in the Moscow railway repair shops in November, one speaker, Fakunin, pointed out that workers there had happily elected party members to the soviet, but concentrated on making sure that non-party people dominated the works committees:

> It's not because they don't trust the communists, no, but because they count on the works committees to defend workers in everyday matters, and ... reckon that if they elect communists to them, then those [communists] will be bound by discipline.[46]

A settlement of sorts

Towards the end of 1923, the finance commissariat, supported by the industrial managers, advocated shifting all wages onto the new currency, the chervonets. Bolshevik trades unionists reasoned that the initial impact on

---

44 The GPU's reports of mass abstentions are at first sight contradicted by the soviet's statistics, which indicate that in November 1923, 594,401 out of 698,884 eligible voters (85 per cent) participated. I suspect that, having held mass meetings to elect soviet delegates, workplace managements and/or trade union organizations submitted voting figures including those who had attended but abstained, and/or absentees. The official history of the soviet states that the turnout of 85 per cent in 1923 fell to 72.5 per cent in the 1925 soviet elections. Aleshchenko, op. cit., p. 251 and p. 255. GPU reports at TsGAMO, 19/1/62/293ob, 294, 294ob, 295ob, 296–98, 312–312ob.
45 TsGAMO, 19/1/62/294, 296ob, 297ob.
46 *Pravda*, 7 November 1923; TsAOPIM, 3/11/85a/138.

wages previously counted in 'goods rubles' would be negative, and resisted the proposal. After discussion at the thirteenth party conference in January 1924, a commission was formed to hammer out a compromise. It agreed that wages would be paid in chervontsy, with a bonus to take account of the increased cost of living, plus flat increases for industries that lagged behind. At the eleventh congress of soviets in 1924, VSNKh president Bogdanov stated that, overall, wages had risen by 3 per cent in the second half of 1923. The Soviet historian A.G. Rashin estimated that real wages in the first quarter of 1924 were 12 per cent higher than they had been in the last quarter of 1923, on account of lower retail prices and greater productivity bonus payments. Although they dipped again in late 1925, real wages continued to rise until 1927, by which time they had surpassed 1913 levels across the economy.[47] Considering the party's decision at the end of 1922 that most wages should be frozen, and the industrial managers' hopes of pay cuts, this amounted to an achievement, albeit modest, of the workers who had participated in industrial unrest. The other side of the coin was the continuing erosion of working-class participation in making decisions. Whereas in 1921 workers had gone to the soviet election meetings in good faith and elected non-party socialists, in 1923 they simply stayed away.

While the party's internal crisis was brewing, in the factories, the social contract was evolving as a set-up in which the working class implemented and passively approved decisions made by the party. Diane Koenker, in her recent study of Soviet printing workers, describes this relationship as a limited democracy, 'approved and supported' by some workers (for example workshop spies and union activists) who were rewarded for 'buying into the system', while the 'silent majority' made their accommodation with the regime, calculating 'that they could promote their interests by delegating their political rights to the appropriate Communist authorities'. Koenker writes:

> The complicated balance between participation and dictatorship ... guaranteed that dissent and resistance would have to manifest themselves in subtle and indirect forms. ... as long as workers stayed within the limits of 'businesslike' exchange of views, dissent was permitted and presumably noticed. ... For the truly committed social democrats, the working people's democracy may have looked hollow indeed; but for many other ordinary workers, ... this socialist democracy was perhaps something they could live with.[48]

47 Rashin, op. cit., p. 6 and pp. 15–23; Carr, *The Interregnum*, p. 130 and pp. 136–38; *Trinadtsataia konferentsiia RKP(b): biulleten'*, Moscow, 1924, pp. 81–83, 91 and 187.
48 D.P. Koenker, *Republic of Labor: Russian Printers and Soviet Socialism, 1918–1930*, Ithaca: Cornell University Press, 2005, pp. 143–73, and especially pp. 171–72.

Koenker points out that the Mensheviks' argument, that this system was solely based on repression, is unsustainable. Workers acquiesced in this system, believing it was the best deal available in the short term. There was worker participation *only* in that sense – a long way short of participation in the sense of collective, creative action, of workers participating in the broader political decisions. A new organizational framework for the conduct of the relations between party and class was created with the mass recruitment of workers to the party from 1924, discussed in the next chapter.

9 The elite takes charge
The party in 1923–24

The need of the party elite, and ultimately the ruling class-in-formation, to remould the party into an administrative machine through which to centralize control of the state and economy, was the underlying determinant of change in the party in 1923–24. The party's political functions – a legacy of its history and of 1917 – now took second place. The disputes of early 1923 pitted the Central Committee of the Bolshevik party's (CC's) leading triumvirate (Stalin, Zinoviev and Kamenev) against senior Bolshevik economic decision-makers, and centred, first, on the division of political power between party and soviet bodies, and, second, on economic policy issues, and the degree to which industrial growth should be prioritized. But in the 'party crisis' of late 1923, brought on by the economic crisis and the formation of the opposition alliance led by Trotsky, Preobrazhenskii and Sapronov, these issues took second place to a more wide-ranging dispute about the exercise of power and the role of the party rank and file. The discussion eventually zeroed in on the question of 'appointism'. The triumvirate was happy to include no end of democratic slogans in resolutions, but the right of the party elite and its apparatus to appoint officials – threatened by the opposition's demand for immediate and regular elections – was a bridgehead it would not surrender. The appointment system was central to the administrative machine that the party elite required the party to become.

The 1923 opposition was a hastily assembled coalition that included the Democratic Centralists (DCs), democratically minded rank-and-filers, economic decision-makers and some industrial managers. While it scarcely admitted its own internal contradictions, the triumvirate exploited them skilfully, in particular by playing on the ranks' suspicion of industrial managers. But the ultimate cause of the opposition's failure was that stronger social forces, whose existence many opposition leaders were reluctant to acknowledge – the rising ruling class and its allies – stood behind the party elite. The opposition's defeat removed the last significant obstruction to the elite's consolidation of control over executive bodies and to its drive to turn the party into a vehicle to carry out its policies. Its next step was the mass recruitment drive of 1924–25, which brought significant numbers of industrial workers into the party for the first time since the revolution – not to broaden participation in decision-making, but to enhance the party's reach in the fields of administration and propaganda. The party doubled in size and achieved the more proletarian social composition to which it had aspired. But the recruits joined an organization qualitatively different not only from the civil-war party but also from that of 1921–23: political initiative was in the elite's hands; discussion of its initiatives in the wider party was reactive, after the fact and subject to censorship; and the ranks' primary function was to implement the elite's decisions.

The twelfth party congress

The debates prior to the twelfth party congress in April 1923 over the distribution of political power between the party elite, the party and state apparatus, and the industrial managers, began with Lenin's famous articles on 'bureaucratism', which the triumvirate unsuccessfully moved to suppress.[1] Lenin, having reiterated his belief that, in building the economy, the Bolsheviks had to rely heavily on specialists and other remnants of the bourgeoisie, proposed that these elements would be kept in check by workers through the beefed-up Workers and Peasants Inspection and reserved places on the CC. Lenin was challenged most vigorously from the left, by the former DC leader Valerian Osinskii. He recalled the eleventh congress, where Lenin had said that workers would have to build the economy 'with the hands of others', i.e. the bourgeoisie. Lenin's new proposals gave these 'others' too much power, Osinskii argued; a workers' state could never surrender its 'decisive influence over industry' via the soviets and their economic bodies. Osinskii's proposals for political reform went further than Lenin's; they sought to reassert the division between party and state (i.e. soviet) functions. Larin and Leonid Krasin also criticized Lenin's proposals. Krasin argued that the best way for the working class to learn about managing production was to do it, not to inspect others doing it; western European industry had always managed without inspection (*kontrol'*), which in its soviet guise had much in common with inspection in tsarist times.

1 On the pre-congress discussion, see E.H. Carr, *The Interregnum 1923–1924*, London: Macmillan, 1978, pp. 13–38 and 257–85, R.V. Daniels, *The Conscience of the Revolution: Communist Opposition in Soviet Russia*, Cambridge, MA: Harvard University Press, 1960, pp. 187–208; E.A. Rees, *State Control in Soviet Russia: the Rise and Fall of the Workers' and Peasants' Inspectorate, 1920–34*, Basingstoke: Macmillan, 1987, pp. 43–57; G.L. Olekh, *Povorot, kotorogo ne bylo: bor'ba za vnutripartiinuiu demokratiu 1919–1924 gg.*, Novosibirsk: izd. Novosibirskogo universiteta, 1992, pp. 79–102; J.R. Azrael, *Managerial Power and Soviet Politics*, Cambridge, MA: Harvard University Press, 1966, pp. 71–77; M. Lewin, *Lenin's Last Struggle*, London: Faber & Faber, 1968; R.B. Day, *Leon Trotsky and the Politics of Economic Isolation*, Cambridge: Cambridge University Press, 1973, pp. 73–87.

It has been suggested, for example by Robert Daniels, that Osinskii, Krasin and Larin effectively constituted a 'managerial opposition'. But although united in calling for greater independence for industrial management bodies, they had important differences. And they offered no defence of industrial managers' privileges, nor expressed their interests as a social group. Larin made scathing criticisms of the growth of privilege in the trusts, and the 'red directors'' stance against rising wages. He was countered by Danishevskii, who made the only explicit defence of the industrial managers' wealth.[2] It was the proposals for political reform, in particular Osinskii's, that provoked a hostile reaction from the triumvirate: Zinoviev and Kamenev accused Osinskii of 'revising Leninism', provoking a fierce counter-attack from Vladimir Smirnov and other leftists.[3] The triumvirate's rage against Osinskii was stoked by the clandestine circulation of an 'anonymous platform', which repeated many of Osinskii's arguments and topped them with a blunt call for the triumvirate's removal. The platform stopped short of identifying the party elite as an agency of hostile class forces, as Workers Truth had, but described a 'petty-bourgeois and bureaucratic degeneration' of the party since the tenth congress, which had brought about 'an end to open discussion', and led to a 'dictatorship' of a group on the politburo. The platform demanded a clear division of party and soviet functions; an end to the 'usurpation' of the CC's power by the politburo and orgburo; and the removal of 'one or two of those most fractionally-minded [and] most amenable to ... bureaucratism under the cover of hypocritical phraseology (Zinoviev, Kamenev, Stalin)'.[4]

The triumvirate's pragmatism in economic policy, and its hostility to planning, reticence in committing investment to heavy industry, and fear of ceding power to economic decision-makers, endangered the economic recovery that was at the centre of the Bolsheviks' state-building project. Trotsky analyzed this problem at the twelfth congress but made no clear proposal to solve it. E.H. Carr argued that a united front between worker communists and industrial managers might have forestalled these dangers, but did not come about largely because of the latter's lack of concern about the impact of the New Economic Policy (NEP) on workers.[5] The lack of such a common cause was evident at the Moscow regional party conference

2 *Pravda*, 25 January, 2, 3, 6, 24 and 26 March, and 4, 5 and 15 April 1923; Daniels, op. cit., pp. 194–96, 200–1; Olekh, *Povorot*, pp. 87–95; D.T. Orlovsky, 'The Anti-bureaucratic Campaigns in the 1920s', in T. Taranovski (ed.), *Reform in Modern Russian History: Progress or Cycle?* Cambridge: Cambridge University Press, 1995, pp. 290–315, especially pp. 295–98.
3 *Pravda*, 5 April 1923; *Dvenadtsatyi s"ezd RKP(b): stenograficheskii otchet*, Moscow: izd-vo politicheskoi literatury, 1968, p. 102.
4 A copy of the platform is among the papers used by Zinoviev to prepare the main report to the twelfth congress. The triumvirate, and historians, speculated that Osinskii wrote it. RGASPI, 324/1/35/158–79.
5 *Dvenadtsatyi s"ezd*, pp. 309–52. See also Carr, op. cit., pp. 82–85; Daniels, op. cit., pp. 202–7.

in March-April 1923. Left dissidents criticized the triumvirate's economic policy, but only conditionally. They saw Krasin as the greater danger: his call for economic bodies to act independently of the party appeared to endanger state control of the means of production. I.N. Stukov, who had been a Left Communist in 1918 and would later in 1923 sign the Platform of the 46, criticized Kamenev for obfuscating the soviet state's relationship with the peasantry, but turned his main fire on Krasin: 'No hint that we would allow our industry ... to be taken out from under state involvement, out from under state regulation, can be allowed'. For Semkov, a left dissident in 1920–21 who had been famously distrustful of NEP, the main target was the 'industrial managers' revolt' led by Smilga: he called this a 'right-wing deviation', culminating with Krasin's proposals, which would turn the Supreme Council of the Economy (Vysshii sovet narodnogo khoziaistva – VSNKh) 'into an [old-regime-style] Supreme Council of Ministers'.[6] Stukov and Semkov both criticized the import of foreign manufactured goods, a staple theme of the Workers Opposition (WO); and both decried the lack of open discussion in the party. But neither they, nor others like them, expressed support for Trotsky's industrial investment strategy or for Osinskii's democratic demands. And if they knew about these senior leaders' disputes with the triumvirate, they kept quiet about them.

The party ranks were largely excluded from this discussion, by a combination of censorship and the unspoken assumption that big policy issues were matters for the leadership. Although the views of Lenin, Osinskii and others were published in *Pravda*, they were only desultorily noted in the cells.[7] The systematic discouragement of discussion amounted to censorship, a 'group of [anonymous] worker members' declared to the CC in early 1923; the inner-party proletarian democracy declared by the tenth congress had become 'democracy for those who agree with the CC'; 'any dissident [*inakomyslie*] ... is considered to be worse than any counter-revolution' and faced possible expulsion and even arrest.[8] Middle-level leaders lived in a bizarre world where opposition views were simultaneously known and unknown. At the Moscow regional party conference in April, Kamenev's report was devoted largely to an attack on the 'anonymous platform', Workers Truth and the Workers Group. Some Workers Truth material had

---

6 TsAOPIM 3/4/1/65–69, 86–89; Iu. Larin, *Intelligentsiia i sovety: khoziaistvo, burzhuaziia, revoliutsiia, gosapparat*, Moscow: Gosizdat, 1924, p. 41; Daniels, op. cit., p. 197. On Smilga's involvement in the managers' organizations, see Chapter 7, p. 179.

7 Most cells whose minutes I read did not discuss the twelfth congress prior to it taking place; one cell noted a formal report and urged unity. On 7 May 1923, a report on its decisions by Kamenev was accepted, unanimously and without discussion or questions, by a meeting of 3000 party members in Khamovniki. TsAOPIM, 88/1/138.

8 V.P. Vilkova et al., *RKP(b): vnutripartiinaia bor'ba v dvadtsatye gody. Dokumenty i materialy 1923 g.*, Moscow: Rosspen, 2004, p. 77.

been reproduced by the emigre Menshevik press, to which higher-ranking Bolsheviks had access, while the other documents only circulated in secret, and the ranks had to surmise their contents from attentive reading of denunciatory articles. In the discussion on Kamenev's report, 13 of 14 speakers referred to various dissident publications, but many added that they had not seen them.[9] The leaders of the 1923 opposition did little to challenge this atmosphere of censorship, and nothing to protest at the repression of dissidents. In October 1923, as the 'party crisis' was brewing, rank-and-filers in Bauman expressed 'disapproval' of the arrests of Workers Group members and 'sympathy' for the Workers Group's 'struggle to restore the party's health',[10] while Trotsky, in the very letters to the politburo in which he fired his first broadsides against the 'unhealthy regime' and lack of internal party democracy, supported repressive action against the far left.[11]

The party crisis

The immediate triggers of the 'party crisis' were the economic and social problems discussed in Chapter 8 – the 'scissors' crisis of trade, financial instability, and the industrial unrest. These events sharpened disagreements on economic policy. Trotsky, who advocated a strategy that combined a gradual closing of the prices 'scissors' with planned expansion of heavy industry and closure of loss-making capacity, found himself in a minority of one in the politburo. His enemies in the triumvirate lined up with the

9 The Menshevik press was an essential source of information for Bolsheviks about their own party. Semkov said he had learned of the dispute between the Russian and Georgian communist leaderships on the national question from the Menshevik press. Sergeev said that had the Menshevik press not published critical material on the weakness of the soviet state trading organizations, the issue would not have been dealt with in the party. TsAOPIM, 3/4/1/72, 88, 116–18.
10 TsAOPIM, 3/11/86/35–35ob; S. Pirani, *The Changing Political Relationship Between Moscow Workers and the Bolsheviks, 1920–24* (PhD diss., University of Essex, 2006), pp. 275–76.
11 In his letter Trotsky welcomed an instruction by Dzerzhinskii to party members immediately to report 'any groupings within the party', i.e. the Workers Group and Workers Truth, not only to the CC but also to the GPU, and emphasized that making such reports was 'the elementary duty of every party member'. G.L. Olekh points out that Pierre Broue and Leonard Schapiro are mistaken in stating that Trotsky opposed this type of reporting of dissident activity. Only Sapronov managed to drop a hint that the arrests damaged the inner-party democracy to which the opposition aspired: at the assembly of active party members in Moscow on 11 December, he complained about the jailing of a party member who had 'accidentally' got caught up in a meeting of Paniushkin's group in 1921. Vilkova et al., op. cit., pp.154–55 and pp. 225–26; G.L. Olekh, *Krovnye uzy: RKP (b) i ChK/GPU v pervoi polovine 1920-kh godov: mekhanizm vsaimootnoshenii*, Novosibirsk: Novosibirskaia gosudarstevennaia akademiia vodnogo transporta, 1999, p. 62; Sapronov in *Documents of the 1923 Opposition*, London: New Park Publications, 1975, p. 19.

finance commissar, Sokol'nikov, who wanted to curtail credits for industry. However the discussion soon broadened out from economic policy to more fundamental issues of power relations in the soviet state. The first of these was the rift between the party and its working-class support base. Responding to Dzerzhinskii's alarmed declaration about the summer strikes, Trotsky argued that the party's failure to maintain support among workers was partly due to its own crippling internal regime, which stifled political discussion. In this context he criticized the 'bureaucratization' of the party apparatus, and in particular the system of appointment of secretaries. These arguments were taken up by the 46 signatories of a declaration to the CC demanding an enlarged plenary session to thrash out a strategy.[12] When the discussion was opened to the party membership, the issues of internal democracy and the apparatus dominated. The triumvirate answered the opposition with a campaign of witch-hunting, censorship and gerrymandering, coordinated through the party's administrative machinery, while simultaneously drawing the sting of some opposition arguments by adopting the 'new course' in internal party affairs in early December, and playing to members' concerns about bureaucracy and privilege with anti-corruption rhetoric.

The opposition leaders shared many ideological assumptions with the CC majority. Notwithstanding their sharp clashes on how to combat deformations of the apparatus, the two sides both attributed these deformations to external class pressures, and considered the party's proletarian character a guarantee against its transformation into an instrument of oppression. The danger that the party elite itself might play a role in the formation of

12 On the party crisis, Carr, op. cit., pp. 292–341; Daniels, op. cit., pp. 209–35; I. Deutscher, *The Prophet Unarmed. Trotsky 1921–1929*, London: Oxford University Press, 1970, pp. 106–40; and R. Sakwa, 'The Soviet State, Civil Society and Moscow Politics: Stability and Order in Early NEP 1921–24', in J. Cooper, M. Perrie and E.A. Rees (eds), *Soviet History, 1917–53*, Birmingham: Macmillan, 1995, pp. 42–77. Recent work by Russian historians includes N.S. Simonov, 'Termidor, Briumer ili Friuktidor? Evoliutsiia stalinskogo rezhima vlasti: prognozy i real'nost", *Otechestvennaia istoriia* 4, 1993: 3–17; A.V. Gusev, 'Naissance de l'Opposition de Gauche', *Cahiers Leon Trotsky* 54, 1994: 5–39; V.A. Shishkin, *Vlast', politika, ekonomika: poslerevoliutsionnaia Rossiia (1917–1928 gg.)*, St Petersburg: 'Dmitrii Bulanin', 1997, pp. 228–29 and 262–71; E.G. Gimpel'son, *Novaia ekonomicheskaia politika i politicheskaia sistema 20-e gody*, Moscow: Institut istorii RAN, 2000, pp. 75–80 and 134–40; Olekh, *Povorot*, pp. 116–81; and I.V. Pavlova, *Stalinizm: stanovlenie mekhanizma vlasti*, Novosibirsk: Sibirskii khronograf, 1993, pp. 73–84. The most important documents to become available in post-Soviet times are in Vilkova et al., op. cit. Relevant memoirs include N.V. Valentinov, *Nasledniki Lenina*, Moscow: Terra, 1991; B. Bazhanov, *Vospominaniia byvshego sekretaria Stalina*, Moscow: SP Sofinta, 1990, especially pp. 65–85; I. Pavlov, *1920-e gody. Revoliutsiia, biurokratiia. Zapiski oppozitsionera*, St Petersburg: 'Peterburg – XXI vek', 2001; G. Grigorov, *Povoroty sud'by i proizvol: vospominaniia 1905–1927*, Moscow: Chastnyi arkhiv, 2005, especially pp. 326–42, and the Zotov notebooks, at the People's Archive, Moscow.

oppressive social relations was aired only by the left dissidents, many of whom were on their way to Siberian exile. The two sides also agreed that the party occupied a privileged vanguard position in relation to the working class, and that 'workers' democracy' was a set of conditional, limited rights that flowed from communists' acceptance of party responsibilities. They clashed over where to set these limits. The most serious disagreements were over economic policy, but here too the dispute rested on shared assumptions about the leading role of the party and the perception of socialism as, first and foremost, the development of state industry. Moreover, the 1923 opposition had little internal ideological coherence, and little connection with the worker support base of previous dissidents. Whereas the opposition alliance of 1920 had been a coming-together of groups, each with its own programme, the 1923 coalition united all who were opposed to the triumvirate's factional approach, and concerned about the economic policy problems and sclerosis of internal party life, on the basis of brief theses such as the Platform of the 46. Beyond the demands for greater inner-party democracy, for constraining aspects of the apparatus, and for a more focused economic strategy, the coalition partners had little in common. The platform's 46 signatories included (i) seven DCs, whose own group's coherence outlasted the 1923 opposition and survived until the early 1930s; (ii) other radicals who had been Left Communists in 1918, such as Georgii Piatakov, Iakovleva and Stukov; (iii) senior Bolsheviks close to Trotsky, such as Preobrazhenskii and Serebriakov, who had lost their leading positions after the tenth congress, and the military commander Nikolai Muralov; and (iv) others previously loyal to the party leadership. Only three of the 46 signatories had a trade union background – Gol'tsman, now working in the VSNKh; Vladimir Smirnov, editor of the trade union newspaper *Trud*; and Mikhail Lobanov, a full-time party official in Moscow who had been an underground metalworkers' union activist before 1917. Lobanov was the only former WO member among the 46; others, including Shliapnikov, distanced themselves from both CC factions, and again raised their own call for stronger trade union involvement in industrial decision-making.[13] On the other hand officials of the VSNKh and its subordinate bodies were strongly represented (12 signatories); these included Danishevskii, who had in 1921 been a supporter of Smilga's extreme anti-democratic proposals. The Platform of the 46 had been prepared in secret and therefore had no rank-and-file signatories. The lowest-ranking signatory was Shmidel', the Kauchuk cell secretary and member of the rubber goods trust management board.[14]

The discussion began in semi-secrecy, at the enlarged plenum of the CC on 25 September. (See Chapter 8, pp. 204–5.) Trotsky's letter to the politburo

---

13 *Pravda*, 18 January 1924; TsAOPIM, 88/1/168/65–79.
14 Vilkova et al., op. cit., pp. 415–48, *Izvestiia TsK KPSS* 6, 1990, pp.194–95, and archival sources, including files of the All-Union Society of Old Bolsheviks (RGASPI, f124).

on 8 October, which formally opened hostilities, was also supposedly secret; news of it spread quickly, but unofficially. The bureau of the Moscow committee (MC) of the Bolshevik party noted on 14 October that it was 'widely known' among members. The triumvirate, and the CC majority that supported it, used control of information to political advantage. The CC discussed the opposition's documents on 25–27 October, and resolved not to publish them, but to raise the issue of the inner-party regime via Zinoviev's sanitized article in *Pravda* on 7 November, which made no reference to the dispute on the CC. The article acknowledged the 'excessive calm, even stagnation, in places' of the party organization, admitted that the biggest problem was that many questions 'go from the top to the bottom already decided', and urged implementation of the many previous resolutions, passed but not carried out, to institute 'workers' democracy' in the party.[15]

A call by *Pravda*'s editors for letters commenting on Zinoviev's article released a pressure cooker valve. Hundreds of communists responded, blaming the party apparatus for undermining inner-party democracy in forthright terms. Sapronov claimed there had been 400 such letters, only a fraction of which were published.[16] A month later, on 5 December, Trotsky and the politburo majority agreed a compromise resolution 'on party-building', which declared the need for a 'new course' in inner-party affairs, and set out practical measures including re-election of some officials and more regular party conferences. The resolution was approved by the CC and Central Control Commission of the Bolshevik party (CCC). A party-wide discussion of the disputed issues followed. Cells responded enthusiastically to the opposition's call for internal party democracy, which had been incorporated into the CC resolution. The triumvirate responded by mobilizing those sections of the apparatus that supported it around its campaign of slander. Stalin led the way, at a meeting on 2 December in Krasnopresnia, making wild allegations that the opposition wanted to 'split the government, and that means destroying Soviet power'. Then followed a personal rant by Stalin against Trotsky, Preobrazhenskii, Sapronov, and Rafail, published in *Pravda* on 15 December, and a public campaign of increasingly foul-mouthed abuse.[17] A.M. Nazaretian, a close collaborator of Stalin's, was put in charge of party discussion items in *Pravda*, which from mid-December were crudely slanted against the opposition; he caused a scandal on the CC by blatantly falsifying an article.[18] Another weapon in the

15 A.V. Kvashonkin et al. (eds), *Bol'shevistskoe rukovodstvo. Perepiska. 1912–1927*, Moscow: Rosspen, 1996, p. 283; Vilkova et al., op. cit., pp. 174–75; *Pravda*, 7 November 1923.
16 *Pravda*, 27 November 1923; TsAOPIM, 1099/1/7/44ob.
17 Vilkova et al., op. cit., pp. 284–85, *Izvestiia TsK KPSS* 12, 1990, pp. 164–65; *Pravda*, 15, 16, 18, 23 and 28 December 1923.
18 Olekh, *Povorot*, p. 141; Bazhanov, op. cit., p. 28; Vilkova et al., op. cit., pp. 345 and 363–66; TsAOPIM, 88/1/170/52.

triumvirate's armoury was the GPU security police. Having been used against the Workers Group and Workers Truth, it was now mobilized, covertly, against the new opposition.[19]

The opposition in Moscow was stronger than in the party nationally, perhaps partly because members there had greater access to uncensored information. But the MC majority, led by Kamenev, supported the triumvirate. Nearly all cell resolutions began with a formulaic welcome for the CC/CCC resolution and the 'new course'; those supporting the opposition then called for re-election of all party officials, while those supporting the triumvirate warned of the danger to party unity and stated that 'groups', as well as factions, were impermissible. Cells further indicated their allegiances either by denouncing the public vilification of Trotsky, or by condemning the oppositionists' 'factionalism'. Many cells were split, for example the Russkabel' no. 3 factory cell, where a CC majority resolution received 26 votes, against 22 for Preobrazhenskii's, or the cell representing office staff at the transport commissariat, which favoured a CC majority resolution over an opposition one, but also complained about *Pravda*'s 'one-sided' reporting.[20] An assembly of active Moscow party members on 11 December became a key forum for the discussion.[21] In the battle for cells' allegiance, the two sides were neck-and-neck in Krasnopresniia, and the opposition achieved a majority in Khamovniki and solid minorities in the other three Moscow districts. The MC and its apparatus gerrymandered to reduce opposition representation at district conferences, and at the eleventh Moscow regional party conference on 10 January 1924. Although the opposition appeared to be winning the votes of nearly half the Moscow membership, it had less than one-fifth of the delegates at that conference.[22] The thirteenth national party conference on 16–18 January 1924, which marked the end of the discussion, was even more thoroughly rigged: only three of several hundred delegates supported the opposition.

19 Vilkova et al., op. cit., pp. 409–14; Olekh, *Krovnye uzy*, pp. 93–97.
20 TsAOPIM 3/11/85a/1, 6.
21 It was implied in *Pravda* that a resolution moved by Kalinin for the CC majority had been passed with an insignificant few against; Sapronov later insisted that of the 1500 people present, 300 had voted for the opposition. TsAOPIM 3/4/36; 88/1/168/52; *Pravda*, 13, 15 and 16 December 1923.
22 Figures on the level of opposition support were sharply contested. The fullest figures, collated by the MC in January 1924 but never published, show that 808 cells with a total of 34,890 members supported the CC majority and 178 cells with 13,442 members supported the opposition. All the statistical material now available suggests that the opposition had the support of 40–50 per cent of the Moscow membership, reduced by gerrymandering to 18 per cent at the regional conference. TsAOPIM, 3/11/85a/11–12; *Odinnadtsataia Moskgubpartkonferentsiia: stenograficheskii otchet*, Moscow: MK RKP(b), 1924, p. 123; Pirani, op. cit., p. 282.

The democratic interlude

The discussion ignited by Zinoviev's article gave party members an opportunity to debate publicly the far-reaching changes in cells' functions since the tenth congress in 1921. Before 1921, the cells had hosted more or less untrammelled political discussion alongside their mobilization and campaigning functions. Afterwards, the cells' political life was curtailed, in parallel with the emasculation of the soviets. Their meeting agendas changed: formal reports on national political issues were often minuted without discussion; administrative issues increasingly dominated. The party's district apparatus transmitted decisions from above and checked on their implementation. Cells developed their own apparatus, i.e. bureaux composed largely of full-time officials. Communists who expressed opinions to non-party workers, even on day-to-day workplace issues, might be rebuked for not confirming in advance the party line. The cells' lifelessness was acknowledged by Zinoviev; he attributed it largely to the membership's 'low political level'. Other discussants blamed authoritarian leadership. A. Bobrov complained that 'our once-vibrant meetings have turned into an onerous chore' because 'the leaders have taken upon themselves the responsibility not only to tell us how to eat, but also to chew the food that's been put in front of us'.[23]

The agreement of 5 December 1923 between Trotsky and the politburo majority – under which the former agreed not to criticize the triumvirate publicly, and the latter adopted the 'new course' resolution approving limited inner-party democracy – was in later years remembered by oppositionists as a ruinous tactical mistake.[24] At the time, though, it produced an unprecedented babel of discussion. Encouraged by this signal from above, some cells met, literally, for days on end. At the Tsindel' textile mill, the scene of one of the summer strikes, the communists talked 'late into the night' every evening for a week. Cell meetings went on until 3.00 am at Krasnyi Bogatyr, until 5.30 am at the 1886 power station and until 6.00 am at a school in Zamoskvorech'e.[25] The 'new course' resolution, which included a phrase acknowledging the undesirability of 'appointism', encouraged some cells to remove long-standing officials, and others to welcome previously unacceptable recruits. A meeting of a large Moscow factory cell reported in *Pravda*, attended by 'many hundreds', threw out a district-committee-approved list of candidates for the Moscow soviet election and replaced it with a list nominated from the floor.[26] The Goznak cell decided to recruit a

---

23 *Pravda*, 7, 22 and 24 November 1923.
24 Sosnovskii, warning in 1928 against the 'hurriedness, exaggerations and illusions' of Preobrazhenskii and others who wanted to return to Moscow and abandon the opposition, cautioned: 'Remember the 5th of December 1923.' *Biulleten' oppozitsii* 3–4, 1929, p. 20.
25 TsAOPIM, 3/11/85a/4–5, 7, 9, 28; V. Kurakhtanova, *Pervaia sitsenabivnaia*, Moscow: izd. sotsial'noi-ekonomicheskoi literatury, 1960, p. 88.
26 *Pravda*, 5 December 1923.

former Menshevik, Gorbachev, who had joined the Bolsheviks during the civil war but left again in protest at the NEP. Such a political record would normally have been a bar to membership, but Gorbachev was unapologetic, defending his campaign against compulsory subscription to the gold loan, and confessing to a 'reputation as a troublemaker' because he 'listened to the mass of workers and defended their interests against the factory committee'. At its next meeting, the cell urged the dismissal of the veteran secretary of the local district committee, Mandel'shtam, and the recall of three other district committee members. Mandel'shtam's counterpart in Zamoskvorech'e, Zemliachka, was targeted by a similar resolution from a joint meeting of the district's hospital cells.[27] One of the AMO car factory cell's founding fathers, Gavrilin, fell victim to his comrades' democratic mood and was deposed from the factory committee.[28] But party members' democratic enthusiasm never extended to involving non-party workers in making decisions. The opposition leaders were as adamant as the CC majority that 'workers' democracy' was a privilege for party members only. While selected comments from non-party workers were published in *Pravda*, both sides remained alert to what Radek called 'the danger that our discussion will be picked up by non-party workers' and opposed to inner-party pluralism in the form of political factions.[29]

The sharp end of the discussion focused on concrete measures to implement inner-party democracy, and, particularly, the re-election of officials. And many cells went further in their demands than the opposition leaders: the Moscow Academy of Mining cell urged not only the re-election of all party committees 'from bottom to top, not from top to bottom', but also a review of all expulsions of worker communists since the tenth congress. The cell demanded that higher party bodies be deprived of the right to initiate disciplinary measures in all but exceptional cases, and urged repeal of the party statute that gave higher bodies the right to confirm the appointment of cell and district secretaries. The Metron factory cell demanded the right of all party members to attend meetings of any committee and an end to the compilation of 'secret profiles' of party members.[30] The apparatus was intransigent in defence of its powers. On 8 December, a full-time party official in Krasnopresnia, I. Shumskaia, warned in a letter to *Pravda* that the apparatus would refuse to carry out the 'new course' resolution. She described how the district committee had instructed oppositionist full-timers to push the CC majority line regardless of their own opinion, and how it sent large groups of full-timers to

---

27 TsAOPIM, 3/11/85a/9; 1099/1/7/48, 50–51.
28 TsAGM, 415/16/317/135; 415/16/318/122–23; and A.P. Churiaev, N.V. Adfel'dt, D.A. Baevskii et al. (eds), *Istoriia Moskovskogo avtozavoda im. I.A. Likhacheva*, Moscow: izd. 'Mysl'', 1966, p. 111.
29 TsAOPIM, 63/1/144/187; 88/1/168/87; 3/4/36/74–76; 69/1/138/20.
30 TsAOPIM, 3/11/85a/90ob-91, 131.

browbeat dissident cells. This provoked a confrontation at a meeting in the district: Preobrazhenskii condemned such practices as 'intolerable'; Belen'kii, the committee's chairman, denounced Shumskaia's 'lies'.[31]

The triumvirate's victory

The opposition was defeated in spite of the support for its arguments on democracy. While scheming, witch-hunting and gerrymandering played their part, there were also political reasons why the triumvirate won support, or at least acquiescence, in the party ranks. The leadership neutralized opposition accusations that economic policy was yielding to alien class forces, with a campaign of repression against NEP's most visible capitalistic excesses; it ably exploited the opposition's failure to address the threat to workers' living standards, thereby depriving it of potential support from among worker communists; and it portrayed the opposition as divisive at a time when the fate of the international revolution hung in the balance in Germany.

The party leadership started its campaign against corruption among party and industry officials, and against speculative trading, in November 1923, just as the party debate became public. The campaign was launched on 17 November by the CCC presidium and the collegium of the Workers and Peasants Inspectorate, Rabkrin. The emphasis was on visible effect: for example, the press featured a spot-check by Moscow police on the use of official cars for private purposes. In December, public trials began of corrupt officials from the Bogorodsko-Shchelkovskii textile trust and the GUM trading house.[32] The GPU coordinated the campaign, and its officers in Moscow saw it as part and parcel of the struggle against the opposition. On 4 December, a gathering of party members in the Moscow region GPU resolved both to resist 'revisionist changes in the internal party line', i.e. the opposition, and to wage a 'decisive struggle with all excesses, distortions of NEP and isolation from the working masses, especially on the part of industrial managers'.[33] Some supporters of the triumvirate counterposed mobilizing the GPU to more democratic forms of struggle as the best means to fight corruption: Andeichin told the 11 December assembly of Moscow party activists that the excesses of NEP had to be combated not by the methods Sapronov proposed, but by the GPU, 'the political organ whose duty it is to defend our interests'; centralism, and appointism, were

---

31 *Pravda*, 8 and 14 December 1923; TsAOPIM, 69/1/138/21–24; 3/4/36/36–37.
32 *Pravda*, 15 and 16 November, 6, 9, 25 and 28 December 1923; 'Marking NEP's Slippery Path: the Krasnoshchekov Show Trial', *Russian Review* 61, 2002: 249–75; Olekh, *Povorot*, pp. 177–78.
33 TsAOPIM, 3/4/37/65.
34 TsAOPIM, 3/4/36/66.

vital for this fight.³⁴ This declaration met with 'loud and prolonged laughter', presumably from oppositionists. They perhaps misjudged its weight: the party leadership proceeded along exactly the lines Andeichin described.

At the end of December, well-publicized raids were carried out against Moscow traders and 'NEP-men', many of whom were imprisoned or exiled. In February-March 1924, after the opposition's defeat and during the 'Lenin enrolment', a show trial on corruption charges was conducted against Aleksandr Krasnoshchekov, head of the Bank of Industry and Trade and member of the VSNKh executive, accompanied by a round of official condemnation of excessive salaries for specialists. The campaign against corruption, like those against the church and the SR party, was organized in a top-down way. When the Duks aircraft factory cell in Krasnopresnia tried in April 1924 to take into its own hands the case of an obviously corrupt party official – Malakhov, who practiced gross *sovmestitel'stvo* – this was perceived by district organizers as a negative fact 'that had heated up oppositional moods'.³⁵ Moreover, the punishment of 'excesses' was selective: as Robert Argenbright has shown, senior party figures were often implicated but spared. The campaign's real importance was agitational: it won support from the party ranks. The AMO cell, for example, complained in February 1924 that the courts were showing 'insufficient harshness ... towards those who embezzle from the economy', and demanded the death penalty for Krasnoshchekov.³⁶ G.L. Olekh, who researched the discussion in the Siberian party, concluded that the triumvirate's anti-*spets* rhetoric and anti-corruption campaign 'made a big impression' on the opposition's left wing, and helped ensure its defeat.³⁷

The triumvirate represented itself as the incumbent leadership, to which credit was due for the successful economic turnaround of the previous two years. The social contract operated inside the party, too: the yearning for stability produced by improved living standards worked against the opposition. Middle-level supporters of the triumvirate expressed fears that the political changes advocated by the opposition would disrupt economic recovery. At a meeting of cell secretaries in Krasnopresnia during the 'party crisis', the secretary of the Krasnyi proletarii factory cell, Kozlov, decried the opposition, saying: 'I am not against democracy as such, but into that democracy crawl those "democrats" who will bring us the [SR] slogan, "long live the constituent assembly". We believe in our CC, and say something else all together: our pay is too low!' At another meeting in the district, Seletskii

---

35 TsAOPIM, 3/4/37/103.
36 Argenbright, op. cit.; Olekh, *Povorot*, p. 177; Carr, op. cit., pp. 120–21. TsAO-PIM, 433/1/19/9, 12; *Sotsialisticheskii vestnik* 1, 1924, p. 13.
37 Olekh, *Povorot*, p. 178. See also *Pravda*, 1, 3, and 4 January 1924; Carr, op. cit., pp. 126–30; *Trinadtsataia konferentsiia RKP(b): biulleten'*, Moscow, 1924, pp. 81–83, 91 and 187.

supported the triumvirate in similarly cynical terms: 'Our rank and file members are backward, very backward. They are consumed by simple material interests.'[38]

The opposition now paid the price for failure to make common cause with the trade unionists and worker communists around its policies for industry. Inside the CC, the opposition offered a long-term strategy to resist the dangers of capitalist revival inherent in NEP; the triumvirate lacked an answer to this, and subsequently incorporated much of it into its own approach. But the party ranks were scarcely made aware of the opposition programme. While it was cursorily rehearsed at some Moscow- and district-level meetings, it was hardly considered in the cells.[39] It was the remains of the WO, rather than the Trotsky-Preobrazhenskii-Sapronov alliance, that pointed to the dangers to workers' living standards implicit in the rise of the party elite and its policies. At a joint meeting of cells in Bauman district, Tul'iakov called for a freeze on factory closures because of mounting unemployment; an end to managers' special pay rates and *sovmestitel'stvo*; and the return of pay to pre-war levels. Other speakers at the meeting complained about the payment of wages in *sovznaky*, perceived injustice in the dispensation of the proceeds of the gold loan and poor spending strategy in industry.[40] But Tul'iakov, like Shliapnikov and Lutovinov on the national stage, was isolated from the opposition leaders. Evidence from the cells supports Carr's argument that the 'lack of sympathy between the leaders of the opposition and those who spoke for the workers' helped crown the opposition's final defeat at the thirteenth party conference. There, the opposition amendments to the CC resolution on economic policy, presented by Piatakov, were heavily voted down, while the dissident trade unionist Lutovinov was elected to a commission to formulate the final draft, and succeeded in adding clauses providing for the increase of below-average wages and the payment of bonuses on all wages paid in chervontsy.

Another of the triumvirate's arguments was that the opposition, by persisting with the political dispute, was weakening party unity and potentially undermining the attempted German revolution. In the ranks, this was a powerful form of emotional blackmail.[41] Behind closed doors, Trotsky

38 TsAOPIM, 69/1/136/33; 69/1/138/36.
39 I estimate that for every 10 cell meetings that considered the inner-party regime, one discussed economic policy. On Moscow discussion, TsAOPIM, 69/1/138/1–22. See also Carr, op. cit., pp. 90–113 and 120–21; Vilkova et al., op. cit., pp. 155–66; K.A. Popov (eds), *Diskussiia 1923 goda: materialy i dokumenty*, Moscow: Gosizdat, 1927, pp. 198–201, p. 207 and p. 275; Olekh, *Povorot*, p. 167.
40 TsAOPIM, 467/1/7/32.
41 The tactics adopted by the Comintern in Germany were not among the issues debated during the party crisis, although some Trotskyists' accounts, with the benefit of hindsight and with Trotsky's subsequent writings in hand, give the impression that they were. See Pirani, op. cit., p. 290; A. Thalheimer, '1923: A Missed Opportunity? – the Legend of the German October and the Real History of 1923', *Revolutionary History* 8: 4, 2004: 90–125; Deutscher, op. cit., pp. 140–51.

protested that freedom of discussion had been incomparably wider 'during the harshest hours of civil war' than it was in 1923 – although Radek, the only CC member to sympathize with the opposition apart from its active participants Trotsky, Preobrazhenskii and Piatakov, believed that the German events were a reason to bottle up the discussion. In the public debate, the triumvirate's pleas for restraint resonated. One party member, K. Rozental', wrote in *Pravda* that 'the German events have the whole party, every member, in the grip of the most terrible tension. This "psychological" mobilization, this heightened revolutionary sensibility, compels us to forget for now the party's "illnesses and sores"'. Other letter writers believed the situation in Germany made the discussion more, not less, urgent, but evidence from cells suggest they were in a minority.[42]

Replenishing the ranks

The party crisis brought to a climax the deep-going changes in the party's structure and modus operandi that had been building up since the tenth congress. It broke the resistance that had obstructed these changes. Together with the mass recruitment campaign that followed it, the opposition's defeat formed a turning point referred to at the time as a 'break' (*perelom*).[43] The relatively simple and transparent hierarchy of the civil-war party had given way to the authoritarian system of command, centralized in the CC apparatus. The backlash against the oppositionists severely limited future protests against this apparatus. The party leadership, by acknowledging the elective principle in words and rejecting attempts to put it into practice, made 'appointism' unchallengeable. The shift in the cells from politics to administration was consolidated. And just as, for non-party workers, the space for discussion had been narrowed by the gutting of the soviets, so the limits were laid down for party members. The character of party membership, and the membership itself, changed: the barriers to recruitment on which Lenin had insisted were lifted and cells undertook mass recruitment for the first time.

Tentative moves had been made towards this type of recruitment in Moscow and other urban centres from late 1922. In the first quarter of 1923, the recruitment of workers in Moscow began consistently to exceed the outflow for the first time since the civil war, in contrast to the decline nationally, which continued until the spring of 1924.[44] The Moscow party recruited 3400 new candidate members, four-fifths of them workers, and the MC and district committees assigned 2000 members to workplace cells. The

---

42 Trotsky, letter to the politburo of 8 October 1923, in Vilkova et al., op. cit., p. 160. Radek, 'Ia zaiavliaiu', *Istochnik* 2, 1998: 42–45; *Pravda*, 25, 27 and 29 November 1923; TsAOPIM, 3/11/85a/29.
43 'Perelom' means a fracture. The same word was used to describe the move to forced collectivization and industrialization in 1929.
44 *Pravda*, 4 April 1923. For statistics on party membership, see Appendix 3, p. 257.

shift from a vanguard party to a wider type of membership was initiated from the top. In April 1923 the twelfth congress loosened the membership criteria that had been tightened a year previously at Lenin's insistence. It decided that workers and peasants could be admitted either with two recommendations from party members of two years' standing, or, in the case of Komsomol members in industry, a recommendation from a party member plus one from the Komsomol district committee – although the upgrading of candidate members of other class backgrounds to full membership was postponed en bloc for a year.[45]

There were significant differences between the civil war recruits and those of 1923. First, and most obviously, the civil war recruits had joined an organization with a much shakier grip on power, membership of which constituted a risk, and implied participation in military action. Recruits of 1923 were joining an organization firmly in control of the state apparatus; the party's capacity thereby to attract opportunists and self-seekers (of all classes) was a subject of constant discussion, and the evidence suggests that, despite preventive measures, they indeed flooded in. Second, the economic recovery, and the party's emphasis on the importance of training and professional qualifications, appealed to young workers whose hearts were with the Bolshevik industrialization and modernization project, not all of whom combined this with a wider socialist vision. Third, the change in the political atmosphere in the party – the frowning on, and then destruction of, open discussion in the party ranks – not only drove committed civil-war communists out of the party but presumably dissuaded politically radical workers from joining.

There is some evidence that in the new wave of recruits, there was a higher proportion than during the civil war of women and young workers, i.e. those routinely dismissed by many Bolsheviks as politically backward and unconscious. On the other hand, the Bolsheviks' favoured constituency – the older, skilled male workers, and 'hereditary' workers who had been born in the city – were apparently resisting recruitment. The statistics are too patchy to confirm this trend, and some of the evidence, i.e. assertions by party activists who saw this as negative, must be treated with caution. But it is sufficient to raise some questions. In August 1923, the Moscow party newspaper interviewed activists about why workers resisted recruitment. Koltsov said that the skilled male workers held back from joining the party from a 'fear of being tied down' and 'love for [their] profession'. Workers he had tried to recruit said they would prefer to spend time developing themselves professionally; 'a worker might be studying, say, astronomy, or some natural science, and he will say: "now I can read a lot, but if I have to go to all those meetings I'll have less time"'. Kul'kov added that workers' standard of living was rising and they were 'becoming more demanding for

---

45 Iu.A. Lipilin and G.A. Sachkovskii, *Leninskii prizyv v leningradskoi partiinoi organizatsii*, Leningrad: Lenizdat, 1984, p. 20; TsAOPIM, 3/11/91/13.

themselves'; 'after work they go home, wash thoroughly and even have something to change into'.[46] The problem of the perceived alienation from the party of 'the skilled, hereditary proletariat' was aired during the party debate. MC secretary Zelenskii acknowledged that the veteran male workers 'either stand to one side, or sometimes even speak against' when mass meetings were urged to support party campaigns; the party cells, rather than engaging in discussion, then turned to the women and young workers. Preobrazhenskii retorted that, given the constraints on discussion inside the party, non-party workers could work things out politically better than members could.[47] B. Lavler, a woman full-timer 'attached' to the AMO cell, wrote that cell leaders – especially ones who are themselves politically 'weak' – assumed the 'more cultured, developed workers, who put forward criticisms' to be opponents, and only talked to younger workers.[48]

An important factor that attracted young workers into the party was that membership was seen as the road to professional and personal advancement. Economic construction required trained personnel. Party leaders began to place less emphasis on the importance of recruits' political reliability and consciousness, and more on their readiness to study. This in turn tapped into workers' strong desire to acquire education and technical skills, which historians have associated with urbanization and class formation from the late nineteenth century.[49] Bukharin declared to the Komsomol's fifth congress in October 1922 that the party needed to rely, first, not on 'nihilist-revolutionaries', but on the sort of young person who 'spits on everything and covers his ears with his hands, so you can't disturb him, [because] he wants to study'.[50] Some Komsomol newspapers, and the Mensheviks, decried the *'rabfak* mood', i.e. a desire above all to attain professional qualifications, among communist youth.[51] But it was in tune with the party's requirements. Cells began to offer technical training courses, in the first place to party and Komsomol recruits. One party activist, Antonov, believed that these would produce not only 'red foremen' but also 'the truest road to communism for the backward mass of workers'.[52]

---

46 *Rabochaia Moskva*, 2 August 1923; TsAGM, 415/16/262/5.
47 *Pravda*, 28 and 29 November 1923.
48 *Pravda*, 14 and 24 November and 8 December 1923.
49 See, for example, R.E. Zelnik, 'Russian Bebels: an Introduction to the Memoirs of the Russian Workers Semen Kanatchnikov and Matvei Fisher', *Russian Review* 35: 3, 1976: 249–89; V.E. Bonnell, *Roots of Rebellion: Workers' Politics and Organizations in St. Petersburg and Moscow, 1900–1914*, Berkeley: University of California Press, 1983, pp. 47–52 and 215–19; V.E. Bonnell (ed.), *The Russian Worker: Life and Labor Under the Tsarist Regime*, Berkeley: University of California Press, 1983, pp. 82–84, 150–52 and 208.
50 *Piatyi s"ezd komsomol'tsev (rechi t.t. Trotskogo, Bukharina)*, Viatka: izd. gubkom RKSM, 1922, pp. 48–49.
51 *Sotsialisticheskii vestnik* 4, 1923, pp. 8–9.
52 *Rabochaia Moskva*, 2 August 1923.

Some new recruits saw professional education in the context of wider socialist ideals: there is ample evidence of this in the memoirs of 1923 recruits who went on to participate in the communist opposition.[53] But others seem to have seen party or Komsomol membership principally in terms of accessing technical skills, without linking this to wider ideas about socialism and modernization. It is striking that several Krasnyi proletarii workers who joined the Komsomol in the early 1920s, when interviewed for the history of factories project about why they had become communists, all referred to the attraction of technical training without mentioning socialism even in passing. R. Romanov, who joined the Komsomol in 1923, said that it had had 'very little' influence among the young people in the factory in 1921–22; young non-party workers were 'no worse, and often better, at tackling production issues' than the Komsomol members. The training school was the key recruitment weapon, and worked on Romanov himself. 'I did not want to be a Komsomolets. But ... you needed to be in the Komsomol to do the organizing work [at the technical school] that I was doing.' Al'brekht, who joined the Komsomol during the civil war, recalled being stung by criticism from skilled workers that Komsomol members were so busy studying politics that they didn't know how to work. The young non-party workers 'were not interested in political questions. They wanted to get qualifications, and to enjoy themselves'. The Komsomol grew when it started training programmes, through which it recruited these young workers. 'They wanted to know how they could get on to a higher tariff band. [In response] we decided to set up a technical training school.'[54]

The Lenin enrolment

With the Lenin enrolment launched straight after Lenin's death in January 1924, the remnants of the vanguard party structure were discarded, and party policy decreed that the workplace cells should move to recruiting groups of workers en masse. The party elite, feeling that its control over the lower bodies was secured, through the CC secretariat and the cadre distribution system, saw the recruitment drive as the next stage of managing the social contract with workers. Mass recruitment was first suggested by the CC majority during the conflict with the opposition, and some historians have made a compelling case that it was conceived as a means of drowning out opposition arguments. There is no definitive proof of this. However, the move to mass membership followed logically from the shift in the party's functions, and Lenin's death came as a fortuitous event around which to launch a campaign already in the making. The thirteenth party conference on 16–18 January had agreed to recruit 100,000 proletarians, and a meeting

---

53 See e.g. Isai Abramovich's memoirs, <http://lib.ru/MEMUARY/ABRAMOWICH/> , and I. Pavlov, op. cit.
54 GARF, 7952/3/98/1, 7, 58, 68; 7952/3/96/8–8ob; TsAOPIM, 412/1/8/13.

of delegates to the eleventh congress of soviets to discuss mass recruitment had been fixed in advance for 21 January 1924, the day of Lenin's death. The Lenin enrolment was approved by the CC 10 days afterwards. The doors were opened for mass recruitment not only of industrial workers but also of workers in handicraft occupations, long considered petty-bourgeois by the Bolsheviks, and of peasants.[55]

The Moscow regional party membership swelled as a result of the three-month enrolment campaign by nearly half, from 53,121 to 76,416, and by the end of 1924 to 88,384.[56] A large number of the recruits were the very workers who had declined to join the party in 1923: older male workers, and in particular those with skills and many years of factory employment. Although the MC's claim that 'up to 80 per cent' of the recruits were highly qualified and/or had long work records seems exaggerated, other evidence suggests that those with pre-war work experience, as well as those who came into the factories in 1914–20, were strongly represented. For example in Sokol'niki district, 60 per cent of those recruited had work records of 5–10 years (i.e. they had started in the factories between 1914 and 1919) and 15 per cent had work records of 11 years or more. The great majority of the recruits were over 25, nearly one-third were over 35, and less than a quarter were 24 or under. More than four-fifths of them were male. More than one-third had served in the Red army; these vastly outnumbered the small minority with experience of the pre-war labour movement (less than one-tenth). There were far fewer former members of other parties than among recruits in earlier periods, and only a handful of the thousands of Bolsheviks who had quit the party, or been expelled, in 1921–23.[57]

Whereas the campaigns of 1922 sought to remould the party's relationship with the non-party workers, this campaign sought to remould the party cells themselves. Long lists of proposed recruits were first approved by the cells' existing members, and often by factory mass meetings. This procedure, along with the acceptance of group applications and the waiver of the

---

55 T.H. Rigby, *Communist Party Membership in the USSR 1917–1967*, Princeton: Princeton University Press, 1968, pp. 116–30; Olekh, *Povorot*, p. 176; Pavlova, op. cit., pp. 104–10.
56 These figures include members and candidates. Nationally, to the 350,000 members plus 122,000 candidates at the beginning of 1924, the Lenin enrolment added about 200,000 (mostly candidates). By the beginning of 1926 total membership had surpassed 1 million. *Leninskyi prizyv v Moskovskoi organizatsii: sbornik*, Moscow: MK RKP(b), 1925, p. 12; MK RKP(b), *Moskovskaia organizatsiia RKP (b) v tsifrakh. K XIV gubpartkonferentsii. Vyp. 2-oi.*, Moscow, 1925; K.I. Bukov, Z.P. Korshunova and N.I. Rodionova (eds), *Moskovskaia gorodskaia organizatsiia KPSS 1917–1988: tsifry, dokumenty, materialy*, Moscow: Moskovskii rabochii, 1989; Gimpel'son, op. cit., p. 127; Rigby, op. cit., p. 127.
57 *Leninskii prizyv*, pp. 11 and 15–17; Sekretariat TsK RKP(b), *Materialy po statistike lichnogo sostava RKP*, Moscow, 1921, pp. 2–3; TsK RKP(b) (statisticheskii otdel), *Partiia v tsifrovom osveshchenii: materialy po statistike lichnogo sostava partii*, Moscow/Leningrad: Gosizdat, 1925, p. 81.

requirement that applicants be recommended by current members, all indicate the extent of the break with the Bolsheviks' traditional vanguardist organizational concept. Some large workplace cells grew several times over: the Serp i Molot cell from 106 members to 257, the Trekhgornaia manufaktura cell from 254 to 617, and the Goznak cell from 136 to 623.[58] The influx strengthened the political position of the triumvirate, and this connection was often made explicit: at Krasnyi proletarii it was noted that 'during the discussion the petty bourgeoisie had been got rid of, and then it was decided to recruit workers from the bench'.[59] Finally, the enrolment reinforced the party's combined status as the country's only legal political organization and the nervous system of state administration.

The motives of the recruiters and the recruits were quite different, and even diametrically opposed. Many joined the party believing that this was the best way to represent workers' interests. The MC recorded instances of enrolment recruits using their new status to press workers' claims against management: at mass meetings in several large factories they 'voted against the cell's proposals, spoke against the cell, and proposed non-party candidates for factory committees'; at the Uritskii factory they supported demands for pay increases of nearly 100 per cent; and at Russkabel' in Rogozhsko-Simonovskii they supported a campaign against the sacking of a Menshevik.[60] But these recruits entered quite a different organization from the recruits of 1917 or 1920. The MC claimed that in the above-mentioned cases of 'a lack of understanding of discipline', once the cell bureau had explained the impermissibility of such actions, the recruits almost always 'admitted their mistakes and tried to correct them'. The sincerity of such confessions may be questioned, but the relationships are clear: the party apparatus, represented in the workplace by the bureau, proposes; the mass of new recruits disposes. On big political issues, the recruits, having broadly professed ignorance of, or indifference to, the 1923 discussion, were claimed to have responded to the discussion of Trotsky's *Lessons of October* in late 1924 by urging 'above all, party unity'.[61]

After the 'break'

The Lenin enrolment recruits played an important part in the 'break' in the party's methods of work. They outnumbered the civil war communists and others in many factory cells, and were often promoted above their predecessors'

58 *Leninskii prizyv*, p. 11; MK RKP(b), op. cit., pp. 3–4 and 16; N.I. Rodionova, *Gody napriazhennogo truda: iz istorii Moskovskoi partiinoi organizatsii 1921–1925 gg.*, Moscow: Moskovskii rabochii, 1963, pp. 151–55.
59 TsAOPIM, 412/1/15/7.
60 *Leninskii prizyv*, pp. 26–27; V.S. Tiazhel'nikova, 'Mekhanizmy "surovogo samoochishcheniia"' (unpublished paper presented at the British Association of Slavonic and East European Studies conference, 2003); A. Pospielovsky, 'Strikes During the NEP', *Revolutionary Russia* 10: 1, 1997: 1–34, here 21–24.
61 *Leninskii prizyv*, p. 28 and p. 33.

heads to the cell bureaux, which had become disciplined purveyors of instructions relayed via regional and district party organizations. Many rapidly became 'responsible officials'. In October 1925, after a campaign to urge cells to re-elect their bureaux, the Moscow organization found that 40 per cent of cell bureau members were enrolment recruits, and almost 60 per cent were soviet or party officials (i.e. administrators rather than workers 'at the bench').[62] The apparatus had from early 1924 directed the cells to purge oppositionists, at least from responsible positions, and the recruits were encouraged to help in this task. The clear-out started at national level, in particular in the Red army,[63] and prior to the thirteenth party congress in May 1924, a corresponding drive was organized in the cells. In Moscow, the MC required district party organizers to submit reports 'on the state of cells that were in the opposition during the discussion', and to distinguish those that had successfully performed the 'break' from those where, for example, 'the old moods have not been superceded' or 'there remains a group of stubborn oppositionists'.[64] In Bauman, reinforcements were brought in to support Aronshtam, who coordinated the attack on the opposition. Lemberg, Stalin's collaborator, was moved into the Ikar cell, the Bauman opposition's most significant remaining outpost. In December 1923 he inspired the sacking of the oppositional factory director, Ivan Petrov, which provoked 'strong dissatisfaction' among workers; in the spring of 1924 he organized the transfer out of the factory of oppositionists such as I.A. Potapov, the cell secretary. The MC admitted subsequently that this witch-hunt had a 'murderous' effect on the cell, producing an atmosphere where anyone who expressed the slightest doubts was pronounced a 'deviationist' and the newly recruited members became 'silent and inward-looking' and 'stopped speaking out at meetings'.[65] In some cells, including those at Goznak and the Manometr factory, uncowed oppositionists lobbied the new recruits from one side, while supporters of the victorious leadership worked on them from the other. In other more frequent cases, though, the newcomers' votes were mobilized to drive oppositionists from cell bureaux: for example at the Semenov dye and bleach works in Bauman, where 'the defeat of the former opposition was achieved with the votes of the Lenin enrolment [recruits], who understood the essence of the cell's illness'. The CC, leaving nothing to chance, waived rules under which candidate members had no voting rights, so that Lenin enrolment recruits participated in the election of delegates to the thirteenth congress.[66]

62 MK RKP(b), op. cit., pp. 28–29.
63 Vladimir Antonov-Ovseenko, who had been rumoured to favour mobilizing the military behind Trotsky, was removed as head of the army's political department, and Frunze, a supporter of the triumvirate, was promoted. Trotsky hung on as war commissar until January 1925, when he resigned on health grounds. Deutscher, op. cit., pp.160–63; Olekh, *Povorot*, p. 175.
64 TsAOPIM, 3/4/37/98–102.
65 TsAOPIM, 63/1/144/256; TsGAMO, 19/1/62/314; *Leninskii prizyv*, p. 23.
66 TsAOPIM, 3/4/37/45, 98–102; Olekh, *Povorot*, pp. 176–77.

The elite takes charge

The way in which the party elite used the new recruits to transform the party organization may be seen as an extension of the social contract. The recruits formed a new layer of a hierarchical structure via which the elite would 'lead', discipline and control the working class through the 1920s. The party of 1920 was a self-declared vanguard – reinforced by the comradeship of the civil war, the moral aspiration to equality among communists and a relatively free internal political regime – that was still consolidating its control, at national level over state institutions, and at factory level over managements and workers' organizations. But in the two years leading up to the Lenin enrolment, a hierarchical structure controlled by the CC secretariat had been created, with a middle layer of endlessly redeployable 'responsible officials', that reached down into the factory cells via the bureaux. The participation of the ranks in political discussion had, after the brief revival of late 1923, been subdued again at the end of the 'party crisis'. The Lenin enrolment was the next step in the party's evolution. The recruits formed a medium through which the party hierarchy, where discussions and decision-making power were concentrated, communicated with and controlled the working class. By bringing them into the party, the elite made full use of those sections of workers that supported Bolshevism politically, to marshal, 'educate' and control others. Political and administrative orders flowing from above were transmitted, via the apparatus and the enlarged cells, to the population at large. In the absence of political democracy in any wider sense, the enlarged workplace cells not only campaigned for production goals and discipline, but also transmitted protests and reactions – on a limited range of issues concerning working and living conditions – upwards to the elite. The civil-war party, a political-military combat organization, had been superceded by an organization better suited to the purposes of the new ruling class.

Conclusions
The impact on socialism

The flames of a richer, more heterogeneous working-class political life, having risen briefly in Moscow in the spring of 1921, had been reduced to embers by 1923 and were extinguished soon after. These flames had not burned brightly for very long. While Marx and Engels had envisaged that socialism would involve a movement towards a public power that supersedes politics, i.e. a negation of, an overcoming of, the state,[1] the movement in Russia during and after the civil war was mainly in the opposite direction. Only small, faltering steps could be made towards overcoming labour alienation, before they were reversed. The movement towards superceding politics, and the state, had no sooner reached the point at which the working class engaged with politics, through collective action, than it started to be pushed back again by the revitalized state.

At the end of the civil war, the working class movement was weakened, but still amounted to much more than the 'empty shell' to which Isaac Deutscher referred. Previous historiography has corrected that one-sided view of the demographic decline of the working class. This book has presented a more detailed picture of that movement's heterogeneous political character. It embraced not only the Bolsheviks, dissidents who left the party, and the semi-legal Menshevik, left SR and anarchist groups, but also a strong non-party socialist tendency that included narodnik, workerist and syndicalist strains, united largely by a belief in greater working-class involvement in government.

The unrest of early 1921 was triggered in the first instance by workers' desperation and frustration with economic hardship, and supply problems in particular. But they were also groping for political solutions. The 'equalization of rations' slogan was indicative. It may have been naïve and illogical

---

1 Marx and Engels wrote: 'When ... class distinctions have disappeared, and all production has been concentrated in the hands of a vast association of the whole nation, the public power will lose its political character'. K. Marx and F. Engels, *Manifesto of the Communist Party*, Moscow: Progress Publishers, 1977, p. 59. See also the discussion in C. Smith, *Karl Marx and the Future of the Human*, Maryland: Lexington Books, 2005, especially pp. 131–42.

in some respects, since workers' concept of 'equality' was class-based and conditional. But it was compelling enough for the Bolshevik party itself to embrace it at the critical moment, in mid January. And it was significant for the unease that it expressed about the appearance of a privileged elite in a supposedly socialist society. Nor did the movement limit itself to the issue of food distribution. The Moscow metalworkers' call in early February for an end to food requisitioning, made independently of the Bolsheviks, was an important factor in compelling Lenin and his comrades to change their minds on the issue. While this call may be attributed in part to the SRs' influence among the metalworkers, they were no more able than the Bolsheviks to win the metalworkers' unequivocal support. The metalworkers wanted to renew trade in the countryside without the corresponding expansion of wealth in the towns that was brought by the New Economic Policy (NEP) when it came.

The main political focus of the movement of early 1921 was for wider soviet democracy, including freedom for non-Bolshevik parties. During the demonstrations and strikes that culminated in the Kronshtadt revolt, these issues were taken up more vigorously in Petrograd and Saratov than in Moscow. In the capital, workers' aspirations to renewing soviet democracy were expressed at the soviet elections, rather than on the streets – suggesting, if anything, a readiness to work with the Bolsheviks in rebuilding the economy. Despite this, when the non-party groups trounced the Bolsheviks in the large workplaces, their pleas for co-operation were spurned. The Moscow workers' relative political moderation, and the lack of both common political demands and of coordination between the various industrial centres, underline that the movement was not united in wanting to overthrow the government. Nor were the Bolsheviks so paralyzed that they were unable to defend their power. So it makes little sense to present the unrest as a 'revolutionary situation'. On the other hand, the movement was anything but non-political, and the aspiration to greater working-class participation in decision-making remained at the centre of non-party socialist politics as long as it could be practised openly.

While in some respects non-party socialism was defined by what it was against, i.e. Bolshevik monopolization of political power, its adherents tried in the narrow political space available to them to articulate alternative views of socialism. This subject would benefit from further research. The Moscow experience needs to be compared with that of non-party socialists in other industrial centres. The extent to which non-party socialism persisted into the Stalinist period is also unclear. Jeffrey Rossman has shown that, the best part of a decade after the organized non-party groups in Moscow broke up, non-party socialists – courageous individuals with no organization, but with clear ideas about the party's usurpation of political power that rightly belonged to the working class – played a role in the resistance in the Ivanovo region.[2] Were they typical? The answers to such questions will enrich the historiography of Russian working-class politics, which has long been dominated by writers who concentrated on the Bolsheviks, Mensheviks, SRs and anarchists, and often sympathized with those political traditions.

The Bolsheviks' vanguardism and statism made them blind to the creative potential of democratic workers' organizations, intolerant of other working-class political forces and ruthless in silencing dissent. But they did not expropriate political power from the working class simply by repression. Central to their political strategy in the early NEP period was the deal that they struck with the majority of workers, who believed that the best that could be hoped for in the medium term was an improvement in living standards and relative stability under Bolshevik rule. Sergei Iarov argues that as workers emerged from their clash with the Bolsheviks in 1921, they concluded that NEP was the best possible outcome in economic policy terms, and moved 'from a mass, politicized, explosion, to conformism'.[3] But there was more to it than conformism: under the social contract struck between the two sides, the party promised – and delivered – a constantly improving standard of living. Workers accepted the responsibility to increase labour productivity, and surrendered decision-making on larger political issues to the party, while limiting themselves to criticisms of workplace management and other local problems. The soviet and trade union bodies in which workers had undertaken political activity in 1917 were brought under tight party control. The particular form of mobilization campaign initiated in 1922 – public displays of support for the government and disdain for its political enemies – displaced and replaced any genuine political activity by workers. The fact that most workers accepted these arrangements hardly denoted enthusiasm, or support, for the Bolshevik monopoly of political power. The cynicism and resignation of the Bromlei workers quoted at the end of Chapter 6 – 'communists at heart, but politically lazy', and well aware that 'every day we slide further and further from what we gained in October' – was presumably an articulation of what many others thought, as they shrugged their shoulders and declined to contribute to the gold loan or even to vote in soviet elections.

The events discussed in this book obviously have bearing on debates about the emergence of the new Soviet ruling class and of the Stalinist dictatorship, and of the roles played by Bolshevik ideology and by the circumstances in which the Bolsheviks operated. The historiography has been dominated by two interpretations. The first, associated with the 'totalitarian' school, was that Bolshevik ideology was the predominant factor, and that the origins of the Stalinist system may be traced back to ideas worked out by the Bolshevik leaders in exile before the First World War. The

2 J. Rossman, *Worker Resistance Under Stalin: Class and Revolution on the Shop Floor*, London: Harvard University Press, 2005, especially pp. 62–112.
3 S.V. Iarov, *Gorozhanin kak politik: revoliutsiia, voennyi kommunizm i NEP glazami petrogradtsev*, St Petersburg: 'Dmitrii Bulagin', 1999, p. 91.

second, radical structuralist approach, taken by left wing historians including Isaac Deutscher, and to some degree E.H. Carr, emphasized the way that the revolution was trapped in a larger historical tragedy from which it could not escape, and that that often left the Bolsheviks few alternatives to the ones they chose.[4] This book has endeavoured to offer a third interpretation, arguing that, while some aspects of Bolshevik ideology played a crucial part in weakening and undermining the revolution, that ideology itself was powerfully impacted by social changes over which it had little control, and to whose operation it often blinded itself.

Shifts in Bolshevik ideology and policy followed the ebb and flow of revolution. In 1917, the revolution's advance radicalized the party. After the February overthrow of tsarism, the Bolsheviks jettisoned long-held assumptions about the types of bourgeois government that would necessarily follow imperial rule and mooted the possibility of soviet power. Under the impact of the peasant revolts that accompanied their seizure of power in October, the Bolsheviks put aside long-cherished principles of land collectivization and issued a land decree that helped bring the peasants, and much of the SR party, over to their side. From 1918, as the revolution retreated, the shifts in Bolshevik ideology and policy were in the opposite direction. The ideas in Lenin's *The State and Revolution*, which was written under the influence of the surge of soviet activity in 1917 and extolled popular participation in government, were dumped. By 1921, as the Red army invaded Georgia to help depose the local Mensheviks, the principle of self-determination of small nations – which had in December 1917 been cited as a justification for granting independence to Finland – was set aside. In the post-civil-war years, the most conservative aspects of Bolshevik ideology – the vanguardism, authoritarianism and statism that had been shaken up in 1917 – were reinforced by the revolution's retreat. Subsequent changes in ideology reflected the hierarchical social relations taking shape, and the growing power of the party elite. The party's organizational structure and membership changed, too. The political-military vanguard organization of 1920 became, by 1924, an administrative tool of the new elite. To sum up the impact of the revolution's retreat on internal party life, three turning-points may be picked out: the defeat in 1921 of the opposition trends that had been buoyed by the mood of the civil-war communists; the shift in Bolshevik ideology in 1921–22 that accompanied the turn to peacetime construction; and the consolidation of the party elite's control over the organization in 1923–24.

4 A recent exposition of the 'totalitarian' case is M. Malia, *The Soviet Tragedy: a History of Socialism in Russia, 1917–1991*, New York: Maxwell Macmillan International, 1994, especially pp. 1–12 and 21–108. See also I. Deutscher, *The Prophet Unarmed. Trotsky 1921–1929*, London: Oxford University Press, 1970, especially pp. 3–22, 126–31, 405–9 and 459–68, and E.H. Carr, *The Russian Revolution from Lenin to Stalin, 1917–1929*, Basingstoke: Palgrave, 1979, especially pp. 186–89.

The first of these turning-points, the defeat of the oppositions, was a victory for centralization, over federalism; for party authority, over the reinvigoration of soviets and unions; and for the party elite, over those who challenged its privileges and its concentration of political power. This is not to suggest that any of the opposition groups had a formula for socialist development that was guaranteed to have worked where the Bolshevik mainstream failed. But failure – by which I mean failure to reawaken the collective working-class creativity that was crucial to the revolution's further progress – was all the more certain once the oppositions had been defeated. For example the Democratic Centralists' (DCs') proposals to broaden the state's combined executive-legislative structure to include local soviets, adopted by the party conference and soviet congress of December 1919 and cynically gerrymandered out of existence by the party apparatus soon afterwards, would surely have strengthened working-class organization and democracy. Indicative, too, was the party leadership's intolerance of essentially loyal rank-and-file oppositionists, such as those in the Bauman district. The apparatus's relationship with the working class was already so antagonistic in 1921, and the atmosphere that settled on the party after the tenth congress so inimical to discussion, that lifelong communists such as Vladimir Demidov and Vasilii Paniushkin were treated as enemies in much the same way as non-party socialists were. The introduction of NEP, and the shift to peacetime construction, obviously created conditions that some of the civil-war communists found politically tough, and the dispersion of most of them into the state apparatus also took its toll. But the defeat of the opposition tendencies that many of them had supported was above all a manifestation of the hierarchical, authoritarian direction in which Bolshevism was moving.

The second turning-point – the shift in ideology in 1921–22 – came as economic reconstruction got underway. It was affirmed that the state would supervise this reconstruction in the workers' name, and broader participation in political decision-making was specifically ruled out. Bolshevik leaders' civil-war-time promises, that such participation could be tried again once the emergencies were over, were forgotten. This approach was justified on the grounds that the working class was insufficiently proletarian; those who argued that it was the state that could not be proletarian were silenced. And as the economic recovery provided opportunities for the industrial and party elite to accumulate wealth, the party's formal barriers to that wealth were removed and aspirations to equality between communists junked.

Lenin and other Bolshevik leaders always emphasized that the soviet state was a 'workers' state', or, at least, a state representing proletarian interests and aspiring to socialism. They frequently argued that its proletarian character was guaranteed not by its relationship with the working class – aspects of which they freely acknowledged were antagonistic – but by the Bolsheviks' presence at its head. The force that this ideology exerted on the party is evident from the experience of the Workers Truth group, mentioned in Chapter 5. It stated in its 1921 manifesto that a 'technical organizing intelligentsia' had risen to the top of Russian society, that it would merge with elements from the old bourgeoisie and form a new ruling class, and that the Bolshevik party was becoming this group's political representative. The manifesto's authors were typical civil war Bolsheviks, and their ideas struck a chord with those of their comrades with whom they spoke before being exiled to Siberia. But in official fora, Workers Truth was harshly denounced by party officials, even though many of them had no access to its documents. Rank-and-file Bolsheviks, at least in the communist universities, were open to the idea, anathematized by the leadership, that the proletarian character of the state might be a fiction. But most of those in the ever-expanding party-state apparatus did their utmost to resist reaching such a conclusion. The balance of social forces in the party itself was changing, in a way that the Workers Truth manifesto highlighted pretty accurately – and which consigned it, and other oppositions, to defeat and isolation.

The same Bolshevik ideology that deemed the non-proletarian state to be 'proletarian', deemed the proletariat itself to be 'petty bourgeois'. This was the cause of Lenin's dispute with Aleksandr Shliapnikov at the eleventh party congress in March 1922, mentioned at the end of Chapter 6. Lenin had declared many times during the civil war that the working class was being 'deproletarianized'. But now he reiterated this claim just as the economy was recovering, and the workers were returning to the factories. The corollary, for Lenin, was that the workers themselves could not be trusted politically, and the party had to rule on their behalf. Shliapnikov's retort, that 'other social forces' stood to gain from such arguments, was prescient. These forces turned out to be the components of the future Soviet ruling class.

Another indication of the ideological shift was the party's acquiescence to inequality in its own ranks, discussed in Chapter 7. Again, the layer coalescing at the top of Soviet society was the beneficiary. The ninth party conference of September 1920 had agreed that such inequality was impermissible, and set up a commission to investigate privilege in the Kremlin. But less than two years later, in August 1922, the twelfth party conference adopted Molotov's resolution that formalized significant material advantages for 'responsible workers'. And another year on, party members in industrial management were accumulating substantial wealth alongside their non-party colleagues. But protests against the breakdown of inner-party solidarity, so vocal in 1920, were by 1922 only heard from a small minority, represented by Vladimir Petrzhek, the AMO car factory worker for whom 'the lack of solidarity and equality among communists themselves was too hard to bear'.

The ideological shifts were accompanied by organizational changes. In place of the ramshackle command centre that had sufficed during the civil war, there grew a large apparatus, staffed by a distinct group of 'responsible officials' and centralized by the CC secretariat. After the tenth congress, constraints were placed on discussion at regional, district and cell level. An elaborate system of administration and cadre distribution took shape. The revival in 1921–22 of the cells, many of which had almost collapsed, was followed by the creation in each of them of a bureau, often dominated by full-timers, that acted more as a coordinating centre for state and management instructions than as a political organization.

The third turning-point was the consolidation of the party elite's control over the party, in 1923–24. This elite had worked, during the first two years of industrial revival, to concentrate in its hands the levers with which to direct the state and the economy. Now it sought to turn the party into a more efficient mechanism of administration and control, which meant shedding many of the functions of a political organization that it had retained. Practices such as 'appointism' were used to strip away lower-level organizations' remaining capabilities for taking political decisions, and turn them into vehicles for unquestioning implementation of directives from above. The left opposition of late 1923 came together principally in response to these changes in the party. It was a diverse coalition of interests – the DCs, people concerned about the rapid erosion of party democracy, industrial administrators critical of bad economic decision-making, and others – that had little in common, beyond a conviction that the ruling 'triumvirate' (Stalin, Zinoviev and Kamenev) were doing things the wrong way. The methods used by the party leadership to settle the 1923 discussion showed how far it had come since 1921. It mobilized the party apparatus, press and sections of the GPU security police in a campaign of slander, frame-ups and vote-rigging unprecedented in its breadth and thoroughness. The workers recruited en masse to the party in 1924–25 thus entered an organization whose authoritarian and hierarchical nature was already well established. The function of the cells they joined was to implement directives from above.

It is striking that supporters of both leadership and opposition in 1923 spoke in terms of the party's 'bureaucratic deformation', or excesses of privilege, but never acknowledged that by defending exploitative social relationships the party could itself be pushing the revolution backward. The danger that the party would become the axis around which a new ruling formation would gather, on the basis of alienated labour and hierarchical social relations, was plain for the Workers Truth group and other isolated oppositionists to see, but inadmissible to Bolshevik discourse. And yet the elements that would make up the new Soviet ruling class were already being drawn around the party elite. With the benefit of hindsight it has been possible to trace the antagonistic relationships between workers and these various social groups, such as industrial managers and lower-level party officials, and the way that the party apparatus began to operate against workers' interests. The process of ruling-class formation would take many more years before a clearly defined social group dominated the Soviet Union by means of Stalinist dictatorship. But in the mid 1920s, even before such a class had taken shape, the exploitative relationships that characterized its rule were evolving.

The question that the Bolsheviks so stubbornly ruled out of their discussions – as to whether it made any sense at all to call their state a 'workers' state' – needs to be reconsidered by socialist theory. It has been demonstrated that this state oversaw the reimposition of alienated labour and hierarchical social relations. It carried out this function in the absence of a ruling class, and then played a central role in ushering that class into existence – a class which subsequently ruled not through its ownership of private property, but through its 'ownership' of the state. That state was antagonistic to the forces that could have best resisted the retreat of the revolution, i.e. the working class. There *was* a sense in which this state acted in workers' interests: in the 1920s it guaranteed them an improving standard of living, and access to education, health care and other material benefits. But it did this at a cost. Workers' collective political creativity was stifled. And when, in the late 1920s, the new ruling class required higher levels of exploitation, many of these benefits were reversed. Meanwhile the concept of a 'workers' state' took on a life of its own in socialist thinking. It pushed the irreconcilable opposition between socialism and the state, which had been at the centre of Marx's thinking, into the distant background. It enshrined the Soviet path, with all its defects, as a model for others to follow, and very often took the form of justifications for the Soviet state's actions.

Could things have been different? It has been argued throughout that in 1921 the Bolsheviks' room for manoeuvre widened. They chose to alter their economic policy in fundamental ways, but not their political methods. They chose to strengthen the party-state rather than revive soviet democracy, not because they were power-hungry, but on the basis of ideologically formed considerations. They believed that their vanguard party was fit to guide the 'workers' state' in a way that workers themselves were not. What if the Bolshevik leaders had encouraged wider soviet democracy, as the non-partyists wanted? What if they had legalized the other socialist parties, as Il'ia Vardin proposed? What if they had accepted the DCs' proposals for reinvigorating soviet democracy? In the long run, it seems unlikely that such choices would have greatly altered the course of Russian history. The rolling-back of socialist aspects of the revolution, and the advance of Stalinism, were conditioned by many powerful factors over which the Bolsheviks had no control: the failure of the workers' movements at the end of the First World War to produce revolutionary change outside Russia; the economic conditions in Russia that were unfavourable for socialist experiments; and the economic imperatives that drove Russia forward to industrialization. Substantially different outcomes would have been produced only if other causal factors, also, had been different. But perhaps different choices in 1921 would have made possible different types of resistance to the reimposition of exploitative class relations and the establishment of dictatorship.

The legacy of the Bolsheviks' actions was not limited to their impact on Soviet history, though. The effect on the political development of the workers' movement internationally was just as important. Authoritarian, vanguardist and statist ways of thinking and assumptions spread out from Moscow – not only directly through the Comintern and the Communist Parties, which for decades influenced radical workers' struggles, but also in many indirect ways. Moscow's instructions to Communist Parties might or might not be obeyed, but, far beyond the ranks of those parties, Bolshevik ideologies clouded, obstructed and diverted efforts to develop socialist ideas and strategies for working-class movements. Bolshevik ideology packed the powerful punch of association with the first successful workers' revolution: it was the great shadow of 1917, hanging over the twentieth century like the shadow of 1789 hung over the nineteenth century, that gave these ideologies force. Socialism was damaged not only by the choices the Bolsheviks made, but by their sincere insistence that those choices were the continuation of the revolution, and by the powerful influence of their ideology on subsequent movements of social liberation.

The dilemmas produced for socialists by the Russian revolution were already under discussion at the time. In 1920, before most of the events described in this book took place, Victor Serge wrote, with reference to the Soviet republic as it emerged from civil war:

> The pitiless logic of history seems hitherto to have left very little scope for the libertarian spirit in revolutions. That is because human freedom, which is the product of culture and of the raising of the level of consciousness, can not be established by violence; [and yet] precisely the revolution is necessary to win – by force of arms – from the old world ... the possibility of an evolution ... to spontaneous order, to the free association of free workers, to anarchy. So it is all the more important throughout all these struggles to preserve the *libertarian spirit*.[5]

Serge defined the task of 'libertarian communists' as being to 'recall by their criticisms, and by their actions, that at all costs the workers' state must be prevented from crystallizing'. A damaging legacy of the choices made by the Bolshevik leaders in 1920–23 was that, in Russia, public enunciation of such questions was stopped almost completely, and the crystallized 'workers' state' became a burdensome shibboleth for the workers' movement.

---

5 V. Serge, 'The Anarchists and the Experience of the Russian Revolution', in *Revolution in Danger: Writings from Russia 1919–20*, London: Redwords, 1997, pp. 81–120.

Appendix 1. Biographical information

Angarskii, Nikolai Semenovich (Klestov). 'Old Bolshevik' and Ignatov oppositionist

?–1941. Started political activity as a narodnik, when still at school. Excluded from gymnasium for distributing leaflets. 1899, became a Marxist. 1902, joined the *Iskra* group in Paris. Arrested and exiled many times. 1905, participated in the military revolutionary committee at Khar'kov. 1906–7, organized the first publication in Moscow of Marx's *Capital*. 1917, worked in the Bolsheviks' Moscow leadership and, in October, in the military revolutionary committee in Khamovniki district. 1918, having spoken against forming 'committees of the poor' in the countryside, was briefly expelled from the party. 1917–29, member of Moscow soviet executive; in the post-civil-war years 'attached' to the Kauchuk factory cell. From 1918, editor of the journal *Tvorchestvo*. 1920, joined Ignatov's group; was the only 'old Bolshevik' intellectual to participate actively in the opposition. Angarskii's published literary criticism included books on Mikhailovskii, Chekhov and Chernyshevskii. 1923, supported the party leadership against the opposition. 1940, arrested and found guilty of a list of lurid charges, e.g. having been since 1898 a tsarist provocateur. 1941, executed after appealing in vain to Stalin to intercede against his death sentence.

Berzina, Mariia Karlovna. Communist district official and Bauman oppositionist

1907, joined the Bolsheviks. Worked as a teacher before and after 1917. 1920, a party district official, in Khamovniki and then Bauman, where she became an opposition leader. 1921, ordered out of Bauman. 1923, worked as secretary of the heavy artillery workshops cell; joined the Workers Group. Her removal, together with that of Demidov, sparked worker protests. September 1923, faced with arrest and exile, corresponded with Nikolai Ezhov, then a district official in Petrograd and a personal friend.

Boguslavskii, Mikhail Solomonovich. Communist regional official and Democratic Centralist

1886–1937. A compositor by trade. 1905, joined the Jewish socialist Bund. 1917, worked on the soviet in Kremenchug, Ukraine. 1918–19, president of the city soviet and Bolshevik city committee in Voronezh; then served in the short-lived Ukrainian soviet government. 1920, briefly headed the transport political department Glavpolitput; transferred to Moscow, became a member of the All-Russian Central Council of Trade Unions (Vserossiiskii tsentral'nyi sovet profsoiuzov – VTsSPS) and president of the red printers' union, set up to break the Mensheviks' hold on the printers' union. Joined the Democratic Centralists (DCs) and signed their platform for the tenth congress. 1922–24, deputy chairman of Moscow soviet. From 1924, president of the Small Sovnarkom, an executive sub-committee of Sovnarkom. 1925–27, supported the united opposition; expelled from the party. 1928, head of the Siberian planning commission. 1930, quit the opposition with Preobrazhenskii and returned to Moscow. 1936–37, arrested and executed.

Chukhanov, Fedor Tikhonovich. Non-partyist at AMO car factory

A metalworker from the age of 12. Came to Moscow from Petrograd, where he worked at the Obukhov factory and in 1917 participated in defending the city against Kornilov. October 1919, started work at the AMO car factory. February 1920, elected to the factory committee and became its chairman, which he remained until 1922. 1920–21, metalworkers' union Moscow presidium member. A leader of the AMO non-party group. April 1921, elected to the Moscow soviet. 1924, joined the Communist party. 1924–32, worked in management of the AMO factory co-op, and back on the factory floor in 1925–26 and 1929–31.

Danishevskii, Karl Khrest'ianovich. 'Old Bolshevik' and communist industry official

1884–1938. 1900, joined the Latvian social-democratic party; from 1906, represented it on the Central Committee of the Russian Communist Party (CC) of the Russian Social Democratic Labour Party (RSDLP). Worked as a professional revolutionary; suffered imprisonment and exile. 1917, member of the Moscow committee (MC) of the Bolshevik party. 1918–19, member of revolutionary military council of the republic. 1921, supported Smilga at the tenth congress. 1921, secretary of the Bolshevik party Siberian bureau; then moved to work in economic management, in the timber industry trust. October 1921, expelled by the Khamovniki purge commission on corruption charges; readmitted in unclear circumstances. 1922, appointed head of the central timber industry authority. Further brushes with control commissions, in Bauman district in 1922 for 'negligence' towards party tasks, and with the Central Control Commission in 1924 for misuse of resources. 1923, signed the Platform of the 46. 1927, took charge of the bank of foreign trade. In the 1930s, worked on the central soviet executive of the USSR. 1938, arrested and executed.

Demidov, Vladimir Potapovich. Communist heavy artillery workshops cell official and Bauman oppositionist

1884–1937. 1907, joined Bolshevik party. 1916, worked politically with Tul'iakov among soldier-workers at the artillery workshops at Brest-Litovsk. 1917, moved with them back to the heavy artillery workshops in Bauman district. During the seizure of power in Moscow in October, served on the military revolutionary committee of the Lefortovo sub-district in Bauman, led a Red guard formed at the workshops and organized shelling of buildings held by counter-revolutionaries. During the civil war, was a divisional commander on the eastern front. 1920, back at the workshops, became a leader of the Bauman opposition group and chaired the 'conspiratorial' meeting which planned its takeover of the district party. 1922, twice called before the Moscow control commission to answer charges of alleged discrimination against party officials transferred into the district. May 1923 expelled from the party; joined the Workers Group. September 1923, arrested and exiled to the Solovetskie islands; at some point, having signed a confession of 'mistakes', was restored to party membership. 1935, arrested and tried, along with other former WO supporters; executed.

Enukidze, Trifon Teimuralovich. 'Old Bolshevik' and communist industry official

1877–1937. Born into a Georgian peasant family. Probably a brother or close relative of Avel' Enukidze, the CC member. A friend of Stalin and Sergei Alliluev, the father of Stalin's wife. Trained as a metalworker; worked in Siemens and other engineering factories. 1899, joined the social democrats' Tiflis organization. Did party work in Tiflis, Baku, Moscow, Petersburg and Vyborg; repeatedly arrested, jailed and exiled. From 1917, manager of the Central Executive Committee of soviets (CEC) print shops. From 1919, director of Goznak, where he had numerous conflicts with the party cell and workers' organizations. 1921, expelled by the Khamovniki district purge commission for alleged anti-worker behaviour, but somehow reinstated. 1927, censured by the CCC for 'bad relationships with workers' organizations'.

Gavrilin, Nikolai Alekseevich. Communist cell leader at AMO car factory

1886–1951. Born in Sharapovo, Moscow region. Went to Moscow to work aged 12; trained as a joiner. Joined the Bolsheviks before the revolution.

1917, together with Semen Smirnov, led the factory committee that took control of AMO. 1919, led a delegation of AMO workers that joined the defence of Petrograd from Iudenich. 1921, participated in repressing the Kronshtadt rising; elected to the AMO party cell bureau. Headed the list of Bolshevik candidates beaten by the non-partyists in the August 1921 elections. 1922, helped organize the non-partyists' electoral defeat. December 1923, voted off a list of candidates for the factory committee and lost his positions at the factory. In the late 1930s, suffered repression and was exiled to Tambov, Beloretsk and finally Serov.

Iakovleva, Varvara Nikolaevna. 'Old Bolshevik' and communist regional official

1885–1941. 1904, joined Bolsheviks. Before 1917, did underground party work in Moscow; repeatedly arrested and exiled. 1916, elected secretary of the Bolsheviks' Moscow district bureau. October 1917, participated in the Bolshevik CC meeting in Petrograd that planned the uprising, and reported to the Moscow party on it; an organizer of the Moscow rising. Worked at the highest level of the Bolshevik party; delegate to its seventh, tenth, eleventh, fourteenth, sixteenth and seventeenth congresses. 1918, signed Left Communist platform. 1918–21, served as a Cheka official, and on the party's Siberian bureau and supply commissariat presidium. 1920, sympathized with the DCs. December 1920 to April 1921, MC secretary. 1923, signed Platform of the 46. From 1922, deputy commissar of enlightenment; 1929, lost that post due to previous oppositional activity. 1937, arrested.

Ignatov, Efim Nikitovich. Communist regional and district official, and oppositionist

1890–1938. 1912, joined Bolshevik party. From 1917, served on executive and presidium of the Moscow soviet. January 1919, won support of Moscow city party conference for democratizing amendments to soviet constitution. 1919, won political control of Gorodskoi district organization. September 1920, elected by ninth party conference, with Ukhanov and Muranov, to a commission to investigate corruption in Kremlin. 1920–21, organized the 'group of active workers in the Moscow districts', which proposed documents on 'party construction' and the trade union discussion to the tenth congress, and coordinated opposition efforts that narrowly failed to win a majority at the Moscow regional party conference. Mid 1921, stopped opposition activity, and was sent to Vitebsk; served as chairman of Vitebsk soviet executive; wrote books and articles on history of soviets. From 1929, director of the CEC higher educational courses in soviet construction. 1938, arrested and executed.

Kamyshev, Petr Dement'evich. SR maximalist leader and bakers' union leader

1879–? 1905, took part in mutiny on the Battleship Potemkin; organized a general strike of Moscow bakers. 1907, joined the Socialist Revolutionaries (SRs) maximalist group; 1917, took an active part in the overthrow of the provisional government; 1918, took part in dissolution of the Constituent Assembly. From 1919, member of the SR maximalists' central council; remained in SR maximalist group until 1924. 1917–21, delegate to Moscow soviet. 1917–19, instructor-organizer in the Moscow Union of Bakers; 1919–21, its president, and member of the executive of the Union of Food Workers. 1920, arrested together with three other bakers' union leaders. From 1924, worked in food industry management. 1924, 1926 and 1927, arrested for alleged anti-soviet activity.

Kuranova, Ekaterina Iakovleva. Communist district official and Bauman oppositionist

1890–1980. 1901, started work aged 11 at a box factory in Rostov-on-Don. 1906, joined Bolshevik party; 1908, exiled for a year. 1917, served in the medical brigade of the Rostov-on-Don revolutionary committee. 1918–20, womens' section organizer in the Lefortovo sub-district in Bauman, Moscow. 1920–21, served on the Bauman party district executive when it was dominated by the opposition, and the Moscow soviet executive. January 1921, signed Ignatov's programme. 1922–25, studied at the *rabfak* of a surveying institute. From 1925, worked in administrative posts. From 1934, district soviet chairman in Krasnyi Kholm, Kalinin (Perm') region. 1937–46, worked in the USSR agricultural bank until retirement.

Kuznetsov. Non-partyist at AMO car factory

1892/93–? Born into a Moscow worker's family; started work aged 12, at an electro-mechanical factory where there was a strong SR organization. 1905, took part in the armed uprising in Moscow; 'it was more out of mischief than conviction; I was a kid', he recalled later. The attack by tsarist forces on workers at Presnia left a lasting impression on him. Became influenced by the Bolsheviks, especially Ivan Smirnov, with whom he became friends. 1908, joined the Bolsheviks, but during a brief prison spell met SR members and joined their terrorist campaign. 1909, injured during a terrorist operation, jailed again. 1910, moved to Petersburg; worked in the Putilov, Lessner and Siemens factories and did illegal trade union activity; arrested and exiled. 1914, returned to Moscow 'with more pronounced SR views'. 1916, started work at AMO when it opened; initiated an underground SR-Bolshevik alliance; both parties recruited rapidly. 'I was opposed to the war from the first day,' Kuznetsov recalled; together with the AMO Bolsheviks he tried to organize political strikes against it. In the 1920s, worked in the assembly shop. 1920–21, participated in the non-partyist group. 1932, was deputy head of the factory's technical training department.

Lass-Kozlova, Polina Ivanovna. Workers Truth group leader

1894–? Born into a Latvian peasant family. 1906–9 worked as a farm labourer. 1913, moved to Khar'kov, Ukraine, became an industrial worker, trained as a lathe operator, and joined the Bolshevik party. During the civil war, worked as a Red army propagandist in Voronezh. 1921, entered the *rabfak* of the Moscow Higher Technical School and was transferred into the Bauman district. 1922–24, was a leader of the Workers Truth group, expelled from the party and exiled. 1927, reinstated to party; worked in the CEC apparatus. 1928–32, studied at the Moscow aviation institute; 1932–35 worked as an engineer.

Lemberg, Gans. Communist district and cell official

1895–19? Born into a family of Estonian agricultural labourers. His father, a drunk, died when Gans was 2; his mother died when he was 7, and he was raised by an aunt. 1906, went to Petersburg with his brother and uncle; started work in the Erikson telephone factory and studied at an Estonian school. 1912, joined the Bolsheviks. In autobiographical notes, related that a love of travel and adventure had encouraged him to become a revolutionary. 1915, conscripted. 1917, when stationed in Odessa, fled to Georgia and linked up with the Bolsheviks there. 1920, worked in underground Bolshevik military organization against the Menshevik government of Georgia. 1921, travelled to Moscow and was assigned to Bauman district; was chairman of Bauman purge commission. 1923–24, 'attached' to the Ikar' (former Gnom i Ron) aircraft factory cell, a dissident bastion. Prided himself on his work against the oppositionists and boasted that he had curbed those at Ikar. 1925, appointed secretary of the sport organization Sportintern. 1926, volunteered to do underground party work in Manchuria. 1930, returned to Moscow to study.

Lysenkov, Afanasii Nikitich. Non-partyist at AMO car factory

Trained as a plane operator. 1918, sent to AMO from the labour exchange and started work in the instrument shop. During the civil war, Lysenkov sent his wife and children to live with her family in Pskov, while caring for his elderly mother. 1920–21, active in the non-party group at AMO, which, he later recalled, had resolved not to undermine discipline at the factory, and to express non-party workers' views in such a way as 'not to cut across government policy or do any harm to the factory's work'. August 1921, stood for the metalworkers' union district committee as part of a list that

248 Appendix 1

defeated the Bolshevik list. Subsequently moved from the shop floor for a year's work on the tariff-setting bureau; then returned to his trade, and worked at it until 1948.

Mel'nichanskii, Grigorii Natanovich. 'Old Bolshevik' and communist district official

1886–1937. Born in Kherson region into the family of a small entrepreneur. 1902, joined the Social Democrats; sided with the Bolshevik faction and did underground party work. Arrested and exiled abroad; from 1910 a member of the American Socialist Party. 1917, returned to Russia with Trotsky. July-December 1917, worked in Moscow metalworkers' union, and then as its secretary. October 1917, represented the unions on the military-revolutionary committee. 1918–24, chairman of MGSPS and member of presidium of VTsSPS; also member of the MC bureau, Moscow soviet presidium and all-Russian central soviet executive. 1925–30, candidate CC member; 1929–31, VSNKh presidium; 1931–34, Gosplan presidium; 1934–36 chairman of new inventions committee. 1937, arrested and executed.

Mikhailov, Sergei M. Non-partyist and Bogatyr factory committee chairman

A metalworker at Bogatyr rubber goods factory. 1917–18, served on the Menshevik-controlled factory committee. 1919, lost his position temporarily. 1920, returned, this time as factory committee chairman (until June 1921), and Moscow soviet delegate (until November 1921). Mikhailov was a consistent non-partyist in a politically divided workforce: he was respected by the Bolsheviks and for that reason was once elected to negotiate with the Cheka to secure the release of arrested workers. April 1921, elected as spokesman of the non-partyist fraction on the Moscow soviet. During the Bolshevik offensive against the non-partyists, colourful but empty allegations against Mikhailov – that he was suspiciously well-off (the legal sale of a small quantity of oats, and purchase of a motor scooter, were mentioned), and that he was a Menshevik (which he was not) – were published in *Pravda*. Thereafter his name disappears from records.

Miurat (or Lezhava-Miurat), Valerian Isaakovich. Communist factory director

1881–1938. Born in Didi-Dzhikhansi in Georgia. Educated at home. Miurat claimed to have joined the Social Democrats in 1902; was described as 'one of the military communists', and treated as such during his spell in the rubber goods industry (1921–23), as manager of the Bogatyr factory and, from 1922, as head of the rubber goods trust. 1923, appointed to a VSNKh commission on workers' conditions and management board of the state bank; then dismissed from all posts during 1923 'party crisis'. January 1924, following a scandal over his relationship with the party, the CCC published a denial that he had been a member, claiming that he had applied for membership three times and been rejected. (Archival records are ambiguous.) Unproven allegations that before 1917 Miurat was a tsarist provocateur, based in the northern Urals, circulated in Moscow and were published by the Menshevik newspaper. Miurat may have been related to A.M. Lezhava (1870–1937), Gosplan chairman in the late 1920s. Worked in Moscow in the 1920s and 1930s, latterly as a port authority inspector. 1937 arrested. 1938 executed.

Paniushkin, Vasilii Lukich. Communist and leader of Workers and Peasants Socialist Party

1888–1960. Born into a poor peasant family in Kochety, Orel region; received a primary education and trained with his father as a metalworker. Became a seafarer in the Baltic fleet. 1907, joined Bolshevik party. 1917, participated in the revolution in Petrograd. Was among the 'Bolshevik cutthroats' who killed seven students found to have tsarist officers' epaulettes, according to a Menshevik memoirist. 1918, Cheka collegium member and special military commissar. 1920, a leader of the Bauman opposition. 1921, left the Bolshevik party and formed the Workers and Peasants Socialist Party. June 1921, arrested; sentenced to two years' hard labour by the Supreme Tribunal of the CEC. December 1921, freed and, after a meeting with Lenin, restored to party membership. From 1922, worked in the VSNKh; 1925–26, in the Orel party committee; 1927–30 in the Soviet trade delegation in Berlin. 1931–37 worked in industrial administration and collective farm management.

Samsonov, Timofei Petrovich. Anarchist turned Chekist

1885–1956. Born in Bessarabia (now Moldova), into the family of an agricultural labourer. Educated at primary school. 1904–19, member of the anarcho-communist party. 1906–7, led a peasant band that organized expropriations and raids against landowners and distributed anarchist literature in western Ukraine. 1907, arrested. 1914, escaped from Siberian exile to the Far East and then England. 1915–17, worked as a docker at Liverpool. March 1917, arrested for making an anti-war speech and deported to Russia. October 1917, member of the Chel'iabinsk soviet. 1918, worked in soviet military counter-intelligence. 1919, joined the Bolsheviks. From May 1919, head of the special department and member of the Moscow Cheka collegium. From September 1920, head of the Cheka secret department. April 1921, helped to organize the infamous beating of political prisoners in Butyrka jail. 1922, represented the Cheka in organizing campaigns to seize church valuables and on the SR trial. 1923, appointed to management post on the Belorussian-Baltic railway. 1924–39, worked in senior administrative posts in the party, VSNKh, Comintern and film industry.

Shteinberg, Isaak Zakharovich. Left SR leader and Moscow soviet delegate

1888–1957. Born at Dvinsk (now Daugavpils), Latvia. Studied at Kazan', Heidelberg (Germany) and Moscow universities. 1917, led the left SR organization in Ufa, Bashkortostan. December 1917–March 1918, commissar of justice in the socialist coalition government; resigned in protest at the Brest treaty. 1918, opposed the left SR rising. 1919, imprisoned for three months and then put under house arrest. April 1921, elected to the Moscow soviet, representing bakers. 1921, asked permission to go abroad and was told he would not be allowed to return; remained in Moscow, often addressing workplace mass meetings. January 1922, re-elected to the Moscow soviet. October 1922, voted off the soviet at the urging of Bolsheviks in the bakers' union. The left SR organization decided that Shteinberg should not participate in the forthcoming tenth soviet congress, reasoning that the Bolsheviks would use his presence there 'as a cover for their crimes'. Late 1922, emigrated. 1933 moved to London; during the Second World War, moved to New York. Wrote several books on the Russian revolution, including a biography of Maria Spiridonova, and studied Jewish history.

Shutskever, Fania Samoilova. Workers Truth group leader

1898–? Born into a family of Jewish leather-workers in Vilnius, Lithuania. Graduated from the gymnasium at Vil'no and the Khar'kov polytechnical institute, Ukraine. December 1916, joined the Bolsheviks in Khar'kov, where she is likely to have met Lass-Kozlova. 1918, a nurse with the Red army; imprisoned by the Czech Whites at Samara; escaped and worked with the underground Bolshevik resistance against the Komuch government. From 1921, taught history at the Sverdlov communist university and studied at Moscow Higher Technical School. 1921–22, joined the Workers Truth group. 1923, expelled from the party. October 1923–November 1924, imprisoned in Moscow, Iaroslavl and Cheliabinsk. 1925–26, worked for the party history commission. December 1926, rejoined the party after signing a confession of 'mistakes'; worked in educational and agit-prop posts. 1932–36 studied aviation. From 1936 worked in the scientific-experimental institute of the Red air forces. 1938, arrested.

Smirnov, Semen Potapovich. Communist cell leader at AMO car factory

1878–1958. Born into a family of poor peasants in Kaluga region. Educated to primary level, plus self-education. 1885, started work aged 11 and trained as a joiner. 1901, signed on at the Mytishchi engineering works; sacked for striking successively from Mytishchi, the rolling stock factory at Tver' and the railway workshops at Velikie Lugi. 1905, joined the social democrats; arrested and exiled. 1916, signed on at AMO, organized the first Bolshevik group there. 1917, together with Gavrilin, led the factory committee that took over AMO. 1917–21, member of the factory committee. 1919, together with S.I. Moiseev, organized a volunteer battalion of workers from Rogozhsko-Simonvskii district; participated in the defence of Petrograd from Iudenich. 1921, supported the Ignatov opposition and signed its programme. May 1921, appointed deputy director of AMO, in the face of worker opposition and accusations of corruption. January 1922, elected to Rogozhsko-Simonovskii district soviet, on a Bolshevik slate that defeated the non-partyists. 1922, returned to work in the joinery shop. 1922–38 worked in various trade union and economic management posts away from AMO. 1946, took ill health retirement.

Tarasov, Georgii Fedorovich. Communist metalworkers' union leader and Workers Oppositionist

1884–1938. Born in Podzolovo village in Moscow region; educated to primary level. 1904, joined the Bolsheviks. 1917, member of Dinamo factory committee. 1918, elected to Dinamo management board. 1920–21, chairman of metalworkers' union Moscow organization. 1920–22, supported the WO. 1922, participated in opposition regroupment efforts. September 1922, brought before the Moscow party control commission along with three others after a binge drinking incident at the metalworkers' union's Moscow headquarters during working hours, which resulted in one worker's death from alcohol poisoning; narrowly avoided expulsion 'in view of the great services he has rendered to the revolution and the party' but barred from responsible posts for two years. In the 1930s, deputy head of the council of co-operatives for the disabled. 1938, arrested and executed.

Tul'iakov, Nikita Sergeevich. Communist regional official

1887–1973. Born in Chertanovka, Simbirsk region, into a poor peasant family. Did not go to school; started work as an agricultural labourer aged 9. 1908–14, worked as a joiner. 1914, conscripted. 1915, sent from the front to the heavy artillery workshops in Moscow. March 1917, joined Bolsheviks; was chairman of the workshops' factory committee and delegate to the conference of military organizations. 1917–25, represented the workshops on the Moscow soviet, repeatedly elected to its executive. 1918–19, took part in suppressing the left SR uprising; was military-political inspector of border regiments on the southern front and then in Moscow, and organizer of special detachments. December 1920, returned to Bauman district; worked as full-time party organizer; sympathized with the Bauman opposition.

1921–25, chairman of Bauman district soviet and member of party MC. Late 1924, made an emotional speech at the heavy artillery workshops cell against the vilification of Trotsky. When asked to switch his membership from that cell, to which he was 'attached', to the cell for soviet *sluzhashchie*, offered to resign from the party all together (this was refused). From 1925, worked in soviet administration. 1936, arrested and sentenced to three years' hard labour for 'counter-revolutionary activity'. 1939, released, without permission to live in Moscow. 1939–46 worked at a railway workers' union rest home/hospital. 1941, during evacuation to Saratov, jumped into the water to save people during a river accident and contracted pleurisy. 1952, ill-health retirement. 1954, readmitted to the party.

Zelenskii, Isaak Abramovich. 'Old Bolshevik' and communist party Moscow regional official

1890–1937. Born into a Jewish tailor's family in Saratov. Educated at home and to primary level; started work in a hat-making workshop. 1906, joined Bolsheviks; worked in the underground revolutionary movement; spent an aggregate of eight years in prison. January 1917, escaped from exile in Irkutsk and reached Moscow. 1917, member of Moscow soviet presidium. 1918–20, worked in Moscow supply department, first on collegium and then as its head; and briefly as MC secretary and on the party CC. 1920, worked in Siberia on supply. April 1921 to late 1924, secretary of party MC and member of the Moscow soviet presidium. March 1921, candidate CC member. 1922, elected a full CC member. From 1924, secretary of the central Asian bureau of the party CC. From 1934, president of the Tsentrosoiuz retail trade organization. 1936, arrested. 1938, executed.

Sources: These sketches, and biographical information in footnotes, are sourced from archives, including TsAOPIM f8654 (personal files), RGASPI f124 (Society of Old Bolsheviks), 'history of factories' project material at TsAGM and the Krylov card index at RGASPI; N.I. Rodionova (ed.), *Soratniki: biografii aktivnikh uchastnikov revoliutsionnogo dvizheniia v Moskve i Moskovskoi oblasti*, Moscow: Moskovskii rabochii, 1985, and other published material. For details see S. Pirani, *The Changing Political Relationship Between Moscow Workers and the Bolsheviks, 1920–24* (PhD diss., University of Essex, 2006), pp. 364–432.

Appendix 2. Districts and workplaces

Districts

In the post-civil-war period, the basic administrative units of the Moscow region (*guberniia*) were the urban districts (*raiony*) and rural districts (*uezdy*). Until June 1920, the city of Moscow comprised a separate administrative unit, but was merged into the region during a national reorganization.

The seven urban districts were: Bauman, Gorodskoi, Khamovniki, Krasnopresnia, Rogozhsko-Simonovskii, Sokol'niki and Zamoskvorech'e. In 1922 the Gorodskoi district, which covered central Moscow, was dissolved and its territory divided between the other six districts.

The 17 rural districts were: Bogorodskoe, Bronnitsy, Vereisk, Volokolamsk, Dmitrov, Zvenigorod, Klimovsk, Kolomna, Narofominsk, Orekhov-Zuevo, Podol'sk, Pavlovskii-Posad, Ruza, Serpukhov, Sergiev, Moskovskii and Mozhaisk.

Workplaces

These workplaces are mentioned frequently.

AMO (i.e. Moscow Automobile Company or Avtomobil'noe Moskovskoe Obshchestvo)

1916, founded in the Rogozhsko-Simonovskii district, by the Riabushinskii brothers, prominent industrialists. During the war, given state support with a view to developing the Russian car industry. 1918, nationalized. During the civil war, produced parts for railway rolling stock. 1921, expansion spurred by a government decision to prioritize car making, and the arrival of a group of communist engineers from America. The workforce was cut in late 1921, but by 1923 had risen to 2000. 1924, produced the 'first Soviet automobiles', trucks and buses based on Fiat designs. Renamed in 1924 after the Italian communist Pietro Ferrero, then after Stalin, and finally after Vasilii Likhachev, head of the Moscow Council of the Economy in 1921–23. Retained the acronym of the Likhachev factory (zavod imeni Likhacheva, ZiL).

Bogatyr/Krasnyi Bogatyr

1887, founded at Bogorodskoe settlement, in the Sokol'niki district. 1910, named Bogatyr. Before the First World War it was Russia's largest rubber goods factory, employing 2180 workers. 1915, the workforce mushroomed to 4100 and the factory added waterproofs, tyres and gas masks to its product range. 1918, nationalized. 1919, production stopped, mainly due to shortages of imported rubber. 1921, restarted. The factory's first Marxist circle was organized in 1895, and Mensheviks, SRs, non-partyists and Bolsheviks were active at the factory during the revolution. 1922, renamed Krasnyi Bogatyr. Continued to produce throughout the Soviet period and up to the present.

Bromlei/Krasnyi proletarii

1869, established as a machine builder in Zamoskvorech'e, by Eduard and Fedor (Friedrich) Bromley, Anglo-German brothers who took Russian citizenship. It was their second Moscow factory; the first had opened in 1857. During the war and civil war, it employed 2–3000 workers and worked on military orders. 1918, nationalized. 1920, slowed to a standstill. 1921, restarted, producing diesel engines. The workforce was a mix of second- and third-generation Muscovites and fresh migrants, including many from Mozhaisk, just outside Moscow. 1922, renamed Krasnyi proletarii. The Ravsak engineering factory now occupies the site.

Dinamo

1897, opened as an electrical engineering works in the Simonovskii (later Rogozhsko-Simonovskii) district. The factory had a strong Bolshevik organization, formed in 1903, which during the civil war contributed a large contingent to the district's Red volunteer force. 1918, nationalized. 1919, closed for several months due to raw material shortages. 1921, began producing equipment for new power stations. During the 1930s expanded to become one of the USSR's largest electrical engineering plants. Still in production today.

Gnom i Ron/Ikar

1912, opened in Bauman district producing French-designed engines; a pioneer of aeroplane engine and propeller manufacture in Russia. 1919, renamed Gnom i Ron. 1922, renamed Ikar. 1927, merged with another aeroplane engine maker, factory no. 4 (which was named Sal'mson until 1920, state aircraft factory no. 6 until 1923, and Amstro until 1924). 1928, the joint enterprise was renamed the M. Frunze factory no. 24. The factory's direct successor, the Saliut aerospace plant at prospekt Budennogo, continues to produce aeroplane engines.

Goznak

Russian state printers have been named Goznak (a contraction of *gosudarstvennyie znaky*, or state-issued notes) since the seventeenth century. 1919, the finance commissariat moved production of bank notes from Petersburg, closed smaller state print shops in Perm' and Penza, and concentrated production at the large works in Moscow's Khamovniki district. In the post-civil-war period the Goznak workforce was 5–7000, mostly women. June 1921, Goznak acquired the premises of the former Brokar' perfume factory in ulitsa Pavla Andreeva, in Zamoskvorech'e, and moved almost all its operations there, where they remain to this day.

Kauchuk

1897, established in Riga by the Freizinger brothers, German industrialists. 1915, evacuated to Malaia Tsaritsynskaia (now Malaia Pirogovskaia) ulitsa in the Khamovniki district in Moscow. Much of the workforce moved too, and although some returned during the civil war, the factory was 'bilingual' in the early 1920s. Both Bolsheviks and Mensheviks were active in the factory in Riga, and again in Moscow in 1917. It became the city's second-largest rubber goods producer after Bogatyr. 1919, the workforce shrank to about 500, but by 1923, with production returning to pre-war levels, it rose again to more than 1000. 1923, renamed Krasnyi Kauchuk.

The heavy artillery workshops (Mastiazhart)

Known by the contraction Mastiazhart (*masterskye tiazheloi artillerii*). 1916, established at Lefortovo in the Bauman district, building and repairing heavy and field guns and other military equipment. 1917, 3000 soldiers evacuated from artillery shops at the western fortresses were posted at the workshops. The Bolshevik cell grew tenfold to 300 after the 'July days', and played an active part in the seizure of power in Moscow in October. During the civil war the workforce was reduced to around 1000, but kept busy by a large volume of military orders. 1941, then named Mastiazhart im. Timoshenko, partly evacuated to Serov. 1942, returned to Moscow. After the war, integrated into the aerospace industry and renamed Vympel. Remains at the same site, ulitsa Veliaminovskaia 34, today.

Trekhgornaia manufaktura

1799, founded in the Presnia (later Krasnopresnia) district, near Moscow city centre; became a vertically integrated textile combine, whose main product was printed cotton fabrics. Trade unions and workers' circles were established in the factory in the late nineteenth century, and in 1905, 16 workers were executed in its courtyard for participating in the Moscow uprising. By

1917 the workforce had grown to more than 6000, of which about half were women. During the civil war, production stopped completely, and restarted in September 1920 on one-eighth of the looms. By 1923 production was approaching pre-war levels and the workforce had again swelled to 6000. The factory flourished through the soviet period and by the 1980s was producing 200 million metres of fabric per year. Named after its founder, Prokhorov, in the nineteenth century, and after Feliks Dzerzhinskii in 1937, it kept only the name Trekhgornaia after the Second World War. 1992, privatized.

Sources: *Kratkii obzor deiatel'nost' Moskovskogo soveta (Vyp.1. 1920)*, Moscow, 1921; A.M. Sinitsyn et al. (eds), *Istoriia rabochykh Moskvy 1917–1945 gg.*, Moscow: 'Nauka', 1983; P.A Voronin et al., *Moskva. Entsiklopediia*, Moscow: Sovetskaia entsiklopediia, 1980; F. Sviatenko, *Zavod 'AMO'*, Moscow: Gos. izd., 1929; A.P. Churiaev, N.V. Adfel'dt and D.A. Baevskii (eds), *Istoriia Moskovskogo avtozavoda im. I.A. Likhacheva*, Moscow: izd. 'Mysl'', 1966; M.Ia. Proletarskii, *Zavod 'Krasnyi bogatyr' (1887–1932)*, Moscow: gos. khim-tekh izd., 1933; A.M. Panfilova, *Istoriia zavoda 'Krasny Bogatyr'*, Moscow: izd. Moskovskogo universiteta, 1958; A.I. Efanov, et al., *Istoriia zavoda 'Dinamo'. Kn. 2. 'Dinamo' v gody stroitel'stva sotsializma*, Moscow: Profizdat, 1964; G.M. Davydov and E.Ia. Knop, *Zavod na Usachevke*, Moscow: Moskovskii rabochii, 1980; Baumanskii komitet VKP(b), *Ocherki po istorii revoliutsionnogo dvizheniia i bol'shevistskoi organizatsii v Baumanskom raione*, Moscow, 1927; I.I. Vernidub, *Na peredovoi linii tyla*, Moscow: TsNIINTIKPK, 1993; P. Podliashuk, *Raduga trekh. gor. Iz biografii odnogo rabochego kollektiva*, Moscow: Moskovskii rabochii, 1967; S. Lapitskaia, *Byt' rabochikh trekhgornoi manufaktury*, Moscow: OGIZ, 1935; archival sources; company websites. Full list in S. Pirani, *The Changing Political Relationship Between Moscow Workers and the Bolsheviks, 1920–24* (PhD diss., University of Essex, 2006), pp. 435–41.

Appendix 3. Wages and currency rates

The steady increase in wages during the post-civil-war period is illustrated in the graph. It is based on calculations by Soviet statisticians, using the 'goods ruble'. There were obvious difficulties in quantifying wages in 1920–21 when they were mainly paid in kind, and further problems in 1922–23, when calculating the 'goods ruble' rate against current forms of payment was an inexact science. The figures are the best that the economists and statisticians could come up with. The scope for error is evident from the difference between the City of Moscow averages worked out by statisticians from the labour commissariat and Gosplan.

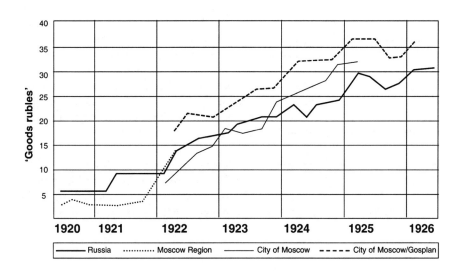

Industrial workers' average wages, 1920–26.

Sources. Russia: *Trud* 15 December 1923; Rashin, *Zarabotnaia plata za vosstanovitel'nyi period khoziaistva SSSR 1922/23–1926/27 gg.*, Moscow: Gosizdat, 1928, p. 6. 1920 and 1921–22 figures were given as averages for the year. Moscow region: Markuzon, *Polozhenie truda v Moskovskoi gubernii v pervom polovine 1922g.*, Moscow: Glavlit, 1922. 1921 figures are estimates for workers on 'reserved' rations. City of Moscow: *Statisticheskii ezhegodnik g. Moskvy i Moskovskoi gubernii. Vyp. 2. Statisticheskie dannye po g. Moskvy za 1914–1925 gg.*, Moscow, 1925, p. 208. City of Moscow (Gosplan): Rashin, op. cit., p. 6. These figures were calculated by statisticians at Gosplan rather than in the labour commissariat.

Note: soviet currencies

During the civil war, notes were printed without restraint, and the volume of money in circulation roughly trebled in 1919 and increased fivefold in 1920. In August 1921 the principle of a state budget was re-established. In November 1921 it was decided to issue a new currency, to replace the civil-war soviet rubles (*sovznaky*) at the rate of 10,000:1. This rate moved to 60,000:1 and, by March 1922, to 200,000:1. The result was a price index currency, which became known as the 'goods ruble'. In March 1922, the finance commissariat, anxious to stabilize the currency, introduced the gold ruble. But other institutions were not prepared to abandon the 'goods ruble' that effectively tied wages to rising prices. Gosplan devised an index of its own, based on the 'goods ruble', that was used in wage agreements. In November 1922 the finance commissariat introduced a stable currency, the chervonets, equal to 10 gold rubles and backed by gold and foreign currency reserves, and proposed to replace *sovznaky* with it. But the government hesitated, fearing the consequences for living standards. The crisis of summer 1923, during which there was excessive issuance of *sovznaky*, brought the arguments to a head. The position of the chervonets strengthened, and by November 1923 it accounted for four-fifths of money in circulation. In 1924 a currency reform was completed, and the *sovznaky* were withdrawn from circulation.

Sources: E.H. Carr, *The Bolshevik Revolution*, London: Macmillan, 1978, vol. II, pp. 257–68, 347 and 350, and *The Interregnum*, London: Macmillan, 1978, pp. 28–29, 69–70, 131–33; M. Dewar, *Labour Policy in the USSR, 1917–1928*, London: Royal Institute of International Affairs, 1956, pp. 94–95.

Appendix 4. Party membership

At no time before the Lenin enrolment of 1924 did the Bolsheviks consider recruitment of members to be an end in itself. On the contrary, once the party had taken power, its leaders worried constantly about the influx of careerists and hangers-on. The party opened its doors wide to recruits only in October 1919, when defeat by the Whites – and the accompanying danger for communists – was a real possibility, and recruits were sent straight to the front. In 1921–22, the only particularly welcome recruits were factory workers, as membership in the factories was at its nadir, and most workers who joined during the civil war had taken up military or administrative posts, or left. But recruitment efforts met with little success. Moreover, under pressure from Lenin, the eleventh congress tightened recruitment criteria (see Chapter 5, pp. 136–7). National membership fell continuously between 1921 and 1924, while the Moscow organization bucked the national trend, expanding from mid 1922, mainly thanks to an influx into the capital of communists from the provinces and from the Red army. The twelfth congress in 1923 loosened the criteria again (see Chapter 9, p. 226), and the Lenin enrolment of 1924 in practice ended most restrictions on recruitment and established the new practice of recruitment en masse.

Records of membership for 1920–21 are chaotic. The statistics improved as a result of the 1921 purge, the 1922 re-registration and the growth of the party apparatus. The best figures available are shown in a table on the next page:

National and Moscow Communist Party membership

	National membership	Moscow regional membership	City of Moscow membership
Mar 1919	211,000 + 70,000 ca.	22,000	17,000
Nov 1919 (after recrtmnt drive)	430,000*	32,600 + 4818 ca.	n/a
Sep 1920	n/a	27,641 + 9557 ca.	23,069 + 2900 ca.
Mar 1921	700,000 +100,000 ca.	48,557**	n/a
Jun 1921	658,938#	40,284 + 10,552 ca.	32,475 + 7886 ca.
Feb 1922 (after rereg'n)	410,430 + 117,924 ca.	31,505 + 4234 ca.	25,225 + 3237 ca.
Jan 1 1923	372,900 + 112,600 ca.	37,328 + 4543 ca.	30,904 + 3549 ca.
Jan 1 1924	328,520 + 117,569 ca.	41,537 + 11,584 ca.	35,244 + 9319 ca.
Jan 1 1925	401,481 + 339,636 ca.##	58,018 + 32,116 ca.	48,246 + 22,241 ca.

ca. = candidate members
*Figure for January 1920. **Figure for April 1921. #Excludes several regions that did not submit figures. ## In addition to this figure there were 57,000 members 'in the military-political organs' registered separately.

Sources. For national membership, *Izvestiia TsK RKP(b)* 15, 1920; S. Ivanovich, *VKP: desiat' let kommunisticheskoi monopolii*, Paris: bib. demokraticheskogo sotsializma, 1928, pp. 31–32, 34 and 76; T.H. Rigby, *Communist Party Membership in the USSR 1917–1967*, Princeton: Princeton University Press, 1968, p. 85; *Vserossiiskaia perepis' chlenov RKP 1922 goda*, Moscow: izd. otdel TsK RKP, 1922; TsK RKP(b) (statisticheskii otdel), *Partiia v tsifrovom osveshchenii: materialy po statistike lichnogo sostava partii*, Moscow/Leningrad: Gosizdat, 1925, p. 5. For Moscow membership, MK RKP(b), *Moskovskaia organizatsiia RKP(b) v tsifrakh. K XIV gubpartkonferentsii. Vyp. 2-oi.*, Moscow, 1925; *Otchet o rabote MK RKP(b) za 1922–23 g.*, Moscow: MK RKP(b), 1923, p. 47; 'Otdelnye dannye kharakterizuiushchii lichny sostav Moskovskoi organizatsii', TsAOPIM, 3/4/5/20; *Moskovskaia gorodskaia i Moskovskaya oblastnaia organizatsiia KPSS v tsifrakh*, Moscow: Moskovskii rabochii, 1972, p. 27; Bukov, K.I., Korshunova, Z.P. and Rodionova N.I. (eds), *Moskovskaia gorodskaia organizatsiia KPSS 1917–1988: tsifry, dokumenty, materialy*, Moscow: Moskovskii rabochii, 1989.

Appendix 5. Communists' occupations

The way in which worker communists were pushed into administrative posts, and the resulting predominance of administrators and soldiers in the party over workers 'at the bench', has been discussed throughout. Statistics compiled by the Bolsheviks do not illustrate this tendency well. The party regularly published information on members' social backgrounds, which included as 'workers' bureaucrats and soldiers who had not worked in a factory for years, if ever (see Chapter 5, pp. 133–4). Information was also collected regularly on the types of cells to which communists belonged. But I have found the results of only two surveys of the party membership by occupation. The first was taken in September 1920, when the reassignment of civil war recruits to peacetime duties was only just getting underway. The second was taken in 1925, when the tiny contingents of communists that stayed in the factories between the civil war and 1923 had been drowned in a sea of new worker recruits. Bearing these weaknesses in mind, it is still worth reproducing the results. See table shown on next page.

Occupation of party members

September 1920			January 1925	Mem.	Cand.
Industry total		8071	Workers performing physical labour	22,826	19,563
Including:					
Responsible officials	204				
Control and accounting staff	322				
Junior sluzhashchie	29				
Workers	7516				
Transport total		1706			
including:					
Responsible officials	229				
Control and accounting staff	230				
Workers and jun. sluzhashchie	1247				
Artisans and small manufacturing (*remesl. i kustarnye prom*)		516	Artisans and small manufacturing	13	13
Agriculture		1009	Agricultural labourers	52	65
			Peasants 'at the plough'	158	250
Red army total		6441	Military	4329	2122
including:					
Political leadership	133				
Senior party officials	104				
Other party officials	1334				
Admin. and medical staff	1090				
Cadets (*kursanty*)	1288				
Troops (combatant units)	2119				
Troops (non-combatant units)	373				
Soviet institutions total		9684	Officials of party, trade union and other organizations	19,491	5467
including:					
Responsible officials	3348				
Control and accounting staff	3638				
Workers and jun. *sluzhashchie*	2698				
Party organizers		1930			
Trade unions total		1042			
including:					
Responsible officials	410				
Factory committee members	596				
Control and accounting staff	35				
Junior *sluzhashchie*	1		Other	60	110
Houseworkers		18			
			Students	9278	3235
Not working		293	Unemployed	239	271
No information given		5782	No information given	1212	665
Total		**35,226**	**Total**	**57,658**	**31,761**

Sources: Sekretariat TsK RKP(b), *Materialy po statistike lichnogo sostava RKP*, Moscow, 1921, pp. 42–47; MK RKP(b), *Moskovskaia organizatsiia RKP(b) v tsifrakh. K XIV gubpartkonferentsii. Vyp. 2-oi.*, Moscow, 1925, p. 12.

Information on the types of cells to which communists belonged in 1921–23 shows a part of the problem, i.e. the preponderance of members in military and administrative cells, rather than industrial ones. It should be borne in mind that, as discussed in Chapter 5, most members in industrial and transport cells were working in administrative posts. Some of them worked not in industrial administration but in government offices and were 'attached' to industrial cells.

Type of cells to which Moscow communists belonged (full members only)

	Oct 1921	Jan 1923	Sep 1923
Industrial	4000	9410	10,245
Transport	2000	2157	2736
Military	6500	7045	3732*
Administrative	15,000	9413	13,005*
Rural/peasant	n/a	1177	1076
Student	n/a	8126	7998
Total	**31,000**	**37,328**	**38,883**

* In mid-1923, party members working in the Red army command, of whom there were at least 2000, were moved from the 'military' to 'administrative' category.

Sources: *Vos'maia gubernaskaia konferentsiia Moskovskoi organizatsii RKP (23-25 marta 1922 g.)*, Moscow, MK RKP, 1922, p. 39; *Otchet o rabote MK RKP(b) za 1922-23 g.*, Moscow: MK RKP(b), 1923, pp. 50-51; TsAOPIM, 3/4/5/210.

Bibliography

Archives

GARF (Gosudarstvennyi arkhiv Rossiiskoi federatsii, State Archive of the Russian Federation)
f393 (commissariat of internal affairs); f5469 (metalworkers' union); f7952 (history of factories project)
Narodny Arkhiv (the Popular Archive)
f389 (Zotov)
RGASPI (Rossiisky gosudarstvennyi arkhiv sotsial'noi i politicheskoi istorii, Russian State Archive of Social and Political History)
f2 (Lenin); f5 (Lenin's secretariat); f17 (CC); f46 (tenth party conference); f70 (Istpart); f95 (Bolshevik fraction in VTsSPS); f124 (All-Russian Society of Old Bolsheviks); f323 (Kamenev); f324 (Zinoviev); f564 (left SRs and maximalists); the Krylov card index
TsAGM (Tsentralnyi arkhiv goroda Moskvy, Central Archive of the city of Moscow)
Workplace archives: f100 (Dinamo); f337 (Krasnyi Bogatyr); f415 (ZiL (formerly AMO)); f425 (Trekhgornaia cotton manufacture combine); f2626 (Goznak)
TsAOPIM (Tsentral'nyi arkhiv obshchestvenno-politicheskoi istorii Moskvy, Central Archive of the Social-Political History of Moscow (the former Moscow party archive))
Party organization archives: f3 (Moscow region); f63 (Bauman district); f69 (Krasnopresnia district); f80 (Proletarskii (formerly Rogozhsko-Simonovskii) district); f88 (Frunzenskii (formerly Khamovnicheskii) district); f412 (Krasnyi proletarii cell); f432 (Dinamo cell); f433 (ZiL (formerly AMO) cell); f459 (Sverdlov University cell); f465 (Vimpel' (formerly heavy artillery workshops) cell); f467 (factory no. 24 'Frunze' (formerly Gnom i Ron) cell); f475 (Kauchuk cell); f634 (Moscow Komsomol); f685 (commission for checking the party, 1921–22); f1099 (Goznak cell); f1300 (Krasny Bogatyr cell); f2867 (Moscow control commission); f8654 (personal archives)
TsGAMO (Tsentralnyi gosudarstvennyi arkhiv Moskovskoi oblasti, Central State Archive of the Moscow Region)
f19 (militia); f66 (Moscow soviet); f180 (MGSPS); f186 (metalworkers' union); f201 (food workers' union); f609 (chemical workers' union)
TsMAMLS (Tsentral'nyi moskovskii arkhiv-musei lichnykh sobranii, Central Moscow Archive/Museum of Personal Collections)
f16 (Boguslavskii); f72 (Kamyshev); f74 (Kaspirovich); f87 (Kubiak); f176 and f177 (material on victims of repression)

Newspapers and periodicals

Biulleten' oppozitsii, 1929–30
Bor'ba klassov, 1931, 1935
Ekonomicheskaia zhizn', 1920–24
Izvestiia, 1920–24
Izvestiia MK RKP(b), 1922–23
Izvestiia Tsk RKP(b), 1920–24
Izvestiia TsK KPSS, 1989–91
Kommunisticheskii trud, 1919–21
Krasnaia nov', 1921–22, 1929
Kuznitsa, 1921
Pravda, 1919–24
Predpriatie, 1923–24
Rabochaia Moskva, 1922–23
Sotsialisticheskii vestnik, 1923–24
Trud, 1922–23

Primary sources: books, articles and documents

Bondarev, N., 'Riadovoi', in *Vagranka. Sbornik literaturno-khudozhestvennogo kruzhka pri Rogozhsko-Simonovskogo raikoma RKP(b)*, Moscow: Moskovskii rabochii, 1921, pp. 61–71.
Briskin, M., 'Perekhod k individualnomu chlenstvu', *Vestnik truda* 1, 1923: 3–14.
Bukharin, N. and Preobrazhenskii, E., *The ABC of Communism: a Popular Explanation of the Program of the Communist Party of Russia*, London: Communist Party of Great Britain, 1922.
Dan, F., *Dva goda skitanii 1919–1921*, Berlin: sklad izd. Russische Bucherzentrale Obrazowanje, 1922.
Dekrety sovetskoi vlasti, Moscow: Gos. izd. polit. literatury, 1986.
Desiatyi s"ezd RKP(b): stenograficheskii otchet, Moscow: Gos. izd. polit. literatury, 1963.
Deviataia konferentsiia RKP(b), sentiabr' 1920 g: protokoly, Moscow: izd-vo politicheskoi literatury, 1972.
Deviataia konferentsiia Moskovskoi organizatsii RKP, Moscow: MK RKP, 1922.
Deviatyi s"ezd RKP(b): stenograficheskii otchet, Moscow: Gos. izd. polit. literatury, 1960.
Doklady na VIII-m Vserossiiskom s'ezde sovetov, Moscow: MK RKP(b), 1921.
Dvenadtsatyi s"ezd RKP(b): stenograficheskii otchet, Moscow: izd-vo politicheskoi literatury, 1968.
Fabrichno-zavodskaia promyshlennost' g. Moskvy i Moskovskoi gubernii, 1917–1927 gg., Moscow, 1928.
Gurevich, A., 'Dobrovol'noe chlenstvo v soiuzakh', *Vestnik truda* 2, 1922: 38–40.
Iaroslavskii, E., *'Rabochaia oppozitsiia', 'Rabochaia gruppa', 'Rabochaia pravda'*, Moscow: Molodaia gvardiia, 1927.
Iurenev, I. [pseudonym for Konstantin Iurenev], *Nashi nestroenie*, Kursk: 'Tsentropechat", 1920.
K otchetu Moskovskoi gubernskoi konferentsii RKP (25–28 iuniia 1921g.), Moscow, 1921.
Kratkii obzor deiatel'nost' Moskovskogo soveta (Vyp.1. 1920), Moscow, 1921.

VK, 'Godovoi opyt professional'noi raboty v novykh uslovyakh', *Vestnik truda* 2–3, 1923: 3–24
Karev, N., 'O gruppe "Rabochaia pravda"', *Bol'shevik* nos. 7–8, 1924: 27–43.
Kerzhentsev, P.M., *K novoi kulture*, Petersburg, 1921.
Klement'ev, V.F., *V bol'shevistskoe Moskve (1918–1920)*, Moscow: Russkii put', 1998.
Krasnaia Moskva, Moscow, 1920.
Kreml' za reshetkoi (podpol'naia Rossiia), Berlin: izd. 'Skify', 1922.
Krylenko, N.V., 'Proizvodstvennaia demokratiia v tsifrakh i faktakh', in *Na Strazhe (biulleten' osobmezhkoma i ekonomicheskogo upravleniia)*, 1–2, 1921: 22–35.
——, *Za Piat' Let 1918–1922 gg. Obvinitel'nye rechi*, Moscow: Gosizdat, 1923.
Larin, Iu., *Intelligentsiia i sovety: khoziaistvo, burzhuaziia, revoliutsiia, gosapparat*, Moscow: Gosizdat, 1924.
Lenin, V.I., *Polnoe sobranie sochinenii (izd. 5-ogo)*, Moscow, Gospolitizdat, 1958–65.
——, 'Ia proshu zapisyvat' men'she: eto ne dolzhno popadat' v pechat'', *Istoricheskii arkhiv* 1, 1992: 12–30.
Leninskyi prizyv v Moskovskoi organizatsii: sbornik, Moscow: MK RKP(b), 1925.
Libedinskii, Iu., *Nedelia: Kommissary: Povesti*, Moscow: Voennoe izd., 1968.
Litvinov, I.I., '"Ptitsegontsvo nadoelo do smerti". Iz dnevnika I.I. Litvinova', in *Neizvestnaia Rossiia* IV, 1993: 81–139.
Machajski, J. (V. Volskii), *Umstvennyi rabochii*, New York: Mezhdunarodnoe Literaturnoe Sodruzhestvo, 1968.
Markuzon, F.D., 'Polozhenie truda v g. Moskve v 1921 godu', *Voprosy truda* 2, 1922: 136–81.
——, *Polozhenie truda v Moskovskoi gubernii v pervom polovine 1922 g.*, Moscow: Glavlit, 1922.
—— (ed.), *Polozhenie truda v Moskovskoi gubernii v 1922–1923 gg.: sbornik materialov biuro statistika truda*, Moscow: MGSPS, 1923.
Mel'nichanskii, G., *Moskovskie professional'nye soiuzy*, Moscow: Glavlit, 1923.
MGSPS, *Otchet o deiatel'nosti MGSPS, gubotdelov i uprofbiuro (mai-avgust 1921)*, Moscow: MGSPS, 1921.
——, *Otchet o deiatel'nosti Moskovskogo gubprofsoveta 1921–22*, Moscow, 1922.
——, *Rezoliutsii i postanovleniia IV-ogo Moskovskogo gubernskogo s"ezda profsoiuzov (5–8 sent. 1922)*, Moscow, 1922.
——, *Piatyi gubernskii s"ezd moskovskikh profsoiuzov. Itogi, rezoliutsiia, postanovleniia*, Moscow: Mosgublit, 1923.
MK RKP(b), *K otchetu Moskovskoi gubernskoi konferentsii RKP (25–28 iiunia 1921) i III s"ezde sovetov*, Moscow: Gos. izdatel'stvo, 1921.
——, *Novye zadachy professionalnykh soiuzov*, Moscow: MK RKP(b), 1922.
——, *Moskovskaia organizatsiia RKP(b) v tsifrakh. K XIV gubpartkonferentsii. Vyp. 2-oi.*, Moscow, 1925.
Moskovskaia gubernskaia konferentsiia profsoiuzov, 14–15 sent. 1921, Moscow: MGSPS, 1921.
Odinnadtsataia Moskgubpartkonferentsiia: stenograficheskii otchet, Moscow: MK RKP(b), 1924.
Odinnadtsatyi s"ezd RKP(b): stenograficheskii otchet, Moscow: Gos. izd. politicheskoi literatury, 1961.
Otchet o rabote MK RKP(b) za 1922–23 g., Moscow: MK RKP(b), 1923.
Otchet o rabote Moskovskoi obshchepartiinoi konferentsii, Moscow, 1920.

Otchet Rogozhsko-Simonovskogo raiona s 3-go maia po 15-e noiabria 1922 g., Moscow, 1922.
Otchet sed'moi Moskovskoi gubpartkonferentsii RKP 29–31 Oktiabria 1921 g., Moscow, 1921.
Perepis' sluzhashchikh sovetskikh uchrezhdenii g. Moskvy 1922 g., Moscow, 1922.
Piatyi s"ezd komsomol'tsev (rechi t.t. Trotskogo, Bukharina), Viatka: izd. gubkom RKSM, 1922.
Pisateli ob iskusstve i o sebe: sbornik statei. no.1., Moscow/Leningrad: 'Krug', 1924.
Pokrovskii, M.N., *Sem' let proletarskoi diktatury*, Moscow: Gos. izdatel'stvo, 1924.
Radek, K., 'Ia zaiavliaiu', *Istochnik* 2, 1998: 42–45.
RKP(b). *Uchet i raspredeleniia rabotnikov (k soveshchaniiu sekretarei i zaveduiushchikh orgotdelami gubkomov)*, Moscow: izd. otdelenie TsK RKP, 1923.
Sapronov, T.V., *Stat'i i doklady*, Moscow, 1920.
Sarab'ianov, V.N., *Metallopromyshlennost' Rossii*, Moscow: Gosizdatel'stvo, 1921.
Sed'moi vserossiiskii s"ezd sovetov: stenograficheskii otchet, Moscow, 1920.
Sekretariat TsK RKP(b), *Materialy po statistike lichnogo sostava RKP*, Moscow, 1921.
Shirokaia konferentsiia fab-zavkomov g. Moskvy 29 okt. 1921, Moscow, 1921.
Smilga, I., *Na povorote: zametki k X-mu s"ezdu partii*, Moscow: Gos. izdatel'stvo, 1921.
Sokol'nicheskaia raionnaia konferentsiia RKP(b). 30–31 maia 1923 goda. Otchet., Moscow, 1923.
Sol'ts, A., 'Communist Ethics', in Rosenberg, W.G. (ed.), *Bolshevik Visions: First Phase of the Cultural Revolution in Soviet Russia*. Part 1, pp. 30–42, Michigan: University of Michigan Press, 1990.
Sosnovskii, L., *Dela i Liudi*, kn. 1, Moscow, 1924.
Statisticheskii otdel Moskovskogo soveta, *Statisticheskii atlas gor. Moskvy i Moskovskoi gub. Vyp. 1. Naselenie.*, Moscow, 1924.
——, *Statisticheskii ezhegodnik g. Moskvy i Moskovskoi gubernii. Vyp. 2. Statisticheskie dannye po g. Moskvy za 1914–1925 gg.*, Moscow, 1925.
——, *Statisticheskii atlas gor. Moskvy i Moskovskoi gub. Vyp. 3. Promyshlennost' i torgovlia*, Moscow, 1925.
Tomskii, M., 'Pervye rezul'taty novoi soiuznoi politiki', *Vestnik truda* 8–9, 1922: 3–11.
Trinadtsataia konferentsiia RKP(b): biulleten', Moscow, 1924.
Trinadtsatyi s"ezd RKP(b), mai 1924 goda: stenograficheskii otchet, Moscow: Gos. izd-vo politicheskoi literatury, 1963.
TsK RKP(b), *Itogi partiinoi raboty za god 1922–23*, Moscow: Krasnaia nov', 1923.
TsK RKP(b) (statisticheskii otdel), *Partiia v tsifrovom osveshchenii: materialy po statistike lichnogo sostava partii*, Moscow/Leningrad: Gosizdat, 1925.
Vlasov, A., 'My vse vidim i vse znaem: krik dushi krasnogo komandira', *Istochnik* 1, 1998: 85–87.
Vos'maia gubernaskaia konferentsiia Moskovskoi organizatsii RKP (23–25 marta 1922 g.), Moscow: MK RKP, 1922.
Vos'moi vserossiiskii s"ezd RKP(b): mart' 1919 goda: protokoly, Moscow: Gos. izd. polit. literatury, 1959.
Vovsi, M. (ed.), *Polozhenie truda sluzhashchikh, ob"ediniaemykh profsoiuzom administrativno-sovetskikh, obshchestvennykh i torgovykh rabotnikov v 1923/24 g. (Statisticheskii sbornik.) Vyp 3-i.*, Moscow: TsK VSASOTR, 1924.
——, *Trud sluzhashchikh v SSSR: statistiko-ekonomicheskii obzor*, Moscow: izd. 'Voprosy truda', 1926.

268   Bibliography

Vserossiiskaia konferentsiia RKP (bol'shevikov) 4–7 avgusta 1922 g., Moscow: izd. MK RKP(b), 1922.

Vserossiiskaia perepis' chlenov RKP 1922 goda, Moscow: izd. otdel TsK RKP, 1922.

Zelenskii, I., 'K ocherednym zadacham partiinoi raboty' in *Izvestiia MK RKP(b)* 3, 1922: 5–13.

Document collections

Alidin, V.I., Velidov, A.S., Polikarenko, I.E. and Ushakov, V.G. (eds), *MChK: iz istorii Moskovskoi chrezvychainoy kommissii: sbornik dokumentov (1918–1921 gg)*, Moscow: Moskovskii rabochii, 1978.

Antonova, N.S. and Drozdova, N.V. (eds), *Neizvestnyi Bogdanov v 3-kh knigakh*, Moscow: AIRO, 1995.

Bernshtam, M.S., *Narodnoe soprotivlenie kommunizmu v Rossii: nezavisimoe rabochee dvizhenie v 1918 godu*, Paris: YMCA Press, 1981.

Diskussiia o profsoiuzakh: materialy i dokumenty 1920–21 gg., Moscow/Leningrad, 1927.

Documents of the 1923 Opposition, London: New Park Publications, 1975.

Felshtinskii, Iu. (ed.), *Arkhiv Trotskogo: kommunisticheskaia oppozitsiia v SSSR 1923–1927* (4 vols.) Moscow: Terra, 1990.

Krasil'nikov, S.A., Morozov, K.N. and Chubykin, I.V. (eds), *Sudebnyi protsess nad sotsialistami-revoliutsionerami (iiun'-avgust 1922 g.). Sbornik dokumentov*, Moscow: Rosspen, 2002.

Kvashonkin, A.V., et al. (eds), *Bol'shevistskoe rukovodstvo. Perepiska. 1912–1927*, Moscow: Rosspen, 1996.

Meijer, J. (ed.), *The Trotsky Papers 1917–1922* (2 vols.), The Hague: Mouton, 1964.

Naumov, V.P. and Kaskovskii, A.A., *Kronshtadt, 1921*, Moscow: Mezhdunarodnii fond Demokratiia, 1997.

Pavlov, D. (ed.), *Soiuz Eserov-Maksimalistov. Dokumenty, publitsistika. 1906–1924 gg.*, Moscow: Rosspen, 2002.

Pokrovskii, N.N. and Petrov, S.G. (eds), *Arkhiv Kremlia: Politbiuro i tserkov' 1922–1925 gg.*, Moscow: Rosspen, 1997.

Popov, K.A. (eds), *Diskussiia 1923 goda: materialy i dokumenty*, Moscow: Gosizdat, 1927.

Shcherbina, V.R., et al. (eds), *V.I. Lenin i A.V. Lunacharskii. Perepiska, doklady, dokumenty*, Moscow: Nauka, 1971.

Sevost'ianov, G.N., et al. (eds), *'Sovershenno sekretno': Lubianka-Stalinu o polozhenii v strane (1922–1934 gg.)*, Moscow: Institut rossiiskoi istorii RAN, 2001: vol. 1 (1922–23)

Vilkova, V.P., et al., *RKP(b): vnutripartiinaia bor'ba v dvadtsatye gody. Dokumenty i materialy 1923 g.*, Moscow: Rosspen, 2004.

Vinogradov, V.K., Kozlov, V.P., Antifeeva, M.A. and Kudriavtsev, I.I. (eds), *Kronshtadtskaia tragediia 1921 goda: dokumenty v dvukh knigakh*, Moscow: Rosspen, 1999.

Secondary sources

'1921 god. Miasnikov, Lenin i diskussiia', *Svobodnaia mysl* 1, 1989: 62–75.

Abramovich, I., *Kniga vospominanii*, HTTP. <http://lib.ru/MEMUARY/ABRAMOWICH/> (accessed 2 May 2007).

Aleshchenko, N.M., *Moskovskii sovet v 1917–1941 gg.*, Moscow: Nauka, 1976.
Allen, B.C., *Worker, Trade Unionist, Revolutionary: a Political Biography of Alexander Shlyapnikov 1905–1922* (PhD. diss, Indiana University, 2001).
——, 'The Evolution of Communist Party Control Over the Trade Unions', *Revolutionary Russia*, 15: 2, 2002: 72–105.
——, 'Alexander Shliapnikov and the Letter of the Twenty Two: A Critical Episode in the Russian Communist Party's Internal Debate over Criticism and Party Discipline', paper presented at the mid-Atlantic Slavic conference, March 2003.
Anweiler, O., *The Soviets: the Russian Workers', Peasants and Soldiers Councils, 1905–1921*, New York: Pantheon Books, 1974.
Argenbright, R., 'Marking NEP's Slippery Path: the Krasnoshchekov Show Trial', *Russian Review* 61, 2002: 249–75.
Ashin, P., 'Wage Policy in the Transition to NEP', *Russian Review* 47, 1988: 293–313.
Astrakhan, Kh.M., *Bol'sheviki i ikh politicheskie protivniki v 1917-m godu*, Leningrad: Lenizdat, 1973.
Aves, J., *Workers Against Lenin*, London: Tauris, 1996.
Avrich, P., *Kronstadt 1921*, Princeton: Princeton University Press, 1970.
——, 'Bolshevik Opposition to Lenin: G. Miasnikov and the Workers Group', *Russian Review* 43, 1984: 1–29.
Azrael, J.R., *Managerial Power and Soviet Politics*, Cambridge, MA: Harvard University Press, 1966.
Baker, M., 'Establishing Soviet Power in the Countryside: Kharkov Province 1918–21' (paper presented at the AAASS convention, Boston, December 2004).
Bailes, K.E., *Technology and Society Under Lenin and Stalin: Origins of the Soviet Technical Intelligentsia 1917–1941*, Princeton: Princeton University Press, 1978.
Baumanskii komitet VKP(b), *Ocherki po istorii revoliutsionnogo dvizheniia i bol'shevistskoi organizatsii v Baumanskom raione*, Moscow, 1927.
Bazhanov, B., *Vospominaniia byvshego sekretaria Stalina*, Moscow: SP Sofinta, 1990.
Beissinger, M.R., *Scientific Management, Socialist Discipline and Soviet Power*, London: Tauris, 1988.
Bennett, G., *Yundong: Mass Campaigns in Chinese Communist Leadership*, Berkeley: Centre for Chinese Studies, 1976.
Berkman, A., *The Bolshevik Myth*, London: Pluto, 1989.
Bonnell, V.E., *Roots of Rebellion: Workers' Politics and Organizations in St. Petersburg and Moscow, 1900–1914*, Berkeley: University of California Press, 1983.
——, (ed.), *The Russian Worker: Life and Labor Under the Tsarist Regime*, Berkeley: University of California Press, 1983.
Bordiugov, G.A. (ed.), 'Kak zhili v Kremle v 1920 godu: materialy Kremlevskoi kommissii TsK RKP(b)', in *Neizvestnaia Rossiia* II, 1992: 261–71.
Borisova, L.V., *Voennyi kommunizm: nasilie kak element khoziaistvennogo mekhanizma*, Moscow: Moskovskii obshchestvennyi nauchnyi fond, 2001.
——, 'NEP v zerkale pokazatel'nykh protsessov po vziatochnichestvu i khoziaistvennym prestupleniiam', *Otechestvennaia istoriia* 1, 2006: 84–97.
Borrero, M., *Hungry Moscow: Scarcity and Urban Society in the Russian Civil War, 1917–1921*, New York: Peter Lang, 2003.
Brovkin, V.N., *The Mensheviks After October: Socialist Opposition and the Rise of the Bolshevik Dictatorship*, London: Cornell University Press, 1987.
——, *Behind the Front Lines of the Civil War: Political Parties and Social Movements in Russia 1918–1922*, Princeton: Princeton University Press, 1994.

Bibliography

Brower, D.R., '"The City in Danger": the Civil War and the Russian Urban Population', in D.P. Koenker, Rosenberg, W.G. and Suny, R.G. (eds), *Party, State and Society in the Russian Civil War: Explorations in Social History*, Bloomington: Indiana University Press, 1989, pp. 58–80.

Bukharin, N., *Ekonomika perekhodnogo perioda*, in Bukharin, N., *Izbrannye proizvedeniia*, Moscow: Ekonomika, 1990, pp. 81–239.

Bukov, K.I., Korshunova, Z.P. and Rodionova, N.I. (eds), *Moskovskaia gorodskaia organizatsiia KPSS 1917–1988: tsifry, dokumenty, materialy*, Moscow: Moskovskii rabochii, 1989.

Bunyan, J., *The Origin of Forced Labor in the Soviet State 1917–1921: Documents and Materials*, Baltimore: Johns Hopkins Press, 1967.

Burawoy, M., *The Politics of Production: Factory Regimes Under Capitalism and Socialism*, London: Verso, 1985.

Buzgalin, A.V., Churakov, D.O. and Shul'tse, P. (eds), *Rabochii klass v protsessakh modernizatsii Rossii: istoricheskii opyt*, Moscow: 'Ekonomicheskaia demokratiia', 2001.

Carr, E.H., *The Bolshevik Revolution 1917–1923* (3 vols.), London: Macmillan, 1978.

——, *The Interregnum 1923–1924*, London: Macmillan, 1978.

——, *Socialism in One Country, 1924–1926* (4 vols.), London: Macmillan, 1978.

——, *The Russian Revolution from Lenin to Stalin, 1917–1929*, Basingstoke: Palgrave, 1979.

Castoriadis, C., 'The Role of Bolshevik Ideology in the Birth of the Bureaucracy' (1964) <http://www.geocities.com/cordobakaf/castbolsh.html> (accessed 2 May 2007)

——, 'On the Content of Socialism', in Curtis, D.A. (ed. and trans.), *The Castoriadis Reader*, Oxford: Blackwell, 1997, pp. 40–105.

——, 'The Social Regime in Russia', in Curtis, D.A. (ed. and trans.), *The Castoriadis Reader* (Oxford: Blackwell, 1997), pp. 218–38.

Cell, C.P., *Revolution at Work: Mobilization Campaigns in China*, New York: Academic Press, 1977.

Chase, W.J., *Workers, Society and the Soviet State: Labour and Life in Moscow 1918–1929*, Urbana: University of Illinois Press, 1990.

Cherniaev, V.Iu. and Makarov, E.I. (eds), *Piterskie rabochie i 'Diktatura Proletariata'. Oktiabr' 1917–1929: ekonomicheskie konflikti i politichestkii protest*, St Petersburg: Russko-baltiiskii informatsionnyi tsentr BLITs, 2000.

Chernyshevsky, N., *What Is To Be Done? Tales About New People*, London: Virago, 1982.

Churiaev, A.P., Adfel'dt, N.V. and Baevskii, D.A. (eds), *Istoriia Moskovskogo avtozavoda im. I.A. Likhacheva*, Moscow: izd. 'Mysl'', 1966.

Clements, B.E., *Bolshevik Women*, Cambridge: Cambridge University Press, 1987.

Colton, T.J., *Moscow: Governing the Socialist Metropolis*, Cambridge, MA: Harvard University Press, 1995.

Cook, L., 'Brezhnev's "Social Contract" and Gorbachev's Reforms', *Soviet Studies* 44: 1, 1992: 37–56.

D'Agostino, A., *Marxism and the Russian Anarchists*, San Francisco: Germinal Press, 1977.

Daly, J.W., '"Storming the Last Citadel": The Bolshevik Assault on the Church, 1922', in Brovkin, V. (ed.), *The Bolsheviks in Russian Society: the Revolution and Civil Wars*, New Haven: Yale University Press, 1997.

Daniels, R.V., *The Conscience of the Revolution: Communist Opposition in Soviet Russia*, Cambridge, MA: Harvard University Press, 1960.
David-Fox, M., *Revolution of the Mind: Higher Learning Among the Bolsheviks 1918–1929*, Ithaca: Cornell University Press, 1997.
Davydov, G.M. and E.Ia. Knop, *Zavod na Usachevke*, Moscow: Moskovskii rabochii, 1980.
Day, R.B., *Leon Trotsky and the Politics of Economic Isolation*, Cambridge: Cambridge University Press, 1973.
Debo, R.K., *Survival and Consolidation: the Foreign Policy of Soviet Russia, 1918–1921*, Montreal: McGill-Queen's University Press, 1992.
Deiateli soiuza sovetskikh sotsialisticheskikh respublik i oktiabr'skoi revoliutsii: avtobiografii i biografii, Moscow: Granat, 1925–26.
Deutscher, I., *The Prophet Armed. Trotsky 1879–1921*, London: Oxford University Press, 1970.
——, *The Prophet Unarmed. Trotsky 1921–1929*, London: Oxford University Press, 1970.
Dewar, M., *Labour Policy in the USSR, 1917–1928*, London: Royal Institute of International Affairs, 1956.
Draper, H., 'The Two Souls of Socialism', *New Politics* 5: 1, Winter 1966: 57–84.
——, *Karl Marx's Theory of Revolution. Volume II: The Politics of Social Classes*, New York: Monthly Review Press, 1978.
Dune, E., *Notes of a Red Guard* (ed. and trans. D.P. Koenker and S.A. Smith), Urbana: Illinois University Press, 1993.
Dvinov, B., *Moskovskii Sovet Rabochykh Deputatov, 1917–1922: vospominaniia*, New York: Inter-university project on the history of the Menshevik movement, 1961.
——, *Ot legal'nosti k podpol'iu 1921–22*, Stanford: Hoover Institution, 1968.
Easter, G., *Reconstructing the State: Personal Networks and Elite Identity in Soviet Russia*, Cambridge: Cambridge University Press, 2000.
Edmondson, C., 'The Politics of Hunger: the Soviet Response to Famine, 1921', *Soviet Studies* 29: 4, 1977: 506–18.
Efanov, A.I., et al., *Istoriia zavoda 'Dinamo'. Kn. 2. 'Dinamo' v gody stroitel'stva sotsializma*, Moscow: Profizdat, 1964.
Engelstein, L., *Moscow 1905: Working Class Organization and Political Conflict*, Stanford: Stanford University Press, 1982.
Farber, S., *Before Stalinism: the Rise and Fall of Soviet Democracy*, Oxford: Polity Press, 1990.
Farbman, M., *Bolshevism in Retreat*, London: Collins, 1923.
Fiddick, T.C., *Russia's Retreat from Poland, 1920: from Permanent Revolution to Peaceful Coexistence*, London: Macmillan, 1990.
Figes, O., *A People's Tragedy: the Russian Revolution 1891–1924*, London: Jonathan Cape, 1996.
—— and Kolonitskii, B., *Interpreting the Russian Revolution: the Language and Symbols of 1917*, New Haven: Yale University Press, 1999.
Filtzer, D., *Soviet Workers and Stalinist Industrialization: the Formation of Modern Soviet Production Relations 1928–1941*, London: Pluto, 1986.
——, Goldman, W., Kessler, G. and Pirani, S. (eds), *A Dream Deferred: New Studies in Russian and Soviet Labour History*, Amsterdam: Peter Lang, forthcoming.
Firsov, S., 'Workers and the Orthodox Church in Early Twentieth-Century Russia', in Melancon, M. and Pate, A.K. (eds), *New Labor History: Worker Identity and Experience in Russia, 1840–1918*, Bloomington: Slavica, 2002, pp. 65–76.

Fitzpatrick, S., *The Commissariat of the Enlightenment: Soviet Organization of Education and the Arts Under Lunacharsky 1917–1921*, Cambridge: Cambridge University Press, 1970.
——, 'The Soft Line on Culture and Its Enemies: Soviet Cultural Policy, 1922–27', *Slavic Review* 33: 2, 1974: 267–87.
——, *Education and Social Mobility in the Soviet Union 1921–1934*, Cambridge: Cambridge University Press, 1979.
——, *The Russian Revolution 1917–1932*, Oxford: Oxford University Press, 1982.
——, 'The Civil War as Formative Experience', in Gleason, A., Kenez, P. and Stites, R. (eds), *Bolshevik Culture: Experiment and Order in the Russian Revolution*, Bloomington: Indiana University Press, 1985, pp. 58–76.
——, 'The Bolsheviks' Dilemma: Class, Culture, and Politics in Early Soviet Years', *Slavic Review* 47, 1988: 599–613.
——, 'The Problem of Class Identity', in Fitzpatrick, S., Rabinowitch, A. and Stites, R. (eds), *Russia in the Era of NEP: Explorations in Soviet Society and Culture*, Bloomington: Indiana University Press, 1991, pp. 12–33.
——, 'Politics as Practice: Thoughts on a New Soviet Political History', *Kritika* (new series) 5: 1 (2004), pp. 27–51.
——, Rabinowitch, A. and Stites, R. (eds), *Russia in the Era of NEP: Explorations in Soviet Society and Culture*, Bloomington: Indiana University Press, 1991.
Genkina, E.B., *Gosudarstvennaia deiatelnost' V.I. Lenina 1921–1923 gg*, Moscow: 'Nauka', 1969.
Getzler, I., *Kronstadt 1917–1921: The Fate of a Soviet Democracy*, Cambridge: Cambridge University Press, 1983.
——, 'Soviets as Agents of Democratization', in Frankel, E.R., Frankel, J. and Knei-Paz, B. (eds.), *Revolution in Russia: Reassessments of 1917*, Cambridge: Cambridge University Press, 1992, pp. 17–33.
Gill, G., *The Origins of the Stalinist Political System*, Cambridge: Cambridge University Press, 1990.
Gimpel'son, E.G., *Formirovanie sovetskoi politicheskoi sistemy 1917–1923 gg.*, Moscow: 'Nauka', 1995.
——, *Sovetskie upravlentsy 1917–1920 gg.*, Moscow: Institut istorii RAN, 1998.
——, *Novaia ekonomicheskaia politika i politicheskaia sistema 20-e gody*, Moscow: Institut istorii RAN, 2000.
Glebkin, V.V., *Ritual v sovetskom kul'ture*, Moscow: Inus-K, 1998.
Goldman, W., *Women, the State and Revolution: Soviet Family Policy and Social Life, 1917–1936*, Cambridge: Cambridge University Press, 1993.
——, *Women at the Gates: Gender and Industry in Stalin's Russia*, Cambridge: Cambridge University Press, 2002.
——, 'Stalinist Terror and Democracy: the 1937 Union Campaign', *American Historical Review* 110: 5, 2005: 1427–53.
Gorinov, M., 'Moskva v 20-kh godakh', *Otechestvennaia istoriia* 5, 1996: 3–17.
Gorsuch, A.E., *Youth in Revolutionary Russia: Enthusiasts, Bohemians, Delinquents*, Bloomington: Indiana University Press, 2000.
Grigorov, G., *Povoroty sud'by i proizvol: vospominaniia 1905–1927*, Moscow: Chastnyi arkhiv, 2005.
Grunt, A.Ya, *Moskva 1917-y. Revoliutsiia i konttrevoliutsiia*, Moscow: 'Nauka', 1976.
Gusev, A.V., 'Naissance de l'Opposition de Gauche', *Cahiers Leon Trotsky* 54, 1994: 5–39.

Halfin, I., *From Darkness to Light: Class, Consciousness and Salvation in Revolutionary Russia*, Pittsburgh: University of Pittsburgh Press, 2000.
—— (ed.), *Language and Revolution: Making Modern Political Identities*, London: Cass, 2002.
——, *Terror in My Soul: Communist Autobiographies on Trial*, Cambridge, MA: Harvard University Press, 2003.
Hatch, J., 'The Politics of Mass Culture: Workers, Communists and Proletkult in the Development of Workers' Clubs', *Russian History/Histoire Russe* 13: 2–3, 1986: 119–48.
——, 'Working-Class Politics in Moscow During the Early NEP: Mensheviks and Workers' Organizations, 1921–22', *Soviet Studies* 34: 4, 1987: 556–74.
——, 'The Lenin Levy and the Social Origins of Stalinism. Workers and the CP in Moscow 1921–28', *Slavic Review* 48: 4, 1989: 558–78.
——, 'Labour Conflict in Moscow 1921–25', in Fitzpatrick, S., Rabinowitch, A. and Stites, R. (eds), *Russia in the Era of NEP: Explorations in Soviet Society and Culture*, Bloomington: Indiana University Press, 1991, pp. 58–71.
Helgesen, M.M., *The Origins of the Party-State Monolith in Soviet Russia: Relations Between the Soviets and Party Committees in the Central Provinces, October 1917 – March 1921* (PhD diss., State University of New York at Stony Brook, 1980).
Herrlinger, P., 'Orthodoxy and the Experience of Factory Life in St Petersburg 1881–1905', in Melancon, M. and Pate, A.K. (eds), *New Labor History: Worker Identity and Experience in Russia, 1840–1918*, Bloomington: Slavica, 2002, pp. 35–64.
Hoffman, D.L., *Peasant Metropolis: social identities in Moscow, 1929–1941*, London: Cornell University Press, 1994.
Holmes, L., *For The Revolution Redeemed: The Workers Opposition in the Bolshevik Party 1919–1921*, Carl Beck Papers no. 802, Pittsburgh: University of Pittsburgh, 1990.
Holquist, P., 'Information is the Alpha and Omega of Our Work', *Journal of Modern History* 69, 1997: 415–50.
Husband, W.B., *'Godless Communists': Atheism and Society in Soviet Russia 1917–1937*, DeKalb: Northern Illinois University Press, 2000.
Iarov, S.V., *Gorozhanin kak politik: revoliutsiia, voennyi kommunizm i NEP glazami petrogradtsev*, St Petersburg: 'Dmitrii Bulagin', 1999.
International Communist Current, *The Russian Communist Left, 1918–30*, London: ICC, 2005.
Istoriia Moskvy (7 vols.), Moscow: izd. Akademii Nauka SSSR, 1952–59.
Ivanovich, S., *VKP: desiat' let kommunisticheskoi monopolii*, Paris: bib. demokraticheskogo sotsializma, 1928.
Izmozik, V.S., *Glaza i ushi rezhima: gosudarstvennyi politicheskii kontrol' za naseleniem Sovetskoi Rossii v 1918–1928 gg.*, St Petersburg: izd. Sankt-Peterburgskogo universiteta ekonomiki i finansov, 1995.
Jansen, M., *A Show Trial Under Lenin*, The Hague: Martinus Nijhoff, 1982.
Johnson, C. (ed.), *Change in Communist Systems*, Stanford: Stanford University Press, 1970.
Johnson, R.E., *Peasant and Proletarian: the Working Class of Moscow in the Late Nineteenth Century*, Leicester: Leicester University Press, 1979.
Kabo, E., *Ocherki rabochego byta: opyt monograficheskogo issledovaniia domashnego rabochego byta*, Moscow: VTsSPS, 1928.
Katznelson, I., 'Working Class Formation: Constructing Cases and Comparisons', in Katznelson, I. and Zolberg, I. (eds), *Working-Class Formation: Nineteenth-Century*

Patterns in Western Europe and the United States, Princeton: Princeton University Press, 1986, pp. 3–41.

Kenez, P., *The Birth of the Propaganda State: Soviet Methods of Mass Mobilization 1917–1929*, Cambridge: Cambridge University Press, 1985.

Khromov, S.S., et al. (eds), *Grazhdanskaia voina i voennaia interventsiia v SSSR: entsiklopediia*, Moscow: Sovetskaia entsiklopediia, 1983.

Kir'ianov, Iu.I., Rosenberg, W. and Sakharov, A.N. (eds), *Trudoviie konflikti v Sovetskoi Rossii 1918–1929gg.*, Moscow: URSS, 1998.

Koenker, D.P., *Moscow Workers and the 1917 Revolution*, Princeton: Princeton University Press, 1981.

——, 'Urbanization and Deurbanization in the Russian Revolution and Civil War', *Journal of Modern History* 57, 1985: 424–50.

——, 'Labour Relations in Socialist Russia: Class Values and Production Values in the Printers Union 1917–21', in L. Siegelbaum and R. Suny (eds), *Making Workers Soviet: Power, Class and Identity*, London: Cornell University Press, 1994, pp. 159–93.

——, 'Factory Tales: Narratives of Industrial Relations in the Transition to NEP', *The Russian Review* 55: 3, 1996: 384–411.

——, *Republic of Labor: Russian Printers and Soviet Socialism, 1918–1930*, Ithaca: Cornell University Press, 2005.

—— and Rosenberg, W.G., *Strikes and Revolution in Russia, 1917*, Princeton: Princeton University Press, 1989.

——, Rosenberg, W.G. and Suny, R.G. (eds), *Party, State and Society in the Russian Civil War: Explorations in Social History*, Bloomington: Indiana University Press, 1989.

Korovina, M.N. and Kogan, T.F., 'Bor'ba za uluchshenie blagosostoianiia rabochego klassa (1921–25gg.)', *Voprosy istorii* 9, 1961: 42–55.

Korshunova, Z.P. (ed.), *Ocherki istorii Moskovskoi organizatsii KPSS, kn. II, noiabr' 1917–1945*, Moscow: Moskovskii rabochii, 1983.

Korzhikhina, T.P. and Fignater, Iu.Iu., 'Sovetskaia nomenklatura: stanovlenie, mekhanizmy, deistviia', *Voprosy istorii* 7, 1993: 25–38.

Kotkin, S., review of Davies, *Popular Opinion in Stalin's Russia*, *Europe-Asia Studies*, 50: 4, 1998: 739–42.

Krasil'nikov, S.A. and Morozov, K.N., 'Predislovie', in Krasil'nikov, S.A., Morozov, K.N. and Chubykin, I.V. (eds), *Sudebnyi protsess nad sotsialistami-revoliutsionerami (iiun'-avgust 1922 g.). Podgotovka. Provedenie. Itogi. Sbornik dokumentov*, Moscow: Rosspen, 2002, pp. 9–144.

Kravets, V.P. (ed.), *Rezinovaia promyshlennost'. kn. 2.*, Moscow/Leningrad: tsentr upr. pochati VSNKh SSSR, 1926.

Kuleshov, S.V., Volobuev, O.V. and Pivovar, E.I. (eds), *Nashe otechestvo: opyt politicheskoi istorii*, Moscow: Terra, 1991.

Kurakhtanova, V., *Pervaia sitsenabivnaia*, Moscow: izd. sotsial'noi-ekonomicheskoi literatury, 1960.

Lane, C., *The Rites of Rulers: Ritual in Industrial Society – the Soviet case*, Cambridge: Cambridge University Press, 1981.

Lapitskaia, S., *Byt' rabochikh trekhgornoi manufaktury*, Moscow: OGIZ, 1935.

Lebina, N.B., *Povsednevnaia zhizn Sovetskogo goroda 1920–1930 gody: normy i anomalii*, St Petersburg: izd. 'Letnii sad', 1999.

Lefort, C., *The Political Forms of Modern Society: Bureaucracy, Democracy, Totalitarianism*, Cambridge: Polity Press, 1986.

Lel'chuk, V.S., (ed.), *Istoriki sporiat: trinadtsat' besed*, Moscow: izd. polit. literatury, 1988.
Leonov, S.V., *Rozhdenie sovetskoi imperii: gosudarstvo i ideologiia 1917–1922 gg.*, Moscow: Dialog-MGU, 1997.
Leont'ev, Ia.V. and Iur'ev, K.S., 'Nezapechatlennyi trud: iz arkhiva V.N. Figner', in *Zven'ia: istoricheskii almanakh*, no. 2, St Petersburg: Feniks/Atheneum, 1992, pp. 424–88.
Lewin, M., *Lenin's Last Struggle*, London: Faber & Faber, 1968.
——, *The Making of the Soviet System: Essays in the Social History of Interwar Russia*, New York: The New Press, 1994.
——, 'Concluding Remarks', in Siegelbaum, L.H. and Suny, R.G. (eds), *Making Workers Soviet: Power, Class and Identity*, London: Cornell University Press, 1994, pp. 376–89.
Lih, L., *Bread and Authority in Russia 1914–1921*, Berkeley: University of California Press, 1990.
Lih, L., 'The Mystery of the *ABC*', *Slavic Review* 56: 1, 1997: 50–72.
——, 'Vlast' from the Past', in *Left Politics*, 6: 2, 1999: 29–52.
Lipilin, Iu.A. and Sachkovskii, G.A., *Leninskii prizyv v leningradskoi partiinoi organizatsii*, Leningrad: Lenizdat, 1984.
Liutov, L.N., *Gosudarstvennaia promyshlennost' v gody NEPa*, Saratov: izd. Saratovskogo universiteta, 1996.
Lunacharskii, A.V., Trotsky, L. and Radek, K., *Siluety: politicheskiie portrety*, Moscow: izd. politicheskoi literatury, 1991.
Lupher, M., *Power Restructuring in Russia and China*, Oxford: Westview Press, 1996.
Luukkanen, A., *The Party of Unbelief: the Religious Policy of the Bolshevik Party 1917–1929*, Helsinki: SHS, 1994.
Malia, M., *The Soviet Tragedy: a History of Socialism in Russia, 1917–1991*, New York: Maxwell Macmillan International, 1994.
Malle, S., *The Economic Organization of War Communism 1918–1921*, Cambridge: Cambridge University Press, 1985.
Mally, L., *Culture of the Future: the Proletkult Movement in Revolutionary Russia*, Berkeley: California University Press, 1990.
Mandel, D., *The Petrograd Workers and the Fall of the Old Regime: from the February Revolution to the July Days, 1917*, London: Macmillan, 1983.
——, *The Petrograd Workers and the Soviet Seizure of Power: from the July Days 1917 to July 1918*, London: Macmillan, 1984.
Marie, J.-J., *Cronstadt*, Paris: Fayard, 2005.
Markevich, A. and Sokolov, A., *'Magnitka bliz Sadovogo kol'tsa': stimula k rabote na Moskovskom zavode 'Serp i molot', 1883–2001 gg.*, Moscow: Rosspen, 2005.
Marx, K., *Wage Labour and Capital*, Moscow: Progress Publishers, 1952.
——, *Critique of Hegel's 'Philosophy of Right'* (ed. J. O'Malley), Cambridge: Cambridge University Press, 1970.
——, 'First draft of the Civil War in France', in Marx, K., *The First International and After*, London: Penguin, 1974, pp. 136–68.
——, 'The Civil War in France', in Marx, K., *The First International and After*, London: Penguin, 1974, pp. 187–235.
—— and Engels, F., *The German Ideology. Part One* (ed. C.J. Arthur), London: Lawrence & Wishart, 1977.

—— and Engels, F., *Manifesto of the Communist Party*, Moscow: Progress Publishers, 1977.
Matiugin, A.A., *Rabochii klass SSSR v gody vosstanovleniia narodnogo khozaistva, 1921–1925*, Moscow: izd. Akademii nauk SSSR, 1962.
Maximoff, G., *The Guillotine At Work, vol.1. The Leninist Counter-Revolution*, Chicago: Cienfuegos Press, 1979.
——, *Syndicalists in the Russian Revolution*, London: Syndicalist Workers Federation, 1985.
Mazaev, A.I., *Prazdnik kak sotsial'no-khudozhestvennoe iavlenie*, Moscow: 'Nauka', 1968.
McAuley, M., *Bread and Justice: State and Society in Petrograd 1917–1922*, Oxford: Clarendon, 1991.
McDaniel, T., *Autocracy, Capitalism and Revolution in Russia*, Berkeley: University of California Press, 1988.
Mchedlov, M.P. and Sovokin, A.M., *V.I. Lenin: biograficheskaia khronika, 1870–1924*, Moscow: izd. polit. literatury, 1985.
Melancon, M. and Pate, A.K. (eds), *New Labor History: Worker Identity and Experience in Russia, 1840–1918*, Bloomington: Slavica, 2002.
Merridale, C., *Moscow Politics and the Rise of Stalin: the Communist Party in the Capital 1925–32*, Basingstoke: Macmillan, 1990.
Meszaros, I., *Marx's Theory of Alienation*, London: Merlin, 2005.
Miasnikov, G., 'Filosofiia ubiistva, ili pochemu i kak ia ubil Mikhaila Romanova', *Minuvshee* 18, 1995, pp. 7–191.
Mikhailov, N.V., 'The Collective Psychology of Russian Workers and Workplace Self-Organization in the Early Twentieth Century', in Melancon, M. and Pate, A. K. (eds), *New Labor History: Worker Identity and Experience in Russia, 1840–1918*, Bloomington: Slavica, 2002, pp. 77–93.
Moskovskaia gorodskaia i Moskovskaya oblastnaia organizatsiia KPSS v tsifrakh, Moscow: Moskovskii rabochii, 1972.
Moskovskii sovet rabochykh, krestianskikh i krasnoarmeiskikh deputatov 1917–27, Moscow: izd. Moskovskogo soveta, 1927.
Murphy, K., *Revolution and Counterrevolution: Class Struggle in a Moscow Metal Factory*, Oxford: Berghahn Books, 2005.
Naiman, E., *Sex in Public: the Incarnation of Early Soviet Ideology*, Princeton: Princeton University Press, 1997.
Narskii, I., *Zhizn' v katastrofe: budni naseleniia Urala v 1917–1922 gg.*, Moscow: Rosspen, 2001.
Nenin, A.B., *Sovnarkom i Novaia Ekonomicheskaia Politika (1921–23gg)*, Nizhnii Novgorod: izd. Volgo-Viatskoi akademii gosudarstvennoi sluzhby, 1999.
Nikoljukin, A., 'A Little-Known Story: Bellamy in Russia', in Bowman, S. (ed.), *Edward Bellamy Abroad: An American Prophet's Influence*, New York: Twayne, 1962, pp. 67–85.
Olekh, G.L., *Krovnye uzy: RKP(b) i ChK/GPU v pervoi polovine 1920-kh godov: mekhanizm vsaimootnoshenii*, Novosibirsk: Novosibirskaia gosudarstevennaia akademiia vodnogo transporta, 1999.
——, *Povorot, kotorogo ne bylo: bor'ba za vnutripartiinuiu demokratiu 1919–1924 gg.*, Novosibirsk: izd. Novosibirskogo universiteta, 1992.
Orlov, I.B., 'Vosstanovlenie promyshlennosti', in Pavliuchenkov, S.A., et al. (eds), *Rossiia nepovskaia*, Moscow: Novyi khronograf, 2002, pp. 121–49.

——, 'Problemy edinoi ekonomiki', in Pavliuchenkov S.A., et al. (eds), ibid., pp. 150–65.
Orlovsky, D.T., 'State Building in the Civil War Era: the Role of the Lower Middle Strata', in Koenker, D.P., Rosenberg, W.G. and Suny, R.G. (eds), *Party, State and Society in the Russian Civil War: Explorations in Social History*, Bloomington: Indiana University Press, 1989, pp. 180–209.
——, 'The Hidden Class: White Collar Workers in the Soviet 1920s', in Siegelbaum, L.H. and Suny, R.G. (eds), *Making Workers Soviet: Power, Class and Identity*, London: Cornell University Press, 1994, pp. 220–52.
——, 'The anti-bureaucratic campaigns in the 1920s', in Taranovski, T. (ed.), *Reform in Modern Russian History: Progress or Cycle?* Cambridge: Cambridge University Press, 1995, pp. 290–315.
Panfilova, A.M., *Istoriia zavoda 'Krasny Bogatyr'*, Moscow: izd. Moskovskogo universiteta, 1958.
Patenaude, B.M., *Bolshevism in Retreat: the Transition to NEP 1920–22* (PhD diss., Stanford University, 1987).
——, *The Big Show in Bololand: The American Relief Expedition to Soviet Russia in the Famine of 1921*, Stanford: Stanford University Press, 2002.
Pavliuchenkov, S.A., *Krestianskii Brest, ili predystoriia bol'shevistskogo NEPa*, Moscow: Russkoe knigoizdatel'skoe izdatel'stvo, 1996.
——, *Voennyi kommunizm v Rossii: vlast' i massy*, Moscow: RKT-Istoriia, 1997.
——, 'Ekonomicheskii liberalizm v predelakh politicheskogo monopolizma', in Pavliuchenkov, S.A., et al. (eds), *Rossiia nepovskaia: issledovaniia*, Moscow: Novyi khronograf, 2002, pp. 15–57.
——, '"Novyi klass" i stanovlenie sistemy gosudarstvennogo absoliutizma', in Pavliuchenkov, S.A., et al., op. cit., pp. 169–207.
——, et al., *Rossiia nepovskaia: issledovaniia*, Moscow: Novyi khronograf, 2002.
Pavlov, D.B., *Bol'shevistskaia diktatura protiv sotsialistov i anarkhistov 1917-seredina 1950-kh godov*, Moscow: Rosspen, 1999.
Pavlov, I., *1920-e gody. Revoliutsiia, biurokratiia. Zapiski oppozitsionera*, St Petersburg: 'Peterburg – XXI vek', 2001.
Pavlova, I.V., *Stalinizm: stanovlenie mekhanizma vlasti*, Novosibirsk: Sibirskii khronograf, 1993.
——, *Mekhanizm vlasti i stroitel'stvo staliniskogo sotsializma*, Novosibirsk: izd. SO RAN, 2001.
Pinnow, K., *Making Suicide Soviet: Medicine, Moral Statistics and the Politics of Social Science in Soviet Russia, 1920–1930* (PhD diss., Columbia University, 1988).
Pipes, R., *Russia Under the Bolshevik Regime*, London: Harvill, 1994.
Pirani, S., 'Class Clashes With Party: Politics in Moscow between the Civil War and the New Economic Policy', *Historical Materialism* 11: 2, 2003: 75–120.
——, 'The Moscow Workers' Movement in 1921 and the Role of Non-partyism', *Europe-Asia Studies* 56: 1, 2004: 143–60.
——, *The Changing Political Relationship Between Moscow Workers and the Bolsheviks, 1920–24* (PhD diss., University of Essex, 2006).
——, 'The Party Elite, the Industrial Managers and the Cells: Early Stages in the Formation of the Soviet Ruling Class in Moscow, 1922–23', *Revolutionary Russia* 19: 2, 2006: 197–228.
Podliashuk, P., *Raduga trekh. gor. Iz biografii odnogo rabochego kollektiva*, Moscow: Moskovskii rabochii, 1967.

Podshchekoldin, A.M., 'Kogda i kem byla 'prodana revoliutsiia'?' (unpublished conference paper, Moscow, 1999).

——, 'The Origins of the Stalinist Bureaucracy – Some New Historical Facts' (tr. Mike Jones). <http://www.revolutionary-history.co.uk/supplem/podsheld.htm> (accessed 2 May 2007).

Poliakov, Iu.A., *Moskovskie trudiashchiesia v oborone sovetskoi stolitsy v 1919 godu*, Moscow: izd. Akademii nauk SSSR, 1958.

——, '20-e gody: nastroenie partiinogo avangarda', *Voprosy istorii KPSS* 10, 1989: 25–38.

Pospielovsky, A., 'Strikes During the NEP', *Revolutionary Russia* 10: 1, 1997: 1–34.

Priestland, D., 'Bolshevik Ideology and the Debate Over Party-State Relations, 1918–21', *Revolutionary Russia* 10: 2, 1997: 37–61.

——, *Stalinism and the Politics of Mobilization: Ideas, Power and Terror in Inter-War Russia*, New York: Oxford University Press, 2007.

Proletarskii, M.Ia., *Zavod 'Krasnyi bogatyr" (1887–1932)*, Moscow: gos. khim-tekh izd., 1933.

Rabinowitch, A., *Prelude to Revolution: the Petrograd Bolsheviks and the July 1917 Uprising*, Bloomington: Indiana University Press, 1968.

——, *The Bolsheviks Come to Power: the Revolution of 1917 in Petrograd*, New York: W. Norton, 1976.

Radek, K., 'The Paths of the Russian Revolution', in Richardson, A. (ed.), *In Defence of the Russian Revolution: a Selection of Bolshevik Writings, 1917–1923*, London: Porcupine Press, 1995, pp. 35–65.

Rakovsky, C., *Selected Writings on Opposition in the USSR 1923–1930* (ed. Gus Fagan), London: Allison & Busby, 1980.

Raleigh, D.J., *Experiencing Russia's Civil War: Politics, Society and Revolutionary Culture in Saratov, 1917–1922*, Princeton: Princeton University Press, 2002.

Rashin, A.G., *Zarabotnaia plata za vosstanovitel'nyi period khoziaistva SSSR 1922/23–1926/27 gg.*, Moscow: Gosizdat, 1928.

——, *Formirovanie rabochego klassa Rossii: istoriko-ekonomicheskie ocherki*, Moscow: izd. sotsialno-ekonomicheskoi literatury, 1958.

Read, C., *From Tsar to Soviets: the Russian People and their Revolution 1917–21*, London: Routledge, 1996.

Rees, E.A., *State Control in Soviet Russia: the Rise and Fall of the Workers' and Peasants' Inspectorate, 1920–34*, Basingstoke: Macmillan, 1987.

Rees, J., Farbman, S. and Service, R., *In Defence of October*, London: Bookmarks, 1997.

Remington, T., *Building Socialism in Bolshevik Russia: Ideology and Industrial Organization 1917–1921*, Pittsburgh: University of Pittsburgh Press, 1984.

Rigby, T.H., *Communist Party Membership in the USSR 1917–1967*, Princeton: Princeton University Press, 1968.

——, 'The Soviet Political Elite', *British Journal of Political Science* I: 4, 1971: 415–36.

——, 'Early Provincial Cliques and the Rise of Stalin', *Soviet Studies* 33, 1981: 3–28.

Rodionova, N.I., *Gody napriazhennogo truda: iz istorii Moskovskoi partiinoi organizatsii 1921–1925 gg.*, Moscow: Moskovskii rabochii, 1963.

—— (ed.), *Soratniki: biografii aktivnikh uchastnikov revoliutsionnogo dvizheniia v Moskve i Moskovskoi oblasti*, Moscow: Moskovskii rabochii, 1985.

Rokitianskii Ia. and Muller, R., *Krasnyi dissident: akademik Riazanov – opponent Lenina, zhertva Stalina*, Moscow: Academia, 1996.

Rosenberg, W.G., 'The Social Background to Tsektran', in Koenker, D.P., Rosenberg, W.G. and Suny, R.G. (eds), *Party, State and Society in the Russian Civil War: Explorations in Social History*, Bloomington: Indiana University Press, 1989, pp. 349–73.

——, 'Russian Labor and Bolshevik Power After October', *Slavic Review* 44: 2, 1985, pp. 213–38.

Rossman, J., *Worker Resistance Under Stalin: Class and Revolution on the Shop Floor*, London: Harvard University Press, 2005.

Rowney, D.K., *Transition to Technocracy: the Structural Origins of the Soviet Administrative State*, Ithaca: Cornell University Press, 1989.

Sakwa, R., *Soviet Communists in Power: a Study of Moscow During the Civil War*, London: Macmillan, 1988.

——, 'The Soviet State, Civil Society and Moscow Politics: Stability and Order in Early NEP 1921–24', in Cooper, J., Perrie, M. and Rees, E.A. (eds), *Soviet History, 1917–53*, Birmingham: Macmillan, 1995, pp. 42–77.

Schapiro, L., *The Origin of the Communist Autocracy*, London: G. Bell & sons, 1955.

Seidman, M., *Workers Against Work: Labor in Paris and Barcelona During the Popular Fronts*, Berkeley: University of California Press, 1991.

——, *Republic of Egos: a Social History of the Spanish Civil War*, Madison: University of Wisconsin Press, 2002.

Serge, V., *Littérature et révolution*, Paris: Maspero, 1976.

——, *Memoirs of a Revolutionary*, New York: Writers & Readers, 1977.

——, *Revolution in Danger: Writings from Russia 1919–20*, London: Redwords, 1997.

Shedrov, S.V. (eds), *Profsoiuzy Moskvy: Ocherki istorii*, Moscow: Profizdat, 1975.

Shishkin, V.A., *Vlast', politika, ekonomika: poslerevoliutsionnaia Rossiia (1917–1928 gg.)*, St Petersburg: 'Dmitrii Bulanin', 1997.

Shkaratan, O.I., *Problemy sotsial'noi struktury rabochego klassa SSSR*, Moscow, 'Mysl', 1970.

Siegelbaum, L., *Stakhanovism and the Politics of Productivity*, Cambridge: Cambridge University Press, 1988.

——, *Soviet State and Society Between Revolutions, 1918–1929*, Cambridge: Cambridge University Press, 1992.

—— and Suny, R.G. (eds), *Making Workers Soviet: Power, Class and Identity*, London: Cornell University Press, 1994.

—— and Suny, R.G., 'Class Backwards? In Search of the Soviet Working Class', in Siegelbaum and Suny (eds), op. cit., pp. 1–26.

Simonov, N.S., 'Reforma politicheskogo stroiia: zamysly i real'nost' (1921–23 gg.)', *Voprosy istorii KPSS* 1, 1991: 42–45.

——, 'Demokratichnaia alternativa totalitarnomu NEPu', *Istoriia SSSR* 1, 1992: 41–56.

——, 'Termidor, Briumer ili Friuktidor? Evoliutsiia stalinskogo rezhima vlasti: prognozy i real'nost'', *Otechestvennaia istoriia* 4, 1993: 3–17.

Sinitsyn, A.M., et al. (eds), *Istoriia rabochykh Moskvy 1917–1945 gg.*, Moscow: 'Nauka', 1983.

Smith, C., *Karl Marx and the Future of the Human*, Maryland: Lexington Books, 2005.

Smith, S.A., *Red Petrograd*, Cambridge: Cambridge University Press, 1983.

Sochor, Z.A., *Revolution and Culture: The Bogdanov-Lenin controversy*, Ithaca: Cornell University Press, 1988.

Sokolov, A.K. and Koz'menko, V.M. (eds), *Rossiia v XX veke: liudi, idei, vlast'*, Moscow: Rosspen, 2002.
Solzhenitsyn, A., *Arkhipelag Gulag*, Paris: YMCA Press, 1973.
Sorin, V., *Rabochaia gruppa ('Miasnikovshchina')*, Moscow: MK RKP, 1924.
Steinberg, M.D., *Proletarian Imagination: Self, Modernity and the Sacred in Russia, 1910–1925*, Ithaca: Cornell University Press, 2002.
Sternheimer, S., 'Adminstration for Development: the Emerging Bureaucratic Elite, 1920–30' in Pintner, W. and Rowney, D.K. (eds), *Russian Officialdom: the Bureaucratization of Russian Society from the Seventeenth to the Twentieth Century*, London: Macmillan, 1980, pp. 316–54.
Stites, R., *Revolutionary Dreams: Utopian Vision and Experimental Life in the Russian Revolution*, Oxford: Oxford University Press, 1989.
Strauss, K.M., *Factory and Community in Stalin's Russia: the Making of an Industrial Working Class*, Pittsburgh: University of Pittsburgh Press, 1997.
Suny, R.G., 'Towards a Social History of the October Revolution', *American Historical Review* 1, 1983: 31–52.
Suvorova, L.N., 'Za "fasadom" "voennogo kommunizma": politicheskaia vlast' i rynochnaia ekonomika', *Otechestvennaia istoriia* 4, 1993: 48–59.
Sviatenko, F., *Zavod 'AMO'*, Moscow: Gos. izd., 1929.
Thalheimer, A., '1923: A Missed Opportunity? – the Legend of the German October and the Real History of 1923', *Revolutionary History* 8: 4, 2004: 90–125.
Thompson, E.P., *The Making of the English Working Class*, London: Victor Gollancz, 1963.
——, *The Poverty of Theory and Other Essays*, London: Merlin, 1978.
Tiazhel'nikova, V.S., 'Samoubiistvo kommunistov v 1920-e gody', *Otechestvennaia istoriia* 6, 1998: 158–73.
——, '"Voennyi sindrom" v povedenii kommunistov 1920-kh gg.', in Seniavskaia, E. S. (ed.), *Voenno-istoricheskaia antropologiia. Ezhegodnik 2002. Predmet, zadachi, perspektivu razvitiia*, Moscow: Rosspen, 2002, pp. 291–305.
——, 'Povsednevnost' i revoliutsionnie preobrazovaniia sovetskoi vlasti', in Sevost'ianov, G.N. (ed.), *Rossiia v XX veke: Reforma i revoliutsiia*, Moskva: 'Nauka', 2002, vol. 2, pp. 84–100.
——, 'Povsednevnaia zhizn' moskovskikh rabochikh v nachale 1920-kh godov', in Sokolov, A.K. and Koz'menko, V.M. (eds), *Rossiia v XX veke: liudi, idei, vlast'*, Moscow: Rosspen, 2002, pp. 194–218.
——, 'Mekhanizmy "surovogo samoochishcheniia"' (unpublished paper presented at the British Association of Slavonic and East European Studies conference, 2003).
Tilly, L. and Tilly, C. (eds), *Class Conflict and Collective Action*, Beverly Hills: Sage, 1981.
Timofeevskii, A.A. (ed.), *V.I. Lenin i stroitel'stvo partii v pervye gody sovetskoi vlasti*, Moscow: Mysl', 1965.
Trotsky, L., *Writings of Leon Trotsky (1933–34)*, New York: Pathfinder, 1972.
——, *The Revolution Betrayed: What is the Soviet Union and Where is it Going*, London: New Park, 1973.
——, *Terrorism and Communism: a Reply to Karl Kautsky*, London: New Park, 1975.
——, *Writings of Leon Trotsky (1935–36)*, New York: Pathfinder, 1977.
——, *How the Revolution Armed: the Military Writings and Speeches of Leon Trotsky* (tr. B. Pearce), London: New Park, 1981.
Trukan, G.A., *Put' k totalitarizmu, 1917–1929 gg*, Moscow: 'Nauka', 1994.

Tsakunov, S.V., *V labirinte doktriny: iz opyta razrabotki ekonomicheskogo kursa strany v 1920-e gody*, Moscow: Rossiia molodaia, 1994.

Tsuji, Y., 'The Debate on the Trade Unions, 1920–21', *Revolutionary Russia* 2: 1, 1989: 31–100.

Tucker, R.C., 'Towards a Comparative Politics of Movement-Regimes', *American Political Science Review*, 55: 2, 1961: 281–89.

Ulrich, J., *Kamenev: Der gemassigte Bolschewik*, Hamburg: VSA-Verlag, 2006.

Valentinov, N.V. (Vol'skii, N.), *Nasledniki Lenina*, Moscow: Terra, 1991.

——, *Novaia ekonomicheskaia politika i krizis partii posle smerti Lenina*, Moscow: Sovremennik, 1991.

Vasiaev, V.I., Drobizhev, V.Z., Zaks, L.B., Pivovor, B.I., Ustinov, V.A. and Ushakova, T.A., *Dannie perepisi sluzhashchikh 1922g. o sostave kadrov narkomatov RSFSR*, Moscow: izd. Moskovskovskogo universiteta, 1972.

Vasil'eva, O.Iu., 'Russkaiia pravoslavnaia tserkov' i sovetskaia vlast' v 1917–27 godakh', *Voprosy Istorii* 8, 1993: 40–54.

Vernidub, I.I., *Na peredovoi linii tyla*, Moscow: TsNIINTIKPK, 1993.

von Geldern, J., *Bolshevik Festivals, 1917–1920*, Berkeley: University of California Press, 1993.

Voronin, P.A., et al., *Moskva. Entsiklopediia*, Moscow: Sovetskaia entsiklopediia, 1980.

Ward, C., *Russia's Cotton Workers and the New Economic Policy: Shop-Floor Culture and State Policy 1921–1929*, Cambridge: Cambridge University Press, 1990.

Weber, M., *Essays in Sociology* (tr. and ed. by H.H. Gerth and C.W. Mills), London: Routledge and Kegan Paul, 1970.

Wheatcroft, S., 'Famine and Food Consumption Records in Early Soviet History, 1917–25', in Geissler, C. and Oddy, D. (eds), *Food, Diet and Economic Change Past and Present*, Leicester: Leicester University Press, 1993, pp. 151–74.

Wood, E., *The Baba and the Comrade: Gender and Politics in Revolutionary Russia*, Bloomington: Indiana University Press, 1997.

Zelnik, R.E., 'Russian Bebels: an Introduction to the Memoirs of the Russian Workers Semen Kanatchnikov and Matvei Fisher', *Russian Review* 35: 3, 1976: 249–89.

Zhiltsov, S., *Smertnaia kazn' v istorii Rossii*, Moscow: Zertsalo-M, 2002.

Zhukov, A.F., *Ideino-politicheskii krakh eserovskogo maksimalizma*, Leningrad: izd. Leningradskogo universiteta, 1979.

Zhuravlev, S.V., *Fenomen 'istorii fabrik i zavodov': gor'kovskoe nachinanie v kontekste epokhi 1930-kh godov*, Moscow: Institut rossiiskoi istorii RAN, 1997.

——, *'Malenkie liudi' i 'bol'shaia istoriia'. Inostrantsy moskovskogo Elektrozavoda v sovetskom obshchestve 1920-kh – 1930-kh gg*, Moscow: Rosspen, 2000.

Zhuravlev V.V., et al. (eds), *Vlast' i oppozitsiia: Rossiskii politicheskii protsess XX stoletiia*, Moscow: Rosspen, 1995.

Index

absenteeism 28–29
Aleksandrovskii, Vasilii 120–22
alienation *see* labour alienation
anarchism 38, 82, 83, 98, 107, 150, 198
anarchist-individualists 198
anarcho-communism 107, 249
anarcho-syndicalism 7, 83, 87, 98, 104
anarcho-universalism 84, 98, 107
Andeichin 222–23
Angarskii, Nikolai 50, 64, 66, 126, 185, 242
Anikeev 84
'anonymous platform' (1922) 164, 213, 214–15
anti-semitism 76, 186, 187n, 203
'appointism' 170, 239; discussions of 57, 125, 211, 216, 220–21, 225
Aronshtam 231
Artem, Fedor 67
Askarov, German 107

Badaev, Aleksei 27
Baranov, Aleksandr 61, 62, 136, 197, 204
Barmash, Vladimir 84
Bauman group 50–51, 59, 61–63, 69, 124–26, 195, 237, 242, 244, 249, 251–52
Belen'kii, Grigorii 134, 222
Bellamy, Edward 54–55
Berzina, Maria 61, 62, 126, 136, 197–98, 242
Bogdanov, Aleksandr 128, 204
Bogdanov, Petr 182, 209
Boguslavskii, Mikhail 50, 64, 66, 67, 98, 101, 204, 243
Bolshevik party: apparatus of 57, 129, 169–70, 172, 216, 225, 231–32; 'attachment' to workplace cells 61, 185; ban on factions by 88–89; cadre distribution by 129–31, 170, 172–73, 228; cells (general) 214, 220–21, 224; cells (industrial workplaces) 39–41, 70, 85, 101, 109, 117, 121, 129–31, 137, 176, 181–85, 185–89, 197–98, 205, 207, 223, 228–30; cells (Red army) 134, 135; cells (state apparatus) 129–31, 134, 136–37; civil war communists in 44–56, 115, 176, 226, 230; discussion of equality in 52–53, 55–59, 121, 174–77; discussion of party's role in state 211–13, 216, 237; discussion of SR trial in 152; disillusionment in 119–23; dissidents in 104–5, 115, 132, 213–15; former members of 81, 182, 196, 207; iconization of leaders 155; and Kronshtadt revolt, 85–87; membership statistics of 44–45, 116, 229, 259–60; 'party crisis' (1923–24) 164, 215–25; purge (1921) 131–37, 259; rank-and-file members of 102, 129–31, 133–34, 136–37, 211, 225–28; recruitment to 137, 185, 210, 211–12, 225–30, 238; resignations from 41, 116–18, 127–28, 176, 229; social composition of 133–34, 136–37, 212, 229, 261–63; super-optimism in 45–52, 122; trade union fractions of 124; women in 52, 121, 161–62; *see also* 'anonymous platform'; Bauman group; democracy, inner-party; elite; left opposition; Lenin enrolment; 'new course'; socialism; Workers Group, Workers and Peasants Socialist Party, Workers Truth
Bolshevik party Central Committee 42, 67–68, 193; enlarged plenum of

(1923) 204–5; and NEP 115; and party membership 136–37, 231–32; and purge (1921) 132; and spring 1921 crisis 75, 81–82, 102; leading 'triumvirate' of (1923–24) 211, 213, 215–16, 218, 231–32, 239
Bolshevik party Central Control Commission 184, 204, 222
Bolshevik party conferences: ninth (1920) 50, 58, 66, 238; tenth (1921) 115–16; twelfth (1922) 170, 173–74, 175, 238; thirteenth (1924) 209, 219, 224, 228–29
Bolshevik party congresses: eighth (1919) 56, 63; ninth (1920) 65, 91; tenth (1921) 40, 58, 63, 67–68, 72, 74, 88–89, 117, 124; eleventh (1922) 124, 133, 137, 156, 158, 162–64, 212, 238; twelfth (1923) 170, 194, 199, 212–14, 226; thirteenth (1924) 231
Bolshevik party, Moscow Committee of 27, 33, 62–63, 66, 70, 119, 193–94; bureau 38, 102, 125, 126; and campaign against church 145; and gold loan 206; and industrial managers 183; and Lenin enrolment 230; and 'party crisis' (1923) 218, 219; and soviet elections 98, 101–2, 106; and spring 1921 crisis 81–82; and state apparatus 129, 170
Bolshevik party, Moscow organization 44, 116; in Moscow soviet 102–6; membership of 137, 225–26, 229, 231; and purge 132–36; and soviet elections (1921) 98–102;
Bolshevik party Moscow regional conferences: (August 1920) 33 (November 1920) 41–42, 49–50, 66–67; (February 1921) 60, 63; (June 1921) 125; (October 1921) 125, 129–30; (March 1922) 130, 137, 175; (June 1922) 152, 179; (April 1923) 177, 192, 213–14; (January 1924) 219
Borovoi, Aleksei 198
Breslav, Boris 135
Bretan 104, 107, 110
Bruno, Genrikh 124
Bubnov Andrei 64–65, 66, 175
Budniak, F.D. 124, 186
Bukharin, Nikolai 9, 49, 66, 88–89, 227
Burdakov K.V. 61, 126
bureaucracy, theory of 166–68
bureaucratization *see* bureaucratism

bureaucratism: campaigns against 190; discussions of 25, 56–60, 66, 132, 216, 238
Butyrka prison 101, 103, 106, 110

Carr, E.H. 213, 236
Castoriadis, Cornelius 168
Cheka 32, 38, 39, 79, 82, 106–7, 118, 134, 249; information reports 17–18; Workers Group of 17; *see also* GPU
chemical industry 22, 100
chemical workers' union 156, 181–83
Chernyshevskii, Nikolai 53, 107, 242
China 142
Chizhevskii, D. 97–98
Chizhikov, O.L. 84, 106, 198
Chukhanov, Fedor 77, 100, 108, 109, 243
church: campaign to confiscate valuables from 143–47; *see also* religion
civil war 6–7, 19; discussions of 120; *see also* Bolshevik party, civil war communists in
collective agreements, *see* labour relations
Collectivist manifesto (1921) 46, 128
Comintern 35, 46, 119, 124, 196
communes 53
communism *see* socialism
Communist party *see* Bolshevik party
Communist International *see* Comintern
corruption 26, 58, 190; discussions of and campaigns against 118, 222–23; *see also* sovmestitel'stvo
currency *see* monetary policy

Dalin, David 42, 139
Daniels, Robert 213
Danishevskii, Karl 89, 134, 213, 217, 243–44
Davydov, Vasilii 82, 100, 108–9
death penalty 105, 148, 151–52, 153–54, 223; passed at Orekhovo-Zuevo trial 190
Demidov, Vladimir 51, 61, 62–63, 197–98, 204, 237, 244
Demidov (AMO worker) 40
democracy 2, 4, 90; inner-party 125, 164, 214, 216–18, 221; and mass mobilization 142–43; soviet 78, 86–87, 96–97, 101, 102–6, 118, 155, 195–96, 209, 220, 234, 235; trade union 69, 156–59; *see also* mass meetings

Democratic Centralist group 42, 55–57, 60, 64–65, 124, 186, 237, 240, 243; and left opposition 211, 217; at tenth congress 88–89; and trade union debate 70;
democratic rights 37, 86, 87, 105, 195, 208; *see also* death penalty
demonstrations 35, 152–55
Deutscher, Isaac 22–23, 233, 236
disabled workers 201
Dorofeev, Iakov 52
Dvinov, Boris 97, 102, 106, 153
Dzerzhinskii, Feliks 204–5, 216

economic policy 19; discussions of 41–42, 51, 115–16, 118, 126, 141, 192–93, 196, 211, 213, 215, 217, 224, 234; *see also* trade union debate, wages
economy: 'war communism' 19–20, 41–43; under New Economic Policy (NEP) 9–12, 88, 90–91, 111–14, 138–41, 192–93, 199–200, 226–27, 237
elite of Bolshevik party 6, 57–58, 162, 166–75, 211–12, 228, 236–39; discussions of 58–60, 117, 125, 126–28, 175–77, 213, 216–17, 234; at local level 188, 189–91; *see also* 'appointism', bureaucratism, privilege
Engels, Frederick 233
Enukidze, Avel' 60, 134
Enukidze, Trifon 134–35, 189, 244
Epifanov 34, 146
'equalization of rations' 31–35, 78–80, 86, 233
Ezhov, Nikolai 242

factories *see* workplaces
factory committees 27, 29–30, 34, 102, 108–10, 157, 188, 194–95; and industrial managers 135, 181–82; and workers' movement of spring 1921, 78–79, 81, 85; 182
famine (1921) 141, 143, 145–47
Figes, Orlando 86
Fonchenko, Vasilii 64
food consumption data 140
food processing industry 22
food supply 26–28, 41–43, 73, 76, 78–79, 111–14, 141; grain requisitioning and tax in kind 75, 76–77, 85, 88; *see also* famine, procurement trips, rations
food workers' union 161, 246

garment industry 22
Gavrilin, Nikolai 30, 54, 69, 108, 220, 244–45, 251
Georgia: invasion of (1921) 72, 236
Gerasimov, Mikhail 48, 120, 122
Germany: revolution in (1923) 222, 224–25
glavki and *tsentry* 30, 33, 34, 77
Glebov, Nikolai 95, 109
gold loan 205–7, 220, 224
Gol'tsman, Abram 31, 33, 217
Gol'tsev, D.S. 31, 40
Golubeva, Vera 161–62
Gor'kii, Maksim 17
GPU 155, 170, 190, 197, 205; and campaign against church 144–45; and campaign around SR trial 148–49, 153; and 'party crisis' (1923–24) 218–19, 222, 238; *see also* Cheka

Halfin, Igal 45
higher education institutions 124–26, 151, 152
'history of factories' project 17, 108*n*, 228
hours *see* labour relations, eight-hour day

Iakovleva, Varvara 40, 82, 217, 245
Iaroslavskii, Emelian 124
Ignatov, Efim 50, 58, 61, 63, 66, 117, 126, 245
Ignatov group 63–65, 67, 124, 126, 242, 245, 246
industrial managers 166, 174–75, 177–85, 189–91, 193; discussion of 213, 214; organisation of 179; and left opposition 211
industry 20, 113–14; production levels 20, 138–39; trusts 113, 199–200; *see also* chemical industry, food processing, garment industry, labour relations, metalworking industry, productivity, rubber goods industry, textile industry, workplaces
Iurenev, Konstantin 56, 60, 65*n*

Kalinin, Mikhail 74, 136, 203
Kamenev, Lev 39, 60, 67, 77, 81, 152, 163; and Moscow soviet 102–3, 105; in 'triumvirate' (1923–24) 184, 211, 213, 214
Kamyshev, Petr 161, 246
Karelin, Appolon 107
Kaspirovich, Anna 85, 184

Kazin, Vasilii 120–21
Kerzhentsev, Platon 48
Kireev, Ivan 77, 100, 108
Koenker, Diane 22–23, 209–10
Kollontai, Aleksandra 162, 204
Komsomol 36, 53, 160, 173, 226–28
Korobitsyn, Nikolai 108, 176
Korzinov, Grigorii 61, 65
Krasin, Leonid 103, 212–13, 214
Krestinskii, N.N. 124
Kronshtadt 93; revolt (1921) 63, 72, 78, 82–87
Krylenko, Nikolai 180, 187–88
Krylov, Aleksei 33
Krzhizhanovskii, Gleb 25–26, 42
Krupskaia, Nadezhda 55
Kuibyshev, Valerian 204
Kun, Bela 175
Kuraev, Vasilii 76
Kuranova, Ekaterina 61, 126, 246
Kutuzov, Ivan 42, 61, 65, 66
Kuznetsov, Nikolai 203–4
Kuznetsov (at AMO) 108, 246–47
Kuznitsa group 48

labour alienation 2, 91, 240
labour relations 77–78, 90–91, 111–12, 139–41, 156, 193–94; collective agreements 141, 193, 194, 195, 202; eight-hour day 139–40; labour compulsion 28, 68, 77; *see also* productivity, 'shock' working, wages
Larin, Iurii 51, 116, 212–13
Lass-Kozlova, Polina 126, 204, 247, 250
Lavler, B. 227
Lebedev, G. 117–18
Lebedev-Polianskii, Pavel 45
Lefort, Claude 168
Left Communists (1918) 217
left opposition (1923) 167, 211, 215, 216–19, 239, 244, 245
left Socialist Revolutionaries 38, 83, 97, 198, 250; and Moscow soviet 98, 100, 103, 106, 155; worker sympathizers 150–51, 164–65; *see also* Socialist Revolutionary maximalists
left Socialist Revolutionary internationalists 38–39
Lemberg, Gans 135, 231, 247
Lenin, V.I. 9, 42–43, 50, 67, 155; and Bolshevik dissidents 117–18, 119; and campaign against church 144; and crisis of spring 1921 51, 73, 86, 101, 205, 234; death of 228–29; on

party membership 136–37, 226; on *spets*-baiting 188; on state and apparatus 25–26, 237; and trade union debate 68–70; and 'triumvirate' 212; on working class 163–64, 238
Lenin enrolment 185, 228–32, 259
Libedinskii, Iurii 52, 120
Lidak, Andrei 64, 108
Lide 176
Likhachev, Vasilii 33, 155
Lisitsyn, N.V. 63
Litvinov, Iosif 127
Lobanov, Mikhail 217
Lozovskii, Solomon 74, 81, 101
Lunacharskii, Anatolii 80, 149, 155
Lutovinov, Iurii 224
Lysenkov, Afanasii 108, 109, 247–48

Machajski, Jan 75, 91; *see also* makhaevism
makhaevism 75, 97
Maksimov, Grigorii 87
Mandel'shtam, Aleksandr 135, 185, 220
Marx, Karl 9, 107, 166–67, 233, 240
Maslennikov, Sergei 136
Maslov, I. 64
mass meetings 35–37, 80, 84, 98–100, 146–47, 151–52, 194, 195, 198, 203, 207, 229
mass mobilization 10–12, 141–55, 235; and the Polish war 36–37, 143; *see also* demonstrations
Medvedev, A.I. 197
Medvedev, S.P. 65, 124
Mel'nichanskii, Grigorii 33, 76, 92, 156, 158, 194, 248
Mensheviks 82, 198; and chemical workers' union 156, 181; and Moscow soviet 98, 100–101, 102–3, 106; and non-partyism 94–95, 97, 107, 109, 208; worker sympathizers of 35–36, 80, 106, 148, 150
Messing, Stanislav 79
metalworkers' union 36, 196, 248, 251
metalworkers' union, Moscow delegate conferences of: (1920) 28, 30–31; (February 1921), 34, 69, 74–78, 234; (1923) 198
metalworking industry 21–22, 28
migration from countryside 21, 159–60, 192
Miasnikov, Gavriil 184, 197
Mikhailov, Mikhail 124, 197

Mikhailov, Sergei 102–4, 181, 248
Mikhailov, V.M. 124
Minkov, Isaak 33, 102
Miurat, Valerian 180–84, 196, 248–49
Mizikin, Nikolai 134
mobilization *see* mass mobilization
Molotov, Viacheslav 116–17, 124, 170, 173, 177, 238
monetary policy 140–41, 193, 194, 199, 206, 208–9, 258
Moscow: administrative districts, 30*n*, 253; demography of 19–20, 21–25
Moscow Council for the Economy (MSNKh) 32
Muralov, Nikolai 217

narodnism 97, 107, 109
Nastas'ian, Vasilii 77, 82, 100
Nazaretian, A.M. 218
naznachenstvo see appointism
Nestroev, G. 198
'new course' 216, 218–19, 220
New Economic Policy *see* economy, economic policy
Nizhnii Novgorod 108, 200
Nogin, Viktor 58, 83
non-party socialists 75, 81, 84, 234
non-partyism 93–96, 107–10
non-party workers' groups 97, 147, 149, 151, 164–65, 188, 207, 234; at AMO factory 77, 81, 107–9, 146, 243, 246–48; and Moscow soviet 98–101, 102–6, 248

OGPU *see* GPU
Oldenborger, V.V. 187–88
Olenov, P.A. 40
Orekhov, Aleksandr 64
Orlovsky, Daniel 23
Osinskii, Valerian 42, 63, 115, 212–14
Ostrovitianov, Konstantin 62

Paniushkin, Vasilii 61, 104–5, 118–19, 237, 249
Pavlov, D.B. 97
Pavlova, Irina 170
peasants 43; delegate conference of 31; relations with state and workers 76–77; organization 94; revolts by 72; *see also* food supply: requisitioning
peasant unions 77
peat industry 157, 201
Petrograd 86–87, 97, 109
Petrzhek, Vladimir 176, 238
Piatakov, Georgii 217, 224, 225

Pil'niak, Boris 46
Pipes, Richard 86
Platform of the 46 (1923) *see* left opposition
Platonov, Andrei 121
Pokrovskii, M.N. 46
Pokrovskii (factory manager) 184–85
Poland: Soviet Russia's war with (1920) 35–37, 46, 50–51
post and telegraph offices 151, 153, 206
Potapov, I.A. 231
Preobrazhenskii, Nikolai 124, 243; and left opposition (1923) 184, 211, 217, 218–19, 222, 225, 227
Priestland, David 10–12, 142
printers' union 37–38
privilege 26, 58, 166, 168–69, 175; discussion of 58–60, 65–66, 125, 132, 146, 173–77, 213, 238
procurement trips 27, 34, 112, 143
productivity 27, 91, 156, 177; bonuses in kind 27, 29, 78
Prokopovich, K.N. 150–51, 198
'proletarian culture' 128
'proletarianization' *see* 'workerization'
proletkult 48, 120, 128; *see also* Kuznitsa group, worker poets

Radek, Karl 221, 225
Radzivilov, K.D. 197
Rafail, R.B. 49, 64–65, 70, 89, 218
Rafes, Moisei 51
railways 80, 87, 106, 143, 202; Kursk line 100, 202; Moscow-Nizhny Novgorod line 121
railway workshops 208; Aleksandrovskaia 38; Kursk 74; former Mikhel'son factory 202, 206; Rogozhsko-Simonovskii 36
rations 26–28, 30, 41, 78–80, 81–82, 111; *see also* 'equalization of rations'
Rakovsky, Christian 167
Red army 36, 135
religious belief 144–46, 155
Remington, Thomas 10
repression: of Bolshevik dissidents 118, 197–98, 204–5, 215, 218–19; of corrupt officials 190, 222–23; of non-Bolshevik parties 38, 82, 100–101, 104, 106–7, 149–50, 198; of strikes 33, 37–38, 43, 86–87, 110, 157
revolution of 1917, 1–3, 94–95, 236
Riazanov, David 101, 124, 152
Rodov, Semen 48, 122

Rossman, Jeffrey 234
Rozenshtein, Aleksandr 95
Rozenshtein, Mikhail 61
rubber goods industry 178, 180–83, 199–200
Rudzutak, Ian 124, 155
ruling class, Soviet 166–68, 211, 235–36, 239–40
Russian Orthodox church, *see* church

samodeiatel'nost see self-activity
Samsonov, Timofei 148, 249–50
Sapronov, Timofei 91; and left opposition (1923) 184, 211, 218, 222
Saratov 86
Sazonov 85
school teachers 24, 157
Seidman, Michael 6–7, 29
self-activity 91–92, 162
Semkov 214
Serebriakov, Leonid 124, 217
Serge, Victor 241
Shapiro, Aleksandr 107
Shliapnikov, Aleksandr 65, 81, 124, 125, 163–64, 217, 224, 238
Shmidel', Oskar 217
Shteinberg, Isaak 103–4, 106, 250
'shock' working 27, 29, 30, 78–80
Shokhanov, G.V. 197
Shumskaia, I. 221–22
Shutskever, Fania 126–27, 204, 250
Skvortsov-Stepanov, I.I. 173, 184
sluzhashchie 21, 23–26, 57–58, 130–31, 160; pay rates of 174
Smidovich, Petr 50
Smilga, Ivar 85, 89, 134, 179, 214
Smirnov, I.N. 164, 246
Smirnov, Semen 64, 108, 245, 250–51
Smirnov, Vladimir 213, 217
social contract 90–91, 110, 111, 153–54, 138, 178, 200, 203, 209, 235
social mobilization *see* mass mobilization
socialism 2; discussion of 53–55, 128, 141–42, 176–77, 217, 228, 234
Socialist International 148
Socialist Revolutionaries 38, 74, 80, 82, 94–95; and soviet elections (1921) 98, 101; worker sympathizers of 34, 75, 77, 80, 106, 149, 188; *see also* left Socialist Revolutionaries, trials
Socialist Revolutionary maximalists 98, 106, 155, 161, 198, 246
Sokol'nikov, Grigorii 206, 207, 216

Sol'ts, Aron 55, 56, 132
Sorokin, Fedor 185
Sosnovskii, Lev 116, 180–81, 184
Sovetov, Aleksei 61, 62, 124, 126
Soviet state *see* state; *see also* ruling class
soviets: elections (1921) 96–102, 119; *see also* democracy, soviet
soviets, congresses of: seventh (1919) 56; eighth (1920) 42, 57; ninth (1921) 106; tenth (1922) 206
soviet, Moscow 35, 41, 73, 78, 102–6, 110, 250; elections (1921) 98–102, 188; elections (January 1922) 106, 110; elections (December 1922) 155; elections (1923) 207–8; and gold loan 206–7
soviets, Moscow regional conferences of: June 1921 113
sovmestitel'stvo 174, 223, 224
Sovnarkom 27, 111, 113
specialists 166, 180–81; discussion of 34, 77, 135, 188–91, 212; false specialists 189; *spets*-baiting 186–88
spetsy see specialists
SRs *see* Socialist Revolutionaries
Stalin, Iosif 169–70, 172, 177, 244; in 'triumvirate' (1923–24) 184, 211, 213, 218
Stalinism 235–36, 240–41
state, Soviet 8–10, 233, 239–40; apparatus of 25, 121, 129–31; discussions of 166–68, 237–38; *see also* Bolshevik party, discussion of role in state
statism 54–55, 235, 236–41
Stefashkin, Ivan 64
Steinberg, Mark 122–23
strikes: (1920) 32–33, 41, 43; (January-February 1921) 63, 73–74, 78–82, 83–84; (March-May 1921) 86–87, 111–12; (1922) 110, 141, 156–57, 182; (1923) 192, 201, 202–3
Stukov, I.N. 214, 217
Sukharevka market 35, 42, 73
suicides by communists 123
Supreme Council of the National Economy (VSNKh) 25, 65, 68, 182–83, 188, 193, 214, 217

Talaiko, N.M. 176
Tarasov, Georgii 30, 251
tax in kind *see* food supply
telegraph offices *see* post and telegraph offices

textile industry 22, 43, 199–200, 202–3
textile mills: Glukhovskaia, Bogorodskoe 141, 157; Narofominsk 112, 156; Orekhovo-Zuevo 92, 112, 157, 200, 207; Trekhgornaia, Moscow 145, 149, 155, 202–3, 208, 230, 255–56; Tsindel', Moscow 202, 220
textile workers' union 156–57
Tikhonov, Vasilii 108, 146
Tiunov, Sergei 204
Tomskii, Mikhail 124
'tops and ranks' *see* Bolshevik party, discussions of equality within
trade *see* economic policy, economy, food supply
trade unions 155–59, 174, 201, 235; All-Russian Central Council of 124, 193; expulsions from 157, 182, 197, 201; and food supply 29; Moscow regional conference of (1922) 160; Moscow congress of (1923) 194; Moscow regional council of 33, 83, 158, 160, 194, 206, 248; 'trade union week' (1921) 83; *see also* chemical workers' union, factory committees, food workers' union, metalworkers' union, printers' union, textile workers' union
trade union debate 67–71
tram depots 32–33, 157; Miusskii 147, 152; Presnenskii 100; Uvarov 152
trials: of Socialist Revolutionaries 147–52, 153–54, 182; of Alekseevskaia water works *spets*-baiters 187–88; of Orekhovo-Zuevo officials 190; of corrupt officials (1923) 222; of Krasnoshchekov 223
Trotsky, Lev 9, 49, 51, 85, 124, 155, 199, 230; and campaign against church 143; and left opposition (1923) 184, 211, 215, 218–19, 225; on Soviet state 167; and tenth congress 88; and trade union debate 68–70; at twelfth congress 213
trusts, *see* industry
Tsektran 69, 136
tsentry see glavki
Tsiurupa, Aleksandr 58, 75
Tsivtsivadze, Il'ia 39–40
Tul'iakov, Nikita 61, 83, 224, 251

udarnichestvo see 'shock' working
Ukraine 97, 177

unemployment 159–62, 192
United Workers party 95, 109
universities, *see* higher education institutions

Vardin, Il'ia 100–101, 240
vanguardism 4, 52, 162–65, 230, 235, 236–39, 241
Vlasov, Anton 53, 59, 121
Vovsi, M. 174
Vyshinskii, Andrei 75

wages 77, 111, 113–14, 139–41, 193–94, 200, 209, 257–58; differentials 174–75, 189, 224
'war communism' *see* economic policy, economy
women workers 36, 145, 160, 161–62, 202–3; at Goznak 78–80
worker poets 48, 120–23
workerism 34, 39, 62, 75, 77–78, 109, 186; *see also* Machajski
'workerization' 57, 63, 133–34
Workers Group 62, 142, 195–98, 203–4, 214–15, 242, 244
workers' movement 22–23, 233–35; (1918) 94–96; (spring 1921) 73–74, 78–87, 200; (summer 1923) 199–203; *see also* mass meetings, non-partyism, strikes
Workers Opposition 65, 68–69, 118, 124, 186, 214, 251
Workers and Peasants Inspectorate 187, 222; discussion of 212
Workers and Peasants Socialist Party 105, 118–19, 249
Workers Truth group 126–28, 204, 213, 214–15, 237–38, 239, 247, 250
working class: formation 4–7, 107; demographic changes 20–23; and education 227; living standards of 19–20, 26–28, 138–41, 223, 226–27; social composition of 24, 158–59, 163–64; views of Bolshevism in 36–37, 100–102, 153–55, 164–65, 205–8, 209; *see also* disabled workers, migration from countryside, social contract, women workers, workers' movement
workplaces, industrial: 1st state drinks factory 74; 1886 power station 30, 106, 146, 220; Alekseevskaia water works 149, 187–88, 206; AMO car factory 17, 35, 40, 53, 100, 107–9,

117, 119–20, 146, 176, 186, 207, 220, 223, 251, 253, *see also* non-party workers' groups; Amstro works 197; Bogatyr (later Krasnyi Bogatyr) factory 35, 95, 180–83, 207, 220, 248, 254; Bromlei (later Krasnyi proletarii) machine-building works 17, 36, 41, 74, 83–85, 106, 131, 164–65, 175, 196, 223, 228, 230, 235, 254; Dinamo 30, 80, 251, 254; Dobrovykh-Navgolts works 41, 192; Duks aircraft factory 36, 223; Gnom i Ron (later Ikar) aircraft factory 61, 231, 247, 254; Goznak works 78–81, 117, 135, 139, 141, 207, 220, 230, 231, 255; Gustav List engineering factory 38, 73, 100, 106; Guzhon (later Serp i Molot) steel works 100, 111, 140, 155, 230; heavy artillery workshops, Lefortovo (Mastiazhart) 51, 61, 63, 65, 69, 126, 197–98, 252, 255; Il'in motor works 100, 150; Kauchuk rubber goods factory 79, 85, 180, 182–85, 217, 255; Kosa metallurgical works 147; Krasnaia Roza textile works 194; Manometr engineering works 61, 80, 231; Merkurii shoe factory 74; Moscow Union of Consumer Associations 197; Oktiabr' engineering factory 197; Podol'sk engineering works 30, 92, 151; Provodnik works 180–83; Russian-American instrument works 197; Russkabel' 219; Russkaia mashina factory 74; Salmson factory 80; Soviet rolling mill no. 1 36; Sytin print works 37–38, 84, 100, 110, 147, 161; Varts Makgill foundry 147, 152; *see also* post and telegraph offices, railways, railway workshops, textile mills, tram depots

Zakolupin, P.V. 61
Zaslavskii, P.S. 102, 116
Zelenskii, Isaak 82, 98, 101, 129–31, 137, 154, 176, 179, 185, 227, 252
Zemliachka, Rozaliia 60, 220
Zetkin, Clara 162
Zinoviev, Grigorii 65*n*, 66, 68–70, 137, 164, 170, 181; in 'triumvirate' (1923–24) 184, 211, 213, 217

Lightning Source UK Ltd.
Milton Keynes UK
UKOW040441091012

200260UK00004B/95/P